URBAN NETWORKS
IN RUSSIA, 1750–1800,
AND PREMODERN
PERIODIZATION

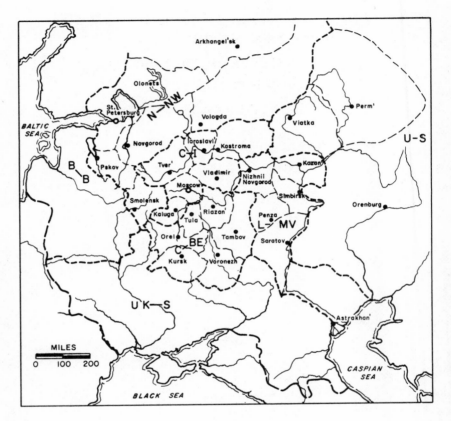

MAP 1.
Regions and Guberniia of the Russian Empire

GILBERT ROZMAN

❉ ❉

URBAN NETWORKS IN RUSSIA, 1750–1800,

AND PREMODERN PERIODIZATION

PRINCETON UNIVERSITY PRESS   PRINCETON, NEW JERSEY

CONTENTS

Tables, Graphs, and Maps   *vii*

Acknowledgments   *ix*

Introduction   *3*

1. Approaches to Periodization   *16*

2. The Establishment of Urban Networks:
   Cities in Russia Prior to 1750   *41*

3. Spatial Divisions in Social Structure:
   Russia as a Stage G Society   *86*

4. Regional Variations in Urbanization:
   Russia in the 1780s   *159*

5. Urban Networks of Advanced Premodern
   (Stage G) Societies   *220*

6. Conclusions   *276*

Glossary   *285*

Notes   *287*

Selected Bibliography   *315*

Index   *329*

TABLES

1. Idealized Consensus of Soviet Historians on the Stages of Russian History   22
2. Definitions of the Seven Levels of Central Places   34
3. The Seven Stages of Premodern Urban Development   35
4. Development of Central Places in Russia   74
5. Development of Central Places in China   75
6. Development of Central Places in Japan   76
7. Development of Central Places in England and France   79
8. The Population of the Russian Empire   99
9. The Regional Population Distribution of Russia   99
10. Estimates of National Income Produced in the Russian Empire in the 1790s   118
11. Estimated Number of Fairs in the Russian Empire   120
12. Number of Marketing Settlements in Three Guberniia   124
13. Distribution of Central Places in 1782   149
14. Central-Industrial Region   162
15. Central-Black Earth Region   171
16. North-Northwest Region   183
17. Lower and Middle Volga Region   193
18. Urals and Siberia Region   202
19. Ukraine-South Russia and Belorussia-Baltic Regions   211
20. The English Urban Network in the 1680s   222
21. The Urban Networks of 9 English Counties and Wales   223
22. England's Regions and Main Cities   226
23. The French Urban Network in the 1760s   230
24. The Urbanization of France's Regions   233
25. Estimates of World Population by Countries in 1800   241

26. The World's Largest Cities in 1800   *243*
27. Comparative Distribution of Central Places in 5 Stage G
    Societies   *245*
28. Measures of the Efficiency of the Urban Hierarchy   *247*
29. Countries Overrepresented at Various Levels of the
    Urban Network   *254*
30. Percentages of Total Urban Population in
    Administrative Centers   *257*
31. Areas of Integration in a World of Stage G Societies   *259*

GRAPHS

1. Prevailing Views on Periodization   *30*
2. The Urban Network View of Periodization   *84*
3. The Premodern World Population   *240*
4. Distribution of World Population in Societies at
   Stages A-G   *240*
5. Cumulative Percent of Central Places in 5 Countries   *246*
6. Cumulative Percent of Urban Population in 5 Countries   *246*

MAPS

 1. Regions and Guberniia of the Russian Empire   *ii*
 2. Major Fairs of the Russian Empire   *128*
 3. Plan of Moscow   *142*
 4. Plan of St. Petersburg   *147*
 5. C-I Region   *161*
 6. C-BE Region   *172*
 7. N-NW Region   *182*
 8. L-MV Region   *192*
 9. U-S Region   *201*
10. England's Regions and Major Cities   *227*
11. France's Regions and Cities at Levels 1-3   *234*

ACKNOWLEDGMENTS

Conceived as a second step in a large comparative project, this book responds to the need for information on Russian urban history in the light of earlier findings on the history of cities in China and Japan and to the opportunity for reinterpreting stages of history on the basis of assembled urban data for five countries. It is based on research carried out in the United States and the Soviet Union, generously assisted by specialists on Russian history and by others with competencies relevant to the comparative contents of the book.

As in my previous work on East Asia, I am most appreciative of the assistance of Frederick W. Mote and Marion J. Levy, Jr., who read this manuscript critically and helped me in focusing the comparative sections. Lawrence Stone made available materials on English cities and offered suggestions on the major section dealing with England. I am grateful also to students who joined me in classroom discussions on comparing societies and to Charles Tilly, who provided detailed criticisms for revising the manuscript.

While in Moscow, I was ably guided in the search for materials by N. B. Golikova and in the analysis of urban data by V. M. Kabuzan, to whom I am particularly grateful for sharing his impressive command over Russian historical demographic materials. The opportunity to do research in the Soviet Union was made possible by Princeton University and by the International Research and Exchanges Board. I also want to thank Marc Raeff, Cyril Black, S. Frederick Starr and David Miller who commented on parts or all of this book from the perspective of Russian historians.

Finally I am indebted to my wife Masha for making it possible for me to improve my knowledge of Russian and for helping to type this manuscript.

Princeton, New Jersey　　　　　　　　　　　Gilbert Rozman
September 1974

URBAN NETWORKS
IN RUSSIA, 1750–1800,
AND PREMODERN
PERIODIZATION

INTRODUCTION

This book is about the development of cities in Russia and of premodern societies in general. It is a continuation of a longer project that began with my book, *Urban Networks in Ch'ing China and Tokugawa Japan*. It employs the same general methodology and explores the same themes in the history of the Russian Empire and, in a much more condensed fashion, in the histories of England and France. A number of refinements in the interpretation of data on urban history including an effort to designate common stages of premodern history serve as a basis for new generalizations. In addition, expanding the scope of comparisons of networks of central places (systems of administrative and marketing settlements) from two countries to five broadens our attempt to identify universal characteristics of social change prior to the nineteenth century or to initial modernization.

Two objectives guide the analysis and presentation of data on urban networks. The lesser objective is to examine the validity of the recurrent theme of Russia's historic backwardness. To accomplish this aim it is necessary not only to trace the development of central places over a period of almost 1,000 years and then to focus specifically on the state of the Russian urban network at a time prior to the creation of extensive contacts with modernizing societies, but also to compare these characteristics with urban data from other societies. At the same time, determination of the extent of Russian backwardness in urban development serves a broader and more important objective. Above all, the Russian case sheds light on the general processes of development in premodern societies. The study of Russian urban networks contributes additional evidence for generalizing about the periodization or common stages of history of premodern societies and for devising an improved framework to reinterpret the development of all countries before their modernization.

What appears to be a book about Russia, thus, turns out, in fact, to be an attempt to generalize about stages of premodern history, using information about the development of cities and smaller marketing centers in the Russian Empire. Chapter 1 develops the framework for this comparative analysis, showing how it relates to other approaches to periodization. Chapter 2 places the information on the evolution of Russia's urban network in comparative perspective through short sections on similar developments in other countries. Chapters 3 and 4 give details on spatial aspects of social structure and on regional variations in cities within late eighteenth-century Russia. Finally in Chapter 5 the focus shifts exclusively to comparisons of societies. Concentration on Russia in Chapters 2 to 4, with the addition of information on England and France in Chapter 5, sets up a scaffolding that, together with the foundation established in the earlier study of China and Japan, provides a much needed environment for constructing hypotheses about general features of premodern development.

The two themes of Russian backwardness and premodern development closely interlock, and each stands in need of an infusion of some stimulant to counteract wearied thinking. The general picture of Russian backwardness before 1800 is misleading. As was true of assessments of Tokugawa Japan (1600–1868) prior to reevaluations of the past 25 years, so the level of development attained by Russia as a premodern society has been repeatedly minimized. Indicative of this general misperception, Russian cities have been credited with just 3–4 percent of the late eighteenth-century national population rather than the correct figure of 8–9 percent.[1]

Recent treatments of evolutionary approaches to social change are also, in my opinion, characterized by a misplaced consensus generally disparaging in its assessment. While opinions differ on the utility of past efforts to divide history into stages of development, no voices proclaim this area of historical sociology as having high priority on the agenda for future studies of social change. Nevertheless, after previously devising an evolutionary framework for comparing stages of urban networks, I became convinced that, inherent in both the Marxist and the prevailing Western European and American approaches to periodization, there exists a common urban-oriented conception of social change. Even if this focus does not lie at the heart of these ostensibly quite divergent camps, I believe that a basis exists for a remarkable convergence of treatments of periodization with special emphasis on urban change. In Chapter 1, I explore the relationship of various approaches to periodization, culminating with a concise statement of a new, empirically rooted approach to stages of history.

The theme of Russian backwardness

The notion that Russia was perpetually backward has been widely propagated, but almost never does one ask: how, when, to what extent, and in comparison to which countries was Russia backward? We read that Russia was a backward frontier for the Varangians and the Byzantines; an isolated sacrifice to the Tatar yoke severed from the ongoing processes of development so noticeable elsewhere in Europe; an emerging centralized state frustrated in its economic development by the twin forces of autocracy and serfdom; and, more recently, a latecomer to modernization encumbered with crude Stalinist measures that are increasingly incapable of sustaining rapid development. At each historical turn, a paramount task is said to have stood between the enormous potential of the peoples somewhat loosely known as Russia and their persistent ambitions to overtake one or more rivals. It has been taken for granted that Russia has remained backward under the great burden of these successive overriding tasks.

For the early centuries of Russian history, the obstacles to catching up to more advanced countries have generally been identified in military or territorial terms, including the requirements of the long struggles to overthrow the Mongols and later to open windows on the Baltic and Black Seas. Yet, it is usually agreed that, even before boundaries were secure, a new set of elusive motivational barriers was primarily responsible for retarded development. According to such views, in the eighteenth century the main cause was the absence of self-government by the commercial population; the nineteenth century was plagued by the lack of personal reward for the agricultural population; unattained goals in agricultural production throughout the Soviet period, and in other sectors of the economy after 1960, resulted from the sacrifice of private initiative to collective responsibility. These recurrent explanations for the presumed Russian backwardness are espoused by both Soviet and non-Soviet writers for the pre-Revolutionary periods and by non-Soviet writers for the contemporary period.[2]

At the root of these explanations of Russian backwardness can often be found certain assumptions about the nature of positive and negative forces in social development. If the negative forces are repeatedly associated with efforts to secure national borders, to maximize the centralization of power, and to utilize labor without providing a wide range of opportunities for consumption or mobility, the positive forces are commonly identified with the great geographical expanse, the large population, and the vast natural resources of the country or to waves of intensive borrowing from abroad. In some instances the very elements listed among the negative forces are said to have served temporarily as factors contributing to increased production, but in the long run the priorities given to collective responsibility over individual initiative and to military preparedness over consumer satisfaction are presumed to have blocked the path of success in the development of production.

While there are common elements in the treatment of the balance of positive and negative forces in the development of Russia right up to the present, it is important to distinguish between analyses of Russian history before 1800 and after 1800. To the extent that assumptions about Russian backwardness after roughly 1800 refer to an international context in which national development can, in some sense, be equated with modernization, these assumptions are at least based on a considerable body of evidence concerning the complicated but unavoidable transformation that has everywhere been set in motion by contacts with modernizing peoples. The process of modernization has been the subject of wide study, in the light of which data on Russia can be interpreted.[3] In this comparative setting, Russia merits classification as one of the few latecomers to rapid modernization; yet it is also clear that Russia started this process slowly and her development has been uneven, with certain sectors lagging conspicuously by contrast with the firstcomers and even with a few latecomers. Despite inadequacies in the state of scholarship concerning the factors that have contributed to or hindered the modernization of Russia, we can conclude that the notion of Russian backwardness in a modernizing world from the early nineteenth century to after World War II is a useful and generally clearly understood comparative statement.

No similarly clear comparative perspective exists for presumptions of Russian backwardness prior to 1800. There is no satisfactory theory of the stages of premodern development against which to evaluate these conclusions. Assumptions concerning an implicit struggle between what are regarded as positive and negative forces have been made against a background of hazy comparative information; indeed, even the concept of development in premodern societies has rarely been defined. Data on aspects of social history have been ignored because scholars were unaware of their significance in a comparative context. In particular, little attention has been given to data on eighteenth-century Russian cities by historians who have assumed that the positive force for development is self-government, and that this was clearly absent in Russian cities.[4]

The presumed balance of forces affecting urban characteristics during the eighteenth century is clearly set forth in writings about Peter I and Catherine II (both called "the Great"), the dynamic leaders of the first and final quarters of the century. Biographers and others who concentrate on the periods of these reigns describe their efforts to introduce such advances from Western Europe as urban self-government, but minimize the results of their efforts because urban areas were not granted adequate freedoms. In the final analysis, urban population data are assumed to have been much lower than was in fact the case, the relative strengths of positive and negative forces are never quantified, and we are left with the vague formulation that one barrier after another obstructed the path of the normal, and presumably rapid, growth that would have resulted had the positive forces been allowed unrestricted development.

Given the glaringly imprecise character of comparative statements about premodern societies in general, it is not surprising that explanations of Russian backwardness before 1800 lack specificity and support. Both to improve the comparative perspective on other premodern societies and to expose elements of myth in the notion of Russian backwardness, it is necessary to draw up a new balance sheet of development before 1800. In it I will discard assumptions that positive forces emerged primarily from geographical conditions or were externally generated, and will reexamine some of the forces that are typically placed in the negative category. In place of unsubstantiated and inexplicit assumptions, a systematic comparative approach will be applied to the history of Russia before she began to experience the heavy fallout from the Industrial Revolution in Western Europe. The year 1800 is chosen as a terminal date because, soon after, improvements in transportation introduced from abroad produced, albeit slowly at first, patterns of long-distance trade indicative of a society with a mixture of nonmodernized and modernized elements.

The conclusion advanced in this book is that by the end of the eighteenth century the Russian Empire had reached an advanced stage of premodern development. The following chapters will show that in important respects the Russian Empire resembled other advanced countries in Western Europe and East Asia. Its urban network had already entered a mature stage with seven distinct levels of central places present, and the percentage of its population living in cities was well above the world average. As periodic marketing started to decline in certain areas of the Russian Empire at the beginning of the nineteenth century, evidence accumulated that Russia's urban network was no more than a century behind those of advanced Western European countries and had pulled roughly even with that of Japan. Similar to these other advanced premodern societies, the Russian Empire had moved ahead of China in the development of a hierarchy of central places.

The theme of premodern development

Comparisons of societies require not only statements of similarities and differences but also methods of classifying those statements. Generally sets of interrelated propositions about aspects of social structure are grouped together in typologies of societies. The dominant typology in Western sociology is "modernized" and "nonmodernized" (also labeled "industrialized" and "nonindustrialized" or "developed" and "less developed"). Relatively nonmodernized societies can be divided further into transitional and premodern examples. Our attention in this volume will be directed at general comparisons of social structure in premodern societies.

Some typologies of premodern societies are based on factors that presumably could arise at any point in history; for instance, Russia before 1800 has been variously classified as a centralized bureaucratic empire and as an oriental, despotic society.[5] Examples of each of these types are alleged to have appeared over thousands of years. Similarly the application of the designation "feudal" has included societies such as China in the first millennium B.C. and Japan immediately before the Meiji Restoration in A.D. 1868.[6] Other typologies are based on the hypothesis that social change, even in premodern societies, is cumulative. While a society may not "advance" in terms of designated criteria over a specified period, the general pattern is one of increasing differentiation of function and specialization. Starting with this notion of the growing complexity of societies, we can designate types of societies with varying degrees of complexity.

There are essentially two, contrasting approaches to what George H. Nadel has identified as the problem of importing "significance to the passage of time in history by identifying and ordering chronological sequences (periods)."[7] On the one hand, there is what Nadel labels the pedagogic approach, in which varying criteria for and configurations of periods are selected to suit the convenience of a particular study. While giving unity to a body of information, the approach is not designed to develop theories of societies. On the other hand, there is a lawlike approach to periodization, differing in respect to determinism. According to this approach, successive stages in history are attributed to the manifestation of underlying forces, for instance to the growing complexity of social relations. It is tempting to follow Nadel's example in contrasting the two major systems of periodization in use today, treating as pedagogic the widely encountered tripartite division of history into ancient, medieval, and modern (early modern if we confine our interests to periods before 1800), and as lawlike the Marxist division of history into primitive communalism, slavery, feudalism, capitalism, and the post-nineteenth-century forms of socialism and communism. In fact, both of these systems have been applied with varying degrees of theoretical sophistication. While the Marxist framework has the advantage of being more explicitly theoretical and the disadvantage of being canonized without the customary verification, both frameworks have contributed to the careful classification of information concerning the growing complexity of societies.

Systematic analysis of evolutionary changes in social structure dates from the nineteenth century. The usefulness of dividing history into stages was discovered more than 2,000 years ago in relatively literate societies such as Greece and China.[8] More recent is the identification of new stages in terms of changing levels of economic development rather than by dramatic events affecting the ruling house such as military conquests and rebellions.

Only as some countries began to experience modernization did the problems of periodization acquire a new focus more applicable to comparisons of societies. To determine which countries would be quickly receptive to the currents of change, attention increasingly centered on existing levels of economic development and related characteristics of social structure. Because societies were not identical, it was also deemed necessary to analyze historical processes to discover whether one society resembled another society in a previous period of its existence. Comparing societies by locating them on a continuum of development became an important part of modern scholarship.

The two major traditions associated with the development of what Nadel labels lawlike periodization have been Marxism in particular and sociology in general. Indeed, with sociologists claiming Marx as one of the outstanding early representatives of their discipline and with Soviet Marxist-Leninists attracted to sociology as a means of bridging the gap between narrow historical specialization and the high-level generalizations of historical materialism, the differences between the two traditions are not always clear. Yet, for more than a century the main currents of these traditions have diverged. Marxists have elaborated on but have not seriously revised a single model of periodization, while the majority of sociologists who have not been Marxists have proposed numerous typologies of societies but have seldom found substantial historical support for their ideas.[9] Increasingly the centers of these respective traditions have become the world's two contrasting major powers, the Soviet Union and the United States, which accounts in part for the lack of cross-fertilization despite the considerable impact of Marxism on the academic milieu of the United States and Western Europe.

During the twentieth century, three interesting parallels continued to refine these two traditions. First, in the early part of the century, V. I. Lenin and Max Weber carried out historical studies that were instrumental in providing new research foci for their respective followers. Assuming the leadership of a dictatorial state, Lenin had a great impact in directing attention toward the study of Russian history through the application of Marx's stages of development. Weber acquired unusual familiarity with the history of many regions of the world, revitalizing detailed cross-societal historical studies. While both men were limited by distinctly inferior resources on social history in contrast to those available today, their ideas remain at the center of attention some fifty years after their deaths.

Despite the intentions of Lenin and Weber and probably to a certain extent because of the shortcomings of their research efforts, the craft of periodization stagnated during the second quarter of this century. This is the second similarity between the two traditions. Under Stalin the extreme was approached whereby the Marxist tenets of periodization were repeated with historical facts presented primarily as illustrations. Meanwhile in the West a reaction set in against grandiose classifications of historical societies; sociologists became absorbed in problems of methodology applied to contemporary local studies.

Finally, during the 1950s and 1960s, historians and social scientists in the United States and the Soviet Union initiated a reexamination of comparative studies and historical methods for treating types of societies. Within roughly a ten-year span in each country, a rash of articles and books appeared with such titles as "Sociology and History" and "History and Sociology."[10] Large studies and collections were devoted to types of societies, including the sociologist S. Eisenstadt's *The Political Systems of Empires: The Rise and Fall of the Historical Bureaucratic Societies*; the earlier *Feudalism in History*, edited by R. Coulborn; and closely corresponding Soviet collections entitled, *Problems of the Appearance of Feudalism among the Peoples of the USSR* and *Paths of the Development of Feudalism*.[11] The third noteworthy parallel between the two traditions is the present agreement that the sociological study of societal types in history merits renewed interest.

In short, after making disappointingly little progress in solving problems of periodization during nearly half a century of partially severed communications both between representatives of these two traditions and between specialists in history and the social sciences within each tradition (the suppressive measures that resulted in the disappearance of sociology in the Soviet Union were especially severe), both sides have now rediscovered interdisciplinary historical studies aimed at developing generalizations about types of societies. At the same time, these interests have not led to attempts to devise new formulations of the stages of premodern history. It is time to draw from the best of both traditions in an effort to identify stages of history.

Among Western sociologists a recent revival of interest in classifying theories of social change has provoked discussion of what approaches are most useful for comparing societies. At one extreme, Robert A. Nisbet rejects all forms of developmentalism, which are alleged to provide generalizations drawn from metaphor instead of historical data.[12] Nisbet assumes that studies that regard social change as continuous, cumulative and directional (i.e. as immanent in existing social conditions) are incompatible with empirically derived generalizations. This book will demonstrate that his assumptions are incorrect. A large number of sociologists classify the search for stages of development under the headings of evolutionary theory, social evolution, or neo-evolutionism.[13] Singling out this category as one of several types of sociological theories of change, they generally point to various flaws in these attempts to identify a process of increasing complexity over time; e.g. these theories are unilinear when they should be multilinear, they cannot be tested, or they are incomplete without being merged with other types of theories. In contrast to these cautious commitments to the study of societal development, this book is an attempt to identify a unilinear process that provides a basis for designating successive stages of premodern development; I argue that the stages so delineated are explicitly rooted in historical data.

This approach derives from central place theory, a framework to which representatives of several social science disciplines have contributed. Central place studies seek a general explanation for the sizes, number, and distribution of cities.[14] Identifying hierarchies of cities, they consider how cities at each level perform functions that are not available in cities at lower levels and how cities at each level have a fixed number of satellite cities at the next lower level. Study of spatial patterns has focused on hexagonal trading zones around each central place. Study of population patterns has drawn attention to the similarities in the number of people in cities that are at the same level in the marketing hierarchy and correspondingly have hinterlands of similar size. From these studies emerges the notion of a rank-size ordering of the population of cities within an area. According to this ordering principle, a consistent relationship must exist between the populations of cities at various levels within a given area. Central place theorists have introduced the concept of networks of cities, have pointed to the cities of a country as constituting a self-contained network and have considered relations between spatial, demographic, and temporal patterns as they pertain to the urban network.

Although no systematic application of the central place approach to the study of stages of development exists apart from my own introduction of the urban networks approach, a number of relevant interpretations of central place theory can be identified. G. W. Skinner has traced the history of central places in China over a period of roughly two centuries, pointing to the existence of an intensification cycle relating the ratio of villages to periodic markets to the level of economic development of an area.[15] Skinner's formulation has been widely cited for a variety of contributions; among these it suggests a framework for studying history in terms of changing interrelationships between settlements of varying sizes and functions. J. C. Russell, C. T. Smith, and E. A. J. Johnson also have written about the pattern of central places at various periods in history, associating a specific network of cities with a certain stage of societal development.[16] Their writings create the impression that successive hierarchies of urban size and function reveal not only transformations of networks of cities but also stages in the development of societies.

The urban networks approach, which will be explained in detail in the final section of Chapter 1, is a revised version of central place theory designed to apply to an unadulterated nonmodernized setting. Central place theory has been criticized for failing to deal with industrial activities, while applying best to the location of tertiary activities, such as commerce.[17] In the premodern setting with little specialized industry for long-distance markets, one might assume that there would be less interference from manufacturing functions in the distribution of cities. Rank-size systems have been found to require a high degree of closure in a society. Again the premodern setting, with less advanced transportation technology and more highly self-contained units, should improve the applicability of an important element of the central place approach. However, while the urban networks approach incorporates the notion that there are regularities within each network in the distribution of cities at distinct population levels, the original rank-size approach that assumes that the population of a city multiplied by its rank in size equals the population of the largest city has been discarded as incorrect. No attempt is made here to examine J. C. Russell's revised formulation of rank-size distributions or G. William Skinner's elaborate treatment of shapes and sizes of hinterlands, both of which deserve further study in a broadly comparative context. Without applying all of the themes of central place theory, the urban networks approach focuses attention on the relationship between city-size distributions and stages of development in premodern societies.

It is frequently stated that Russia was between East and West. An examination of China and Japan in the East and England and France in the West enables us to consider the accuracy of that statement with respect to urban development. In 1800 these five countries together contained more than two-fifths of the total world population and at least one-half of the total urban population. If we compare these countries (England before 1750; France before 1790; Russia before 1800; and China and Japan before 1850), on the eve of early modernization or extensive contacts with modernizing states, they provide a convenient, well-documented historical juxtaposition—our laboratory for comparative study. Data on and analysis of the networks of central places in these five countries should establish a foundation for generalizing about the stages of premodern development.

APPROACHES TO PERIODIZATION

The search for standard stages of premodern development invariably shifts back and forth among: 1) single-country studies, 2) direct comparisons between societies, and 3) general statements of uniformities among large numbers of societies. The raw materials from all three of these fields of inquiry must be in ample supply before a satisfactory theory of the stages of history can be produced. In the absence of findings from any one of these fields, the explorations of the other two cannot realize their full value. It is only when various signs of development observed in one country are explicitly and systematically compared with similar signs in one or more other countries and simultaneously a general framework is developed for interpreting the relationships between indicators of social change that generalizations carefully rooted in empirical data become possible.

Previous studies of periodization have not incorporated a proper balance between these three types of inquiry. The liveliest phase of evolutionary studies during the nineteenth century approached an extreme—one-sided statements of uniformities in historical stages with scant attention to careful historical documentation. Optimistic assessments of rational man's potential for discerning universal sequences of large-scale social change led to bold statements and imaginative interpretations, yet these attempts at ordering history occurred at a time when, in comparison to today, the historical records of many major countries were poorly understood. Later, under the onslaught of contradictory historical findings and criticisms of methodological shortcomings, social scientists turned away from this task of generalization although sporadic efforts to substitute a new theory of historical stages continued to draw attention, and the best of the early formulations survived with modest revisions, occupying what would otherwise have been a vacuum. That state of affairs continues to this day. As the introduction pointed out, single-country studies are guided primarily by the Marxist and tripartite taxonomies of history.

So far the twentieth century has witnessed a vast outpouring of single-country studies. Historical writings on most major countries have become voluminous, adding immeasurably to our knowledge of only a few decades past. There is still little awareness that efforts to specify patterns of development in a single country are limited by the absence of knowledge of corresponding patterns elsewhere. The ordering of historical data requires a framework for determining what is of importance, and that framework must develop in a comparative context. The issue of periodization raised for the history of a single country with, at most, vague references to patterns elsewhere quickly leads to an impasse in interpretation accompanied by either a hesitancy to generalize or a propensity to write non sequiturs.

Of the three essential steps in the study of periodization, least attention has been given to direct comparisons of societies. This necessary link between generalizations about uniformities and detailed study of a single country has been persistently ignored. Without it, the empiricists can correctly regard the generalizations as vague and unsupported, and the generalists can with equally smug aplomb reject detailed studies as leading nowhere. What is vitally needed in the field of historical sociology and related disciplines is systematic comparisons of societies, incorporating the findings of single-country studies and directed at generalizing about standard stages of development.

Russian history has two main attractions for the student of periodization. First, more so than the historians of any other country, historians writing about Russia have assiduously applied general schemes of periodization. Beginning with the writings of Karl Marx, undoubtedly the dominant figure among all who have sought to establish a universal taxonomy of societies, the historians and social scientists of the Soviet Union have been organized under a system that permits only one perspective in print. Without challenging that perspective, they have produced a vast literature recently filled with lively debate.[1] By turning to these numerous materials on the periodization of Russian history, we can benefit from the intensive cultivation of the seeds planted by Marx.

Second, one cannot but be aware of the oft-noted paradox of modern Russian history. In Marxist terminology, Russia is a country that passed through the capitalist stage of development in only a little more than half a century. From a tradition of serfs and state peasants, whose obligations in many respects resembled those of serfs, Russia quickly emerged as one of the most rapidly modernizing nations. One of the few similar examples of a successful latecomer to modernization is Japan. In both countries, the essential ingredients for moving swiftly ahead to the next stage of development can be traced back to the last stable period before the onslaught of modernizing influences. The failure of current schemes of periodization is nowhere better seen than in their inability to account for the modernization of these two countries.

In the past half-century, Russian history has been the focus of intensive efforts to determine the evidence for stages of development within a single country. In this light, it probably serves as well as any other country the purpose of providing a well-documented record of processes of change within a single country. It also provides the single case examined in greatest detail from the perspective of a general formulation of stages of development. If we agree that Marx was a leading theorist in the field of historical sociology, and that Russia is the principal example studied by those who have applied Marx's theory, then the Russian record takes on added significance. Finally, to the extent that comparisons of societies have been attempted, the Russian case has appeared with unusual frequency. Soviet social scientists have used Russian history as a standard against which to measure other histories and, of course, the recurrent theme of Russian backwardness is premised on at least an implicit comparative approach. We should begin our treatment of approaches to periodization by considering how Soviets have interpreted Russian history.

Soviet Periodization of Russian History

Since Soviet social scientists have considerable experience in the use of periodization as a method of comparing societies and since most studies of Russian history are carried out in terms of Soviet periodization, it will be helpful to recapitulate the Soviet treatment of the pre-modern stages of Russian history. Marx described three precapitalist forms of societies: primitive communal, slaveholding, and feudal. Although a possible fourth variant has been discussed, i.e. Asiatic despotic societies, this can be set aside here because it has not been seriously applied to the specific study of Russian history.[2] After some initial disagreement, a consensus was achieved under Stalin that Russia had not experienced a slaveholding stage.[3] At the time that the primitive communal formation was beginning to be replaced by a class society, the productive forces available were already sufficiently advanced to permit the direct establishment of a feudal society. Thus the entire span of Russian history until the middle of the nineteenth century is divided into two periods: 1) an almost totally undocumented, vaguely understood, primitive communal period; and 2) an approximately 900–1,000 year-long feudal period. The same problem of a long, unwieldy feudal period plagues Marxist studies of China, but at least in China many records exist of the preceding period before the more than 2,000 years of "feudalism" began. The great length of the feudal era in Russia as in China means that the task of establishing the general characteristics of the period can be only a preliminary step in specifying its major subdivisions.

According to Marx, the salient features of any society are the forces of production and the relations of production, the latter involving ownership and conditions of employment.[4] The forces of production of a feudal society are distinguished, on the one hand, from the primitive technology of the preceding stage of society and, on the other hand, from the widespread presence of manufacturing in the succeeding capitalist period. The application of varied animate sources of power in agriculture, small-scale crafts, and transport and even some limited use of inanimate power such as windmills are apparently typical of feudal societies. Relations of production in these societies reflect the principal reliance on agriculture. Engaging in farming, most of the population produce primarily for their own consumption and secondarily for a minority who specialize in crafts, trade, religious activities, and administrative or military pursuits. The property system, the system of rents, and the system of taxes all promote the concentration of wealth among individuals removed from production and create a potential, on the one hand, for the accumulation of capital, and, on the other hand, for large-scale rebellions. Yet, for the most part, a self-sufficient local economy prevails; most goods are consumed within the village or local area in which they are produced, and marketing is weakly developed. Merchants, craftsmen, and other urban residents compose a small proportion of the total population.

This general description of a feudal society is static, noting the common features of countless societies and of numerous points in the development of a single society hundreds or even as many as two thousand years apart. Marxists have also portrayed feudal development as a generally linear process: technology gradually improves, new craft specialties provide signs of a widening division of labor, increasing numbers of people become involved in commercial transactions.[5] These dynamic characteristics of feudalism are particularly interesting because they provide a basis both for specifying subdivisions within the rubric of the feudal period and for demonstrating different paths through feudalism. It is the former task that has especially absorbed the energies of Soviet scholars.

There is agreement in the Soviet Union on the criteria for subdividing feudalism, but not on either the names or the dates of these subdivisions. Reviewing the historiography of Russia during the ninth to fourteenth centuries, L. V. Cherepnin found at least nine names being used for subdivisions, including pre-feudal, proto-feudal, early feudal, and the period of the genesis of feudalism.[6] Similar differences in terminology are evident in Soviet writings on the later phases of Russian feudalism from the fifteenth to the nineteenth centuries.[7] Disagreements in terminology are frequently related to differences of opinion regarding the timing of the major landmarks in development. For the earlier period, the dispute concentrates on the extent to which remnants of the primitive communal phase were present; for the final centuries of feudalism, the debate centers on the timing of the appearance and the rate of growth of the roots of capitalism.

Rephrasing this debate on the stages of Russian history in idealized, quantitative terms, we can say that at one point 100 percent of the basic features of Russian society could be accounted for by the presence of primitive communalism, but over many centuries that percentage dropped to zero as a corresponding rise in feudal phenomena occurred, and subsequently an inverse relationship between feudalism and capitalism began to become apparent, although until 1800 an overwhelming percentage of the characteristics of Russian society could still be attributed to feudalism. In these idealized terms, a society that was 100 percent primitive communal was steadily replaced by one that was 100 percent feudal, which in turn was giving way to a capitalist society. This is the framework of stages of history through which Soviets categorize aspects of social structure during each century.

Actually, debate in the Soviet Union never achieves this degree of precision. First, there is little consensus about the meaning of many of the principal historical terms. Second, Soviet authors disagree about the degree of development achieved at a particular time. We can speak in general terms about a consensus regarding the percentages given here for successive points in time, but there is no unanimity and, of course, the Soviets have never presented their views in terms of this explicitly quantified form.[8]

For clarity, I have schematized the conclusions based on this idealized presentation, trying to represent accurately the most frequently expressed opinions pertaining to the extent of feudalism, century by century, in Russian society. Of course, there should be no doubt that for individual authors the figures would be altered in one direction or the other by 10 percent or 20 percent, but a sufficient consensus does exist within the Soviet Union to argue that the variation from the figures in Table 1 is not large.

We can divide this period into four phases according to the balance of the primary and secondary societal types present: 1) P/F (9th–10th centuries); 2) F/P (11th–13th centuries); 3) F (14th–16th centuries); and 4) F/C (17th–18th centuries). During the first phase, when the primitive communal (P) social structure prevailed, Russian society had a tribal appearance; scattered rural settlements were weakly integrated into larger territorial entities, and there was little specialization of labor. Nonetheless, the growing weight of feudal

TABLE 1

Idealized Consensus of Soviet Historians on the Stages of Russian History
(as expressed by the percentage of basic features of the society accounted for
by the presence of each stage of development)

Century	Primitive Communalism	Feudalism	Capitalism
9th	80	20	
10th	60	40	
11th	40	60	
12th	20	80	
13th	10	90	
14th	5	95	
15th	0	100	
16th		95	5
17th		90	10
18th		80	20

(F) characteristics was visible both in the emergence of cities and in the appearance of princes demanding tribute from an increasingly agricultural rural population.

The breakdown of the independent rural community became particularly apparent during the F/P phase, when feudal elements were in the majority. Cherepnin identifies the twelfth century with the completion of the genesis of feudalism within the rubric of the previous form of society, and he traces the disappearance of the lingering, so-called "free community" to the following two centuries.[9] According to him, feudalism was secured as large cities emerged, villages increasingly consisted of the landless and the relatively prosperous, and land ownership became sharply fragmented among the prominent subordinates of local princes.

The decelerated decline of primitive communal elements (what some regard as even a temporary reversal of the generally linear process of development) during the thirteenth and fourteenth centuries is attributed by Soviet authors to the retarding influences of the Mongol invasions and subsequent rule.[10] Nonetheless, they generally argue that Russia continued to progress in many ways and that the last traces of pre-feudal society disappeared in roughly the fifteenth century.

During the fourteenth to sixteenth centuries, nonfeudal elements were least evident in Russian society. The waning traces of primitive societal forms finally disappeared, and the initial signs of capitalism became visible only gradually. Russia had achieved its most purely feudal form.

According to many Soviet Marxists, the sporadic beginnings of the capitalist means of production originated in Western Europe during the fourteenth and fifteenth centuries, but in Russia not until the sixteenth or seventeenth century.[11] At about this time, monetary and commercial relations were beginning to spread from the city to the countryside, and within cities crafts were being converted from production for orders to production for the market. Yet, these processes were still not sufficiently advanced to signal unambiguously the onset of capitalist elements.[12] Without a precise definition of capitalist elements, Soviets are especially prone to disagreement over the timing of their appearance and early development. Recent scholarly attention has focused on identifying a later point, when the capitalist presence was large enough to exert a substantial impact, what they call the capitalist *uklad*. The authors of a collective conference report entitled *The Transition From Feudalism to Capitalism in Russia* agree that this turning point occurred during the second half of the eighteenth century and, for some, more specifically during the 1760s.[13] Thus, it is probably accurate to quantify the appearance of capitalism in Russia, as seen by Soviet eyes, as a gradual process beginning in the sixteenth century and reaching a noticeable boundary near the end of the eighteenth century. Limited degrees of penetration of commerce, of large-scale craft production, of hired labor, and, in general, of forces disrupting the closed character of the peasant economy were all consistent with a feudal society; however at some time the combined effect of these forces achieved a level where the rise of a new epoch can be observed. The significance of the period 1750–1800 to many Soviets is that this is the time when the roots of capitalism plunged deep into Russian soil.

Before leaving Table 1, we should note that the rate of change in the stages of history was more rapid before the thirteenth century than afterward. The slow rate of development of Russia after this date is a problem for which Soviet scholars are constantly giving explanations. Blame is assigned not only to the Mongols but also to European states, which intervened in Russia during the seventeenth century. In addition, both the proponents of widespread capitalist features in the sixteenth or seventeenth century and their critics, who observe these changes only in the eighteenth century, agree that the development of capitalism was slowed by special factors of Russian feudalism, two of which were the continued spread of the feudal system to new territory as the boundaries of the empire widened and the relative absence of international trade.[14] Most writers emphasize, however, that the major inhibiting factor was serfdom, a relationship between landowner and cultivator that generally prevented the latter from either freely redividing his holdings or freely leaving the area in which he was registered. The fact that a large part of local production went directly to serfowners is seen as having retarded the differentiation of labor in rural areas. Regardless of the explanation emphasized, the duration of six centuries in which Russia remained overwhelmingly (in my terms at least 80 percent) feudal is viewed as unnecessarily long by Soviet writers.[15]

While Soviet research on Russian history has been consistently guided by these broad interests in periodization, historians have increasingly prided themselves on the careful accumulation and analysis of facts pertaining to a single area during a few decades. The quality of specialized monographs has improved considerably during the past two decades. In addition, the 1960s might properly be labeled the decade of collections of articles (*sborniki*). Volumes such as *Absolutism in Russia, Problems of the Genesis of Capitalism in Russia*, and *Cities of Feudal Russia* as well as the 1959 collection, *Monographs on the Economic History of Russia in the First Half of the Nineteenth Century*, and the 1970 collection entitled *Problems of the Socio-economic History of Russia* have contributed to a collective assessment of the state of historical scholarship. Regrettably, the contents of these joint efforts are too disparately focused to provide much information directly pertaining to the central problems of periodization, and, as many Soviet scholars have correctly pointed out, high quality research has tended not to be cumulative. In my opinion, the opportunity remains to register the gains of recent research in a dramatic way, but for that a suitable approach has yet to be found.

Certain minimum requirements for a new approach to periodization have been articulated by Soviet writers. When the postwar periodization debate flared at the end of the 1940s, many, in an effort to overcome the intensity of existing disagreements, raised the call "to the archives."[16] From that time, there seldom has been any doubt that a solid foundation in historical documentation is an inescapable necessity for any general approach. In the succeeding decades, practically every one of the acknowledged controversial issues has been the subject of tens of specialized studies; yet, for the most part, the same, unresolved issues remain. N. I. Pavlenko summarized the state of the field in 1965 with this comment: "Narrow specialization also has a negative influence when the in-depth study of local questions from a chronological, territorial, or thematic perspective is not supplemented by synthesizing works. The latter have almost disappeared from the literary market."[17]

In accord with this appeal for eclectic studies building on the best of recent Soviet research are those demanding new standards of precision and clarity as well as improved applications of comparative methods. In the report published in 1969 of the 1965 conference on *The Transition from Feudalism to Capitalism in Russia*, A. L. Shapiro argued that, without quantitative analysis, problems of the timing of the genesis of capitalism cannot be resolved.[18] Quantification is necessary to show how this process differed century by century and region by region. Seconding Shapiro's argument, V. K. Iatsunskii also affirmed the necessity of comparative historical methods, which "can clarify a great deal."[19] A. M. Sakharov called specifically for comparisons "not only with England and France, but also with countries of the East."[20]

Of course, these opinions are selected from a variety of suggestions for future research priorities. The fact that some prominent Soviet historians assert the need for the kind of study that I have undertaken in no way indicates that they and their colleagues would approve of this specific work. Certainly the absence of references in this book to the class struggle as a critical factor in the periodization of Russian history is one issue about which all would be publicly critical.

Direct justifications for the study of urban development in order to clarify periodization are also not uncommon in Soviet works.[21] Indeed, one oft-repeated quotation from Marx is to the effect that the history of all societies is summarized in the movement of the contradictions of city and countryside.[22] Expanding on this theme in the synopsis of his 1970 doctoral dissertation entitled, "The Socio-economic Development of the Cities of Belorussia in the Second Half of the 17th and 18th Centuries," A. M. Karpachev wrote that "the evolution of a feudal society was defined to a significant extent by the development of cities."[23] He further argued that analysis of changes in cities is important for the study of substages of feudalism. Similarly, Iu. R. Klokman's *Notes of the Socio-economic History of the Cities of Northwest Russia in the Mid-18th Century* contains the conviction that "Marxist-Leninist historical science views the city as a definite economic and socio-political category. The character of a city, its specifications and development is limited above all by the socio-economic structure of the society."[24] Klokman added that the "Investigation of the socio-economic history of the city is extremely important for resolving the problem of the genesis of capitalism in Russia. . . . The appearance of the city as an economic center of a designated territory is a natural result of the development of the forces of production and the relations of production, the sum of the attained level of the social division of labor."[25] Finally we note A. L. Shapiro's suggestion for making concrete, i.e. measuring, the process of separation of city from countryside and V. K. Iatsunskii's call for carefully determining urban population data as a prelude to further analysis of cities.[26]

Mention of the separation of city from countryside almost inevitably introduces consideration of the development of marketing, a subject to which Soviets have been continually attracted in an effort to attach meaning to a quotation from Lenin concerning the timing of the establishment of a national market in Russia.[27] Fortunately, perhaps, for productive research, there has been disagreement over whether Lenin meant that, during the seventeenth century, small, local markets began to concentrate into a single national market or that the formation of such a market was actually completed during this time. In any case, study of the widening of market ties has probably contributed more than any other research to improved understanding of subdivisions within the feudal era and of changing interrelationships between settlements. Any analysis of Russian urban networks must be indebted to these materials.

In sum, Soviet conceptualizations of periodization and related research, especially on cities and marketing, point the way to new, eclectic, quantified, and comparative studies. Soviet scholars have forcefully argued that the rise and fall of Russian feudalism over ten centuries was mirrored in the transformation of cities and rural-urban relationships and that the same processes were present in other societies. Although they have made surprisingly little progress in demonstrating these assertions, in the absence of superior studies of periodization in other areas of the world, their work remains worthy of close attention. Indeed, as we shall shortly see, the presence of common elements in this and other treatments of premodern social change raises the possibility of convergence in the study of history.

Periodization of World History

Unlike the problem faced by Soviet scholars of applying predetermined periods to the actual historical events and processes that continue to be revealed, the task elsewhere has been primarily a groping effort to find useful periodizations. This has occasionally taken the form of devising new systems of periodization, but more frequently has involved reconciling traditional chronologies with the tripartite and Marxist approaches or identifying turning points in history. Specialists on various countries have applied these approaches differently. As a result the histories of Western Europe, China, and Japan have become identified with somewhat different traditions of periodization.

Diverse traditions of the histories of individual countries form the starting point for systematic efforts to compare stages of two or more societies. Comparisons of Western European countries are facilitated by a consensus of historians using both the tripartite and Marxist approaches. Most historians of Western Europe have clung to the three stages of ancient, medieval, and modern. Agreeing that the ancient stage ended around the fifth century A.D. with the collapse of the Roman Empire and that the medieval stage gave way to an early modern period around 1500, they have not engaged in the acrimonious disputes concerning dating that have characterized Soviet scholarship. Disagreements have centered more directly on the rate of social change in designated centuries or even briefer periods. Using the same indicators of development as the Soviets, including growth in agricultural production, commerce, craft production, and cities, specialists on England and France have identified particular centuries of major progress such as the tenth, thirteenth, sixteenth, and seventeenth as well as intervals of relative stagnation or even partial decline. For convenience they too have chosen subdivisions of periods, e.g. the medieval stage is divided into an early phase before 1000, a middle phase to about 1350, and a late phase to roughly 1500.[28] The fact that successive subdivisions are approximately one-half the duration of the previous subdivision indicates the accelerated pace of development identified in Western Europe. Finally the brief early modern period, lasting until the inception of the Industrial Revolution, is only about one-quarter as long as the medieval period.

Following Marx and Engels, Marxist historians of Western Europe including Soviets have found correspondences between the following labels: 1) slaveholding = ancient; 2) feudal = medieval; and 3) capitalist uklad = early modern. These parallels are understandable since both systems of periodization are based on the histories of Greece, the Roman Empire, and Western Europe. The two great discontinuities observed for these areas of the world became generalized into the end point of the ancient world and the starting point of the early modern world. The medieval period (or middle ages) and Marxist feudalism were initially conceived as residual categories beginning with the decline of Western Europe after the fall of Rome and ending with the demographic and economic crisis that followed the outbreaks of the Black Death from the mid-fourteenth century.

During the past century, these labels of periods derived from European experience have been transferred to societies that were neither conquered by the Romans nor devastated by the fourteenth-century plague. Efforts to achieve a consensus on the dating of the stages of history in many of these countries have been unsuccessful. Disagreement on the periodization of China has been particularly noticeable. Familiar with the dynastic blocks into which Chinese history has been traditionally divided, representatives of the five major contemporary schools of sinology have tried to group the dynasties into stages and even to divide some dynasties between two stages. Applying the tripartite classification most avidly, although at times disclaiming the parallels with European experience, the prolific Japanese historians of China have clashed to the point that some of them place the start of the middle ages as late as the eighth to twelfth centuries while others identify the start of the early modern period with some of these same dates.[29] Chinese communist historians also diverge sharply, ranging on the timing of the start of feudalism from the eleventh century B.C. to the first century A.D.[30] Spokesmen for the rapidly maturing Soviet school of sinology originally relied primarily on periods identified by the Chinese communists but have been eager to reject proposals that the periods in China preceded comparable periods elsewhere, for instance, that the "sprouts of capitalism" can be traced back to the Sung dynasty (960–1280).[31] Finally the amorphous but at times boldly interpretative Western sinology and, to a lesser extent, the traditional Chinese studies still alive on Taiwan have occasionally referred to problems of periodization without producing any widespread interest in either the tripartite or Marxist approaches.

In the case of Japanese history, the tripartite scheme quickly became associated with specific dates that the Marxist scheme lacks. The customary division of Japanese history is as follows: 1) ancient, seventh–twelfth centuries; 2) middle ages, thirteenth–sixteenth centuries; and 3) early modern, seventeenth–nineteenth centuries. Marxists have tended to shift the feudal period back to the seventh century and to postpone the capitalist uklad until after the seventeenth century; however, there is still no formal position on the exact dates for Japan. As I. G. Pozdniakov wrote in 1962, "At the present time it is not possible to come to a final decision on the question of the chronological limit of the beginning of feudalism in the country."[32]

No one has yet unraveled the confusion of comparisons of societies based on two systems of periodization applied by diverse schools of historians and social scientists to separate countries. Objecting to both systems for imprecise definitions of historical stages and for terms of Western origin and Western connotations, some scholars have been tempted to discard these universal systems of periodization. Yet, so much research has been carried out in terms of these viewpoints that the loss would be a severe setback for comparisons if we were to abandon hope of salvaging and restating more explicitly chronological indicators of tripartite or Marxist development.

Graph 1 combines the most widely encountered statements of the Marxist and tripartite systems of periodization. Where researchers

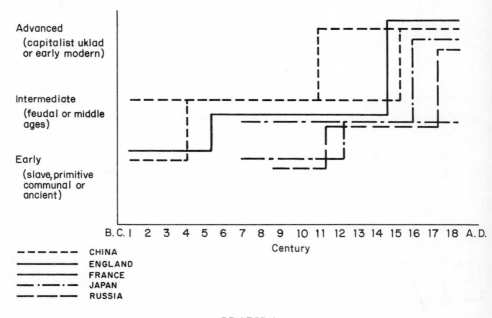

Advanced
(capitalist uklad
or early modern)

Intermediate
(feudal or middle
ages)

Early
(slave, primitive
communal or
ancient)

B.C. 1 2 3 4 5 6 7 8 9 10 11 12 13 14 15 16 17 18 A.D.
Century

- - - - - - CHINA
—————— ENGLAND
—————— FRANCE
— · — · — JAPAN
— — — — RUSSIA

GRAPH 1.
Prevailing Views on Periodization

using each of these systems agree, as for England and France, a single line demonstrates the chronological path through three stages of history. Where there is disagreement among those who apply the two systems and, indeed, among those who share a single system, as for China and Japan, the graph reveals alternate paths to represent the main lines of disagreement. For Russia, the line on the graph represents the consensus argument presented in the previous section. In broad strokes, these lines show the current state of comparative knowledge concerning the stages of history in these five countries.

If we think of historic societies as more or less developed, Graph 1 gives the impression that China was ahead of the other four countries in reaching the second stage and perhaps in reaching the third stage of premodern periodization as well. England and France follow China; in fourth place is Japan; and bringing up the rear is Russia, the last to reach feudalism (or the medieval phase) and to set up the capitalist uklad (or to enter the early modern phase). Closer examination of the graph reveals that Russia passed through the first two stages more quickly than any of the other four countries. The image of Russia conveyed in this graph is of the most backward but also the most rapidly developing country.

A frequent theme in comparisons of stages of history is the changing nature of cities. Studies of cities combine concepts of linearity and discontinuity in history. Discontinuities resulting from invasions, rebellions, and plagues are said to separate one period from another, although the underlying differences between stages of societies are usually acknowledged to be associated with such evolutionary processes as growth in the percentage of population in cities, and increase in the diversity of urban occupation. Another conception of discontinuities is the identification of leaps forward along an evolutionary path such as that H. Pirenne has identified as the rise of medieval towns in Western Europe and D. Twitchett has referred to as the transformation of cities and marketing in T'ang China (618–906).[33]

Indeed, much of the research related to the dating of stages in history has involved urban characteristics. The deterioration of European cities in the fifth and fourteenth centuries is contrasted to the revitalization of these cities in the tenth to thirteenth and sixteenth to seventeenth centuries. The arguments in favor of sprouts of capitalism in Ming China (1368–1644), as the discussion of the capitalist uklad elsewhere, gravitate around changes in urban environment.[34] There has been general recognition that changing cities are a perpetual sign of new stages or substages in history. Herein lies the convergence of approaches to periodization.

Comparisons of cities in East and West have generally focused on the degree of autonomy of urban governments from rural-based lords or national administrators.[35] A rise in merchant associations of urban self-government is usually associated with an acceleration of the movement of Western European societies through the second pre-modern stage. Lacking autonomous cities, Eastern countries are portrayed as slowly passing through the second stage. An example of a recent Soviet comparison of cities in East and West is provided in the following statement by B. F. Porshnev.

> An important turning point in the economic development of Western European feudal society was the separation of city from countryside and the wide distribution of feudal cities. Actually, the separation of city from countryside had already been realized in the preceding stage of development of society in the slaveholding society, but in the West in the early period of feudalism the economic significance of cities almost disappeared and then it somehow rose again. In contrast, in countries of the East we do not observe such a sharp break in the history of the development of cities: here even in the early middle ages cities were preserved and played a notable economic role.[36]

Accepting Max Weber's view that in the East there is nothing similar to the sharp turning point associated in the West with the rise of cities during the feudal period,[37] Porshnev emphasizes that cities in the West were acquiring new economic activities. He distinguishes between early feudal cities, dependent mainly on long-distance luxury trade, and later feudal cities, developing in the West but not in India, supported by the direct participation of peasants and craftsmen in local commerce. Other Soviet authors such as E. P. Stuzhina have not accepted such a sharp division, pointing out that cities in some Eastern countries such as China also were acquiring local marketing functions indicative of a widening division of labor.[38]

Since Soviet historians generally agree that cities were developing in the same direction in East and West, their disagreement can be restated as whether the advance of Western European cities in the medieval period indicated that England and France surpassed China or whether, despite the absence of urban self-government, Chinese cities remained superior as centers of exchange until the next European spurt in the sixteenth and seventeenth centuries. This focus on cities and commerce has been increasingly regarded as a useful way of comparing periods in history.

The Urban Networks Approach

An urban network is a hierarchy of settlements differentiated according to population or commercial and administrative functions. Those settlements included in the urban network are called central places and can be distinguished from ordinary villages by the presence of an administrative seat or a periodic market. Premodern societies vary greatly in the degree of complexity of their urban networks, ranging from large numbers of tiny nonurbanized societies to a small number of sizable eighteenth-century commercialized countries including the five selected for this study. Beginning with the hypothesis that it is possible to find a method of measuring this growing complexity in patterns of settlement, I have defined levels of central places and have sought to divide history into stages according to the number and variety of levels present.

I have selected seven levels of central places and two sets of definitions for them.[39] One set of definitions is based entirely on commercial and administrative functions and therefore can be used to specify the number of levels present at any time for which descriptive materials are available, even when population statistics are unknown. The second set of definitions is based on population data, except for the distinctions between levels 6 and 7 (settlements at both levels have fewer than 3,000 residents, but level 6 has an intermediate market while level 7 has only a standard market) and between levels 1 and 2 (cities that must be larger than any level-3 cities present, defined as having 30,000 to 300,000 residents, but which differ in that level 1 is the national administrative center). This second set of definitions can be applied to periods in which all seven levels are present, using the considerable volume of population data available for such countries as China, Japan, Russia, England, and France. The second set of definitions given in Table 2 is a modified version of the orig-

33

TABLE 2

Definitions of the Seven Levels of Central Places

Level	Definition I	Definition II
1	National administrative center	National administrative center and more populous than any level-3 city
2	Regional center or a capital of a decentralized state	Regional center and more populous than any level-3 city
3	Elevated administrative center or a major port linking a level-1 or 2 city to distant areas	Population: 30,000–299,999 and not classified at levels 1 or 2
4	Second lowest administrative center or a major regional port	Population: 10,000–29,999
5	Lowest administrative center	Population: 3,000–9,999
6	Intermediate marketing settlement	Population: fewer than 3,000 people and an intermediate marketing settlement
7	Standard marketing settlement	Population: fewer than 3,000 people and a standard marketing settlement or an administrative center without a periodic market

inal definitions used in the study of China and Japan. These definitions include the older set and are more useful for comparisons among all five of these countries.

In place of the three stages of premodern history described by the two major systems of periodization, I have grouped settlement patterns into seven stages. Whereas the Arabic numerals 1–7 are used to identify seven types of settlements, the capital letters A–G are used to identify seven types of societies. The initial stage, called stage A, can be simply described as pre-urban. Although some differences in the distribution of activities within settlements in societies of this kind can be identified, no single settlement attracted a high degree of

TABLE 3

The Seven Stages of Premodern Urban Development

Stage	Number of levels present	Usual levels present	Characteristic
A	zero	—	pre-urban
B	one	2	tribute city
C	two	1, 5 or 2, 5	state city
D	two, three, or four	1, 4, 5 or 2, 4, 5 or 2, 3 or 1, 3, 4, 5	imperial city
E	four or five	1, 3, 5, 7 or 1, 3, 4, 5, 7	standard marketing
F	five or six	1, 3, 5, 6, 7 or 1, 3, 4, 5, 6, 7	intermediate marketing
G	seven	1, 2, 3, 4, 5, 6, 7	national marketing

concentrated commercial or craft production. Within these societies, the evidence indicates that there was a relatively undifferentiated mass of villages or earlier settlement forms.

Stage B is the first phase of urban development. Generally isolated urban centers are loosely integrated into a national setting. Surrounding villages send tribute in support of military, religious, and administrative functions in these centers.

Only in stage C societies does a formal administrative hierarchy appear. The existence of two levels of cities facilitates the regular movement of goods and manpower from scattered areas in which there are lower level cities to a small number of higher level cities. Larger territories can be integrated into one administrative system, improving the capacity to support populous cities.

The continued increase in centralization based on a hierarchy of administrative centers culminates in stage D societies. While the number of levels present ranges from two to four in these societies, in each case there is an unusual concentration of population in one dominant city, often reaching hundreds of thousands of people. Also included in the stage D category are the relatively decentralized societies that seem in each instance to have followed the heyday of the great empires. In most cases a single imperial center was replaced by several competing regional centers or by a fragmented map of local cities cut off from any great regional center. In the case of China, the stage D category applies also to the early T'ang dynasty, when centralized forms had been reestablished and four levels of administrative cities were in existence. The great centralization of resources in T'ang Ch'ang-an is undoubtedly the peak of the long process of administrative centralization in world history. Ch'ang-an during the seventh to ninth centuries was the level-1 city of China and probably the largest city in world history before 1800.[40]

It is important to distinguish stages A through D from subsequent stages of premodern urban history. The principal force behind the maturation of the urban network was administrative centralization. Commerce did exist and was even an important factor in the concentration of population in many cities, and, indeed, some ports grew up as major transshipment centers of revenues in kind or of goods destined for absentee lords. Yet, commerce was a secondary factor, and it was almost entirely confined to closely regulated sections of administrative cities.

Stage E marks the beginning of what I call commercial centralization, although it should be noted that advances in commerce furthered administrative control in some respects just as advances in the establishment of a hierarchy of administrative centers had benefited commercial growth. The widespread appearance of periodic markets in settlements miles removed from administrative centers is the mark of the onset of a stage E society. Life in most villages must have been significantly affected by the development of nearby markets making it possible regularly to buy and sell goods.

Stage F societies had larger numbers of periodic marketing places, but also a new level of intermediate marketing centers. The flow of goods from villages to administrative centers was improved by the greater integration of local standard markets under more substantial intermediate markets. Higher level administrative cities acquired correspondingly greater commercial activities as the centers of the expanding networks of markets.

Finally, stage G societies are those that have all seven levels of central places or, in the case of societies which are too small to sustain a complete urban network, are fragments of a potentially complete seven-level system that is missing levels 2 or 3 or both. Goods forwarded from centers at levels 4–7, and in the case of complete systems level 3 as well, support very large cities at levels 1 and 2. The existence of both level 1 and level 2 in a given society is a sign that separate regions are integrated into a national market.

We can now review the commercial centralization of premodern societies. Just as stages B, C, and D designate phases in the maturation of an essentially administrative hierarchy, stages E, F, and G refer to the maturation of a commercial hierarchy even though many of the major commercial nexuses are found in cities that also have administrative functions. From the time standard periodic markets begin to appear, with the start of stage E until well after the beginning of stage G, the number of level-7 markets continues to proliferate. Correspondingly, after the emergence of level-6 central places from among level-7 centers, there is a persistent expansion of intermediate markets, limited primarily by the size and population in administrative units centering on level-5 cities. In countries that do not have as many as four administrative levels, the missing levels are filled in during stage F. Zones of large-scale commercial interchange gradually widened to encompass, first, level-5 cities then level-4 cities, and finally cities at levels 3 and 2, signifying the inception of stage G societies.

Sharing the hypothesis of Marxists and various social scientists that indices of urban growth are a useful measure of societal development, we now have a system for measuring change from century to century and for comparing stages of history in all premodern countries. Other frequently mentioned signs of development such as the differentiation of labor, the centralization of power, and the commercialization of agriculture are undoubtedly related to changing patterns of central places. Our goal will be to define precisely many of these processes and to determine the degree to which they correspond to changing settlement patterns. However, for the present, our attention will focus on the division of history into stages in terms of urban growth.

The lack of systematic criteria in applying the tripartite and Marxist approaches is revealed by comparing the overlap of stages according to these approaches and the urban networks approach. By all three approaches, stage A societies are classified as ancient or primitive communal, but the beginning and end points of the medieval/

feudal stages and early modern/capitalist uklad stages have no constant referents in the development of urban networks. The beginning of feudalism or the medieval period is identified for various countries experiencing stages B, C, D, and even E. The rise of the capitalist uklad or the inception of the early modern period occurs in stage F, at the beginning of stage G, or even many decades after the beginning of stage G. My impression is that any other specific identification of criteria for evolutionary historic development would also expose the confused bases for identifying stages in the present two widely used approaches.

With the urban networks approach, detailed comparisons can be carried out for advanced premodern societies, which have already reached stage G. Now our techniques must change, for these societies are potentially identical in the number of levels of central places present. The interesting problems for stage G societies are to identify the distribution of central places at each level, to specify regional variations in these patterns, and to examine concomitant characteristics of the social structure such as the distribution of social classes and the organization of trade. Using the second set of definitions based primarily on population, we can carry out intensive studies of societies such as late eighteenth-century Russia on the eve of initial modernization. By concentrating on this period, we will be trying to determine to what degree of societal development Russia had advanced by the end of the eighteenth century.

The urban networks approach provides an alternative to existing approaches to large-scale change in premodern societies. Other approaches account less satisfactorily for similarities and differences between societies. Frequently they emphasize diffusion instead of independent appearance of social phenomena. While in some cases the origin of a phenomenon was a result of borrowing, the stages of its development could proceed independently of foreign infusions. Moreover, questions of origin often preoccupy us when for systematic comparative purposes our attention would be better focused on long-range parallels in subsequent development. Tracing the movement of ideas and the migration of skills is undoubtedly a challenging pursuit, but it is not cumulative. Each example of diffusion that must be tracked down is a singular case of copying or conquering. The more interesting explanation for societal uniformities is that they arise from similar conditions. Once we identify the necessary conditions, we can generalize to all societies in which these conditions prevail.

Approaches that assume independent processes of development also may not choose strategies conducive to systematic generalizations about social change in large numbers of societies. New religious movements, new urban commercial organizations, or strong national leaders become identified as the main forces giving rise to differences between societies. Without contesting the occurrence of historical accidents or the influence of a strong leader or new type of organization on the process of premodern development, I take the position that in order to understand the impact of these differences one must first be aware of underlying similarities. It is important to try to explain as many facts as possible in terms of parsimonious factors such as the degree of development of urban networks. Once the similarities are specified, it will be appropriate to turn to the sources of differences.

The choice of the urban networks approach is based on two expectations, already to some extent borne out in the earlier comparison of China and Japan. First, I expect this approach to be a handy way of identifying similarities and differences between settlement patterns in premodern societies. Identification of levels of central places provides a method to compare stages of urban development and regional variations in two or more countries. In this light, the urban networks approach should prove a valuable tool in the vital task of comparing societies. Second, I anticipate not only that aspects of the social structure of premodern societies do not vary at random to the development of urban networks, but, in a positive vein, that powerful interdependencies can be ascertained between generalizations about changing central place distributions and other social phenomena. Specific attention is directed to patterns of commercialization and centralization, with some mention of urban land use and social stratification as well. While this book, as only the second step in the formulation of the urban networks approach, is focused primarily on demonstrating the utility of the approach for ordering data on Russian society and utilizing data from five countries for conceptualizing the stages of urban history in a new way, an effort will be made in Chapter 5 to investigate the interrelationships between various social phenomena and stages of urban change. Although considerable additional study is necessary before we can state precisely which aspects of societies can be explained in terms of periodization based on central place development, it is hoped that the evidence presented here will be persuasive that the urban networks approach qualifies both as a useful method of comparing societies and as a much needed general framework for interpreting stages of history.

✳ *2* ✳

THE ESTABLISHMENT OF
URBAN NETWORKS:
CITIES IN RUSSIA PRIOR TO 1750

In less than one thousand years the Russian landscape evolved by steps from separate clusters of dwellings without any central places to villages joined by an integrated network of many hundreds of central places under the prosperous cities of Moscow and St. Petersburg. The progression from stage A to stage G can be traced through the earliest phase of urban development, the Kievan era, the Tatar rule, and then the Muscovy and Tsarist periods up to 1750.[1] Determining the order and rate of appearance of the seven levels of central places (using the first set of definitions in Table 2), we can relate these changes to other transformations in the social structure of Russia.

By examining the course of urban history in Russia while all seven levels were being established, we emerge in a position to compare this experience with the maturation of the urban networks in China and Japan in the East and with England and France in the West. Having already described these Far Eastern countries elsewhere,[2] I refer again to their urban histories frequently, but briefly, throughout the chapter. At the conclusion of each section of the chapter, additional attention is devoted to the urban histories of England and France, which have never been examined in terms of this approach. Identification of similarities and differences in the urban histories of all of these countries should enable us to attach meaning to the observations concerning the development of cities in Russia.

At the end of Chapter 2 we can at last address ourselves to a precise explanation of the meaning of Russian backwardness for roughly 900 years before 1750. It becomes clear that Russia's urban system consistently trailed those of the other four countries; but it also becomes apparent that the rate of change in Russia was unusually rapid. Russia gained steadily on China, which until roughly 1600 probably maintained its hold on first place in the world, and generally narrowed the gap with the other countries as well. The only country to which Russia lost ground during its first five hundred years of urban history was Japan, but the differences between these two countries began to narrow by the sixteenth century. Although I argue that as late as 1700 Russia remained the only one of these countries that had not yet entered stage G, the overall conclusion to be drawn is that the reality of backwardness must be tempered with an awareness of dynamism. Russia continually reduced the gap separating it from the world's most developed society. Russia entered stage G in the early eighteenth century after moving from stage to stage in the briefest time of all of these countries.

Stages A and B: pre-Kievan Russia

Although some non-Slavic peoples occupying areas of what is today the vast expanse of the Soviet Union had at times established cities, the uninterrupted tradition of urban development that is rightly associated with Russian history began only in the eighth or, at the latest, the ninth century.[3] The first Russian cities were established along a roughly north-south line extending from Novgorod to Kiev. Clearly, the Eastern Slavic inhabitants of this region were familiar with people from previously urbanized areas. Countries not many hundreds of miles distant to the northwest, the west, the southwest, and the southeast had already entered the urban age—in some cases more than 1,000 years past. Moreover, just south of the Black Sea was located the center of the Byzantine Empire, one of the principal urbanized areas of the world. Yet, despite the presence of traders and warriors from foreign lands, the establishment of urban settlements in ancient Russia should be seen as essentially a local achievement for it followed the consolidation of the Eastern Slavic tribes, the marked development of craft skills, the spread of agriculture, and the emergence of multitribal political centers.[4] After many centuries of societal development, the Slavic people of this area successfully adopted urban forms of which they were aware.

During the ninth and tenth centuries some tens of fortresses appeared along the Novgorod-Kiev axis. Generally located on a bluff overlooking a river or a river junction, a fortified settlement primarily served the ruler who received tribute from the local population of surrounding territories. Many of these settlements were undoubtedly only in the initial stage of urban development;[5] they lacked merchants and artisans and were sustained chiefly by local agricultural goods paid in kind and by corvée labor. Some of these settlements, however, were also supported by the accumulation of such goods as furs, honey, and wax for long-distance commerce and by trade in transit. In the vicinity of these more prosperous fortresses, there were likely to be scattered clusters of artisans, producing adornments, weapons, and other metal products for consumption largely within the walled area where the local prince and his principal supporters resided in relative security.[6] Depending on one's definition of urban, one could argue, as some Soviet scholars do, that the first fortresses were still pre-urban and that cities appeared only at the turn of the tenth century when built-up areas with merchants and artisans were being established just beyond the walls of some of the fortresses.[7] Nevertheless, because the continuity between the two types of fortified settlements can be clearly shown and because it is customary to trace the history of Chinese and Japanese cities back to the earlier fortified forms, I accept here the viewpoint of M. N. Tikhomirov, who was a prominent scholar of these early Russian settlements, that they do qualify as cities.

As indicated above, prior to the widespread settlement of areas just beyond fortress walls and surrounding moats during the eleventh century, we can divide cities into two types: 1) those with just a *kreml'* or fortress, and 2) those with both a kreml' and a *posad*, an area inhabited by craftsmen and traders. Yet, similar to the earliest cities in China and Japan, all of these fortress cities should be properly labeled level-2 central places. They were highly independent of each other, functioning as centers of almost entirely self-sufficient local areas. Even when their lords fought one another in an effort to capture additional cities or joined in alliance, no formal urban hierarchy appeared.

Already by the late tenth century, major level-2 central places were becoming distinguishable. In an embryonic form, they displayed the characteristics of large cities during the next phase of urban development. Located along lively river routes, these cities benefited from greater access to the production of large areas and from foreign trade.[8] Their development was spurred also by the regularization of demands on the local population as new procedures were devised for securing rural payments and new points were designated for efficiently collecting goods owed to the prince. The lords of these cities vied first to subjugate other cities and then to use effectively these other fortresses for the support of their own cities.

Some comparisons with the initial period of urban growth in China and Japan should clarify the above descriptions. In many respects, the introduction of Russian cities appears to have been intermediate between the extremes observed in the other two countries. First, Russian cities were the products of diffusion of foreign knowledge, but were not copies of what existed abroad. In contrast, the earliest Chinese cities have not been traced to foreign models, while the first Japanese cities not only were based on knowledge of foreign cities but were even directly modeled after those in China. Russian contacts encompassed a diversity of foreigners, and no single awe-inspiring center of civilization loomed in the distance as did China for the Japanese. Second, the period during which only level-2 cities had formed reached 1,000 years or more in China and less than 100 years in Japan as opposed to the roughly 200 years in Russia. Beginning with level-2 cities that had already been established for 150 or 200 years in Japan, the Russians fell somewhat further behind, but nonetheless in comparison to China demonstrated remarkable progress in a brief span of time. Third, while the number of level-2 cities proliferated in China to 100 or more in striking opposition to the single city at this level in Japan, some tens of distinct fortress-cities were scattered through Russia before efforts at unified control succeeded. Finally, we should note a basic similarity between Russian and Japanese cities. Both societies were seemingly ripe for a sharp transformation by the time their cities were first established. Pre-urban settlement patterns and metal objects uncovered by Russian archaeologists indicate that considerable development had already taken place by the eighth century. Of course, China in 2000 B.C. had far less opportunity to benefit from the diffusion of foreign achievements than did Japan and Russia during the first millennium A.D.

The universal stages A and B provide an obvious sequence of premodern social change in Russia as elsewhere. From the time of the first appearance of man in this portion of Eurasia, a series of pre-urban stage A societies in some of their many metamorphoses had been in existence. Similar to other stage A societies, undoubtedly a majority of all societies in world history, these collectives were primarily hunting and gathering peoples characterized by the shifting locations of recognizable ethnic groups. While, during a period of more than 1,000 years, these stage A societies may have occasionally yielded to abortive attempts to establish cities, the firm imprint of an urban stage B society, which served as a foundation for subsequent societal development, can be traced only to a period of about 200 years ending with the rise of Kiev.

Of course, the distinction between stages A and B as between all of these stages is continuous and not dichotomous. At the time stage A was drawing to an end, specific settlements must have already developed a gradual concentration of administrative and ceremonial functions. Similarly, the weak control over resources in the countryside from the early cities of stage B presumably yielded to a more hierarchical distinction between some of the increasing number of cities. One or more cities arose from among the mass of urban centers as superior points in the concentration of resources.

Stages C and D: Kievan and Tatar-ruled Russia

By the early eleventh century, Kiev had emerged as the foremost city of Russia. A period of more than 200 years is commonly identified as "Kievan Russia," which indicates the predominance of this one center, "the mother of Russian cities." Population estimates vary both for the country as a whole and for its central city, but if we tentatively accept the frequently encountered estimates of 5 million people in all of Russia and 50,000 or at most 100,000 people in Kiev, we find that this city contained 1–2 percent of the national total.[9] A level-1 national administrative center now existed in Russia.

Kiev's prosperity rested on a foundation of numerous local urban centers. Tikhomirov calculates that by the end of the eleventh century nearly 100 fortress-cities had been founded, and that the total continued to climb, reaching almost 300 at the time of the Mongol invasion in 1237.[10] These figures should undoubtedly be reduced somewhat in order to obtain the number of cities existing simultaneously during this period of frequent territorial realignment. In addition, we should note that some of these were fortresses without posad, which ought no longer to qualify as cities at a time when new levels of central places existed. In any case, even if these figures are reduced by half, they still reveal a considerable proliferation of local cities. Some five to ten of these cities are identified by Tikhomirov as major centers with more than 1,000 inhabitants, and Novgorod, easily the second city of the country, is credited with a population of about 20,000.[11] Altogether these figures add up to an estimated 3–4 percent of the population in cities during the Kievan period. The first two cities of the land held at least one-third and, perhaps, as many as one-half of all urban residents. Scattered resources were being transported to these national centers via local cities.

A two-step administrative hierarchy existed during the Kievan period. At the bottom level were local cities, corresponding to the definition of level-5 central places. Above them was Kiev, the national center. The classification of Novgorod poses a problem similar to one faced previously with regard to the secondary national capitals of Han China. To be consistent, we must classify Novgorod in the same manner as these Chinese cities, i.e. as an offshoot of the level-1 city. At a time when transportation was poorly developed and techniques of central control were still considerably dependent on personal relationships, establishing a secondary capital eased the task of ruling a large territory. Later when Kiev fell into decline, it co-existed with Novgorod as level-2 cities in a more decentralized setting without any level-1 city.

During the eleventh century, churches and monasteries were built in large numbers. Tikhomirov's estimates of the number of these religious structures in various cities provide us with a handy criterion for comparisons of cities. Kiev, with hundreds of churches, contrasted with other principal cities in which there were only tens. Of the seventy monasteries in Russia, the seventeen in Kiev were rivaled only by an equal number in Novgorod.[12] That monasteries were predominantly located in cities is one indication of the special importance of urban areas during the Kievan period before new dispersed patterns became widespread.

Similar to early empires, Russia achieved a high degree of centralization of urban population in one or two cities without much commerce. Since the appearance of markets in settlements other than administrative cities was still several centuries away, the only regular exchange within a princedom occurred in the tightly regulated level-5 city market. Cities characteristically now had two centers, the kreml' residence of the local prince who was subordinate to the great prince in Kiev, and the market within the posad. Kiev with its large population was permitted at least two markets.

Among the settlements established as administrative centers at strategic locations, an increasing number displayed what was becoming the standard urban plan. Primary among urban elements was the walled fortress. In the eleventh and again in the twelfth centuries the number of notable fortresses approximately tripled. No less essential for the settlement's vitality was the marketing square. As a rule, this commercial zone developed just outside the fortress wall. The market's importance can be judged from the assertion by G. P. Latysheva and M. G. Rabinovich that, "The main danger for a city—was not destruction by an enemy, but loss of its local market."[13] This danger could arise from any major reorientation of local trade or revenues in kind. Extending out from the market, the posad area registered the most growth, but its position could be jeopardized whenever the fortress area required expansion, resulting in an encroachment on former posad land. In big cities, an outer wall enclosed much or all of the posad in addition to the inner wall around the kreml' (or *detinets*).

While sharing some of the features of early empires, Kievan Russia was in many respects not an empire. Despite the unification of the country under Kiev, there is no record of the establishment of an extensive state bureaucracy, and local cities were not well-integrated in a formal hierarchical system. In fact, reliance on local princes who controlled most territory from their fortified cities guaranteed that the pyramid of support on which Kiev's prosperity rested would be short-lived.

Two opposing tendencies are apparent in rural-urban relations of the Kievan period. On the one hand, princes strengthened their control over the local population. Princes' cities took on new significance for surrounding territories not only through the establishment of city markets but, even more importantly, through the expansion of administrative demands and services. Symbolic of the new city was a broadened line of fortifications to protect both a larger urban population and a part of the rural population in case of attack.[14] On the other hand, techniques of governing large rural areas were not well developed. In order both to improve overall capacity to extract agricultural production and to satisfy pressures from associates seeking rewards for services rendered, princes parceled out direct control over much of their holdings. Estates known as *votchiny* were granted to members of the prince's family, to his principal subordinates, and to church and monastery heads.[15] Differentiation of the population in rural settlements was promoted first by strengthening the prince's direct control over them and then by the division of that control among his associates.

The century before the Mongol invasion was a period of decentralization. Stunned by a series of wars, Kiev declined in population as its lords lost their claim to a share of the production from many areas. After being sacked in 1169, Kiev never fully recovered and continued only as the nominal capital, i.e. as a level-2 city. Decentralization did not, however, signal a reversion to pre-Kievan settlement patterns. Centers of the now hereditary princedoms remained as level-5 cities, directly subordinate to a growing number of level-2 cities. Russia was becoming divided into clusters of level-5 cities, centering on level-2 cities whose lords vied for power. Decline in the shipment of goods between clusters of cities was probably compensated for by increased trade among the cities of each cluster and by rising consumption of the owners of the rapidly proliferating votchiny. The fact that many votchiny owners were concentrated in the level-2 central cities of princedoms undoubtedly encouraged trade and kept the urban population of the country from falling sharply.

The impact of the Mongol invaders who seized Russia in 1237 is often exaggerated.[16] True, more than other invaders, they killed and plundered. Furthermore, they ruled Russia for almost two and one-half centuries, which Table 1 indicates was as much as half of the period when Soviets classify Russia as most purely (more than 90 percent) feudal. Yet, unlike in China, the Mongols ruled from afar, demanding little more than tribute and acquiescence to their rule. Even without the Mongol invasion, we can expect that decentralization would have continued and that territorial readjustments would have accompanied Kiev's final fall as the national center.

Probably the most misleading impression of Mongol rule stems from the fragmented political map of the period. Rather than interpreting this fragmentation as due to the serious blow to trade and crafts caused by the Mongols, we can also find evidence that some previously urban-based activities were now being performed in rural areas and that new growth of agriculture and commerce was contributing to a changing pattern of central places.[17] As in China, Japan, England, and France, centuries of decentralization permitted the preconditions to form in rural areas for the widespread emergence of periodic markets.

The arrival of the Mongols hastened some processes and slowed others. The terrifying Mongol sweeps through Russian lands undoubtedly accelerated the migration of Russians to the relatively secure and also centrally located Tver', Moscow, and Vladimir regions, collectively known at the time as the Northeast. Furthermore, the Mongol demand for continuous payment of tribute must have helped princes to consolidate their hold on local areas, gradually overcoming the forces of decentralization to even tinier holdings. Nonetheless, for at least the remaining decades of the thirteenth century, the Mongol devastation certainly disrupted the performance of urban crafts. Indeed, stone construction in Russia was completely halted for roughly five decades.

The frequent rise and fall of cities was more characteristic of the two and one-half centuries of subordination to the Tatars than of any subsequent period in Russian history. Even before 1240, local princes eager to consolidate their control over enlarged territories had begun to build satellite cities and to convert existing cities into satellites of their own cities.[18] New cities were founded along rivers and roads were built leading out from the major centers or were constructed near the boundaries of princedoms in an effort to create a base for extending those boundaries. For example, Moscow, alleged to have been established in 1131 but actually originating even earlier, emerged as a city straddling the boundary of Prince Yuri Dolgoruky's holdings. During the twelfth and thirteenth centuries, cities were also founded along the Volga river as control was extended eastward and southward. The new cities of Moscow and Nizhnii Novgorod at the junction of the Volga and the Oka rivers provide examples of settlements that replaced their parent cities as centers of princedoms.[19]

Almost as common as the building of new cities was the abandonment of existing ones. With the great loss of territory in the west, the population actually settled in what is often called appanage Russia under the Tatars was no doubt less than the peak figure for Kievan Russia; yet, despite intermittent wars and some severe epidemics, the total was definitely rising. Increased densities of population in the core area of the Northeast provided favorable conditions for urban growth. Considerable improvement in agricultural techniques and expanded trade further enabled cities to acquire a more diverse economic foundation. Fortresses that did not attract increased trade were unlikely to withstand the competitive conditions of the new era. Other cities that proved their worth were well situated to serve as the centers of large hinterlands. During this period, the patterns were formed for local units of administration known as *uezd*, which persisted to the twentieth century. Uezd cities at level 5 became the building blocks of a new hierarchy of central places.

The Mongol period is widely known for the rivalry of princes who, using the terminology of this approach, resided in level-2 cities around which were grouped level-5 cities. Competing for large numbers of level-5 cities, princes considered the strategic advantages of locations and were frequently willing to build new cities at more advantageous locations or simply to gather their supporters in fewer, better situated centers. Thus the emergence of clearly recognized hierarchies of cities in princedoms promoted the efficient distribution of centers of consolidated local areas. Often attacked, subject to destruction by fire, and transferred back and forth with the constantly changing boundaries of major princedoms, level-5 cities persistently struggled for survival. Simultaneously, level-2 cities underwent repeated change. The most fragmented conditions of feudalism in which cities along with other territorial holdings had been divided among heirs as personal property resulted in the frequent transference of cities from owner to owner. During the fourteenth and early fifteenth centuries, small princedoms gave way to larger ones, which in turn competed for supremacy. Networks of cities absorbed isolated centers. Succeeding both in mobilizing resources from their surrounding territories and in gathering a major share of interregional commerce, the capitals of the newly enlarged princedoms emerged as centers with 10,000 or more inhabitants as opposed to level-5 settlements with populations rarely in excess of 1,500.[20]

The era of Moscow's rise corresponds to the entire history of Mongol rule. Beginning as a minor fortress-city (with a population of a few hundred), the city became first the center of a small princedom (population: 1,000 or more); then a rival of Tver' for preeminence among appanage cities (population: 10,000 or more); and finally, in the early fifteenth century, the undisputed first city of Russia (population: many tens of thousands).[21] Indicative of the steady rise in the significance of this city was the frequent enlargement of its kreml', appearing as the first stone fortress during the 1360s.[22]

Cities that can be distinguished as a third type on the seven-level hierarchy first appeared during the fourteenth century. Supported not by a single area's production, but to an unprecedented extent by long-distance commerce en route to (and, to a lesser extent, from) level-2 cities, settlements such as Nizhnii Novgorod are properly classified as level-3 central places. Expansion of shipments along the Volga and other rivers made their appearance possible.

Additional description of the changing pattern of the accumulation of goods may help to explain the growing network of cities. Ownership of votchiny was divided between clerical authorities representing churches and monasteries, nobles who owed definite numbers of horsemen in times of combat, and the prince himself. At least in the Novgorod region, not part of appanage Russia and perhaps developing more rapidly due to extensive foreign trade through the Baltic

Sea, there was also an intermediate group of nobles in possession of estates so small that they had to engage in farming themselves.[23] Surpluses for cities came primarily from big votchiny, whose owners frequently had urban residences. Goods in kind sent to absentee owners and urban religious institutions and corvée in the form of transportation of these goods and construction within the city contributed to the urban economy.[24] Increasingly, however, direct supplies from estates could not meet the needs of urban populations. Toward the end of this period when large cities were developing, nearly half of the 3–4 percent of the Russian population in cities could be found in central places at levels 2 and 3, which required support from wide areas. Many of the major religious institutions and *boiars* (nobles) in these cities held scattered votchiny in distant areas. It was often more profitable for them to sell produce from their lands in local cities than to send it directly to their urban residences. In addition, many of their growing needs could not be supplied from their own votchiny, but required money for purchases in the city market. In these conditions of growing commercial involvement, many estate owners fell into debt, while others, including certain monasteries, adapted to the changed circumstances by securing grants of land in still unsettled areas or through rights of inheritance from private owners seeking salvation, by engaging in usury, or by taking advantage of monopoly trading rights in such goods as salt and fish. By the middle or late fifteenth century, votchiny had lost a considerable part of their self-sufficiency, and trade was replacing direct shipments to landowners in cities.[25]

During the final decades of Tatar rule, cities continued to be divided between a kreml' and a posad. A rich prince could take pride in the great circumference and firm construction of his kreml'. Inside its wall, he placed his military and administrative offices, storage facilities, major churches, cathedrals, and monasteries, and residences of the chief personages in the princedom. Some kreml' were large enough to include many additional residences and, perhaps, some vacant land. The posad was normally the low part of the city, with winding streets sloping down from the bluff above which peered out the high towers of the kreml' wall. At least thirty cities were noted for their sizable posad and many of these even had a wall around the posad, albeit of distinctly inferior construction to the kreml' wall.[26] The most prominent buildings in the posad as in the kreml' were religious structures, lavishly adorned and rising high above the densely packed residences. Some of these monuments to God, at least five or ten of which could be found in any major city, were even built of stone in contrast to the wooden huts all around. Parts of the city were likely to be the private holdings of boiars, whose household economies frequently included craftsmen working directly to supply their patron's needs. Other craftsmen were settled in clusters according to their specialization and they, too, produced mainly for orders. Many streets were named after the type of craft located there.[27] Finally it should be mentioned that there were agricultural lands within many cities.

In conclusion, these third and fourth phases of Russian urban development, encompassing the Kievan and Mongol periods, lasted about 450 years, only half as long as the similar stages in China and, perhaps, 50 years less than the similar stages in Japan. In each society, the period began with levels 1 and 5 present; subsequently level 2 replaced level 1 as a time of division was reached; and eventually level 3 appeared (see Table 3) as commerce was rising. Again Russia's resemblance to Japan in many respects is striking. The early centralization in each country produced a prominent national center that lent its name to the period as a whole. Heian (Kyoto) contained at least twice as many residents as Kiev at its peak, but ninth- and tenth-century Japan was also probably somewhat more populous and densely settled than Kievan Russia, and Heian did not have to share its prosperity with a secondary capital such as Novgorod. In both countries, this early period of city building did not result in a lasting infrastructure of cities for use in the subsequent evolution of the urban network. Heian Japan's level-5 cities disappeared during the initial centuries of decentralization, and in Russia the shift from Kiev to the Northeast also required the consolidation of new level-5 cities, but this transition occurred quickly in Russia, and level-5 centers of local princedoms and later uezd cities remained a continuous part of the urban network, as in China. The position of Japan and Russia was reversed, however, in regard to populous cities. Institutions of national control were less firmly established in Russia, and, during the period of decentralization to estates, more than two centuries passed before a city comparable to Kiev emerged. In contrast, in Japan as in China large cities remained an active force.

From this comparative perspective, we can reevaluate the thirteenth and fourteenth centuries in Russia as an unusually brief interlude between the early phase of centralization under a big city and the subsequent shift away from weakly integrated, scattered estates to a new network of cities based on greater commercialism. All of these three societies experienced decentralization with two or three levels of cities present, but Russia, with the most extreme decline of large cities, also was the quickest to move ahead in building the urban network. One common factor in Russia and Japan that may have contributed to overcoming the forces of decentralization was the rapid transplantation of foreign religious institutions, which became associated with urban control over the countryside first by maintaining close ties to urban institutions and then by providing a continuous source of goods to cities during the time when rural estates were proliferating. Experiencing less decentralization, the Chinese were the slowest to expand their network of cities.

A major difference in timing of the decisive struggle for urban survival gives the end of this period in Russia special importance. The term "warring states" applied to China properly refers to the fifth to third centuries B.C., the time when in the struggle for supremacy a realignment of urban hierarchies resulted, which proved to be a pattern that endured until modern times. When this term is applied to Japan, it refers to the constant fighting during the sixteenth and, perhaps, the end of the fifteenth centuries, the time when at last a stable network of cities appeared. If such a term existed for Russia, it would undoubtedly be applied to the fourteenth and fifteenth centuries. The basic division into uezd administrative units was achieved in conditions of continuous conflict. The principal integration of Russian territorial units into a lasting administrative system dates from this period.

The comparable periods in England and France date from the time that these countries were part of the Roman Empire to the ninth or tenth centuries A.D. During more than eight hundred years, a highly centralized system under the hegemony of Rome was set up and then quickly gave way to an unusually decentralized system in which the urban presence was only faintly discernible. Even more disruptively than during the Mongol period in Russia, these countries became divided into tiny local units that for a long time were not reintegrated into any larger system. As in Russia, Christian religious institutions were increasingly active in accumulating resources in rural areas during this phase of decentralization. Eventually, efforts to reorganize the movement of local resources together with various improvements in rural conditions would result in the widespread emergence of periodic markets.

The advance from stage B to stage C is signaled by the establishment of a hierarchy of urban centers. However, the distinction between stages C and D is less readily apparent. Indeed, it appears as if the only one of these five countries that experienced a clearly discernible stage C is China. For more than 500 years before the establishment of an imperial system, China was divided into states with their own two-level hierarchies of local administrative centers and state capitals. In contrast, England, France, and Japan borrowed from or were colonized by stage D societies. Through a rash of city building, they seemed to have passed directly from stage B to stage D. There was no noticeable intermediate stage of scattered networks with two levels of cities.

Russia's apparent direct leap from isolated cities characteristic of stage B to a single national administrative center over local centers typical of stage D also may be a consequence of its relative backwardness with respect to neighboring societies. As in England, France, and Japan, there were probably some transitional decades suggesting a stage C society with competing networks of level-2 and level-5 cities, but then Kiev quickly emerged as the predominant center, perhaps following the model of Constantinople. According to this system of classification, both Kievan and Mongol Russia should be treated as stage D societies.

Of all the stages in the maturation of the urban network, latecomer societies were best able to bypass stage C. Yet, in each of the four cases where we have witnessed this phenomenon, the stage D urban network was conspicuously fragile. As appendages of a huge imperial system centering on distant Rome, England and France failed to maintain most of their cities after the collapse of the empire. Similarly, Japanese level-5 cities disappeared with little trace, although a large level-2 city persisted. In each of these countries, but not in China, the decentralization of the second phase of stage D was the time of a precipitous decline or disappearance of level-5 cities. The recovery from this nadir was quickest in Japan and Russia. The remarkable fact of the Mongol period in Russia was that, in spite of great territorial displacement and occupation by a power regarded as more barbarous than the invaders who overran Western Europe following the Roman Empire, Russia recovered with alacrity to move quickly into stage E.

In the continuity of its cities, Russia ranks intermediate between China and Japan. Urban bases in Russia often disappeared if they lacked functions to give them continued importance. Yet, this did not reach the extreme found in Japan, where the first generation of cities was largely eclipsed by a later generation built in response to the need for new functions. Nor did the Russian situation approach the stability of Chinese cities, where existing urban bases acquired new functions as demanded. The ephemeral prosperity of many cities in this early phase of urban history seems to be a consequence of administrative instability in the period when cities reflect primarily the growth of administrative centralization.

Stages E and F: Muscovy Russia

The two hundred years from the middle of the fifteenth to the middle of the seventeenth centuries comprise stage E and part of stage F in Russian history. The remainder of stage F will be treated separately in the following section on the transition to stage G.

Shortly before the beginning of this period Russia was essentially reunited, with cities at levels 1, 3, and 5. During the next two centuries, autocratic government in Moscow continued to be strengthened,[28] other cities were steadily placed under central control and, first, level 7 and then level 6 were added to the existing hierarchy of central places. At the time of the *ulozhenie* (code) of 1649, which confirmed that cities had become pillars of central control, Russia's urban network resembled China's in the late fourteenth century and those of Japan, England, and France in the late fifteenth or early sixteenth centuries. The gap between these countries was narrowing.

Territorial expansion and population growth marked most of these two hundred years in Russia. Beginning with an area of less than 200,-000 square miles in 1462, the area of Russia under one government expanded to at least six times this size by the 1530s and then doubled again by the end of the century.[29] Acquisition of the autonomous Novgorod and Pskov regions in the Northwest and of Smolensk along a principal trade route to European countries was an essential step in the early consolidation of a populous and comparatively developed core area. Also rapidly secured and settled were areas to the north of Moscow, providing access to the Volga river and eventually to trade routes expanding through the White Sea to Western Europe and through the northeast to Siberia. With the conquest of Kazan' and Astrakhan' in the middle of the sixteenth century, the Volga river became an entirely internal waterway boosting the already extensive commercial relations to Asia. Finally toward the end of the sixteenth century, the settlement of western Siberia was begun. Continuing through the seventeenth century, Russian colonization pushed across the vast expanse of Siberia in search of furs. Especially significant during the final decades of this period was the gradual movement of fortified lines of settlement southward, making possible the first widespread migration into the fertile black-earth zone. While continued expansion to the south and new annexations in the west remained to be carried out in the eighteenth century, the Russian Empire by the middle of the seventeenth century had completed most of its outward thrust. Whereas in ancient Russia and in the Kievan and Mongol eras, Russia occupied relatively little territory mainly along one or two river systems, this third period saw Russia become by far the largest country in the world, occupying essentially the territory of today's Russian Republic.

Annexations were not accompanied by corresponding increases in population. While some of the initial new territory in the west was as densely settled as the old Muscovite areas, most new lands remained sparsely inhabited. According to Ia. E. Vodarskii, the population of Russia increased from 6.5 million in the mid-sixteenth century to just 7 million toward the middle of the seventeenth century, when population growth began to accelerate. A. I. Kopanev offers higher estimates, dating a population of more than 10 million from at least the early seventeenth century.[30] In my opinion, a figure of 10–12 million for the second half of the century is most consistent with the widely accepted data available for later years.

Vast expansion of political boundaries far in advance of significant colonization into those territories seems to be unique to Russia among the five countries. Only in the eighteenth century did China initiate a similar expansion in response to Manchu policies.

A sudden sign of the shift in the geographical focus of development occurred during the 1570s and 1580s. Prior to this time, mainly areas to the west and north were commercially integrated with Moscow. The largest cities after the capital were mostly spread along an arc between Smolensk, Pskov, Novgorod, and Iaroslavl'. Then a serious crisis partly due to the loss through war of access to the Baltic Sea struck these areas; population declined as some villages were deserted and the number of households in many cities dropped sharply.[31] Despite considerable recovery in the production of these areas by the end of the century, the balance of economic forces was soon altered. Areas to the south and east of Moscow were now better represented by the increasingly prosperous cities of Astrakhan', Kazan', and Nizhnii Novgorod along the Volga and by an expanding network of lesser cities.

The number of uezd centers rose from roughly 100 in 1500 to 160 or 170 in mid-century and finally to as many as 230 by the early part of the following century.[32] Many of the first new uezd cities appeared in the north beyond the Volga river, later as many as 20 new cities were established in the east and southeast in the vicinity of the Volga river and at the end of the sixteenth century up to 15 new cities were founded in Siberia. Especially numerous were the cities built as fortresses in the steppes to the south in an effort to block frequent Tatar raids, which in 1571 even succeeded in reaching Moscow. By the first half of the seventeenth century some of these fortress cities were gradually being transformed into typical uezd cities, serving as centers of agricultural hinterlands.

Non-Slavic minorities inhabited many of the areas brought into the Russian Empire during the sixteenth and seventeenth centuries. As nomadic peoples in the south and east, they generally retained the right to reside in the areas where they had long lived, although their ways of living gradually succumbed to the influences of Russian administration and economic pursuits. Incorporating the troops of minority groups into their armed operations, Russian authorities at the same time insisted on strict rules limiting internal battles among the separate nationalities. Meanwhile fortresses founded by Russians in these areas attracted trade and encouraged specialized activities for the Russian market such as livestock breeding. In return, the local populations received luxury items and other products from central areas of the Russian Empire.[33]

With the growing authority of the tsar in Moscow, uezd cities were transformed to better serve his military, administrative, and fiscal needs. An essential step was to transfer cities from the control of private individuals into state property.[34] Ivan III, in the late fifteenth century, was especially active in this effort. His successors continued to strengthen central control, but at the end of this period there remained many private settlements not inferior to uezd cities. Private *slobody* (suburbs) on the outskirts of uezd cities were slower to be converted, but by the middle of the sixteenth century many had already been placed under state control, and in the early seventeenth century new rules significantly limited the rights of owners in these urban areas. Finally with the ulozhenie of 1649, private slobody were in large part abolished.[35] Steadily, the commercial and artisan posad population was gaining a new legal status under the direct rule of the tsar. Cities at one time fragmented into sections whose residents varied in privileges depending on the standing of their lords were gradually becoming single units.

Throughout these two centuries, approximately one-third of the urban population lived in the flourishing capital of Moscow.[36] For a time, Novgorod and Pskov each may have contained about a quarter of the population of Moscow, while several other cities consistently contained up to 10,000 inhabitants; however, for the latter part of this period there was probably no city other than distant Astrakhan' that held as much as 10 percent of Moscow's total of 150,000 to 200,000 people.[37] According to one estimate, by the mid-seventeenth century there were 254 cities in Russia, of which some fifteen consisted of 500 or more households.[38] With most uezd cities having no more than 1,000 inhabitants, it is likely that Russia was about 5 percent urban.

Moscow's domination rested on superior trade connections as well as administrative precedence. Merchants from Asian and European lands met in this city. Moreover, the tsarist government made special efforts, including forced resettlement of rich merchants from Novgorod, Pskov, and Smolensk, to improve Moscow's marketing ties with all areas of Russia.[39] Sections of the capital bore the names of the cities from which residents had originated. Among the city population, the old aristocracy of boiars and the newly emerging gentry called *dvoriane* were both well represented. Political unification as well as economic integration was attracting large numbers of wealthy individuals to the city.

Moscow's population grew rapidly at the end of the fifteenth and the beginning of the sixteenth centuries.[40] Its kreml' became a residential center for boiars and dvoriane, and the posad area expanded greatly. The sixteenth century was a time of Moscow's most furious wall construction; three outer walls appeared in succession as did fortified monasteries on the city's outskirts. The city acquired the form and even approached the population which in basic respects would remain unchanged until the nineteenth century. The Kremlin became the political and religious center of Russia. The Kitai *gorod* (literally "city," but in this case referring to a section of the city enclosed by a wall) just beyond it combined the character of a great residential center for the city's magnates with the magnetism of Russia's liveliest trading area. As both of these inner city enclosures gained central functions, their day-time population increased, and the number of night-time residents decreased; houses of magnates were moved out of the Kremlin, in some cases to the Kitai gorod, and craftsmen and merchants no longer could retain residences so close to the city center.

The precise date of the appearance of periodic markets outside of uezd cities is difficult to establish, but by the middle of the fifteenth century a few of these marketing settlements were recorded, and, clearly, by the end of the century many had been founded in various areas of the country.[41] Prior to the emergence of these markets, the inhabitants of an uezd had the opportunity regularly to market their goods and make purchases only in the administrative center, which was often located as far as twenty or thirty miles away. Now one or more of their villages could be selected as a site for monthly or weekly gatherings at which itinerant merchants stopped. Actually many of the early markets were not located in typical villages, but were found outside the walls of monasteries, which as owners of large estates had long served as gathering points for craftsmen and as accumulation points for goods.[42] Most often these new locations of markets were along rivers and major roads.

During the sixteenth century, fairs also appeared in conjunction with annual festival days at monasteries and churches.[43] Unlike the weekly markets, which largely served the purposes of intravillage trade and local intervillage trade, annual fairs became agencies noted for the exchange of goods from wider areas. Offering more varied goods to larger crowds, fairs helped overcome the former isolation of princedoms.

In Russia as elsewhere, level-7 local periodic markets eventually gave rise to intermediate level-6 marketing settlements. In China, up to three and one-half centuries were required between the time level-7 settlements became widespread and the time that the larger, level-6 markets became noticeable. In Japan the same progression occurred twice as rapidly. The process was even further shortened in Russia, as many major periodic markets in nonadministrative settlements probably developed by the end of the sixteenth century. Since no special term was given to these settlements and no previous attempt has been made to apply this analytic distinction between types of nonadministrative central places to Russia, the dating of the appearance of level-6 marketing settlements poses a problem. Yet, during the seventeenth century we can observe such signs of their presence as more frequent marketing days and significantly more populous settlements among places with periodic markets. Moreover, various writings on the sixteenth century suggest that, in the northwest, tiny periodic markets emerged in rapid succession followed by a contraction in the latter part of the century when a small number of settlements continued to prosper, i.e. what seems to be the appearance of level-6 markets from among level-7 ones.[44] Similar to fairs, these more substantial centers promoted commercial ties between separate areas. Their development is undoubtedly related to the substantial increase in commerce between various regions of Russia that occurred at this time.[45]

We know that the system of serfdom formally evolved during the sixteenth and seventeenth centuries. According to A. L. Shapiro, rising trade and the conversion of rents in kind to payments in cash accompanied and contributed to the spread of the serf system. Although Shapiro also asserts, without presenting comparative evidence, that the development of bourgeois relationships in the countryside was slowed by serfdom, the information he provides may be used as a further indication of a substantial growth in peasant commercial production during this period.[46]

The maturation of uezd cities can be attributed in large part to their growing commercial significance during this period. Goods flowed into many uezd centers from level-7 and level-6 marketing settlements as well as from nearby villages. A. L. Khoroshkevich states that Russian cities preserved their agrarian character until the late fifteenth century, but during the first half of the sixteenth century commerce and crafts developed rapidly, resulting in a sharp increase in the proportion of the posad population engaged in commercial activities.[47] Changing patterns of land use and increasing inequalities in property within the posad accompanied the growth of market forces. Iu. A. Tikhonov argues that the first half of the seventeenth century was a time of further development especially for cities along the Volga river and in the north of Russia.[48] Notable gains occurred in the specialization of production in certain cities for distribution to distant areas. Although the density of level-7 and level-6 central places remained low in many regions, improved ties between rural and urban areas spurred specialization.

As in other countries, the evolution of periodic markets coincided with structural changes in administrative cities. Marketing areas now appeared outside the gates of these walled cities, facilitating trade between city and countryside. In some cases, city merchants were even protected against rural competition by rules forbidding rural markets, but such measures could not prevent the eventual realization that some areas of the uezd were too distant to be served properly by the city. Within large uezd cities, this was also the period of greatly expanded street trade. Freed from the confinement of designated market areas, commerce spread to stores along main streets. Another sign of widened exchange was the construction in big cities of *gostinyi dvor* or enclosed rows of stores for the orderly conduct of trade with merchants from other cities. Utilizing these three new types of commercial locations, the gostinyi dvor in the city center for intercity trade, stores along streets primarily for retail trade, and periodic markets often near the city wall for rural-urban trade, merchants and artisans increasingly worked for a relatively impersonal market.[49] Where peaceful conditions prevailed, especially in the middle of the seventeenth century, the fortifications of a city often fell into disrepair as attention turned to the commercial uses of the urban area.

A. A. Zimin has identified four regional patterns of urban fortifications for the sixteenth century.[50] In the north, where monasteries owned much city land, cities remained unfortified. Even during the first half of the seventeenth century, rising prosperity in such cities as Ustiug Velikii did not lead to large expenditures for defense. Of course, the situation of these cities far from Russia's vulnerable borders enhanced their security. In sharp contrast were the border fortresses in the south, which continued to be threatened by frequent raids. Although some of these cities were attracting posad residents by the mid-seventeenth century, when Russia's borders were gradually shifting further south, most of them maintained the tenure of predominantly military service population with part-time agricultural and commercial pursuits within the vicinity of the fortress. The northwest was also noted for its border fortresses without many merchants or artisans except in a few old cities such as Novgorod and Pskov. Zimin's fourth region is the commercially advanced central area around Moscow, where walled fortifications could be found but did not shape the character of city life.

Comparisons between what I have designated as stages E and F of urban development in Russia (1450–1700), China (750–1550), and Japan (1200–1600) again give us a clearer idea of the changes in progress in each country. A shift in geographical focus from the northwest to areas closer to the center and southeast occurred in China as in Russia. In both countries, the northwest areas were removed from the most fertile agricultural regions and were subject to invasion. A large, relatively secure capital city based increasingly on marketing rather than on tax shipments was conveniently located in a central area with good transportation connections. Similarly in Japan we observe during this period the abandonment of the northeastern capital of Kamakura in favor of Kyoto, located in the commercial and agricultural center. The common experience of these countries was a noticeable shift in geographical focus in response to differential improvements in agriculture and to the widespread development of commerce. While Moscow remained the first city of Russia, it was becoming less reliant on northwest Russia.

Certain similarities can also be found in population estimates for the three countries. If we discount annexations of settled areas, Russian population seems to have been rising to almost twice its previous peak. Likewise in both China and Japan, population rose during this period by about 50–75 percent. All these countries remained approximately 5 percent urban, including an exceptionally great concentration of residents in a single principal city. Indeed, in both Russia and China, the national administrative center was now as large as any city would become until at least the end of the eighteenth century, and Kyoto contained an even greater percentage of its country's population than did the first cities of the other two countries. Larger than the level-1 cities of the previous stage of urban development (with the exception of Ch'ang-an which straddled stages D and E), the new, centrally located capitals in each country rested on a recently developed commercial network as well as on an improved fiscal system.

A further similarity is the changing land use patterns in administrative cities. Streets, rows of shops, and market squares reached an advanced premodern state essentially similar in all three countries.[51] New walls around sections of Moscow reveal a capacity to order cities in Russia that was probably greater than the reduced capacity in China and Japan, but, even in Russia, cities were becoming more disorderly.[52]

Of course, the appearance of levels 7 and 6 is the most obvious basis for identifying this period common to all three countries. Nonadministrative commercial centers quickly covered the landscape. Russia with levels 1, 3, and 5 was intermediate between China and Japan in the number of levels already present when nonadministrative marketing settlements appeared. In Japan, the presence of local markets with levels 4 and 5 missing seems to have produced divisive, uncontrollable forces corresponding to the inability to concentrate resources now being accumulated in local areas. The contrasting ease of integration in China, except for some decades in the tenth century before level 6 joined level 7, can be attributed to the prior presence of a complete network at middle levels. Russia passed through this period with many signs of divisive tendencies yet without losing central control. For more than a century the urban pattern of levels 1, 3, 5, and 7 undoubtedly made the movement of commerce up every other step of the ladder difficult, but this proved to be an adequate foundation for centralization. Level 6 came during repeated disorder from the middle of the sixteenth century to the early seventeenth century when Russia was racked by wars with Lithuania, the dreaded terror of Ivan the Terrible, decades of economic decline, and finally the Time of Troubles. Vigorous efforts directed against localism were supported by the completion of the urban network within the uezd.

In England and France the development of level-7 central places was also followed by a tremendous expansion of level-5 cities, the appearance of substantial local centers at level 6, and the emergence of a single unrivaled national administrative center. Resembling the growth of the Russian urban network through most of the sixteenth century, the course of urbanization in these Western European countries displayed exceptional dynamism during the thirteenth and early fourteenth centuries. The probable parallel to the decentralization and disorganization associated with the Time of Troubles is the 100–150 years of crisis identified with the Black Plague and its aftermath in Western Europe. City populations suddenly declined although commercial activities continued on a significant, though perhaps reduced, scale in rural areas.[53] Similarly, the resurgence of urban growth that followed these temporary recessions had common properties. The network of local central places in these three countries survived this stage F disorder essentially intact although many small markets disappeared.[54] As centralized patterns were reconfirmed, the development of cities persisted virtually without interruption until the realization of a stage G society.

The actual duration of stages E and F in Russia was roughly 260–270 years until the initial growth of St. Petersburg under Peter the Great. The final two-thirds of a century of stage F will be treated in the next section, but it is possible at this point to draw a brief comparison of these stages in the five countries included in this study. The most striking conclusion is that Russia passed through these stages much quicker than any of the other countries, shaving from 300 to 550 years off the duration of stages E and F in China, England, and France and more than 100 years off the Japanese pace. The maturation of the urban network was accelerating in Russia.

The Transition to Stage G

From the political perspective, we would ordinarily divide the century between 1650 and 1750 in Russia into three periods: pre-Peter, Peter's active reign, and post-Peter. In other respects too, these three periods serve as a convenient sequence: most of the second half of the seventeenth century can be characterized as the final phase of stage F; the period of Peter I's leadership was the time of the emergence of stage G; and the final quarter of a century constitutes the first period after stage G was securely established. Like the Japanese case, where the leadership of Tokugawa Ieyasu and his two renowned predecessors can be identified with the appearance of the stage G society, the imposing rule of Peter the Great accompanied the appearance of stage G in Russia.

Once again I am struck by the rapidity of Russian development. According to the calculations that I will describe more fully at the end of this chapter, this century-long realization and maturation of a stage G society in Russia corresponds to much longer periods in each of the other four countries: 1) in China to a period of 400 years centering on the mid-sixteenth century; 2) in Japan to a period of about 200 years centering on the first decades of the seventeenth century; 3) in France to a period of about 200 years centering on the year 1600; and 4) in England to a period of roughly 150 years also centering on the year 1600, but ending by the mid-seventeenth century. While China was the first country to enter this transition, England was the first country to emerge from it. Russia trailed China by more than 150 years, England and France by more than 100 years, and

Japan by roughly 100 years in the appearance of a stage G society; but Russia was continuing to reduce the degree of its backwardness, as measured by the maturation of the urban network.

Focus on this century straddling stages F and G will enable us to take a primarily static approach in subsequent chapters to the urban network of Russia as a stage G society. As in China during the Ming dynasty and in Japan during the Sengoku and early Tokugawa periods, the late stage F and initial stage G societies established or reconfirmed the basic institutional contours of the following period. Already, shortly after the death of Peter I, the pace of reform was slowing in Russia. The legacy of this pivotal century provided the foundation for the change within tradition during the period of a mature stage G society after 1750.

The dynamic developments of the period 1650 to 1750 fall into two categories: 1) the rise of absolutism based on and simultaneously contributing to the reorganization of relationships between social strata; and 2) the growing complexity of society as revealed by the further differentiation of production and commerce and the evolution of the urban network.[55] Events contributing to the strengthening of absolutist government during this period, including the further consolidation of serfdom following the ulozhenie of 1649, the bureaucratization of the state administrative apparatus, and the reforms of Peter I do not require repetition here.[56] In the section on stratification in Chapter 3, we will observe some of the consequences of these developments. Here we will consider briefly some of the realignments in social strata appearing with the rise of absolutism.

In numerous respects, class identification was simplified under absolutism. Serfdom was gradually consolidated as nearly all rural residents except dvoriane and clergy were identified as either private serfs or state peasants. Previously there had been motley distinctions between the extremes of independent peasant and full serf. Now the legal categories of the farming population became increasingly homogeneous.

The fiscal foundation of the Russian state required intermediaries in the form of officials and estate owners to supervise peasant production and to collect rural revenues. The effort to transform the dvoriane into educated and experienced administrators in government service and into agents for the government in the management of their own estates was high among Peter's priorities.[57] Responsible for producing increased revenues, the dvoriane also were becoming a uniform body possessing equivalent legal rights.

Also acquiring a separate identity in the emerging absolutist system were the urban residents of the posad. By no means the entire urban population, indeed frequently a minority of all city residents, the officially registered posad residents included the principal participants in the commercial life of the city.[58] Repeated efforts by Russian leaders to improve the organization of merchants and, to a lesser extent, artisans affected the posad.[59] Peter I's reforms in 1699 and 1720, especially, gave active leadership to the dual task of forming a prosperous and a dependent bourgeoisie.[60]

Cities consisted of sharply delineated areas. In addition to the walled fortress and the posad, separate clusters of built-up areas called slobody formed on the outskirts of cities. Located on state or private land, they housed specialized groupings of individuals often engaged in a single craft. Despite their official registration, these individuals often competed with the posad population, whose anger at this illegal activity was compounded by the slobody's exemption from the collective tax obligation of the city's posad. On private lands, monastery serfs and other private peasants engaged in crafts and trade. On state land, many slobody were formed from service personnel attached to the city's garrison. Obliged to prepare for the possibility of combat, the service population actually spent most of their time in commercial pursuits. In Moscow alone during the 1680s more than 20,000 *strel'tsy* lived in slobody while working primarily as merchants and artisans, often elsewhere in the city.[61]

Similarly to Japan during this period of its development, Russian society became more finely stratified with a simplification and a rigidification of the privileges and duties of nearly all elements of the population. Innovations were enacted such as the poll tax, the table of ranks, the passport system, the periodic enumeration of the population, the posad system of registration, and the merger of the *pomest'ia* and votchina methods of landholding. Reforms in the systems of military recruitment and administrative organization were premised on a sharp rise in state revenues. Direct control based on a centrally directed reorganization of social strata enabled even further expansion of the government apparatus.

Reforms in administrative divisions during this period presage the reforms of Catherine II's reign, to be treated in the next chapter. Beginning in the first quarter of the eighteenth century, Russia was divided first into *guberniia* and then also into provinces.[62] Altogether there were 10–15 guberniia, including the two whose administrative centers were St. Petersburg and Moscow. Most guberniia cities were among the fifteen largest in the country. Provincial cities were subordinate to the administrative centers of guberniia and the number varied greatly from one area to another. Vodarskii has noted that the number of cities with more than 1,000 males registered in the official posad population rose from 30 in 1652 to 60 in 1722.[63] It was primarily these 60 cities that in 1719 were chosen to serve as either guberniia or provincial seats. The vast majority of cities with fewer than 1,000 males registered in this category remained as uezd centers. This three-tiered administrative hierarchy crowned with St. Petersburg and Moscow at levels 1 and 2 stood above an increasing number of nonadministrative settlements at levels 6 and 7.

While in many ways the policies of Russia's leaders recognized and contributed to the growing complexity of society, direct evidence of societal development exists independent of state policies. Numerous Soviet monographs on the production and commerce of this century have presented ample evidence of this dimension of development.[64] Among the topics they have treated are: 1) the developing specialization of labor; 2) the emergence of a national market; 3) the rise of manufacturers; and 4) the growth of an urban presence. I will not try to recapitulate their arguments concerning each of these factors, but will focus instead on how changes in these factors related to the maturation of the urban network.

Several new categories can be added to the labor force of Russia by 1750. Among the peasants we can single out at least three emerging categories: part-time merchants; compulsory, serf industrial labor; and free, hired labor. Despite official limitations on peasant participation in trade within recognized posad, restrictions were difficult to enforce. Growing involvement in local marketing activities enabled some peasants to compete successfully even in large uezd cities against the posad population. Other peasants were forced to work in industries that employed serf labor. Finally, a sharp increase has been noted for at least part of this period in the number of hired laborers, many of whom worked seasonally in transportation.[65]

Among the city populations, new categories were also being strengthened. Soviet scholars have pointed to merchants involved in the primary accumulation of capitalism and artisans producing for a wide market rather than for direct orders as evidence of greater differentiation. Without worrying whether such categories as hired laborers, capital-accumulating merchants, and gentry-industrialists signaled the advent of capitalism, we can still agree that there were substantial signs of growing specialization of the labor force between 1650 and 1750.[66]

Lenin distinguished a new period dating from the seventeenth century in which the various regions of Russia amalgamated into a single national market. "This amalgamation . . . was brought about by the increasing exchange among regions, the gradually growing circulation of commodities, and the concentration of small local markets into a single all-Russian national market."[67] Although I would identify the integration into a national market with the completion of the seven-level hierarchy in the first quarter of the eighteenth century, I think that Lenin was describing an important advance in premodern development. By the early eighteenth century, goods of mass demand including basic grains flowed annually in large volume between the regions of Russia.

All regions of the Russian Empire gained substantially from the improving economic conditions of the period. The Northwest benefited as the site of the hurriedly constructed capital of St. Petersburg, which quickly became the country's major port for foreign trade, and was joined to the Volga river by a newly constructed canal. Military expenditures were concentrated in this region. The Central-Industrial region around Moscow prospered as a center of crafts, including the rapidly expanding textile industry. Widening ties between Moscow and all of the regions of Russia leave little doubt that this city was the national center for commerce.[68] Also during this period, settlement of the Central-Black Earth region was carried out at a rapid pace, prompted in part by the growing demand for grains in the nation's first two cities.[69] Further east, the Middle and Lower Volga regions remained less closely integated into a national grain market, yet shared in the growing prosperity through expanded river transportation. The single greatest fair in Russia, the Makar'evskaia fair near Nizhnii Novgorod, was located in this region.[70]

Finally, the eastern areas of the Urals and Siberia made the most dramatic progress. During the first half of the eighteenth century, the metal and mining industries developed at an unprecedented rate, leading to the construction of many new cities in the Ural region. Meantime, Siberia was losing its character as a frontier area dependent on the old settled areas of Russia even for such necessities as grain.[71] With the rapid growth in trade with China and the partial exhaustion of the fur supply from relatively accessible areas, Siberian exchanges with the core areas of Russia became more regular. An exceptional feature of Russian long-distance trade was the great reliance on a succession of huge fairs through which interregional contacts were channeled.

The rise of manufacturers is probably the most studied, but the least significant of these factors for urban growth before 1750. Russia had relied on imports from European countries to the west and northwest for manufactures and metals, but during the first half of the eighteenth century it was able to substitute domestic products. Also during this period, several cities joined Moscow as centers for the production of light industrial products, especially textiles.

Small-scale craft production also experienced notable progress in this period.[72] Within central places at levels 5-7 and even in some pure villages, production for periodic markets and fairs provided a growing source of revenue to many families. Certain guberniia became widely noted as areas of specialized production. For instance, Vladimir guberniia in the Central-Industrial region had already emerged by the late seventeenth century as a center of small-scale craft production.[73] Internal tariff reform made it easier for goods produced in one city or region to be sold in another.

The most detailed treatment of rural crafts during this period is by L. L. Murav'eva. She argues that the second half of the seventeenth century was marked by significant progress in all spheres of the economy, especially in the intensive transformation of village crafts to small-scale commercial production. Within the C-I region, clusters of production centers emerged, specializing for a wide market. By the late seventeenth century, noticeable regional specialization had occurred. Relating this specialization to the spread of markets and fairs and the growth of rural to urban migration, Murav'eva counts within only 20 uezd of this region about 400 nonurban settlements with a recorded population engaged in commerce or crafts.[74]

A number of special circumstances during the first quarter of the eighteenth century probably contributed to urban development. G. D. Kapustina lists several factors, including the government reforms under Peter I, the creation of a regular army and navy, the Northern War, and the building of St. Petersburg.[75] At the same time, long-run factors also promoted the growth of production and commerce. While increased taxes demanded by Peter I stimulated the involvement of peasants in monetary relations, the general process of converting taxes in kind to cash payments and of widening market ties was evident both before and after Peter's reign.

All of these changes were reflected in growing urban populations. The final century before the period 1750 to 1800 was a time of rapid increases in city populations. From an urban total of probably no more than 600,000 in the 1650s, Russia's city population total steadily rose to roughly 800,000 to 900,000 at the turn of the century and to a figure of nearly 1.5 million by 1750.[76] Of course, the total population was also rising from roughly 10–12 to almost 20 million, but the urban increase seems to have been proportionately greater.

Urban population growth was less due to the creation of new cities than to increased population in existing cities. Vodarskii's list of cities shows an increase from 160 posad in 1652 to only 189 posad in 1722.[77] Uezd cities omitted from his list because they lacked a posad were predominantly fortresses in newly developed areas of the south and east.[78] Although their number also was not increasing quickly, many of these frontier cities gained in population as soldiers and service residents found new access to commercial pursuits and as the military justification for these cities declined. In the more established cities, population growth occurred partly as a consequence of the sudden build-up of St. Petersburg and of the continued expansion of

Moscow's commercial functions. By 1750 centers for long-distance or intraregional commerce had added many thousands to their populations.

As cities became more populous, land use patterns continued to change in directions already discernible in the previous period. One of the most extensive studies of land use is provided by N. B. Golikova for the city of Astrakhan' at the turn of the eighteenth century.[79] First she notes the increased specialization of function within the kreml' manifest in the governor's order to remove private residences and other non-stone structures such as earthen churches from the area. Second, she points to the concentration of wholesale trade in the urban area just outside the kreml' as retail trade was dispersing throughout the city, including the spread of stores in merchants' and artisans' homes along main streets. Third, she indicates that many slobody were attracting a diverse population, losing any distinctive occupational character, and blending in with surrounding built-up areas. All of these land-use features also characterized Moscow and probably to some extent other large cities of the Russian Empire.

This transitional period in Russia saw a new formal differentiation of cities by administrative function paralleled by the spontaneous emergence of prosperous trading centers. Indeed, the selection of a provincial or guberniia administrative seat was generally a confirmation of the presence of a large commercial population, the core of which was the official posad population. From 1646 to 1678, the registered posad male population climbed from 83,000 to 134,000 and by 1744 this total had reached more than 282,000.[80] If we keep in mind materials, such as Golikova's carefully documented study of Astrakhan', which show that there were no firm barriers preventing members of most urban strata from engaging in the same range of activities as posad members, we learn that the number of persons not registered in the posad but in fact actively participating in trade also spiraled in the same period.[81]

Comparisons with China and Japan

During the course of almost 1,000 years to 1750, Russia's urban network took shape. At first, the network of central places changed slowly; a given configuration of levels lasted for as long as two centuries before evolving into a new pattern. Eventually, new levels were added more quickly, reaching a rate of change of once or even twice a century. It can be seen in Table 4 that if repetitions from century to

TABLE 4

Development of Central Places in Russia

Levels	Centuries									
	9th	10th	11th	12th	13th	14th	15th	16th	17th	18th
1			X	X			X X	X	X X	X
2	X	X			X	X				X
3						X	X X	X	X X	X
4									X	X
5			X	X	X	X	X X	X	X X	X
6								X	X X	X
7							X	X	X X	X

century are not counted, then there were nine distinct combinations of central places beginning with the isolated presence of level 2 and ending by 1725 with the complete formation of all seven levels.

In this chapter I have grouped the seven stages of premodern urban history into four broad periods. The first period, consisting of stages A and B, extends back to an indeterminate past before cities appeared and includes the ninth and tenth centuries. To the extent that an urban presence existed during this time, it consisted of no more than a score or so settlements that amounted to at most a few tens of thousands of urban inhabitants. The second period, consisting of stages C and D, encompasses the eleventh to mid-fifteenth centuries. The urban presence was rapidly enlarged to more than a hundred thousand residents distributed among one hundred or more cities. A period of just 200 years comprises stage E and about half of stage F. Supported by a growing network of nonadministrative cities, the urban total rose to at least 600,000 people in an increasing number of central places. The fourth period, lasting a century, witnessed a further rise in the number of central places and in the total urban population to nearly 1.5 million. By 1750 approximately 8 percent of the Russian population resided in cities (including by definition all people in levels 1–5 and one-half of the population in level-6 settlements). Throughout this chapter we have used the first set of definitions of central places introduced in Table 2; now in preparation for the switch to the second set of definitions in subsequent chapters, we should note that the figure of 8 percent in 1750 approximates both the total population in administrative centers and the number of residents of central places with a minimum of 3,000 persons plus one-half the population of level-6 centers.

The Chinese and Japanese urban experiences can be schematized in precisely the same manner as was done for Russia in Table 4. We see in Tables 5 and 6 that China and Japan also passed through approximately eight or nine distinct combinations of central places. Most combinations in China lasted at least four centuries. The more than 1,000 years during which only level 2 was present are not fully recorded since Table 5 commences with the ninth century B.C. instead of the nineteenth century. In contrast, Japan resembles Russia

TABLE 5

Development of Central Places in China

	Centuries													
	B.C.									A.D.				
Levels	9th	8th	7th	6th	5th	4th	3rd	2nd	1st	1st	2nd	3rd	4th	5th
1							x	x		x	x			
2	x	x	x	x	x	x	x					x	x	x
3														
4							x	x		x	x	x	x	x
5		x	x	x	x	x	x	x	x	x	x	x	x	x
6														
7														

Levels	6th	7th	8th	9th	10th	11th	12th	13th	14th	15th	16th	17th	18th
1		x	x	x		x	x	x	x	x	x	x	x
2	x			x							x	x	x
3		x	x	x	x	x	x	x	x	x	x	x	x
4	x	x	x	x	x	x	x	x	x	x	x	x	x
5	x	x	x	x	x	x	x	x	x	x	x	x	x
6						x	x	x	x	x	x	x	x
7			x	x	x	x	x	x	x	x	x	x	x

TABLE 6

Development of Central Places in Japan

	Centuries											
Levels	7th	8th	9th	10th	11th	12th	13th	14th	15th	16th	17th	18th
1		x	x	x							x	x
2	x				x	x	x	x	x		x	x	x
3					x	x	x	x	x x	x	x	x
4									x	x	x	x
5		x	x	x					x	x	x	x
6									x x	x	x	x
7							x	x	x x	x	x	x

with initial combinations that lasted from one to three centuries giving way to a rapid succession of urban patterns in the fifteenth and sixteenth centuries. The urban networks of Japan and Russia were rushing forward with similar rapidity, gaining on China's sluggish network of cities.

Stages B, C, and D refer to the phase of administrative centralization. This phase lasted roughly 2,500 years in China as opposed to 550–650 years in Japan and Russia. Each country began with level 2, passed through a period when levels 1 and 5 or 2 and 5 were present, and reached the point where levels 1 and 3 or 2 and 3 were simultaneously present.

The final urban combination before level 7 was introduced indicates the differences between the stage D societies in the three countries. Levels 2, 3, and 5 were present in Russia. As outposts of central control, level-5 central places enabled officials to oversee local activities. Level 3 cities permitted some local resources to be sent to a national center. This combination of cities facilitated considerable control from a national center. In this respect, China with levels 1, 3, 4, and 5 was similar to Russia. Ch'ang-an, even more than Moscow 700 years later, was a great administrative center. Japan's stage D pattern consisted of only levels 2 and 3. No level-5 centers existed in local areas. The development of feudal patterns of decentralized control contrasts with the growth of centralized bureaucratic systems in China and Russia.

In fewer than 300 years, Russia added levels 7, 6, 4, and 2 to complete the urban network. Japan took a century longer to add levels 7, 6, 5, 4, and 1. The phase of commercial centralization witnessed a rush of urban transformations, in the Russian case without upsetting the framework of cities that already supported a centralized system and in the Japanese case with the establishment of entirely new cities at all levels creating a new framework for centralization. Comparable in their dynamism, these two countries differed in their degree of centralization.

The transition to stage G occurred first in China during the mid-sixteenth century, second in Japan at the turn of the seventeenth century, and third in Russia at the turn of the eighteenth century. In a broad sense, this transitional phase encompassed from roughly 1550 to 1700 in Japan and from roughly 1650 to 1750 in Russia. In China, continued commercial centralization was not accompanied by urban growth. The population in cities remained about 6–7 percent of the total. In Japan the growth of urban populations was astounding, at least doubling to 16–17 percent of the total. Russia was intermediate with an urban rise about 50 percent faster than the rise of the general population, reaching 8 percent of the total. This transitional period was most dramatic in Japan, but briefest in Russia.

At one level of generalization, we can say that China in the second century B.C. was similar to Japan in the eighth century A.D., which in turn was similar to Russia in the eleventh century A.D.; that, subsequently, China in the eighth century A.D. resembled Japan in the thirteenth century and Russia at the end of the fifteenth century; and that, finally, China in the late sixteenth century paralleled Japan in the early seventeenth century and Russia in the early eighteenth century. Use of the seven levels of central places and the seven stages of premodern history points to these commonalities. At a lower level of generalization we can observe certain differences in the patterns of central places present. China and Russia exhibited centralized networks as opposed to Japan's weak local control. Nevertheless, it is Japan and Russia that are similar in most respects. The Heian and Kievan periods, following with unusual rapidity after cities were first established, both gave way to extensive decentralization, from which Russia emerged more quickly. Most importantly, during all phases of urban development and especially after local markets appeared, Japan and Russia contrasted with China in the rapid completion of their urban networks.

Comparisons with England and France

Six distinct phases of urban development are generally identified in English and French history and in the history of other Western European countries: 1) early indigenous urban centers, 2) garrisoned cities of the Roman Empire, 3) urban remnants of the Dark Ages, 4) revived cities of the Middle Ages, 5) reduced cities of the post-Plague era, and 6) flourishing cities of the early modern period. The first phase corresponds to stage B, a time of loosely integrated level-2 cities following the origin of cities in northwest Europe under the influence of the diffusion of the Aegean civilization. The absorption of France and then England into the Roman Empire resulted in a rapid transition from stage B to stage D. Presumably, stage C was quickly passed in the process of adapting the urban forms of a centralized stage D society under the great administrative center of Rome. Decentralized patterns of a stage D society correspond to the third commonly identified phase of European history. Stage E and the early part of stage F occurred during the late tenth to early fourteenth centuries. Then a decentralized phase of stage F appeared in the aftermath of the arrival of the Bubonic Plague. Finally, the sixth phase was the time of the transition from stage F to stage G and was followed by the presence of a full-fledged stage G society in England and France. Table 7 represents the century-by-century addition of new levels of the urban network in England and France, which seem to have diverged by no more than one-half century in their rate of change and to have been identical in the order in which levels were added.

The history of cities in Western Europe can be traced back to the cities of the classical world, which, in turn, reveal a continuous history dating from the world's earliest urban civilization in Mesopotamia. According to M. Hammond, the gradual centralization of systems of cities was seen in the evolution of the Greek city-state, forming a loose league under the hegemony of Athens, then in the following Hellenistic states in which single city-states lost their inde-

TABLE 7

Development of Central Places in England and France

Levels	B.C. 1st	A.D. 1st	2nd	3rd	4th	5th	6th	7th	8th	9th	10th	11th	12th	13th	14th	15th	16th	17th	18th
													Centuries						
1		x	x	x										x	x	x	x	x	x
2	x				x	x	x	x	x	x	x	x	x					x	x
3			x	x	x									x	x	x	x	x	x
4			x	x	x												x	x	x
5		x	x	x	x					x	x	x	x	x	x	x	x	x	x
6													x	x	x	x	x	x	x
7											x	x	x	x	x	x	x	x	x

pendence to federated leagues, and finally in the Roman Empire when local administration throughout some 45 provinces with up to 70 million people centered on the great imperial city of Rome.[82] These changes reveal a shift from a stage C to a stage D society. England and Gaul were colonized as part of the stage D network of settlements under Rome.

Norman J. G. Pounds describes in greater detail the urbanization of the classical world.[83] Identifying about 600 city-states along the Aegean Sea or in inland Greece at the peak of Athenian power, Pounds sees new city-states appearing in distant areas, even as far away as south England. With a population varyingly estimated at 125,000 to 250,000 at its peak, Athens was at the top of the urban hierarchy. During this period of city-states, new cities were laid out according to a set of expectations concerning the site, the use of walls, and the incorporation of a fortress, certain public buildings, and temples. Although not all cities satisfied these expectations and indeed cities at the periphery may have been only slightly influenced by them, these elements became important in man's consciousness of the urban phenomenon. Another set of expectations concerned the rights and privileges of urban citizens. Unlike China, the focus in designating individual responsibilities was at the level of the city, not the state.

The extension of planned, integrated cities into England and France occurred in the first centuries A.D. Earlier level-2 tribal centers, about which little is known, were transformed into Roman style cities fairly evenly spaced across France and England. By the second century A.D. Gaul had about sixty-three centers at level 5, ten at level 4, and four at level 3, while Britain supported thirty centers at level 5 and eight at level 4.[84] Both countries were part of the vast Roman Empire in which cities at levels 1, 3, 4, and 5 were present.

Britain and Gaul were unable to maintain their urban settlements when the empire broke into fragments. Both Hammond and Pounds single out the third century A.D. as a time of increasing decentralization, which persisted in subsequent centuries as long-distance commerce declined in favor of relatively self-sufficient manorial economies. During the fifth century, many cities ceased to exist, and the nadir of stage D urbanism was reached in the sixth and seventh centuries. The presence of only one or two levels of central places during these several centuries of decentralization may indicate a reversion to a previous stage of development. At the very least, it requires further exploration of the range of variation tolerable in the definition of stage D societies.

During various stages of premodern history, the population of France was roughly one-tenth that of China and the population of England was roughly one-thirtieth that of China. During the zenith of their stage D development, France with nearly one hundred central places and England with half as many contrasted with China during the Han dynasty in which there were one thousand or more cities. In all three countries, this core of cities served as the foundation for all urban growth until the period of modernization.

In England and France a period of recentralization of urban patterns occurred that is properly included in stage D. Peter King points out that three-quarters of the Roman town sites in England were reoccupied by the eighth century and urban population grew rapidly in subsequent centuries.[85] Marguerite Boulet-Sautel argues that an urban regrouping was under way at a similar time in parts of France, and that by the ninth century suburbs were being added around the walls of some prosperous abbeys.[86] In both England and France, the revitalization of old cities continued into the tenth to thirteenth centuries, and, at least in certain core areas, this process was far along by the eleventh century. It seems that by 1100 England was about 6 percent urban, and by 1300, if not earlier, France was also at least 6 percent and probably closer to 7 percent urban.[87]

Stage E societies in England and France may date from as early as the tenth century. The reestablishment of periodic markets at the sites of old cities from the eighth or ninth centuries should not be confused with the entirely new process of adding periodic markets at locations that did not qualify as central places in other respects. It seems that originally in the tenth and eleventh centuries new centers not the product of long-distance commerce but rather the foci of feudal and ecclesiastic purchasing power acquired marketing functions.[88]

By the early thirteenth century England and France had become stage F societies. J. C. Russell argues that in 1250 to 1350 functional regions had formed in Western Europe; in each region, cities offered a descending order of sizes indicative of a high level of regional integration of economic activities.[89] Russell equates the 3.7 million people of England with one region and the roughly 11 million people of France with four regions—5.2 million in the Paris region, 3.4 million in the Toulouse regions, 1.1 million in the Dijon region (including part of Switzerland), and 1.3 million in the Montpellier region. Paris with 80,000 and London with 60,000 people were followed by Montpellier, Toulouse, and Rouen with 30–40,000 people as the major cities of these two countries. Although Russell's effort to determine regions by rank-order hierarchies of cities and at the same time to supplement incomplete urban data by arguing that regions exhibited such hierarchies of city sizes seems circular in places, it serves as the most complete effort to incorporate and interpret urban data for large areas of Europe during the premodern period.

Stage F in England and France, as stage D before it, can be readily divided into a centralized and a decentralized phase. During stage D, the centralized phase based predominantly on administrative controls had yielded to the extremely decentralized conditions of the period known as the Dark Ages. The reverse pattern occurred in each of the stage F societies; decentralized patterns such as those of the Time of Troubles in Russia and of the late fourteenth and fifteenth centuries in Western Europe were replaced by new heights of centralization, this time supported by substantial commercial development. In both England and France the completion of the seven-level hierarchy followed more than a century of revived centralization of previously scattered functions.

The equivalent to the century (1650–1750) of transition to a fully developed stage G society in Russia was the centralized phase of stage F and roughly the first half century of stage G in England and France, i.e. the period from about 1500 to 1650. The rapid population growth of Paris and London both preceded and made possible the consolidation of regional commerce into a national market. Whereas in the first phase of stage F, markets and fairs proliferated, spurred by the speculation of lords of rural manors in the future of local settlements, the granting of urban charters sharply declined by 1500 and the regularization of trade resulted in the growth of certain well-situated markets and the decline or disappearance of many peripheral markets.[90] As Clark and Slack have noted, between 1500 and 1700 the economic functions of almost all English towns were transformed.[91] Local craft functions often receded before wider trading networks. Gradually cities acquired new importance also as social centers for the consumption and secondary residences of rural lords. Dorothy Davis points to the century from the 1550s to 1660s as a time of transformation in the methods of supplying consumer goods to London; while local fairs and markets were still relied on for the movement of goods, shops began to serve a much greater clientele.[92] Similarly this period in France witnessed a consolidation of scattered functions and substantial growth of major cities.

Summary

We are now prepared to replace Graph 1, which was based on a variety of attempts at periodization using the tripartite or Marxist stages, with Graph 2 showing the seven stages according to the urban networks approach. Throughout history until about 1600 China either was in a more advanced stage than the other four societies or was in the same stage, but can be presumed to have been further along in that stage since it was the first to enter it and also the first to move ahead to the next stage. England and France were second to China. Japan and Russia followed similar accelerated paths from stage to stage as they steadily narrowed the leads of the frontrunners. By the eighteenth century, all five countries had entered stage G.

Through this new chronology of our five examples, we can examine the stages of premodern societies with special reference to Russia's relative performance. Stage A extends back to an indeterminate past before cities emerged. In societies at this stage, gradually the preconditions appeared for moving ahead to stage B: agriculture was developed, a variety of crafts was practiced, and intertribal political integration was achieved. Similarly to Japan, Russia seems to have proceeded further than China and probably than England and France in establishing advanced features for a pre-urban society. Here we can hypothesize that there were advantages to latecomers that came into contact with societies as advanced as stage D. Even before they introduced cities under foreign influence, they benefited from the diffusion of numerous other technological and organizational feats.

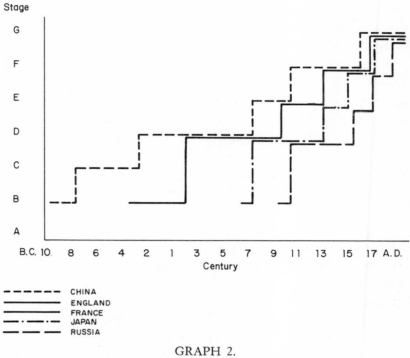

GRAPH 2.
The Urban Network View of Periodization

Stage B in Russia as in England, France, and Japan was quickly replaced by stage D. Although Russia and Japan, unlike England and France, were not conquered by and absorbed into the administrative framework of stage D societies, they borrowed extensively from abroad and set up their own stage D urban systems. The administrative centralization focused on Kiev and Kyoto was not sustained, any more than the English and French colonial urban networks focused on distant Rome were long able to outlast the existence of the imperial system. In contrast to China, which overcame a period of decentralization with the reimposition of a stage D urban network quite similar to what had previously existed, the four societies that had essentially skipped stage C all succumbed to highly decentralized divisions, with only Japan proving successful in preserving a large national center.

Whereas the beginning of the stage D Kievan period came nearly 1,200 years after China's imperial system, about 900 years after the Roman Empire embraced England and France, and nearly 300 years after Japan's centralization following the Chinese model, the shift to stage E in fifteenth-century Russia came only about 750 years after the spread of periodic markets in China, 500–600 years after corresponding changes in England and France, and no more than 250 years later than the inception of stage E in Japan. Russia's backwardness continued to diminish in stages E and F until the seven levels of the urban network were completed by the early eighteenth century, only 150–175 years later than in China, 100–150 years later than in England and France, and about 100 years later than in Japan.

SPATIAL DIVISIONS IN SOCIAL STRUCTURE:
RUSSIA AS A STAGE G SOCIETY

Unlike Western conceptualizations of the takeoff into modernization, which concentrate almost exclusively on the sudden, disruptive transformation in social structure, Soviet historians following a Marxist scheme of periodization give special attention to the earlier, less perceptible process of building a runway from which the takeoff could be launched. Much of their effort to describe the initial laying of this runway—or, using the appropriate vocabulary introduced in Chapter 1, the emergence of the "capitalist uklad" in the throes of Russia's "advanced feudalism"—centers on the second half of the eighteenth century. Russian social structure during this period, while lacking the striking consequences typical of initial modernization, appears to have moved convincingly away from old forms of interaction and hesitantly toward new, though as yet vaguely defined, forms.

Between 1744 and 1811 the population of the Russian Empire climbed by more than 24 million to almost 42 million. The urban population increased even faster as it rose roughly 250 percent and reached more than 3½ million, and the volume of domestic and foreign trade multiplied many times, accompanied, at least in the early decades, by a proliferation of periodic markets and fairs. While annexations of territory contributed to the rising figures, the basic dynamics of growth, differentiation of function and integration of territorial units inhered in longstanding evolutionary processes as outlined in Chapter 2.

Using the system of periodization adopted here, we can identify Russia as a premodern society firmly embarked onto stage G of development. These developments may then be considered against the backdrop of change in other stage G societies. According to my calculations, the years between 1750 and 1800 in Russia merit comparison with these corresponding periods: 1750 to 1850 in China; 1700 to 1850 in Japan; 1650 to 1750 in England; and the late seventeenth century to 1790 in France.[1] These periods represent the final phase of unadulterated premodern development in stage G societies. They acquire added significance for comparative studies as the preparatory phase determining the capacity for subsequent responses to the new forces of modernization. Before we compare these societies in Chapter 5, it is necessary to describe Russian social structure in some detail.

Interest in eighteenth-century Russia generally focuses on both ends of the century at the expense of the middle period. The first quarter of the century was dominated by the towering figure of Peter I, whose military policies, financial reforms, and other innovations are recognized as the principal effort to change the course of Russian history until the 1860s. The final third of the century, ending in 1796, is remembered as the reign of Catherine II, another leader credited with a stream of innovations. The reigns of these two reform-minded rulers also brought strategic annexations of territory to the Russian Empire, as Peter's wars secured access to the Baltic Sea and enabled the founding of St. Petersburg and Catherine's policies supported by military strength led to firm control of the northern border of the Black Sea and, through the partitions of Poland, to the acquisition of populous areas of the west. Moreover, during the entire three centuries of rule by the Romanov dynasty, the most extensive redrawing of administrative boundaries occurred during the reigns of these two tsars and, as a reaction to them, immediately after their deaths. Clearly, those who conceive of history as a succession of leaders who exert a great impact on events rightfully single out these two reigns.

Unfortunately, fascination with the policies of memorable leaders obscures evolutionary processes overlapping reign periods, especially during this critical century. Evidence of the continued development of marketing, of the further differentiation of the peasantry, of a widening territorial specialization in production, and of the steady transformation of cities is no less visible during the middle part of the century than at either end.[2] The scope of these changes will emerge in the separate examination of aspects of social structure most relevant to urban networks. While much of the quantitative data presented here pertain to the 1780s, the boundaries of time chosen for observing processes of change reach back to the second enumeration of the Russian population in 1744 and forward to the fifth enumeration in 1795 and occasionally even to the beginning of the nineteenth century.

A brief overview of Soviet sources helps to identify some noteworthy changes during the second half of the eighteenth century. Among the writings on urban history, works by P. G. Ryndziunskii and especially by Iu. R. Klokman give considerable attention to the new cities of this period. Klokman, who studied the far-reaching administrative reforms of the 1775–1785 that resulted in the addition of more than 200 officially designated cities,[3] argues that during this half-century the Russian city began on the road of capitalist development. Emphasizing the new role acquired by the city through expanded ties with its rural hinterland, Klokman indicates that the creation of so many administrative centers both confirmed the rapid development of cities already evident from at least the middle part of this century and exerted great influence in spurring further development. Although inconsistent and, for national figures, wildly in error in estimates of urban population, and without a systematic approach to marketing functions, Klokman proves insightful in concluding that the competition of small markets did not hinder urban development. He notes that "On the contrary, their rapid growth in this period was a convincing expression of the process of development of a domestic market, of the appearance of a large number of local centers of commercial production and exchange which in turn served precisely as 'fertile soil' on which in the middle eighteenth century the number of new cities increased."[4]

Examination of fairs has been carried out by, first, N. L. Rubinshtein and later by G. L. Vartanov. Rubinshtein divides these annual commercial gatherings into various types, pointing to the increasing number of locations with fairs and also to the appearance of multiple fairs during the year in some settlements.[5] Vartanov more systematically classifies fairs and compiles figures on the central part of Russia showing a manifold increase in the number of fairs between the 1740s and the 1780s.[6] He concludes that this period saw a significant widening of the internal market. Less attention has been given to periodic markets in Russia, but detailed local studies such as A. M. Razgon's work on Vladimir guberniia provide much evidence of the expansion of this element of marketing networks too.[7]

Soviet sources also point to other major changes in the production and distribution of goods and in the relations of individuals to their labor. Studies of foreign trade indicate that the value of exports, which together with imports totaled about 10 million roubles just before midcentury, had risen to over 60 million roubles in the first years of the nineteenth century.[8] Moreover, during the second half of the eighteenth century, the value of manufacturing production tripled, and during just the final two decades many guberniia witnessed a rise in the value of agricultural production of as much as 60–100 percent, which, if we subtract for the inflation of currency, still easily exceeds the growth in population. N. A. Rubinshtein even refers to the second half of this century as the setting up of the "capitalist uklad" in agriculture.[9] Other studies reveal a sharp rise in the number of people engaged in hired labor.[10] By the standards of premodern societies, Russian development between 1750 and 1800 must surely have been remarkable.

While emphasizing these elements of societal advance, Soviet authors find difficulty in generalizing about the second half of the eighteenth century.[11] As I. A. Bulygin writes, "This was a complicated and contradictory period in the history of Russia. On the one hand, the feudal-landlord yoke reaches its apogee, and serf peasants are lowered to the position of slaves. The strengthening of the yoke of landlord arbitrariness leads to a sharp exacerbation of class conflicts and to the peasant war of 1773–1775 under the leadership of E. Pugachev. On the other hand, this was a time when on the base of an ever more developing commercial production in the country a capitalist uklad began to form. All branches of the economy including agriculture experience profound changes. Landlords with the aim of adapting to the new conditions were placed before the necessity of restructuring their economy."[12]

Bulygin is not alone in painting a picture of a rapidly advancing society burdened by contradictions and by increasingly oppressive class relations. For our purposes we can divorce the issue of class conflict from the evidence of societal development, concentrating solely on the latter, to the extent that it pertains to the themes incorporated into the urban networks approach. In the following sections of this chapter, wide use is made of Soviet sources that document the changing spatial divisions in various aspects of social structure that most clearly reveal an evolutionary course of development.

The Geographical Setting

At the beginning of the eighteenth century, the Russian Empire had already approached the area of the U.S.S.R. today except for a stretch of land near Manchuria in the Far East; a large section of Central Asia that remained inaccessible until the mid-nineteenth century; most of the Caucasus, which joined the Empire at the turn of the nineteenth century; parts of the south near the Black Sea; and areas along the western border that in some cases had once been annexed, then relinquished and were to be reannexed. Blocked in their efforts at expansion by four formidable opponents—China, Sweden, Poland, and the Ottoman Empire—Russians successively overcame the last three of these powers and finally took advantage of China's growing incapacity during the mid-nineteenth century to complete their territorial aggrandizement. The areas secured during the eighteenth century were especially significant because of their strategic locations along the Black Sea, the Baltic Sea, and the trade routes across Eastern Europe. Although for brief periods during military campaigns, raids by nomadic neighbors, and peasant revolts, control over some territories was undermined, these represented only temporary interludes not seriously affecting the continued strengthening of imperial authority. In short, the period 1750–1800 can best be characterized as a time when vast territory now made more valuable by strategic outlets and relatively weakened neighbors became increasingly integrated and exploited by central administration.

Until the building of railroads and steamships in the nineteenth century, the huge territory of the Russian Empire could be conquered but not well integrated. In the east, the enormous expanse of Siberia remained largely inaccessible for permanent settlement, while a settled belt along the southern fringes with some outposts stretching to the north along major rivers provided the principal link to trade with distant Peking and to furs ever further eastward from Siberia.

Separating Asia from Europe, the region of the Urals also remained sparsely settled as late as 1700, but possessed rich mineral resources and some fertile agricultural zones that were increasingly exploited during the eighteenth century. Also poorly integrated into a single commercial network were some of the newly annexed areas of the frontier south and some of the old but sparsely settled areas of the north, which, in fact, lost trade as the routes to Siberia shifted further south. Most of the better integrated central core of the country can be divided, as is the custom, into a swath of fertile black-earth and a belt of less productive soil to the north largely covered by forests.

Variations that fully reflect the untold diversity of this enormous slice of the globe cannot be recounted at any length here. Indeed, as we examine the regional variations in urban data presented in Chapter 4, we shall find that, as in modern societies, geographical differences did not play a decisive role in influencing variant patterns of city growth on a regional level, and that the absence of mountain barriers from most populated areas and the gradual expansion of settlement outward from the core regions produced a remarkable sameness outside of the newly annexed Baltic, Belorussian, and Ukrainian areas. In comparison to the population of China and even to the population of comparatively small but densely settled Japan, the Great Russian portion of the population occupying most of the empire was remarkably homogeneous in language, in custom, and in the supremacy of national affiliations. Areas settled by migrants originating from the central parts of Russia mostly during the sixteenth to eighteenth centuries did not become very distinct in their traditions.

The comparative suitability of geographic and climatic conditions for transportation is important in the study of premodern cities. The virtual absence of oceanic transportation of domestic commerce necessarily penalized Russians at a time when it was much cheaper to transport goods by water than by land. However, the core areas of the country were conveniently connected by several river systems, which, when joined by a few well-placed canals built during the eighteenth century, permitted close ties between numerous major cities for at least half of each year. During the other half of the year, except for up to two months of impassable mire in the fall and spring, the ground hardened and the rivers froze so thoroughly that sleighs could move easily across large distances. Thus land transportation in winter was superior to that in summer, but inferior to movement by river. In short, transportation conditions were obviously inferior to the water-locked islands of Japan and England but for the most settled regions may well have been equal or superior to prevailing conditions in large settled parts of China.

The overall impression of Russia is that of a country with land in vast supply, although much of it was infertile, subject to frequent droughts, and relatively inaccessible. Given the prevailing agricultural technology, soil conditions, and climate, much larger areas of land per capita were needed than in East Asian and Western European countries; many uezd possessed five or more acres of arable land per capita, and uezd existed in some areas with total land surfaces of as many as two or three million acres on which resided a population of barely 60,000 or 70,000.

Low population densities contributed to large distances between cities. Yet, during the eighteenth century, densities were rising, and improved transportation routes increased the accessibility of wide areas. The geographical setting became decreasingly hostile to urban development. These conditions did not offer the same opportunities as existed in Japan to register tremendous urban population increases, but they did make possible a widening of exchange and an upsurge in urban growth.

Administrative Divisions

Within the enormous boundaries of the Russian state, the principal ordering of settlements, as seen in Chapter 2, followed the evolution of administrative divisions and the development of production and distribution. Deliberate intervention to reform administrative boundaries offered the possibility of realigning the balance of local and central control and the correspondence of commercial and administrative functions. In effect, the changing geographical setting could be better or worse utilized for the mobilization of resources depending on the boundaries selected.

The history of local administrative boundaries reveals, according to P. G. Ryndziunskii, that a major reform was long overdue by the final quarter of the eighteenth century.[13] For at least the first half of the preceding 1,000 years, local administration was held primarily by the princes, who sought to secure as much territory as possible around their fortress-cities. While these local authorities frequently responded to changing strategic conditions and to developing trade by transferring their headquarters to better situated cities, they could not be expected collectively to select a network of administrative centers wholly appropriate for more centralized and commercialized conditions. During the fifteenth and sixteenth centuries, as large numbers of uezd cities received designation as outposts first of large princedoms and then of central administration, boundaries changed to meet broader needs and new cities appeared; yet the old cities brought with surrounding territories under the authority of Moscow remained the bulwark of the developing urban system. Finally, with the establishment of guberniia and provinces after 1700 a new system of higher administrative units came into existence, but without a corresponding attempt to redraw uezd boundaries. Without any comprehensive effort at redistricting, uezd boundaries were essentially unchanged before 1775. Beginning with hinterlands of varied size and development, these uezd diverged greatly during centuries of unequal population growth and marketing proliferation.

Peter I began to reorganize administrative divisions to enable central authority to penetrate more easily to the uezd level. Under him, the first guberniia were established in 1708–1710, and provinces were added in 1719 as an intermediate level between the large guberniia and the numerous uezd. Although Peter's reforms temporarily weakened the uezd level and left unclarified the precise powers permitted to officials at the three administrative levels, they proved to be the single noteworthy step over a period of more than 200 years before 1775 to alter sharply the administrative boundaries of Russia. In 1727, shortly after his death, further reforms reversed some of the efforts of Peter I to strengthen city governments and to create a set of checks and balances, but they perpetuated the three administrative levels. For the final half-century before the reforms of 1775–1785 the Russian Empire was divided into 14–20 guberniia, 47–66 provinces (approximately two-thirds of their administrative centers were not simultaneously guberniia cities), and roughly 250 uezd cities (approximately three-quarters of which did not serve as seats of higher administration).

Readjustments in administrative boundaries before 1775 were largely confined to the guberniia and provincial levels. Prosperous and advantageously located uezd or provincial centers could merit selection as centers of higher administration at various times when the number of guberniia and provincial cities was increased, and these changes, in turn, elicited shifts of uezd from one higher administrative unit to another, but increasingly during the middle of the century such realignments proved insufficient to preserve the monopoly of administrative centers over large-scale commerce and the efficiency of control over resources in the uezd. As new marketing settlements appeared in rapid succession throughout wide areas of the country, uezd cities became integrated in various ways into the hierarchy of commercial shipments. Small, sparsely settled uezd with at most some 20,000 scattered inhabitants often could not even support a market in the administrative seat. Already in 1764 instructions were sent out to the governors in guberniia cities to combine such small uezd under a single city.[14] Even though these instructions were widely ignored, they show the growing concern with the inefficiency of tiny uezd. At the opposite extreme, large uezd comprised populations sometimes in excess of 200,000. Frequently within the boundaries of these administrative units could be found one or more large marketing settlements that already served as commercial centers for surrounding areas. As we observe the flow of goods from rural areas to regional and national centers, we find that some uezd centers functioned in a subordinate way to others or even to nonadministrative settlements, and likewise cities at the center of guberniia and provinces varied greatly in commercial significance.[15] While the total populations of administrative areas did not necessarily correspond to the commercial importance or populations of their officially designated cities, this was a major factor affecting these latter features. One step toward simplifying administration would be to equalize the population of administrative units of a single type.

Administrative reform was accomplished in two stages with the most important changes occurring during the first stage from 1775 to

1785.[16] The second stage, from 1796 to 1803, consisted of a reexamination of the results of the earlier reforms with Tsar Paul I, who replaced Catherine II, eliminating many uezd cities, following which his successor Alexander I restored some.[17] In contrast to the 216 new administrative cities created during 1775 to 1785, results of the zigzag course ending in 1803 brought a reduction of only 39 cities.

The 1775–1785 reform began in the central regions of the country and then was extended during the early 1780s to the Ukraine, the Baltic, and Siberia. Unlike previous reforms, all administrative boundaries including those at the uezd level were now subject to change. Provinces were eliminated, and the country was now divided into new smaller guberniia, which in turn were divided into uezd. First came the appointment of a governor-general, usually given jurisdiction over two new guberniia, whose task was to recommend which settlements would most suitably serve as guberniia and uezd centers. Carrying with him a list of factors to consider when choosing cities, the new appointee toured the area of his jurisdiction.

What guidelines did the governor-generals follow in drawing up proposals for their superiors in St. Petersburg?[18] New guberniia cities were to be centrally located in areas with roughly 600,000–700,000 people each. Preferably the area should be compact and not much larger than similar areas across the country unless the density of population was low as in the north and in Siberia. In many areas, the choice of a single guberniia city was obvious since one of the former guberniia or provincial cities had previously outdistanced other cities in population growth. Elsewhere, however, careful examination was required of trade, transportation routes, and the number of dvoriane in various cities, and of the so-called "posad" population of registered merchants and artisans. Concern for equalizing the population of administrative units exerted a great impact on the choice of uezd cities. Boundaries around each uezd center had to be drawn to encompass about 50,000 people and simultaneously to serve as the boundaries for neighboring uezd with similar populations. Special attention was given to keeping intact within a single uezd the cluster of villages belonging to an individual serfowner. In the selection of uezd centers, old administrative cities received preference, followed by settlements belonging to the state; last came settlements under private owners. These definitions of personal property clearly affected the social structure in ways more like those of Europe than of East Asia. Thus, after these reforms there continued to be some private settlements with greater prosperity than officially designated administrative centers; yet in the course of the reforms, many old fortress settlements that had previously been uezd centers were replaced by locations with more active trade and larger populations.

By 1787, 499 administrative cities had been chosen, most of which had previously functioned as administrative centers. Over 90 percent of administrative centers now served solely as uezd centers, lacking any higher administrative functions. In the territory of some new guberniia, this transformation necessitated as much as a threefold increase in the number of cities, effected by dividing old large uezd. Elsewhere, where small uezd already prevailed, as few as 25 percent new cities were added to a patchwork of former uezd and provincial cities taken from two to four old provinces. After these reforms, the administrative levels of cities more closely corresponded to their commercial importance.

Less extensive reforms of administrative boundaries in 1796–1797 and 1802–1803 improved somewhat the alignment of administration and marketing by removing some uezd centers that had not experienced anticipated growth, but also exacerbated the already widening inequality between uezd populations. Sustained population growth during the final two decades of the eighteenth century and the early part of the following century favored some uezd over others. With the absorption of the 39 dismembered uezd by their neighbors, further inequalities developed.

Following the example of V. M. Kabuzan, I have chosen the administrative boundaries of 1806 to 1816 for consideration of regional and local conditions.[19] Although these dates fall just beyond the period under study, boundaries remained basically unchanged from 1782 to 1858, and population data for the 150 years to the 1860s have been carefully analyzed in terms of these boundaries.

For purposes of comparison, I have divided the Russian Empire into seven regions, fewer than is customary.[20] While the choices made here correspond for the most part to generally recognized combinations of guberniia used for designating regions, I am aware of no single source that divides Russia in entirely the same way. 1) The Central-Industrial (C-I) region included six guberniia, which centered on the cities of Moscow, Kaluga, Tver', Iaroslavl', Kostroma, and Vladimir. 2) The Central-Black Earth (C-BE) region also contained six guberniia, whose major cities were Tula, Riazan', Orel, Kursk, Voronezh, and Tambov. 3) The hybrid North-Northwest (N-NW) region consisted of seven guberniia, including the administrative centers of Vologda, Arkhangel'sk, Olonets, St. Petersburg, Novgorod, Pskov, and Smolensk. 4) The region of the Lower and Middle Volga (L-MV) stretched from north to south across six guberniia, comprising the administrative cities of Nizhnii Novgorod, Kazan', Penza, Simbirsk, Saratov, and Astrakhan'. In addition to the above 25 guberniia in the four core areas of the Russian Empire, three regions comprising about 21 guberniia can be designated as peripheral areas. 5) The region of the Urals and Siberia (U-S) provided the greatest expanse, at first counting five guberniia cities at Viatka, Perm', Orenburg, Tobol'sk, and Irkutsk. 6) During the late eighteenth century, the region of Belorussia and the Baltic (B-B) was adding new territory, reaching for a time a total of eight guberniia. 7) Finally, the Ukraine together with newly annexed southern areas near the Black Sea (UK-S) also contained a resilient eight guberniia. No specific listing is given here for these last two regions since they are not examined in as great detail as the other regions.

Together, these 46 or so guberniia (having increased from a total of 39 in 1785 mainly because of the further partition of Poland) contained more than 550 uezd cities. Typical guberniia held 10 to 14 lower administrative centers plus the guberniia city.

The example of Viatka guberniia indicates the land use characteristics of administrative divisions. The area of this guberniia measured 15.5 million *desiatin'* (1 desiatina = 2.7 acres). The largest of the 13 uezd equaled roughly four times the area of the smallest, Viatka uezd, which counted fewer than 500,000 desiatin'. Viatka, however, was the most densely settled area, with roughly 13 times the figure of the least densely settled uezd in 1782.[21]

During the 1780s, shortly after uezd boundaries were readjusted to equalize population as much as possible, relatively little variation existed in most uezd populations. In order to reduce differences in population a considerable range in land area was found acceptable. The uezd in their newly designated boundaries operated as the smallest units in the hierarchy identified here of uezd, guberniia, region, and nation.

Demographic Structure

Basic information on the population of Russia is preserved in a succession of ten enumerations dating from 1719 to 1858. Although much (but by no means all) of the data from these enumerations have long been known, until recently they had been subjected to little careful analysis. Fortunately, due to the efforts of the contemporary Soviet demographer V. M. Kabuzan, we now have a much clearer understanding of the population of the Russian Empire during the period of these enumerations. Kabuzan has analyzed the data from the enumerations and other materials with the aim of properly dating them, determining the total national population at successive times, showing the territorial distribution of the population, pinpointing the distribution of the various social strata, and specifying the number of people in cities.[22] His studies based on archival materials place in doubt, to a greater or lesser extent, all other writings that refer to the dynamics of the Russian population over this period of one and one-half centuries. Population data on Russia presented in this and the following chapter are taken directly either from Kabuzan's writings or from archival sources which by virtue of his previous exploration were made readily usable.

The enumerations that mostly encompass the period of this study are the second, third, fourth, and fifth, with some supplementary need for the sixth. Interpolating from the figures in Table 8, we can determine that the population of Russia approximately doubled during the second half of the eighteenth century from roughly 20 million in 1750 to almost 40 million in 1800. About half of this population increase can be attributed to territorial expansion and to population growth in areas annexed after 1719. The considerable increase in the population residing within the old boundaries of Russia is evident from the fact that in the territory included in the first enumeration

TABLE 8

The Population of the Russian Empire[a]

Enumeration	Date	Number of Males	Estimated Total Population
1	1719	7,789,000	15,578,000
2	1744	9,103,000	18,205,000
3	1762	11,618,000	23,236,000
4	1782	14,205,000	28,410,000
5	1795	18,707,000	37,414,000
6	1811	21,353,000	42,706,000
7	1815	21,944,000	43,888,000
8	1833	25,950,000	51,900,000
9	1850	28,441,000	56,882,000
10	1858	29,634,000	59,268,000

[a] V. M. Kabuzan, *Narodonaselenie Rossii v XVIII- pervoi polovine XIX v. (po materialam revizii)*, 164–65.

(excluding some areas in the west recently brought into the Empire) the population rose from 15.1 million in 1744 to 28.2 million in 1795.[23]

Table 9 shows the regional distribution of the population of the Russian Empire excluding the regular army. Most of the growth through annexation occurred in the Belorussia-Baltic region and in

TABLE 9

The Regional Population Distribution of Russia (millions)[a]

Region	1744	1762	1782	1795
C-I	4.083	4.380	5.060	5.227
C-BE	3.780	4.191	5.425	5.928
N-NW	2.520	2.808	3.386	3.565
L-MV	2.521	3.026	3.754	4.886
U-S	1.895	2.268	3.321	3.783
B-B	.649	2.004	2.202	5.395
UK-S	2.403	3.084	4.231	8.237

[a] V. M. Kabuzan, *Izmeneniia v razmeshchenii naseleniia Rossii v XVIII- pervoi polovine XIX v. (po materialam revizii)*, 71–117. These data are taken from Kabuzan's tables, but are rearranged to refer to the regions used in this study of urban networks. These figures omit the regular army.

the Ukraine-South Russia region. Among the other five regions, the areas distant from Moscow grew more rapidly, especially the Urals-Siberia region and the Lower and Middle Volga region. The least growth in population occurred in the Central-Industrial region, which still managed a 28 percent increase in 51 years.

The dynamics of population fluctuations from region to region and area to area involving differential rates of natural increase and migration have scarcely been studied. Kabuzan's brief observations on the causes of varying rates of population growth offer the most tentative conclusions of his work, limited to some general comments on the classification of the agricultural population as serfs, state peasants, or other categories, on the availability of arable land and on the frequency of famines, epidemics, and wars. As do other Soviets, he argues that a high rate of natural increase was facilitated by the less severe obligations of state peasants and that low population densities per amount of arable land contributed to both high rates of natural increase and of in-migration. In the Central-Industrial region, with a high percentage of serfs and a dense population per amount of arable land, population rose relatively slowly, while in the Lower Volga area, with a "fertile soil, warm climate, comparatively low percentage of serfs and relatively great security,"[24] the population climbed from 287,000 in 1744 to 992,000 in 1795. Excluding annexed territory, the annual rate of increase reached an unusually high level between 1762 and 1782 but then fell sharply during the next 13-year interval between enumerations. Kabuzan indicates that this unexpected rise and fall may have resulted in part from less precise methods of calculation used in the third enumeration.[25]

Based on the data from 1782, we can specify the population of the administrative units at the guberniia and uezd levels. Most guberniia ranged in population between 500,000 and 1,000,000. In the C-I region, the six guberniia each counted at least 750,000, while none much exceeded 900,000 inhabitants. Similarly in the six guberniia of the C-BE region, no guberniia fell short of 795,000 people and only one barely exceeded one million. Five of the six guberniia of the Volga region ranged between 581,000 and 816,000, with only Astrakhan' far below the mean with 194,000 people. More difficulty is encountered in generalizing about the N-NW region and the U-S region, where some guberniia with enormous areas supported tiny populations; in the former region the range extended from 902,000 in Smolensk to 170,000 in Arkhangel'sk. If we wish to keep in mind a general figure for guberniia population, we should choose 900,000 for the C-BE region, 800,000 for the C-I region, 700,000 for the L-MV region and, admitting more variance, 600,000 for the U-S region. No breakdown is attempted for the B-B and UK-S regions, where guberniia boundaries were less stable.

As has already been noted, uezd established during the reforms just prior to the fourth enumeration were explicitly shaped more or less to equalize population. In outlying guberniia, where densities varied sharply, considerable inequalities were tolerated, but in guberniia with similar conditions the range of difference in all uezd was only a few thousand people in 1782.[26] By 1795 the range had widened as some uezd experienced greater population growth than others. In Moscow guberniia, where population grew by fewer than 10 percent between 1782 and 1795, ten of the thirteen uezd (if we exclude the city of Moscow) ranged between 60,000 and 77,000 in 1795, and the other three all exceeded 45,000. In all of Russia for the remainder of the eighteenth century after the reforms beginning in 1775, few uezd fell below 40,000 or exceeded 100,000 in population, and, in most guberniia, the range in uezd populations was considerably less than a 2:1 ratio.[27]

The study of the geographical distribution of large agglomerations of persons such as guberniia and uezd populations is more advanced for this period in Russian history than is the study of fertility, mortality, and other subjects of demographic interest. Next to aggregate data on individuals, the smallest unit for which data are preserved is the household. For many uezd, the number of households or houses is given, as is the total population. For instance, in Briansk uezd (Orel guberniia) there were 5,964 households with roughly 54,000 inhabitants; in Ardatov uezd (Simbirsk guberniia) there were 8,370 households with roughly 59,000 inhabitants; and in Aleksin uezd (Tula guberniia) there were 5,682 households with roughly 59,000 inhabitants.[28] In each case, these figures refer to persons registered as peasants outside of the uezd center and omit households of dvoriane.

Iu. A. Tikhonov has studied data on households in an estate consisting of 9 settlements in Kashira uezd (future Tula guberniia) in 1716.[29] The population of the area totaled 1,594, of whom 52 percent were aged 15–60. Altogether there were 185 households. The common size of a household was 7 persons (31 households), and 141 of the 185 households ranged between 5 and 11 persons. Rarely did any household exceed 14 persons or fall below 4 persons.

Other data on uezd indicate that the number of persons per household continued to be large at the end of the eighteenth century.[30] Most uezd averaged 6 to 10 persons per household. Since Russian stem families presumably averaged roughly the same size as those in other countries (about 4–5 persons), these data suggest that not only were extended families common but that unrelated persons often resided in a single household.[31] Detailed studies of village populations are required to untangle the confusion caused by such unexpectedly large household figures.

Social Stratification

The population of the Russian Empire, rising from about 20 to nearly 40 million during the second half of the eighteenth century, consisted of roughly half females and half males, each of which category included 50–60 percent in the generally able-bodied ages of 15–60. Family status derived first of all from the official classification of working-age males, the 5–6 and later 10–12 million persons among whom were counted the heads of most households. These males with the exception of a few privileged categories of the population were treated as the bearers of *tiaglo*, an unofficial unit by the second half of the eighteenth century on the basis of which tax obligations within the village were distributed. The government and serfowners assigned quotas for payment on the basis of the total number of males in the settlement, and these quotas were met by the settlements as a whole by dividing the obligations according to the number of tiaglo per household as well as to some consideration of the wealth of households. Actually, a full tiaglo usually meant a husband and wife both able to work, and efforts were made to calculate partial tiaglo, for instance for children under 16 or 17 who already participated in strenuous work.[32]

Data from the enumerations of the Russian population were based on a classification of the population into as many as ten or fifteen categories. Excluded from this system of classification were the tsar and members of the imperial family, at the top of the stratification system. Population figures also were not regularly reported for the dvoriane, the hereditary and nonhereditary service nobility who were legally eligible to own serfs. Among the other categories of the population, several were not subject to the standard forms of direct taxation: the clergy, members of the civilian and military bureaucracies who were not dvoriane, retired soldiers, and *raznochintsy*, an indistinct category including primarily urban residents not registered in other categories.

Two sets of categories have been the subject of most studies of stratification: the urban and rural registered *podat'* population, both owing the poll tax or some replacement for it. It has been incorrectly concluded that the urban podat' population may be equated with the actual urban population and that the rural podat' population refers to an essentially homogeneous body of persons engaged in farming. The diversity of strata in Russia is not fully revealed by these official categories, but analysis of data on the number of persons registered per category and on their distribution in urban and rural settlements can signify a preliminary step toward an examination of the actual occupational structure and the distribution of wealth.

A quantitative breakdown of the population should begin with the various categories that comprised the rural podat' population or what is widely known as the peasant population. At the time of the fourth enumeration in 1782, the total subsumed by these categories represented roughly 92 percent of the population of Russia exclusive of the armed forces.[33] Included in this total are 4.64 percent of the national population who were court peasants (on lands directly controlled by the imperial court); 9.58 percent who were "economic" peasants (on lands that had been secularized in 1764, having previously belonged to monasteries and churches); and 28.74 percent who were state peasants, a category which for some areas of Russia can be subdivided. Together, these three categories, which were becoming more similar to each other, comprised roughly 43 percent of the national population. In 1782, the remaining 49 percent of the population regarded as peasants were classified as serfs.

Of course, these aggregate figures conceal differences between regions, guberniia, and uezd. While serfs constituted 59 to 78 percent of the total population in the six guberniia of the C-I region and 44 to 77 percent of the total population in the six guberniia of the C-BE region, they comprised only 0.56 percent of the population in the Siberian area within the U-S region and were also scantily represented in such outlying guberniia as Arkhangel'sk, Astrakhan', and Viatka. Figures for the other categories of peasants also fluctuated wildly. For instance, there were no court peasants registered in some guberniia, while in a few guberniia as many as 10 or even 20 percent of all peasants were in this category. Within the C-I region, the range reached from less than 1 percent in Kaluga to greater than 13 percent in Kostroma guberniia. "Economic" peasants were most numerous in northern guberniia, where monastic institutions had been active in early settlement, and near the cities noted for their resplendent churches, monasteries, and nunneries; more than 20 percent of the population in Novgorod, Tver', Moscow, Vladimir, Arkhangel'sk, and Iaroslavl' guberniia belonged to this category.

Quantitative breakdowns of the urban podat' population are available for many of the enumerations. One category frequently listed is that of *tsekhovye liudi*, craftsmen formally organized into guilds. Since this category was not applied systematically and omits artisans in cities and professions in which guilds were not established, for most purposes it should not be treated separately. These craftsmen should be counted as part of the category of *meshchane*, sometimes translated as townsmen, which included most of the posad population. Merchants, craftsmen, and those engaged in many other occupations were listed as meshchane. Relatively wealthy urban posad residents could qualify instead for the category of *kuptsy*, often translated as merchants, of which three guilds were differentiated according to the amount of declared capital required for entry. The first guild with the fewest members required the most capital. Altogether 3.07 percent of the Russian population in 1782, exclusive of the armed forces, registered in the categories of the urban posad population, with kuptsy accounting for roughly one-fourth of the total.

The remaining 5 percent of the population of the Russian Empire consisted of persons in the dvoriane, clergy, and other categories, each with relatively small numbers. Actually, in certain outlying areas, persons in these minor categories were numerous, reaching a maximum of 91 percent of the total population in the slightly settled Astrakhan' guberniia, 38 percent in Orenburg guberniia, and 13 percent in Tobol'sk guberniia. Members of nomadic ethnic minorities in outlying areas generally numbered among this residual percentage. Most guberniia in the C-I, C-BE, N-NW, and L-MV regions ranged between 2 and 4 percent in all of these non-podat' categories. Indeed, if we exclude from the 5 percent of the population not obligated as part of the podat' system such groups on the periphery of the country as the Cossacks, we are left with categories constituting about 3 percent of the total population.

Archival data permit a separate breakdown of the population in many strata into urban and rural residents. The population registered in cities totaled between 8 and 9 percent of the inhabitants of Russia.[34] The breakdown for the rural population is relatively simple; fewer than 1 percent of the total were clergy and dvoriane, a fraction of one percent were soldiers quartered in villages, and almost all of the remaining 99 percent of rural residents, with the exception of a few outlying guberniia, registered in the various categories of peasants. The composition of urban areas was more complex: about 35 percent of the total were kuptsy and meshchane; 32 percent registered in the various peasant categories despite their established urban residence; 7½ percent were clergy, dvoriane, and officials; and the remaining quarter of the population belonged to such miscellaneous categories as retired soldiers and raznochintsy.

The entire population of meshchane and kuptsy registered in administrative centers. Normally registration in a given city was hereditary and could not be transferred easily to another city or to the countryside, although merchants often lived temporarily in places other than those in which they registered.[35] In general, the distribution of the combined total of meshchane and kuptsy gives an important clue about the relative sizes of cities in Russia, which, however, should not be construed as the actual urban population or even the population engaged in crafts and commerce. According to the archival data from the 1782 enumeration, only in the B-B region did as many as one-half of the urban population register in these categories, while in other regions, except the C-I and U-S areas, each with 44 percent so listed, kuptsy and meshchane comprised one-quarter to one-third of urban residents.[36]

Both in urban and rural locations persons registered as peasants frequently engaged in nonagricultural activities. As household personnel of serfowners, as hired laborers, as permanently assigned factory workers, or as self-employed full-time or part-time craftsmen and merchants, peasants could find alternatives to farming on an annual as well as a seasonal basis. State peasants and serfs on *obrok* (owing an annual sum) are thought to have been more mobile than serfs on *barshchina* (owing labor service), but no quantitative statement of this difference has yet been given.[37]

Many of the miscellaneous categories in the residual 5 percent of the population refer primarily to urban residents. The military was stationed predominantly in cities; civil servants were assigned to urban posts; and most raznochintsy and so-called retired soldiers could find no satisfactory alternative to urban occupations. The two strata most widely interspersed in diverse settlements were the dvoriane and clergy; yet both were disproportionately urban. In 1782, between 35 and 40 percent of the roughly 170,000 persons in the dvoriane strata (within all but newly annexed areas, which results in a smaller total than on the next page) lived in cities. Approximately half of these urban residents lived in the central cities of St. Petersburg and Moscow.[38] The total number of clergy probably exceeded that of dvoriane, but the total in cities was very nearly the same, with a higher percentage of the clergy in cities other than the two national centers.[39] It should be noted that the population of dvoriane in cities was rising through the nineteenth century much more rapidly than that of clergy.[40]

In order to penetrate beyond these figures on the official categories of the population, we must examine the actual involvement of the population in production, distribution, and consumption of wealth. Two apparently contradictory processes were at work in Russian society. On the one hand, simplification and standardization of rights and obligations continued to accompany the growing concentration of power in the central government. A single dvoriane stratum formed, various categories of peasants merged into the classification of state peasants, differences narrowed between state peasants and serfs, and fewer limitations interfered with commercial pursuits of persons registered in many urban social strata. The equalization of fiscal burdens by category and the reduction in the number of categories continued into the nineteenth century. On the other hand, the process of increased differentiation and interdependence of activities persisted, accompanying the growing output of goods and services. Great differences in income can be observed among members of each of the major official strata in society. While legally there was a narrowing of differences in rights and obligations, actual differences in wealth and power within strata were widening.

Throughout this period, the actual and ideal systems of stratification were topped by the tsar, who had great power and wealth, and by members of the imperial family by virtue of their relationship to the tsar. Their wealth, derived from court lands and the labor of court peasants in many parts of the country and by funds from the national treasury, rose by the end of the century to 14 percent of all budgeted expenditures.[41] The splendor of their palaces in St. Petersburg and Moscow and the large number of persons serving them set the small number of members of the imperial family apart in their lavish consumption.[42]

Members of the dvoriane stratum, of course, also received support from peasant labor on landed estates. The number of dvoriane was increasing more rapidly than the total population during most of the eighteenth century, with the biggest jump coming between 1782 and 1800, when the figure for the entire Russian Empire rose from 216,000 to 726,000.[43] Most of the increase is accounted for by the annexation of areas in the Ukraine, Belorussia, and Lithuania in which two-thirds of the dvoriane population now lived. Indeed, just in the newly annexed right-bank section of the Ukraine lived some 135,000 persons classified as dvoriane, 7.8 percent of the total population. In contrast, in areas long before incorporated into the Russian Empire there were 84,000 dvoriane in 1782 and 112,000 in 1795, a rise from 0.64 to 0.77 percent of the population.

Quantitative analysis of the dvoriane strata by V. M. Kabuzan and S. M. Troitskii provides a breakdown of the number of dvoriane in each guberniia for 1782 and 1795. Apart from the newly annexed regions, the country was becoming more homogeneous in the percentage of population in this stratum. The C-I region and Nizhnii Novgorod guberniia, which together had been somewhat over-represented, dropped from 0.70 to 0.63 percent, while the previously under-represented C-BE region rose from 0.48 to 0.72 percent. In the L-MV region, which started off below 0.30 percent, indicative of the growing number of dvoriane was an almost fivefold increase of the number in Saratov guberniia. In addition to a sharp increase in the number of dvoriane through the inclusion of local lords in newly annexed settled areas in the west, a further, though small, increase resulted from the high rate of natural increase of the dvoriane population, from ennoblement of individuals active in the settlement of the Black Sea area and also from the granting of dvoriane status to members of the state bureaucracy.

There were two kinds of dvoriane status: hereditary and personal. Persons with the latter status could not pass on their rank or serfs to their children, and many relied for support principally on state salaries. In the C-BE and L-MV regions, hereditary dvoriane predominated. In contrast, personal dvoriane were especially numerous near St. Petersburg and Moscow and comprised well over half the male dvoriane in these cities, according to data for 1816.[44] The corresponding figure for the C-BE region was only 39 percent. One explanation is that individuals were named personal dvoriane in recognition for their work in the two central cities, where they continued to reside, and, if they were granted estates, these generally consisted of few serfs and were located near the city of their work. Personal dvoriane typically did not rank among the wealthiest dvoriane in these cities.

The approximately 40,000 dvoriane households in the major part of the Russian Empire in 1782 were scattered among numerous settlements. A guberniia of 800,000 people counted about 1,000 dvoriane families, while an uezd of 60,000 people typically counted more than 100 homes of dvoriane, about one-quarter of which lacked dvoriane occupants since their owners maintained other residences elsewhere. In Kaluga guberniia in the C-I region, some 1,358 dvoriane homes divided into 11 uezd, ranging from about 50 to 250 homes per uezd.[45] Tarusa uezd, in which there were 48,000 serfs in 268 privately owned settlements, was fairly typical with 145 dvoriane homes.[46] More out of the way was Penza guberniia in the L-MV region. Here there were 1,012 serfowners (exclusive of their families) of whom somewhat more than half lived outside of the guberniia. In this area of relatively large estates averaging 366 serfs per owner, just 20 to 50 dvoriane households resided in a typical uezd.[47]

It is customary to classify dvoriane according to the number of male serfs living in the settlements on their estates, as in the following classification that divides dvoriane into five levels of ownership: 1) very large = 1,000 or more male serfs; 2) large = 500–999; 3) middle = 100–499; 4) small = 21–99; 5) very small = 20 or fewer male serfs. Those dvoriane who lacked estates qualify for the "very small" category. Estates were often scattered in many guberniia. For instance, in 1783, one family classified in the very large category possessed 119 settlements scattered in 30 uezd of 13 guberniia.[48] The most concentrated of these holdings were 17 settlements in one uezd. In Smolensk guberniia, we find that from one-half to two-thirds of the owners were in the "very small" category, another 20–25 percent were in the "small" category and fewer than 1 percent possessed more than 1,000 male serfs.[49] The high percentage of small owners in this guberniia is atypical, however, since for the entire Russian Empire the mean population of a serfowner's holdings fluctuated around 100 male serfs, with larger estates becoming more common in the L-MV and U-S regions and smaller estates persisting in the N-NW region, and, to some extent, in the C-BE region.

Data for the first and eighth enumerations (1719 and 1833) have been analyzed by N. M. Shepukova, providing a perspective from which to estimate the distribution of serfowners during the late eighteenth century.[50] Over this period of more than a century, the percentage of dvoriane having 1–20 male serfs fell from 60 to 54. Owners with 21–100 male serfs also declined relatively from 32 to 28 percent. At the same time, the number of owners with hundreds or thousands of serfs was increasing. Of course, the percentage of serfs belonging to owners at each level was sharply at variance with the percentage of owners at that level. For instance, in 1719 only 0.3 percent of the serfowners had as many as 1,000 male serfs, but together they owned 17 percent of all serfs. The changes in holdings were minor from 1719 to 1833 in comparison to the rapid changes during the next quarter of a century to the tenth enumeration, when owners with fewer than 21 souls (as male serfs were called) dropped to 39 percent, while those with more than 1,000 souls rose to more than 3 percent.[51] These very large owners now possessed 41.5 percent of all serfs as opposed to 26 percent in 1833.

In addition to rankings according to the number of serfs on their land, dvoriane can be usefully compared in terms of the compactness of their holdings, the quality of their land, and the accessibility of markets. Areas varied in the amount of land that was customarily distributed to serfs for their own use; in most uezd this figure was 60–70 percent of the total land, but in some places it was only 50 percent or even as low as 33 percent.[52] The principal obligation of a serf was either barshchina, to spend a certain number of days each week farming the lord's land, or obrok, to pay a certain fee for the year, which could be raised by selling goods from the land distributed for the serf's use or from other activities. The choice was rarely left to the serf; over 80 percent owed obrok in the north and over 60 percent in the C-I region but fewer than 25 percent in the C-BE region. In the nineteenth century, estates increasingly moved to a mixed system, but barshchina continued to be applied to more than twice as many serfs as obrok.

Most small and very small serfowners received, at best, enough crops or cash to supply their own needs but not so much as to sell a regular surplus on the market or to afford a second home in a city. Their ties with the market were episodic. Large owners participated more actively in commercial production, organizing their holdings for a commercial crop, developing craft production or secondary specialization in the production of alcoholic beverages, using hired labor if needed and arranging for shipments to major cities.[53] Since buying and selling land (and with it serfs) was difficult, the dvoriane were in competition not so much at the expense of each other as at the expense of their serfs, whose labor provided the principal source of their wealth.

Secondary sources of dvoriane wealth included salaries and rents from urban properties. The number of persons in the military and civilian bureaucracies rose sharply during the eighteenth century. By the 1770s and 1780s the number of officials in the civilian service, about half of whom were dvoriane, reached 18,000, with about 400 to 480 men located in each guberniia.[54] In St. Petersburg in 1804, the majority of the 5,416 officials were dvoriane.[55] Even more numerous in the city's population were dvoriane who were currently serving or had retired from the military. It became especially stylish to serve in the imperial guards. Also typical of St. Petersburg was the large amount of property rented out by dvoriane, providing further evidence that by the late eighteenth century dvoriane were already finding more diverse sources of income, shifting from serf payments in kind to various sources of cash revenues.

Many dvoriane aspired to lavish consumption. Rich dvoriane, generally from the category of very large serfowners, had multiple estates that resembled palaces in which worked hundreds of household serfs and, in some cases, hired employees. Large and middle level dvoriane also needed household staffs in order properly to display their wealth. It was costly to maintain a house or an apartment in St. Petersburg or Moscow, but that provided the best opportunity for a luxurious life style. This centrifugal force of life in the capitals drew in resources from the provinces and exerted a demonstration effect that penetrated to guberniia cities, uezd cities, and rural estates. Even small and very small serfowners who could not afford to leave their country houses increasingly grasped for elements of the expensive life style introduced in the capital cities. Constituting less than 1 percent of the population in most areas of Russia, the dvoriane probably had available for personal consumption as much as 10 or 15 percent of the value of the national income. These along with government expenditures represented the major share of the funds in Russian society that were not primarily used for sustaining life and maintaining existing levels of production.

The non-dvoriane members of the government bureaucracy and the clergy generally received payments for services performed by virtue of their specialized education and training. Indeed, in the provinces sons of priests were a major source of literate manpower for the career civil service.[56] The incomes of these officials and priests were for the most part inconsiderable, while the expenses of the officials in major cities were often comparatively substantial.

The posad population availed itself of more varied sources of income although it was denied the right to own serfs or land outside the city. Long protected against dvoriane and peasant encroachment on its commercial activities, posad income derived mainly from urban sources but also from trade in rural areas. Members of the three guilds of kuptsy took advantage of these monopolistic privileges to dominate certain spheres of trade. The first guild, comprising 7 percent of the total, included individuals engaged in large-scale shipments of goods, in foreign trade and in interregional trade. Much of their trade was conducted in St. Petersburg and Moscow. The 25 percent of the kuptsy in the second guild were more circumscribed in their range and scale of activities, moving goods to and from neighboring cities and within the uezd of their own city. They often owned stores in uezd and guberniia cities. Finally, the 68 percent of the kuptsy in the third guild engaged in small-scale trade, mainly in local edibles with many of the goods purchased in or destined for local markets and fairs within or just beyond the borders of their uezd. They lacked capital to venture into major operations and often rented stores or stalls and worked as hired laborers.[57]

These proportions did not apply everywhere. In Moscow the distribution in the 1760s was 11 percent, 40 percent, and 49 percent, respectively, while in small cities the first and second guilds were relatively under-represented. Actually, most kuptsy resided in the few major cities of a guberniia, e.g., in Tver' guberniia, three cities held 59 percent of all kuptsy.[58] In general, among the kuptsy were the wealthiest of the commercially active population, including the largest property owners of both commercial and residential units. In St. Petersburg during the 1780s, of 1,204 shops registered under 327 merchants, about one-third belonged to men who owned at least 18 shops, with one man owning 91 shops.[59] Data from 1843–1844 show that kuptsy had also become landlords of property equal to one-third of the entire value of real estate in the city.[60]

Meshchane shared the general posad rights to engage in commerce and crafts, but unlike the kuptsy, were not subdivided into various guilds according to measures of their wealth. They generally engaged in mundane commercial activities such as setting up stalls in markets, peddling goods on carts, and making handicraft items for a mass market.

A. A. Kizevetter provides the most detailed study of the posad population during the eighteenth century. He traces back to the ulozhenie of 1649 the basic principles by which the posad was governed until the reign of Catherine II, although noting frequent changes in the rights and obligations of posad members, especially during the reign of Peter I. Among the underlying principles throughout this period were restrictions on the trade and craft activities of persons not eligible for posad membership, prohibitions on the permanent departure of members of one posad to a posad elsewhere or to some other kind of settlement, and requirements that the posad population pay taxes and meet other obligations imposed by the central government.[61]

Actually, since these principles were restated in various forms throughout most of the eighteenth century, their specific application was frequently altered. In particular, posad members felt threatened by rival efforts of rural dvoriane, peasants, and other urban residents to engage in trade and craft activities. In limited areas associated mainly with foreign trade, competition came also from foreign merchants. The competition from these sources did not subside, although access to membership in the posad population remained tightly controlled. In the long run this meant that, while trade and craft production rose rapidly, the percentage of the national population registered in the posad remained quite constant. Thus the percentage of the urban population in the posad categories fell.

The activities of the posad population were limited first of all by monopolies granted at various times to the dvoriane on the making of such products as iron, potash, salt, and alcoholic beverages. Especially the monopoly granted in 1754 on alcoholic beverages sold in taverns guaranteed a substantial income to dvoriane.[62] Their factories and the workshops on their estates also competed with posad producers. As large-scale producers, sellers, and even buyers, the dvoriane could exert a considerable impact on a local market or could bypass the market, shipping goods directly to major cities. As a rule, however, dvoriane did not engage in wholesale or retail commerce, freeing this increasingly lucrative activity for individuals from other social strata.

While some dvoriane vied with merchants and artisans through the large scale of their production or consumption and enjoyed a monopoly of certain widely used products and items for export, serfs and state peasants competed for the control of small-scale commerce. Persons registered as peasants and subject to various obligations engaged in the same occupations as did other urban residents, including transport, construction, hired household service, and employment in shops and factories. Due to their vast numbers, within a given city they often dwarfed the posad population of kuptsy and meshchane. Many stayed in a city for ten or more years, while others avoided the need to register with the police by staying for only one season, perhaps returning to their home settlements for the farming season. In some areas in which few persons registered in the posad, commerce was carried on almost entirely by those registered as peasants.

An article by G. L. Vartanov explores the conflict between merchants and trading peasants in the central part of European Russia during the second half of the eighteenth century. He notes that, following the removal of local customs barriers in 1753, peasant trade grew rapidly as markets and fairs appeared outside uezd cities and peasants brought products into cities. The main items of trade in rural and urban areas were the products of the peasant economies, and these were often first accumulated by peasant traders, who knew local conditions best. Vartanov postulates three levels of conflict: in small cities peasants won out, sometimes by channeling local trade away from the uezd city; in middle-size cities the battle was fiercest with the posad merchants struggling to keep the peasants out of the city trade; and in large cities, except for some trading peasants who became well established, peasant activities were confined to the least lucrative shares of the market.[63] Vartanov points to the second half of the eighteenth century as a time when the posad population continued to dominate Russian trade, but less successfully than during the previous century.

The other category that contributed many individuals who engaged in commerce was the largely urban non-podat' population, especially those classified as retired soldiers and raznochintsy. The old strel'tsy military population had furnished many craftsmen and traders until early in the eighteenth century.[64] In many regions of the Russian Empire where service categories such as the strel'tsy initially dominated trade, even after the elimination of these categories the posad population never increased to its level in the long-settled northern regions. Instead, individuals reclassified in other miscellaneous urban categories continued to meet urban production and distribution needs. In general, in southern and southeastern areas, where the percentage of the total population in posad strata was 2.0 or 2.5 as opposed to percentages often exceeding 4.0 in northern areas, more non-posad urban residents engaged in commercial activities.[65]

The actual occupations ordinarily grouped as merchants, artisans, and urban hired laborers were filled not only by kuptsy and meshchane, i.e., the posad population, and by non-podat' urban residents such as raznochintsy, but also by persons officially registered as peasants. Many peasants came to cities temporarily and without means; consequently they held the least rewarding jobs. In the capacity of household personnel, transportation or factory workers, and craftsmen or traders, serfs and state peasants found work in both urban and rural areas. Serfs on obrok and state peasants enjoyed more mobility than serfs on barshchina, who had little choice of occupation or residence. Owing an annual fee, state peasants and serfs on obrok were relatively free to find the most attractive means for raising the necessary cash and for improving their own livelihood. Indeed, in some guberniia where a large percentage of registered serfs was seasonally or more permanently away in pursuit of nonagricultural employment, their serfowners resembled labor bosses who receive a payment in return for allowing workers to be hired out.

Peasants were limited in their freedom of action by the poll tax paid through their lord or local administrator and his staff of police, by obligations to the government such as providing recruits for military service and quartering recruits, by obligations to their lords including barshchina or obrok or the equivalent obrok owed by state peasants, and by various regulations affecting their private lives such as the internal passport system, marriage fees, restrictions on trade, and the local custom concerning the partition of land. Some serfs even changed hands several times as their land passed from lord to lord, as they were forcibly resettled, or as they were assigned as workers to factories. While in some respects these limitations on the accumulation of wealth may have weakened personal initiative, there were still opportunities available. Despite the rules against peasant trade in land, in some areas much obrok land was rented out to other peasants, rich peasants even bought land in the name of their owner, and long-term assignments of land from the village commune were often tolerated. Through widespread land transactions between peasants, some even became hired laborers for others.

Other means of enrichment existed besides the accumulation of disproportionate amounts of land. In some areas, peasants rented mills or organized crafts, and trade constituted another prevalent source of nonagricultural income. Despite legal barriers, a small number of peasants became wealthy through various forms of commerce, especially trade in grain. Free to enter cities as purchasers or as sellers to wholesale dealers, peasants often also engaged in large-scale wholesale trade and in direct retail trade.

To a generally unrecognized extent, the interests of serfs and serf-owners did not conflict. Of course, many of the obligations to their lords impinged on the serfs' freedom to make a better than minimal living. Lords who imposed additional days of barshchina or who arbitrarily interfered with the private lives of peasants could seriously threaten the serfs' efficient use of time. Yet, many facets of village life were regulated by custom, rural settlements were self-governing for most purposes and the intervention of the lord might either be a rarity or a largely predictable occurrence. Where obrok prevailed, and it was chosen by most lords near Moscow and St. Petersburg and along major transportation routes accessible to these cities, lords or their stewards approved the departure of peasants for nonagricultural jobs and found it pointless to return a man from the city if he were earning more money than he would earn at home and thus could pay the full obrok. Indeed, where obrok fees were high despite the scarcity of land, nonagricultural activities were obviously indispensable. Owners often cooperated with relatively well-off peasants in efforts to improve their state in life.

Another way of looking at stratification in Russian society is to estimate the value of national income produced and to consider how this was divided among various strata. Using much scattered information on this for Russia in the 1790s, I make a preliminary attempt in Table 10 to estimate the value of national income produced.[66] Rapid inflation both before and after the 1790s makes these figures inapplicable beyond a very short time span, and even for the 1790s these are only crude approximations that deserve careful refinement.

The annual family budget of the wealthy Russians reached the thousands or tens of thousands of roubles. In St. Petersburg persons with incomes of about 3,000 roubles per year are said to have employed about twelve servants in the late eighteenth century, and by the early nineteenth century choice 5–10 room apartments in the city could cost as much as 1,000 roubles per year.[67] Kuptsy of the first and second guilds with capital of 10–50 thousand roubles and 5–10 thousand roubles, respectively, from 1784 to 1794 also had annual budgets in the thousands of roubles, but most small traders in cities operated with budgets only in the tens of roubles. For instance, of the 167 males classified as posad traders below the kuptsy level in Tiumen' city (Siberia) in 1789–1791, the capital of most was assessed between 5 and 30 roubles; these individuals traded in stalls or worked for others.[68] Hired laborers found seasonal employment for 20 or 30 roubles and peasants in the villages sold grain and other products each year for 10 or 20 roubles, persons in both categories using part of their income in cash to pay obrok of 4–5 roubles for each male by the late 1790s.[69]

Fairs and Markets

Fairs (*iarmarki*) were annual events (with the possibility of separate fairs occurring at various times during the year) lasting anywhere from a single day to a few months. In some localities, a brief fair provided the only authorized commercial transactions during the year; elsewhere two or more fairs might occur annually as well as weekly markets and daily exchange in stores and stalls. The significance of a fair for a settlement depended, above all, on the proportion of the total annual commercial turnover that occurred at the fair.

Until 1785, government approval was required in order to establish a fair at a given location at a particular time. Yet, even after the government permitted the unrestricted opening of fairs in cities and in

TABLE 10

Estimates of National Income Produced in the
Russian Empire in the 1790s[a]

Sources of Income	Value (millions of roubles)	Percentage of Total
Primary Production	490–530	64–72
grain production	350	
other agricultural production	100–130	
other primary production	40–50	
Secondary Production	60–80	8–11
Tertiary Production	150–190	20–26
Total	700–800	
Government Revenues	70–75	
poll tax	26	
indirect taxes on wine and salt	30	
Net value of obrok and barshchina to serfowners	40–50	
Value of domestic commerce and exports	140–70	
exports	35–40	
turnover at fairs	30–40	
to St. Petersburg	30–40	
declared capital of merchants	72	

[a] An estimate of 350 million roubles for the annual value of grain production is given in the *Geographical Dictionary*, 309–10. The total amount of grain produced was 96 million *pud* per month (1 pud = 36 pounds) and the average price is calculated at 30 kopecks per pud. In another source, grain production for the beginning of the nineteenth century is given as 160 million chetvert' (1 chetvert' = 6–10 pud depending on the grain), of which 16 million chetvert' are said to have been marketed. See I. D. Koval'chenko, "O tovarnosti zemledeliia v Rossii v pervoi polovine XIX v.," 484–85. On the same pages of the *Geographical Dictionary*, estimates are given for the production of other commodities, totaling almost 200 million roubles. Elsewhere in this encyclopedic dictionary we learn that great fairs at this time had a trade turnover of one or more million roubles as did major guberniia cities, while small fairs had less than 5,000 roubles in turnover and minor uezd cities had at most a few tens of thousands of roubles in turnover. Within two or three decades the value of internal trade turnover was to reach 900 million roubles, exports were to jump to more than 200 million roubles, and the amount of turnover at each of 64 fairs was to exceed 1 million roubles. See M. K. Rozhkov, "Torgovlia," in M. K. Rozhkov, ed., *Ocherki ekonomicheskoi istorii Rossii pervoi polovine XIX veka* (Moscow, 1959), 246–75.

those villages labeled *sela*, there continued to be many annual commercial gatherings, especially in small villages, that were not formally certified as iarmarki.[70] Many such gatherings coincided with the day the local church congregation celebrated its annual festival. Although the number of these festival days remains unknown for many guberniia, large gatherings generally appear to have been included in the lists of iarmarki.

Fairs in Russia as elsewhere served many purposes.[71] They gave access to a variety of goods to the population of relatively inaccessible areas. They corresponded to the seasonal character of supply and demand among the peasants of specified areas. They supplemented daily trade in large cities and periodic trade in the markets of smaller cities by bringing together merchants from a wider area with larger assortments of goods or with the goal of purchasing in large volume a special, local product. They supplied stores and stalls with goods for resale and provided an occasion for recreation. Noteworthy of Russia as opposed to China and Japan is the development of large fairs that facilitated the flow of goods not only between local areas but even between regions.

Data on the number of fairs in eighteenth-century Russia are incomplete, but gradually become more complete for later periods. At the beginning of the 1860s, nearly 6,000 fairs were recorded in European Russia.[72] In the years 1817 to 1820 the total was probably at least 1,000 less, based on data from 40 guberniia showing approximately 4,000 fairs.[73] The steady increase in the number of fairs can be traced back further, too. For seven guberniia in the C-I and C-BE regions there were 448 fairs in the 1830s, 316 in the 1780s, and a far fewer but not precisely known number in the 1740s.[74] In the three left-bank guberniia of the Ukraine, where the number of fairs was most dense, at least 100 new fairs were founded between 1790 and 1815.[75]

Although M. Chulkov lists 1,637 Russian fairs for the 1770s, the actual number was undoubtedly somewhat higher.[76] Using Chulkov's data and the figures from the Commission on Commerce, N. L. Rubinshtein provides an admittedly incomplete chart with more than 900 fairs in 23 guberniia.[77] If we choose a not unlikely sum of 2,800 fairs for the 1770s, we find the interesting result that the number of fairs increased roughly at the same rate as the population until the 1820s with a constant ratio of approximately 10,000 people per fair. If this trend had prevailed for the undocumented early period of the eighteenth century, then the number of fairs in Russia would have failed even to reach 1,000 at the beginning of the century. Table 11

TABLE 11

Estimated Number of Fairs in the Russian Empire

Year	Number of Fairs	Year	Number of Fairs
1475	35	1675	600
1525	75	1725	1,200
1575	150	1775	2,500
1625	300	1825	5,000
		1860	6,000

shows the approximate figures for fairs based on the assumption that the number doubled every 50 years until 1825. Relying on Vartanov's evidence for the central part of the country,[78] we should conclude that, indeed, the rate of increase accelerated in the half-century before the 1780s and the ratio of population to fairs declined throughout most of the seventeenth century from a peak of over 20,000. In addition, the annexation of new areas of the Ukraine with a dense distribution of fairs probably offset a decline in the rate at which new fairs appeared elsewhere from 1775 to 1825.

The development of fairs did not proceed uniformly in all regions. M. K. Rozhkova argues that fairs are a typical form of trade in the period of developed feudalism, but then steadily lose significance as capitalism is accompanied by a reorganization of trade in stores.[79] Already in the beginning of the nineteenth century and, perhaps, even somewhat earlier, there were areas in which commerce in fairs declined relative to other trade. Improved transportation ties, especially in areas close to Moscow and St. Petersburg, resulted in fewer fairs. Rozhkova points out that after 1817 the contrast between regions became strikingly visible in the fate of large fairs. For example, the large C-I regional fair at Rostov actually experienced a reduction in turnover, while Russia's largest fair, the L-MV Makar'evskaia fair (now moved about 50 miles to Nizhnii Novgorod), increased its turnover four times and the largest U-S regional fair at Irbit jumped by 1861 from seventh to second place among all fairs, with a fifteen-fold increase in the volume of turnover.[80]

Rozhkova poses the question: what changes in the organization of internal trade occurred during the first half of the nineteenth century in relation to the breakdown of feudal structure and the formation of capitalist relations? While noting the growth of store trade, she argues that fairs continued to be the basic form of certain kinds of commerce with three qualifications: 1) already at the beginning of the nineteenth century, the industrial regions experienced a comparative decline in trade at fairs; 2) the appearance of new fairs and the growth of old fairs after 1800 occurred mainly on the outskirts of the Russian Empire; and 3) daily trade increased at the expense of fairs while the character of some fairs changed sharply.

Classification of fairs is important in the analysis of urban networks. Rozhkova distinguishes 64 very large fairs in 1817 with a turnover of at least 1 million roubles each. Nearly two-thirds were located in the Ukraine and the C-BE region. For Voronezh, Arkhangel'sk, and Olonets guberniia, she refers also to about 26 large fairs with exchange either in the hundreds of thousands or the tens of thousands of roubles. Presumably there were hundreds of such large fairs in all the guberniia of Russia. Of the remaining fairs, small ones such as many of the 52 fairs of Novgorod guberniia experienced a turnover of a few hundred roubles and intermediate ones, probably including the majority, ranged up to 10,000 or more roubles (higher than corresponding figures in the eighteenth century).

Vartanov provides a more explicit classification of fairs located in administrative cities, which in the century before the 1860s constituted about one-fifth of all fairs. Among the 61 urban fairs in the seven guberniia examined for the 1780s, he ranks 12 fairs as interregional, 17 as intercity, and the remaining 32 as local.[81] The range of goods, volume of exchange, number of people in attendance, distance of cities from which merchants regularly came, and social class of participants all distinguished fairs of one group from those of another. The large fairs provided supplies from a wide area for purchasers from a small area, especially those active in supplying Moscow, and mainly occurred in cities with about 1,500 to 5,000 inhabitants, although Mikhailov (Riazan' guberniia) and Rostov were both somewhat larger. Intermediate fairs attracted merchants from many nearby cities and often were noted for a special good traded in large volume. Local fairs rarely exceeded 5,000 roubles in exchange, and most goods were purchased for the personal use of inhabitants and for small enterprises of the same uezd. If we add small rural fairs as a fourth category and locate other rural fairs corresponding to their prosperity among the above three categories, we will have obtained a classification system for all fairs in the second half of the eighteenth century.

The significance of the hierarchy of fairs for the pyramid of central places was relatively slight. Goods came to fairs both from periodic markets and direct producers as well as from other fairs, and they likewise were forwarded to a variety of consumers, wholesalers, and retailers. Thus fairs provided a point of accumulation and redistribution at any stage of the commercial process. As a rule, fairs were most abundant during the spring and fall in the central parts of Russia and in the winter in areas with cold climates, where transport moved by sleigh. They could result in a temporary congregation of large numbers of people, but not in the permanent build-up of a settlement. The best example of this minimal effect on permanent population is Russia's largest fair, the Makar'evskaia (at Makar'ev uezd city in Nizhnii Novgorod guberniia). While this settlement counted only 384 permanent male residents, second tiniest of the 13 uezd cities in its guberniia in 1782, it burgeoned during the three or four weeks of the summer fair to fill completely 829 stores and hundreds of other hastily set up trading locations.[82] The settlement 17 miles from Kursk guberniia city in which the largest fair of the C-BE region took place for about ten days each year lacked even the title of a uezd city, being known merely as Korrenoe village (Korrenaia fair). Further proof of the inconsequential contribution made by fairs to urban population is that large cities frequently had no fairs at all or, as Iaroslavl', had inconsequential fairs easily dwarfed by the volume of weekly trade conducted in stores.

The decision not to count settlements whose trade occurred primarily at fairs as central places does not mean that we should completely ignore the impact of fairs on city populations. Close examination of Vladimir guberniia in the 1780s reveals that 75 settlements in which 88 fairs took place can be divided as follows: 1) 47 with a single fair annually and no market; 2) 5 with two or three fairs and no market; and 3) 23 with one or more fairs as well as a periodic market.[83] Among the 14 uezd cities, nine offered both markets and fairs, three offered only periodic markets, and two just offered fairs. In these 23 cases where both one or more fairs and a market were present and in the two uezd cities with only fairs, we should eventually seek to observe the relative effect, however minor, of each fair on the prosperity of the settlement.

Periodic markets continued to appear in Russia during the eighteenth century. As in the case of fairs, markets which met generally once, twice, or three times each week either were absent or had little significance in the daily life of the largest cities. However, in central places at levels 5, 6, and 7, periodic markets ordinarily provided the hub of commercial activity. Kuptsy, meshchane, other urban residents, and peasants from nearby settlements converged on the day of the market to buy and sell goods. Stores and stalls that otherwise were empty or scarcely active came alive on market days. As in East Asia, Western Europe, and in other parts of the world, periodic markets in late eighteenth-century Russia served as the regular commercial and social centers for the majority of the population.

Complete data have been published on the marketing centers of three guberniia. Including administrative cities, almost all of which supported markets, the three guberniia together accounted for 145 marketing settlements. In Table 12 various information on these settlements is used to estimate their distribution according to levels of central places.

This presumably complete listing of the marketing settlements in three guberniia provides a basis for tentatively generalizing to a wider area of Russia for which data remain incomplete. These three guberniia in 1782 with roughly 2,100,000 rural residents living in 41 uezd constituted somewhat in excess of 10 percent of the 18 million rural dwellers and the 301 uezd in the four core regions of Russia, i.e., the C-I, C-BE, L-MV, and N-NW regions. Extrapolating from

TABLE 12

Number of Marketing Settlements in Three Guberniia[a]

Guberniia	Levels of Central Places			Total Rural Population
	7	6	5	
Vladimir	46 (2)[b]	13 (8)	5 (4)	856,000
Moscow[c]	16 (4)	5 (5)	5 (5)	640,000
Penza	36 (0)	10 (4)	9 (9)	600,000
Totals	98 (6)	28 (17)	19 (18)	

[a] A. M. Razgon, "Promyshlennye i torgovye slobody i sela vladimirskoi gubernii vo vtoroi polovine XVIII v.," 152–54; *Istoricheskoe i topograficheskoe opisanie gorodov moskovskoi gubernii* (Moscow, 1787); and I. A. Bulygin, *Polozhenie krest'ian i tovarnoe proizvodstvo v Rossii: vtoraia polovina XVIII v.*, 78–80.

[b] In parentheses are the number of administrative cities at these levels.

[c] Moscow city is omitted.

the total of 143 central places above, we would expect at least 1,000 but no more than 1,400 central places in these four regions. My tentative estimate is that in the 1780s the lower figure more closely approximates the actual total; in addition to nearly 300 uezd cities, at least 700 other central places dotted the countryside of this core portion of Russia. Few marketing settlements had appeared in Moscow guberniia, perhaps a consequence of the proximity of the great national center to which peasants and numerous serfowners in this area forwarded their commercial surplus. In contrast, the other two guberniia supported unusual numbers of nonadministrative central places, from all available evidence well above the average of barely two per uezd city in the rest of the core area.

Marketing settlements in Russia were called *torgi* or *torzhki*. Information on individual torzhki can be obtained from the 1787 source used to determine the number of markets in Moscow guberniia, the *Historical and Topographical Description of the Cities of Moscow Guberniia*, and from the 1801–1808 seven-volume *Geographical Dictionary of the Russian State* as well as from recent studies of markets in local areas such as the sources cited on Vladimir and Penza guberniia. In general, markets met once every seven days. In a wide area around the city of Moscow incorporating 29 uezd of the Central-Industrial region including Moscow and Vladimir guberniia plus other nearby uezd, 1/7 markets (those which met once every seven days; correspondingly, 2/7 refers to twice each seven days and 3/7 to three times) met every day of the week except Wednesday. Some of these markets opened in uezd cities, while others met in nonadministrative centers. Similarly the nine 2/7 markets in this area appeared in both uezd centers and other central places. Southeast and northeast of Moscow, they met on Monday and Thursday, and to the northwest they met on Sunday and Thursday, Sunday and Friday, or Tuesday and Friday. In addition, 3/7 markets prospered in the major uezd cities of Pereiaslavl'-Zalesskii and Serpukhov and in Tver' guberniia city.

Detailed descriptions of the uezd around Moscow give a relatively complete picture of marketing activities.[84] Located about 20 miles south of Moscow, Nikitsk uezd center provides an unusual example because it lacked a periodic market for its mere 747 residents, while two other settlements on major transportation routes did sprout 1/7 markets. Twelve miles from Nikitsk and just over 20 miles south of Moscow, Podol' uezd center counted about six times as many kuptsy and meshchane as in Nikitsk, a total population of 856, some 13 stores offering trade mostly in edibles, and a 1/7 market. Elsewhere in this uezd, a second market operated once each week. Interestingly, the four markets in these two adjacent uezd met on consecutive days from Thursday through Sunday, presumably enabling itinerant merchants to visit each in turn. Slightly more than 30 miles from Moscow and roughly 15 miles southeast of Nikitsk, Bronnitsy uezd city provided a more lively commercial image. In comparison to the 47 kuptsy and 52 meshchane homes in Podol' city, there were 63 and 106 homes of these respective groups in this city of 1,542 people. Here a 2/7 market met while a second settlement in the uezd also supported a 1/7 market.

To the north and west of Moscow, a similar pattern had emerged of several 1/7 markets in nonadministrative settlements and uezd centers grouped around each 2/7 market. Dmitrov, about 40 miles from Moscow, served as the 2/7 center for the surrounding 1/7 markets including the uezd center of Klin 30 miles to the northwest and 50 miles from Moscow.

In other areas of Russia, similar circuits of markets existed, with complementary days and a hierarchy often consisting of markets with varying frequencies of activity. A. M. Razgon refers to one weekly circuit of markets in Vladimir guberniia.[85] Similarly in Saratov guberniia, six settlements of Kuznetsk and Khvalynsk uezd, all within about 20 miles of the uezd city of Kuznetsk, formed a weekly commercial circle operating year-round as markets met in turn on consecutive days of the week.[86] Guberniia cities, often with 3/7 or daily markets, normally served as centers for networks of 1/7 and 2/7 markets across Russia. In the C-BE region, nearly all markets outside of uezd centers met 1/7; about one-half of the uezd center markets also met 1/7; most of the rest met 2/7; and a small number met 3/7 as did several guberniia city markets. Circuits of 1/7 markets under a 2/7 market often encompassed two or more uezd since a population of 60,000 or 70,000 in a single uezd normally was insufficient to sustain an intermediate market. Only in a few unusual uezd such as Morshansk in Tambov guberniia could as many as five markets, including the uezd center, coexist.[87]

N. L. Rubinshtein makes the general observation that, whereas a fair remains a distinct organism independent of the territory on which it is held, a market is part of a superior organism on which it is dependent.[88] Yet, to an unusual extent fairs in Russia usurped this function normally associated with markets. Concentrated in the seasons of greatest commercial activity, fairs attracted merchants from longer distances as well as larger crowds of local residents. Comparisons of fairs and markets reveal that at Gorokhovets (Vladimir guberniia) uezd city's 1/7 market, up to 700 persons normally participated, while at Griazovets (Vologda guberniia) uezd city's 3–4 day fair in March, 4,000–6,000 persons attended.[89] At the four marketing settlements in Kovrov uezd (Vladimir guberniia) 300–700 persons regularly attended; while fairs in the uezd attracted up to 1,000 persons, including merchants from nearby uezd. The largest fair in December brought in 1,000–2,500 persons plus merchants from the biggest cities of the guberniia and nearby guberniia.[90] At Moshki in Sudogda uezd of Vladimir guberniia, 100–500 persons attended the market on Mondays, while every year on June 29 up to 2,000 persons appeared for the fair.[91] Likewise, at Viazniki uezd center (Vladimir guberniia), 1,000 persons were attracted on Tuesdays, while July's two-day fair drew crowds of up to 2,000.[92] Where fairs lasted longer, the attendance at markets was even further surpassed.

The most important and unusual respect in which Russian fairs infringed on trade in stores and markets was in their development as centers of interregional commerce. Big fairs of this sort emerged in the late seventeenth century and prospered in the eighteenth century. Referring to this period, Soviet scholars point to the integration of scattered commercial activities into a single national exchange of goods. An increase of the number of markets and fairs reflected the development of an all-Russian market.[93]

The most complete study of the character of the national market has been carried out by B. B. Kafengauz for the first third of the eighteenth century. He has focused on several large fairs, which in terms of the quantity of interregional commerce were important elements in national exchange.[94] For the remainder of the century, the pattern Kafengauz identifies persisted; an annual cycle of large fairs contributed greatly to interregional commerce, with the focal point of traffic being the Makar'evskaia fair. These major fairs of the Russian Empire are identified in Map 2.

The most distant major fair, held in December in Kiakhta on the Chinese border, and the several lesser fairs in out-of-the-way Iakutsk, far to the northeast of Irkutsk, occupied the periphery of the fair system. Furs from Iakutsk arrived in time for the August fair in Eniseisk, and Chinese textiles passed through Irkutsk in time to join caravans headed west. Many months' journey was necessary before the goods from these fairs reached Tobol'sk, the great gathering place of products from Siberia and European Russia. Goods from Siberia arriving at the fall fair in Tobol'sk were then forwarded to one of the major fairs of the Russian Empire, the Irbit fair (in Perm' guberniia of the Urals region), which met at first in January and later from mid-February to mid-March.[95] A second fair in Tobol'sk in the spring was the occasion for the dispersion of goods originating in European Russia, including cargos unsold at the Irbit fair, which were then brought here for sale.

In another part of the Russian Empire, heavy winter traffic produced lively fairs. The Vazhskaia Blagoveshchenskaia fair in Arkhangel'sk guberniia registered a substantial trade turnover during

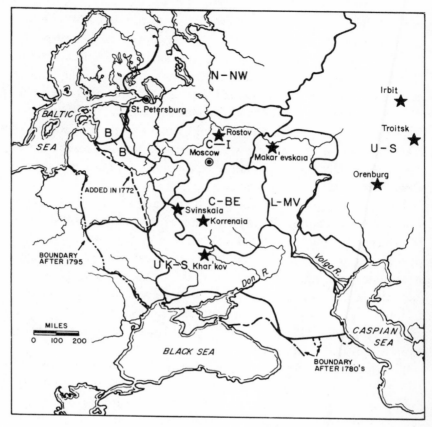

MAP 2.
Major Fairs of the Russian Empire

its 10-day session in early March, when it provided a link between the port of Arkhangel'sk and various cities in the north and in the C-I region.[96] Trade included large quantities of textiles. A portion of the goods available here had arrived from other fairs, and some goods were to be forwarded to major fairs across Russia.

In spring and early summer heavy traffic from the central areas of Russia headed for the Makar'evskaia fair in Nizhnii Novgorod guberniia.[97] From the Urals region, goods flowed from the Irbit fair to blend with goods from Central Asia passing through the considerable fairs at Orenburg and Troitsk. Along the lower and middle Volga river, vast quantities of goods from fairs, markets and daily trade, including Near Eastern and Indian products from Astrakhan', joined an ever-growing volume of traffic. Textiles and other manufactured products occupied a prominent place among goods arriving at the Makar'evskaia fair from Moscow, St. Petersburg, and cities along the upper Volga. The large Rostov fair in the spring was a major source of goods and also belongs on the list of Russia's foremost fairs.

While many textiles and other manufactured products traded at the Makar'evskaia fair were forwarded to the south and east, for most cargos the principal pattern of flow was to Moscow and St. Petersburg to the west and northwest and also to the 10-day Svinskaia fair to the southwest, which began August 15. Located near Briansk in Orel guberniia, this fair was an important link between the Ukraine and Russia. Similarly, the late spring or early summer Korennaia fair near Kursk also deserves recognition as a meeting place of Ukrainian and Russian traders high on the list of the most prosperous fairs in the country.[98] Within the Ukraine, big fairs in Khar'kov and elsewhere also gradually became integrated into this national system of exchange.

While fairs represented an important part of the national flow of goods, their locations were predicated on the existence of, first, Moscow and, later, Moscow and St. Petersburg, the two centers of the national market. Kafengauz stresses the role of Moscow and especially the gostinyi dvor of the Kitai gorod in Moscow as the center of internal exchange. Among various goods, fish arrived here from the lower Volga region via the Makar'evskaia fair, from the upper Don river across the C-BE region, from the White Sea and other waterways in the north, and from uezd near Moscow, especially to the north. Grain arrived in large quantities from the C-BE region. Cattle and livestock products came from the Ukraine. By the mid-eighteenth century, St. Petersburg probably deserved equal billing as a center of national exchange, drawing goods from many of the same localities. For the most part, major fairs facilitated the accumulation of goods for both of these cities. Throughout the eighteenth century, these basic patterns of flow including the hierarchies of fairs, markets, and cities preserved their essential features as they expanded rapidly.

Cities as Systems

By the late eighteenth century, the concept of a city as an ordered arrangement of structures and spaces and as a collection of persons engaged in specified activities had evolved through roughly 1,000 years of Russian history, from time to time infused with new meaning by an awareness of changing European cities and by the progression of Russian society. The impact of foreign models took on immediacy during the final decades of the century when Catherine II commissioned model city plans showing the monumental scale of stone buildings, spacious streets, and public squares current in various European cities.[99] Even prior to this intensive, but on the whole unsuccessful, effort to reshape guberniia and uezd cities, St. Petersburg had been planned as an imposing capital on the style of the major European cities. Its increasingly monumental baroque appearance made evident the enormous discrepancy from this ideal elsewhere in Russia. Likewise spanning the reform initiatives from Peter I to Catherine II was a consciousness of the absence of European-style corporate organizations of merchants and artisans. Later historians were to evaluate the efforts to set up new organizations, including the division of kuptsy into three guilds based on assessed wealth, as unsuccessful attempts to give vitality to commercial organizations without granting the autonomy from state government that had long been customary in European cities.[100] Consciousness of these ideal conceptions concerning the physical plan and the social organization of Russian cities served to shape expectations, yet for the most part perceptions of cities were not determined by the elaborately constructed plans and reforms relegated to the occasional commission reports but by the actual appearance and organization of cities inherited from the past.

Soviet historians have given little emphasis to changes in cities copied from abroad, referring instead to the second half of the eighteenth century as the period of the early evolution within Russia of the feudal city into the capitalist city.[101] According to this reasoning, alterations in the physical appearance of cities and in the social composition of their populations are accounted for by the increasing role of cities as points in a national trading network and by the improved ties of cities to their surrounding rural areas. Particularly noteworthy is their impression that on the foundation of the "feudal" character-istics of small-scale crafts and local trade were beginning to be added factories, especially those engaged in the manufacture of textiles. Further, these sources observe the decline of cities that were primarily fortresses and military-administrative points, to be replaced by cities that effectively integrated the economic activities of the surrounding area. While acknowledging that these changes were uneven and that the insubstantial formation of the antagonistic forces of the prole-tariat and bourgeoisie reveal the slow process of evolution in Russian cities, these Soviet sources generally take a positive attitude toward eighteenth century urban development and provide an orientation point for studying actual changes in cities independent of the new city plans.

The *Geographical Dictionary*, written shortly after 1800 and based primarily on data from the 1780s and 1790s, conveys a wealth of in-formation on individual Russian cities. Using this information, we can determine the characteristic arrangements of the physical and human components of cities at various levels. Separate mention must also be made of the common elements in administrative cities as op-posed to the nonadministrative central places.

We return now to the seven levels of central places, beginning with the smallest settlements. Level-7 central places are not cities. Accord-ing to the second set of definitions of the seven levels of central places (see Table 2), they are settlements with fewer than 3,000 inhabitants differing from level-6 central places in the smaller scale of marketing activities (and normally of the hinterland that their markets serve). Ordinarily, level-7 settlements were less populous than level-6 settle-ments, and in Russia, where village populations were considerably smaller than in East Asia, few level-7 settlements exceeded 1,000 per-sons and most probably ranged from 300 to 800 inhabitants. Included also as level-7 settlements, following the precedent set in the study of China and Japan, are a small number of administrative centers that had so little commerce that they could not even sustain a 1/7 periodic market. These uezd centers reveal a similar population range. As has already been noted, Nikitsk uezd center (Moscow guberniia) had 747 inhabitants. Among other administrative centers without a periodic market, Sudogda (Vladimir guberniia) counted 243 inhabitants exclusive of a small number of gentry, officials and clergy and Kerensk (Irkutsk guberniia) consisted of 87 houses,[102] suggestive of a population intermediate between those of Nikitsk and Sudogda. In the case of Kerensk, located in the north of Siberia, the uezd population of fewer than 13,000 was exceptionally sparsely settled over a large area and included many persons engaged in hunting and fishing. In contrast, the uezd centers that lacked markets in the C-I region and in other populated areas were outrivaled by other settlements. Each of the two uezd centers in Vladimir guberniia without markets was surrounded by four or five marketing settlements within its uezd, and Nikitsk, which may have been hampered by its proximity to Moscow, counted two markets within its uezd. Some of these level-7 administrative centers are described as being too small to be divided into sections, with the perimeter of Sudogda measuring only 450 *sazhen'* (754 sazhen' = one mile).

Almost all level-7 central places were nonadministrative settlements that qualify under the definition of standard marketing settlements. Rarely described in detail, these places consisting of roughly 50 to 150 houses often took on a generally linear shape, along both sides of a road or a river. It is likely that these settlements were physically quite indistinguishable from ordinary villages; indeed, in many level-7 central places agriculture remained the major activity of local residents. However, evidence exists for some of these settlements that the amount of arable land per capita was low, revealing a population relatively separated from cultivation of the soil. Furthermore, at least in some areas, level-7 residents were primarily on obrok, which gave them more flexibility in the use of their labor.[103] Part-time or full-time trade-related or craft activities occupied them even on the days when the market was not functioning. Elsewhere where the population was mainly engaged in agriculture, marketing day changed the normal routine as the main road through the settlement became converted to a row of stalls or display areas attracting peasants from surrounding villages and at least a few itinerant merchants, often from the local uezd city or another nearby level-6 center.

In this classification system, level-6 central places are defined as one-half urban. While occasional nonadministrative marketing settlements merit this classification, the majority of level-6 central places were uezd centers with up to 3,000 residents and with integrative commercial functions for most or all of their uezd and, perhaps, for part of an adjoining uezd. The nonadministrative settlements that achieved this distinction were often called sela or slobody. For instance, a selo (singular of sela) about 15 miles from Vologda guberniia city on the main road to Belozero uezd city consisted of rows of shops built to serve the 1/7 market, and a sloboda (singular of slobody) in Kursk guberniia's Khotmyzhsk uezd, which lined both sides of the river, counted more than 1,000 inhabitants, some stores and a 2/7 market.[104] In general, centers at level 6 can be distinguished by more frequent marketing days, by the presence of a number of stores, and often by the occurrence of several fairs during the year. Populations generally exceeded 600 and not infrequently were greater than 1,000.

Uezd cities that ranked at level 6 varied in their administrative histories. Some had been provincial cities before the reforms beginning in 1775, but had not been chosen as centers for the newly organized guberniia and thus dropped to the level of the uezd cities. Many, indeed, a majority of those with fewer than 2,000 inhabitants, had been originally chosen as uezd cities only a few years before the 1782 enumeration and therefore were still scarcely affected by the efforts to restructure them in the image of other uezd cities. Others had served as uezd cities since the first part of the eighteenth century or even earlier.

Descriptions of administrative cities most frequently mention the following physical elements: the urban perimeter, walls and fortifications; churches and monasteries; public buildings; stores, the gostinyi dvor, and public squares used for marketing; big and small streets (*ulitsy* and *pereulki*); and houses, often differentiated into stone and wooden ones. The social composition of the city is given as the number of houses belonging to members of each stratum, as the separate male and female population per stratum, or as the total city population. Sometimes only the data for males are listed, requiring a doubling of the figures for approximate totals. Inconsistencies and inaccuracies in these data presented in the *Geographical Dictionary* can be corrected by reference to the actual archival statistics for the fourth enumeration.

The skyline of Russian cities was dominated by cupolas and towers, the former topping churches and monasteries and the latter rising from gates and other points along the city walls. Since the perimeters of these level-6 centers rarely exceeded three miles, with an average side ranging from about one-fifth of a mile to slightly over one mile in exceptionally large instances, the landmarks of these cities were frequently visible from all around. Recently established uezd centers generally lacked towers and walls, containing at most one or two stone churches along with one or more wooden churches. Older uezd cities presented a more awe-inspiring skyline, which marked the seat of secular and religious authority. Despite a meager population of 734, Zvenigorod in Moscow guberniia counts among these old uezd centers with an impressive skyline, dominated by a fortress one-third of a mile in perimeter rising above the steep bank of the Moscow river. In addition, on the edge of the city there was a sizable monastery enclosed by a stone wall with seven towers.[105]

Some older cities were divided into sections or precincts in spite of their small areas. The three sections of Zvenigorod were characteristic of these old administrative centers: 1) fortress, 2) lower posad with the main square and public buildings, and 3) upper posad across the river consisting of former private settlements called slobody. Klin (Moscow guberniia) also contained an old fortress, and the city was divided by a river into two other sections. Through an unusual plan, Klin was separated into quarters for its six distinct strata: dvoriane, kuptsy, meshchane, soldiers, clergy, and raznochintsy.[106] These cities, however, were exceptions; due to the small scale of cities at this level, the most common pattern was not to divide the urban area into sections.

Commerce and crafts in level-6 central places were conducted in either 1/7 or 2/7 periodic markets as well as in one or more annual fairs and in stores. The ratio of population to stores ranged from about 10:1 to 150:1 exclusive of blacksmith shops, which were counted separately. Ratios between 20:1 and 40:1 seem to have been most common. For instance, in the new uezd city of Myshkin in Iaroslavl' guberniia, 27 stores served 634 residents; in Ladoga uezd city in St. Petersburg guberniia, some 69 stores served 1,786 residents.[107] Ladoga numbered among the few cities at this level with a gostinyi dvor; in this case its perimeter measured 180 sazhen'. Another of these large enclosures in Bogoroditsk uezd city of Tula guberniia encompassed 25 stores, which, together with 26 shops on a marketing square and an additional 40 stores in the homes of merchants and artisans, contributed to a total of 87 stores for 2,816 residents.[108]

These small uezd cities at level 6 consisted of roughly ten or twenty streets, each with some tens of houses or sometimes even fewer. One to four main ulitsy (big streets) were the sites of comparatively numerous houses as well as of shops, while the smaller and more numerous pereulki (small streets) often contained as few as ten or twenty wooden houses. In cities at this level, an average of nearly six persons per house was common.

Usually 5–10 percent of the population in small uezd centers belonged to one of the three non-podat' strata of dvoriane, clergy, and officials. In Moscow guberniia, Podol'sk uezd center (population: 718) counted two dvoriane homes, 4 clergy homes, and one home of an official; Ruza uezd center (population: 1,818) had 4 dvoriane homes, 18 clergy homes, and 8 homes of officials; and Volokamsk uezd city (population: 2,054) contained 13 dvoriane homes, 23 clergy homes, and 9 homes of officials.[109] Variations in the distribution of other officially recognized social strata primarily followed regional lines.

The presence of agricultural activities in Russian cities is sometimes emphasized.[110] Particularly on the fringes of level-6 settlements, land planted to grain could be found. Since these settlements are treated as half urban here, this phenomenon causes no concern over whether Russian cities were indeed urban. The widespread presence of gardening in cities and the fame acquired by certain cities for special fruits or vegetables also should not be surprising. Comparative information on China and Japan reveals the existence of vegetable farming in small cities and to a limited extent in large cities, too, but as in Russia this made only a minor contribution to urban employment and did not impart an agrarian character to cities. Perhaps, as F. W. Mote has suggested to me for China, gardening should be conceived as an aspect of the urban character of premodern cities.

Level-5 central places are defined as cities. Only a tiny percentage of these settlements with 3,000–10,000 inhabitants did not function as administrative centers. These were exceptional cases of private sela, either inadvantageously located to be chosen as uezd centers or purposely by-passed in this selection because of the costly compensation due the owner. Examples include Ivanovo (in Shui uezd of Vladimir guberniia), a city of textile factories, wide and straight streets, and more than 1,000 houses, many constructed of stone, and Pavlovo selo (in Nizhnii Novgorod guberniia), also a craft center described as more like a city than a selo.[111] Both of these settlements of 4,000 to 6,000 population belonged to one of the richest men in Russia, Count Sheremetev.

Administrative centers of 3,000–10,000 population are the most representative of late eighteenth-century Russian cities. They were full-fledged urban concentrations in contrast to the level-6 central places and were far more numerous than cities at higher levels. They functioned as local cities at a distance of no more than 40 miles from most inhabitants of European Russia. They generally encompassed an area of one or two square miles with a perimeter ranging from about three to eight miles. Frequently, these cities were divided into three or four sections. Older cities centered on a fortress or kreml', elevated on a river bank or surrounded by a moat and enclosed by a wall. The 35-foot high earthern wall of the kreml' in Balakhna (Nizhnii Novgorod guberniia) measured two-thirds of a mile in perimeter, intermediate among the fortresses in the five level-5 cities in Moscow guberniia, whose perimeters ranged from one-third of a mile to well over a mile.[112] In many cities, the kreml' wall had fallen into disrepair or, if wooden, had burned down. In the case of the large earthen wall extending 1,037 sazhen' (more than 1⅓ miles) in Pereiaslavl'-Zalesskii (Vladimir guberniia), its moat on three sides had become filled with grass and swampy.[113] In this city, the kreml' counted three gates and twelve wooden towers, and inside its wall stood large churches and government offices. From the many descriptions of fortresses in the *Geographical Dictionary*, we can conclude that not only were outer walls rare in Russian cities but inner walls enclosing kreml' were preserved only in some older cities and were often in disrepair. After the kreml' lost any military significance, these old enclosures whose interiors occupied as little as one percent of the urban area often collapsed from inattention.

Roughly one percent of the urban structures served primarily religious purposes. Indeed, in a few cities noted for their traditional Greek Orthodox functions, such as Kostroma and Pereiaslavl'-Za-lesskii, the figure reached up to 3 percent. In areas outside of administrative centers, the percentage of all principal structures that were churches or monasteries varied from about 0.5–1.5. Usually the percentage was less than in the administrative cities. In Kursk guberniia, where 7.75 percent of the population resided in administrative centers, some 105 churches stood in these cities as opposed to 630 outside of them; the administrative centers accounted for a ratio of churches to population more than twice that of other settlements in their uezd.[114] The contrast between stone and wooden churches in this guberniia was even sharper; 38 of the 105 urban churches were constructed of stone as opposed to 42 of the 630 rural churches. In Tula guberniia, in which only 5.97 percent of the population resided in administrative centers, 86 of 851 churches stood in these cities, including 71 of the 357 stone churches.[115]

Level-5 cities consisted of roughly 500 to 2,000 houses. Almost all of the houses were one-family dwellings built of wood, but by the 1790s in many cities at this level from 1 to 10 percent of the houses had been rebuilt of stone, including a disproportionate number of dvoriane and kuptsy residences. Stone construction still had barely spread to some regions, for instance only 3 of the 1,697 houses in Penza guberniia city were not of wood.[116] City planners under Catherine II advocated stone foundations as the next best thing to stone dwellings. While just 56 of the 1,163 houses in Elets uezd city of Orel guberniia were built of stone, 123 additional houses boasted a stone foundation.

Cities at this level dominated the commerce and crafts of areas generally as large as one, two, or three uezd. In most cases, they counted more than 50, frequently more than 150, and in some instances more than 250 stores. A stone gostinyi dvor often enclosed one-half or more of these stores. In Zaraisk (Riazan' guberniia) there were 136 stores, and in Rzhev (Tver' guberniia) some 113 stores lined the inside of the gostinyi dvor.[117] Level-5 cities also were centers of periodic markets, often meeting with frequencies of 2/7 or 3/7, and in some cases of relatively large fairs. The 3/7 market in Rzhev was supplemented by two fairs, each of which lasted for one week and registered about one percent of the total annual exchange in the city.

The number and variety of artisans is known for many cities, including two in Kursk guberniia at the opposite ends of the population range for level 5. In Novoi Oskol', a city of barely 3,000 inhabitants and only one big street, among 19 registered craftsmen, there were 8 tailors, 5 shoemakers, and 5 blacksmiths.[118] In Putivl', a city of more than 8,000 inhabitants with three main streets, the total number of registered craftsmen reached 158, including 36 carpenters, 35 tailors, 31 shoemakers, and 15 blacksmiths, the same professions that predominated in other cities.[119]

Aside from Moscow and St. Petersburg, large Russian cities ranked at level 4, with only a few exceptions at level 3 barely exceeding the minimum of 30,000 people. For the most part, these level-4 and level-3 cities of 10,000–35,000 people functioned as guberniia centers. Their perimeters ranged from about 6 to 12 miles, suggesting a total of 2–9 square miles. The number of houses inside these cities generally exceeded 2,000 with Kazan's total in excess of 3,000 and Tula's as high as 4,570.[120] Again we find numerous small pereulki in many Russian cities; Kursk was crisscrossed by 182 streets of all sizes, and Tula boasted 106 streets. Many cities at this level contained 20 or 30 churches in addition to several large stone churches noted separately as *sobor* (a cathedral), and perhaps even one or two monasteries or nunneries. The gostinyi dvor of each city sheltered a great number of stores; the two in Irkutsk each comprised 224 to 243 stores, while those in Tver', Tula, and Kazan' harbored 342, 746, and 777 stores, respectively. These huge enclosures occupied several ordinary city blocks, e.g., in Orenburg the rectangular gostinyi dvor measured more than one-half mile around.

In nearly every respect, these level-4 cities had the same basic characteristics as level-5 cities, but on a more bountiful scale. The number of registered craftsmen was higher in these cities, reaching 405 in

Kursk and 470 in Tver'. Similarly, there were more dvoriane homes and many more residents serving in official positions or in garrisons; together, these service categories totaled 1,213 persons in Tver' and 1,584 persons in Kursk.[121] Correspondingly, there were more public buildings. In Novgorod, 12 of 17 public buildings were constructed of stone. Perhaps, only to the extent that in some level-5 cities the new city plans had begun to be implemented, including even the building of some four-story structures in Kazan', did they contrast markedly with cities at lower levels.

Some cities on the outskirts of the Russian Empire had unusual characteristics. Foreign influences were visible in Central European-style stone housing in Riga and in Near Eastern-style religious structures in Astrakhan'—both level-3 cities. Astrakhan' also boasted an exceptionally large kreml', whose walls measured roughly 20–35 feet high and 9–15 feet wide, with towers soaring to heights of 50 feet or more. Three of the towers enclosed gates, which were guarded and closed at night.[122]

The new plans for cities at all levels were designed to provide permanence and grandeur to urban structures. Until this time, except for the kreml' and stone religious structures, almost all buildings were of recent construction. For instance, a description of the houses in Tula notes that most had been standing for about 20 years although some that had been built as many as 30 years before were still in good condition.[123] Fires contributed to the frequent turnover in houses; in Tula, big fires in 1779 and 1781 burned down as many as 450 houses. Even more important was the fact that houses and stores, many of which were located in houses, were not built for permanence; these one-story, single-family wooden dwellings could be replaced without great cost. Data assembled from the *Geographical Dictionary* on the number of houses in the cities of 13 guberniia reveal that in all but two guberniia the ratio of urban population (using archival figures) to number of houses ranged between 5.7 and 6.2, indicative of the small size of dwellings.

Streets had appeared somewhat haphazardly over the years. The new city plans called for widening ulitsy to 70 feet and establishing a regular gridiron pattern of blocks. In many cities this regularization of the street pattern had long been planned. The authorities in Astrakhan' had initiated an effort to rebuild, straighten, and widen the dusty streets of the city in 1746.[124]

Some urban dwellings assumed the shape of courtyards (*dvory*). The concept of a courtyard conveys the image of more than one structure. In Russia, compounds might enclose a stable, a barn, a workshop or other structures that served the productive activities of the resident family. Many courtyards comprised two or three *izba* (roughly translated as house), suggesting the presence of more than one family. Evidence that this was indeed the case is found in Astrakhan', where many dvory were subdivided between two owners, or portions of the total area were rented out. N. B. Golikova observes that, in an outer area of this city where land was more abundant, every courtyard had a garden.[125] Rich dvoriane often owned huge courtyards beautified with orchards; however, in general, urban courtyards ranged in area from only about 1,200 to 2,100 square feet.

Moscow and St. Petersburg loomed on a much vaster scale than other cities of Russia. In most respects the old capital exhibited the same basic characteristics of smaller cities magnified many times. In contrast, the newly established capital city of the eighteenth century was constructed with tighter restrictions under the guidance of Western European architects and modeled on contemporary European city plans. St. Petersburg represented an ideal against which Russians measured the reality of other cities, while Moscow provided a sample of reality by which they judged the actual conditions of other cities.

These two great cities were more densely populated than other Russian cities, but as the *Geographical Dictionary* notes in regard to St. Petersburg, they were only moderately populated relative to the density of big cities in other countries.[126] High densities prevailed within built-up areas of St. Petersburg, but the total planned area of the city included many bodies of water and expanses of open land. The population of Moscow was more evenly dispersed within the 25-mile perimeter of the Kamer'-Kollezhskii wall on a total built-up area measuring twenty square miles. The contrast between the two cities is evident from the number of dwellings, some serving as apartment buildings. The total for St. Petersburg had peaked by 1762, when some 460 stone residential dwellings were interspersed among

4,094 wooden houses.[127] By 1783 the number of stone residential buildings had risen to 1,094, while the number of wooden houses had dropped sharply to only 2,734. Already in 1787 the ratio had declined to 1:2, and the total number of structures had slipped below 3,500. By contrast, despite the fact that Moscow's population was smaller in 1787, it counted 8,554 houses. In many sections of Moscow the ratio of stone to wooden housing remained as low as 1:10.[128] Although the ratio of stone to wooden houses for the city as a whole also had recently been rising, as yet it still hovered around 2:9. That these two cities each boasted many multiple dwelling units can be seen in the average population per residential building or house: a figure well in excess of 50 persons in St. Petersburg and of 20 persons in Moscow.

Each city was divided into sections or precincts (*chasty*) and quarters or wards (*kvartaly*). The number of chasty in St. Petersburg had increased from 5 in 1737 to 10 in 1782 and finally to 11, still considerably short of the 20 sections in Moscow, a total up from 14 in the middle of the century. In St. Petersburg the chasty contained 3 to 5 quarters, resulting in a total number of kvartaly roughly half the figure of 88 found in Moscow.[129] Moscow's five walls marked its most prominent boundaries, lacking any parallel in St. Petersburg and only partially duplicated in other old Russian cities. As seen in Map 3, the areas within these walls were called the four cities (goroda) of Moscow. The innermost imposing stone wall enclosed Moscow's Kremlin, an area of palaces, religious centers, and government buildings in the center of the city. The second wall around the Kitai gorod, demarcated the smallest and most centrally located of the so-called cities after the Kremlin. Containing roughly 0.5 percent of the built-up area and 1.8 percent of the buildings in the city, the densely packed Kitai gorod boasted large multifamily dwellings, numerous churches, and rows (*riady*) of stores. In the two gostinyi dvor located on Red Square just outside of the Kremlin stood some 53 riady with a total of 3,732 stores and stalls.[130] Both the central wholesale and retail trade functions of Moscow were concentrated in the Kitai gorod.

The third wall formed the boundary for about 12 percent of the city's built-up area and somewhat more than 10 percent of its buildings and courtyards. It surrounded the Beloi gorod, second only to

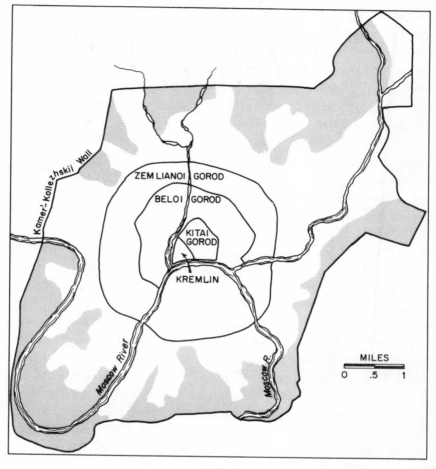

MAP 3.
Plan of Moscow

the Kitai gorod in the proportion of the total amount of the land area
on which buildings or courtyards stood and in the percentage of all
courtyards or buildings which were large (more than 50,000 square
feet) or medium (more than 17,500 square feet).[131] For many purposes these two areas are treated together as a kind of central city,
which along with the Kremlin formed the nucleus of Moscow.

Residential areas of the Kitai gorod and the Beloi gorod, surrounding the administrative and religious center of the Kremlin and the
dense concentration of stores in Red Square just outside the Kremlin

within the Kitai gorod, attracted many wealthy dvoriane and kuptsy. Even in the eighteenth century the pattern described by P. G. Ryndziunskii for nineteenth-century Russian cities had, at least to some extent, appeared; well-constructed dvoriane and bourgeois residences predominated in the central city, while on the outskirts the shabbier dwellings of workers' regions clustered in the vicinity of a growing number of factories.[132] However, the extent of segregation by officially recognized social strata was far less than the segregation by wealth. Data for 1810 reveal that a minimum of 193 dvoriane resided in each of the city's twenty sections.[133]

Already in the 1760s there were plans to tear down the wall enclosing the Beloi gorod in order to replace it with a boulevard. In the 1780s and 1790s the boulevard gradually appeared.

Another walled enclosure dating from the sixteenth century—as did the walls of the Kitai gorod and the Beloi gorod—was the Zemlianoi gorod. Similarly to the wall of the Beloi gorod before its removal, this wall often fell into disrepair, not being a solid stone structure as were the walls around the Kremlin and the Kitai gorod. The Zemlianoi gorod included about 33 percent of the built-up area in the city and 35 percent of the dwellings and courtyards. Between 1737 and 1771, this area had experienced changes in physical appearance and social composition that caused it to resemble the areas of Moscow closer to the center. For instance, during a 28-year period the number of pereulki (small streets) dropped by 25 percent and the number of courtyards by more than 30 percent, testifying to the decline in small dwelling units as larger tracts were consolidated by wealthy dvoriane and merchants choosing to live further from the center of the city than was previously the custom. As in the Beloi gorod a few decades before, stone construction was coming to predominate on main streets, while wooden houses remained common on pereulki. The Zemlianoi gorod, the Beloi gorod, the Kitai gorod, and the Kremlin should together be treated as the inner city of Moscow. In an area of 7–8 square miles this inner city comprised about half of the courtyards in Moscow, including 76 percent of the stone courtyards and 63 percent of the 33,000 rooms in 1775, a total that would rise to 50,000 by 1801.[134]

The sprawling area of the outer city reached in places to the

Kamer'-Kollezhskii wooden wall and along a few major roads even beyond the wall. Despite large, open spaces, the area built-up outside the Zemlianoi gorod exceeded that of the more densely settled inner city. In 1799 some 4,133 courtyards stood beyond the Zemlianoi wall but within the Kamer'-Kollezhskii wall, and another 293 courtyards existed even beyond this outer perimeter. By this date the city's outermost wall had begun to fall apart, to some extent losing its usefulness as a barrier against the free movement of goods into the city.

Individuals registered in five strata were legally allowed to own urban land. The distribution of courtyards owned by members of these strata reveals important differences between the inner and outer cities of Moscow.[135] Clergy and dvoriane concentrated in the inner city; only 26 and 31 percent, respectively, of their holdings were located in the outer city. The courtyards and houses of the kuptsy and meshchane combined were fairly evenly distributed; 47 percent stood in the outer city. Finally, more than two-thirds of the raznochintsy, who owned 40 percent of the courtyards and houses in Moscow but only 20 percent of the rooms, lived in the outer city. Courtyards and houses in the outer city were smaller than those in the inner city, consisted of fewer rooms, and were owned by poorer individuals. The contrast is especially sharp in the Kitai and Beloi sections. Moreover, lodgers, who along with household serfs made up roughly one-third of Moscow's permanent population, found rooms primarily with poor owners, adding substantially to the population of the outer city.

During the long winters the population of Moscow rose as high as 400,000.[136] The dvoriane returned from summer sojourns at their estates, bringing with them household serfs and, perhaps, a small part of the produce needed for personal consumption. At least in the eighteenth century, dvoriane preferred to buy homes in Moscow, considering it demeaning to rent or stay in an inn.[137] State peasants and serfs on obrok found cheap quarters in the city while working as hired laborers. Other serf laborers were bound to the owners of factories, which in Moscow predominantly produced textiles.

The annual winter influx of up to 200,000 persons together with the inclusion in the summer population figures of roughly 60,000 lodgers testifies to the abundant employment opportunities for temporary residents of Moscow. One growing source of jobs was the manufacturing industry, which in 1784 included 147 factories and 233 plants (generally smaller enterprises such as breweries and leather processing companies). In 1780, after all the factories had been relocated from the Kitai gorod because they were out of character with the prevalent land use, there were 25 factories in the Beloi gorod, 69 in the Zemlianoi gorod, and 64 in the outer city. The smaller industrial plants were absent also in the Beloi gorod; roughly 55 percent of them stood in the Zemlianoi gorod and 45 percent in the outer city. The changing distribution of blacksmith shops gives some insight into the smaller craft enterprises in Moscow. There were 373 of these shops in 1780; 46 of 77 in the Kitai and Beloi areas were constructed of stone as opposed to all 207 in the outer city having been built with wood. By 1796, the number of shops had declined to 337, but the stone shops had increased from 87 to 199, including all 49 in the Kitai gorod and Beloi gorod and almost one-half of the shops in the outer city.[138] As in the decline of small courtyards, large stone blacksmith shops and sizable factories were replacing smaller wooden structures.

Commerce and related transportation functions offered a more important source of employment. In the mid-1780s Moscow counted 9,646 stores located in 134 riady divided by type of good, including the riady of the gostinyi dvor mentioned above, plus 1,174 scattered stores generally lacking such specialization.[139] Around the city, often located next to gates in the various walls, stood 13 riady of meat stores and along the city's rivers appeared 8 riady of lumber stores. In the Zemlianoi gorod alone markets on five city squares attracted peasants from the surrounding countryside periodically bringing firewood, charcoal, lumber, hay, and edibles, while ten other marketing areas consisted of 151 stone and 427 wooden stores.[140]

Eighteenth-century Moscow was not a rapidly growing city; except for a possible, temporary decline after St. Petersburg's founding, the city's permanent population hovered around 200,000. Yet, the above description indicates that Moscow was in many respects a changing city. The annual winter influx grew as employment opportunities became available. The number of streets and courtyards dropped considerably during the middle third of the century, suggesting a process of consolidation. Thus with respect to population dynamics and land use Moscow was becoming less similar to smaller Russian cities. In the size of its courtyards and in the average population per residential building, Moscow was gradually coming to resemble St. Petersburg. Even in the central city some of the smaller wooden churches were being demolished as part of the consolidation effort. Despite the presence of 377 churches,[141] as many as one for every 35 urban residential structures, the average population per church remained roughly as in other cities. The quartering of soldiers was also changing in the city. Following an edict issued in 1765 to house all soldiers in barracks, progress in this regard was eventually made at the end of the century, freeing almost all families from the burden of quartering soldiers.[142]

While these changes made Moscow a city intermediate between the mass of smaller Russian cities and the new West European-style of St. Petersburg, they did not result in the carefully planned city originally anticipated. Despite the proclamation of a new city plan in 1775, so many exceptions and qualifications were eventually permitted that the development of the city can best be described as spontaneous and unplanned. To some extent the city plan was realized in the central areas and in areas devastated by fire, but this was the exception rather than the rule. By the contemporary standards of European cities, Moscow remained a settlement of wooden single-story structures, low in population density with numerous gardens and green spaces and tightly sealed by walls with guarded gates and protected by watchmen manning the 1,056 public boxes dotted along its streets.

Because of hurried construction and rapid expansion, St. Petersburg, too, did not correspond precisely to what had been envisioned in its foreign-inspired plan; much remained to be accomplished by the planning apparatus of Catherine II. The first flush of construction had continued until 1737, and the limits of area built up by that time prevailed for the remainder of the century.[143] These built-up areas on this city of islands can be seen on Map 4. Even here pereulki measured only 21–35 feet in width, although ulitsy, which in Moscow generally remained 42–56 feet wide, frequently reached widths of

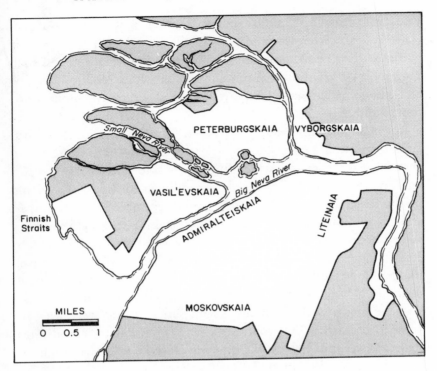

MAP 4.
Plan of St. Petersburg

more than 100 feet. Planning called for perspectives of long, straight streets bordered by stone buildings of a uniform size and distance from the street. Much was done to realize these plans after 1762 although as late as 1787 residential buildings of three and four stories were still the exception and many houses boasted large gardens and orchards. Even in the 1790s, in some areas of the city, numerous wooden houses remained.

The special functions of a national capital in various ways distinguished St. Petersburg from Moscow. First the number of state buildings far exceeded the total of 59 in Moscow. Second, the military population was larger, including more than 11,000 persons in families associated with the navy and well over 30,000 persons in families associated with the army. Third, the investment in residential housing in St. Petersburg had no parallel elsewhere; its total value was calculated as 70.6 million roubles in the late eighteenth century.[144] In certain poor sections of the city, the value of housing was quite low, with some small wooden houses valued at less than 200 roubles. In contrast, the central areas in which wealthy dvoriane and kuptsy congregated displayed rows of expensive multistoried stone buildings.

In concluding this section, we should consider what distinguished cities from rural areas in Russia. Clearly, the most impressive urban element was the kreml', which measured up to 7,000 feet in perimeter. The best known of these, the Kremlin in Moscow, boasted imposing towers, some used as gates, spaced several hundred feet apart and rising 100 to 200 feet. Yet, most cities including St. Petersburg lacked kreml'. A second urban element was the city wall. Not many Russian cities had a wall in addition to a kreml', and those city walls that had long existed, as the one in Tula, delimited only a small part of the total built-up area and had already fallen into disrepair. Unlike the stone walls of many kreml', these walls were typically wooden or earthen. Of course, the wall of the Kitai gorod represents an exception. Made of stone with towers 30–90 feet high and spaced 350–450 feet apart the wall was an impressive sight.[145] The walls of the Beloi gorod and Zemlianoi gorod, and the more hastily constructed Kamer'-Kollezhskii wall around outer Moscow also stand out because of their long perimeters, but not so much because of any effort to make their appearance imposing.

With the exception of a few cities, most urban architecture was indistinguishable from rural architecture. Housing was largely wooden and one-story, stores were small, and streets were often irregular and short. Although monasteries and nunneries were predominantly located in cities by this period, with rare exceptions cities had only one or two of these large religious compounds. In general, the physical appearance of cities differed from that of rural settlements primarily as a result of the greater density of construction, the larger area of settlement and the smaller amount of land used for gardening and other agricultural purposes. However, the preservation of certain stone churches, and buildings within kreml' and the development primarily in the eighteenth century of large-scale stone construction of residential housing did attach an aura of permanence to the physical features of urban areas that was lacking in rural areas.

Systems of Cities

In the preceding section I compared central places at each of seven levels in order to generalize about the physical and social characteristics typical of settlements at each level. According to the explanation of the urban networks approach presented in Chapter 1, similar conditions in cities result in large part from similarities in their position in the urban hierarchy within a single country. In this section the emphasis switches from individual cities to the interdependence of settlements. I focus on the distribution of central places at each level in order to generalize about their locations in the pyramid of commercial and administrative centers. Settlements at each level fit into local, regional, and national systems of cities. Table 13

TABLE 13

Distribution of Central Places in 1782[a]

	Russian Empire		Four Core Regions	
Level	No. of Central Places	Urban Pop. (millions)	No. of Central Places	Urban Pop. (millions)
1	1	.30	1	.30
2	1	.21	1	.21
3	4	.13	2	.06
4	28	.42	18	.25
5	210	1.05	110	.57
6	300	.22[b]	180	.12[b]
7	1100	—	700	—
Est. Totals	1650	2.3	1000	1.5

[a] Based on data (presented in detail in Chapter 4) on the number of persons in cities. The principal source of data is the archival records of *TsGADA*. The writings of V. M. Kabuzan, insofar as they pertain to materials on the size of the population of the cities of the Russian Empire, have been of great assistance in using these archival records and in compiling this table.

[b] Consistent with the definition given for urban population, the total population in level-6 central places has been divided by two in calculating the figures in this table.

gives the estimated distribution of central places first for all of the Russian Empire and then separately for the four core regions, the C-I, C-BE, N-NW, and L-MV.

The four areas designated as the core regions contained roughly 65 percent of the population of the Russian Empire and 25 of the 41 guberniia in 1782. Excluded are the U-S region in the east, with about 12 percent of the national population and 9–10 percent of the urban population, and the B-B and UK-S regions in the west, with roughly 24 percent of the national population and 25 percent of the total urban population. The statements below on the general characteristics of central places at each of the seven levels are based on information from the core regions and do not necessarily apply to the vast stretches of the U-S region, in which special frontier conditions existed, or to cities in the B-B and UK-S regions, which had developed under separate governments. In Chapter 4, attention will be given separately to cities in each guberniia of the core areas and the U-S region.

Level-7 central places rank at the bottom level in the hierarchy of settlements. Having 1/7 markets, they served in Russia as loci for the local redistribution of agricultural and livestock products as well as of village crafts; however, by the late eighteenth century their commercial functions were rarely limited to local exchange. Along with rural settlements that offered fairs, they represented the first step in a wider network of redistribution. Local peasants and kuptsy, meshchane and others from the uezd city appeared on marketing days and at fairs to buy agricultural products and handicrafts, which could be resold at higher level central places. Evidence of the involvement of outsiders is found in records showing which uezd cities were represented at local markets and by references to cycles of neighboring markets each of which met on a separate day of the week, making it possible for traders to visit all of them in turn.[146] Frequently, level-7 marketing settlements were located roughly 5–20 miles upriver from or along the same road as a superior level-6 center.

Table 13 estimates the number of level-7 central places in the four core regions at 700. This represents an average of 2⅓ level-7 settlements per uezd. In Moscow guberniia the average reached barely one per uezd, while in Vladimir guberniia the figure exceeded three, and in Penza guberniia it approached three per uezd.[147] A typical uezd of 60,000–70,000 inhabitants and several hundred settlements supported three central places, including two at level 7, each directly serving about 20,000 persons.

The level-7 settlement qualifies as a central place because its weekly market brought together representatives of households within an area normally of some 200 to 400 square miles and even larger in sparsely settled uezd. This settlement often offered other activities that attracted outsiders; for instance, unlike Western Europe, markets located near a church often met on Sundays after the service. Yet, some tens of churches stood within a typical marketing area and most markets did not occur on Sunday. Fairs on religious holidays more frequently became associated with church attendance. Among other facilities in marketing settlements, but not necessarily restricted to these places, were taverns and blacksmith shops.

Nonadministrative settlements were divided by name into different categories of settlements. Those labeled sela and also slobody were most likely to be distinguished by one or more stores, a major church, an atypically large population, and central place functions. A. M. Razgon differentiates between three types of sela and slobody according to the type of labor utilized in craft production: 1) free hired labor; 2) serf labor working for someone other than their serfowner; and 3) serfs working directly for their owner.[148] In Vladimir guberniia, 26 of 44 sela and slobody with primarily craft production belonged to the first type, 12 to the second type, and 6 to the third type. These figures are probably exceptional, however, since in rich agricultural areas with many big estates, the third type appears to have been most common. Frequently, sela that served as the centers for the management of large estates developed serf industries and were favored as periodic marketing locations, especially after dvoriane rights for setting up markets and fairs were expanded in 1785.[149]

Level-6 central places were present in somewhat more than half of all uezd, with an occasional uezd having two settlements at this level. A typical guberniia supported roughly seven or eight level-6 central places. These settlements with up to 3,000 persons differed from level-7 central places in having more substantial marketing activities. In Russia they often served approximately 100,000 persons, providing the standard marketing functions also available in level-7 centers for a neighboring population of 20,000 or more and intermediate marketing functions for persons directly served by level-7 settlements within 20 or 30 miles.

Although further study of local spatial patterns is necessary before regularities can be fully ascertained, it appears that Russian patterns were irregular. In some uezd, the administrative center at level 6 served a large population of up to 60,000 directly and through local fairs without the assistance of any level-7 markets within the uezd, while in other uezd the level-6 city was supported by several additional weekly markets. Of course, marketing did not observe uezd boundaries; level-6 and level-7 markets often served parts of two or more adjoining uezd.

The population is known for each of the uezd cities at level 6 in the four core regions of Russia. There were 36 administrative centers with 2,000–3,000 population and 70 additional uezd centers with 1,000–2,000 population. Also at level 6 by virtue of their combined administrative and marketing functions were more than half of the 65 uezd centers that counted fewer than 1,000 residents. Together these uezd centers comprised more than three-quarters of all level-6 central places.

To the list of intermediate marketing centers should be added nonadministrative settlements. Less satisfactory data are available on the number and population of these central places, but there seem to have been at least ten and probably considerably more of them with 1,000–3,000 inhabitants and marketing functions. An additional twenty or more nonadministrative centers achieved sufficient prosperity to rank as intermediate markets although their populations did not exceed 1,000. In Nizhnii Novgorod guberniia alone there were seven nonadministrative locations singled out in the *Geographical Dictionary* as major settlements, including at least one that ranked at level 5.[150]

The total population of the roughly 180 settlements at level 6 in the core regions reached approximately 240,000. At least 200,000 of these persons resided in uezd centers. Consequently the choice of a definition of *urban* that counts half of the population in all level-6 central places (i.e., 120,000 persons) results in a deficit of 80,000 as compared to the widely used definition based on the assumption that all persons registered in administrative centers were urban. The figure of 120,000 urban residents in level-6 settlements is equal to 8 percent of the total city population in these regions of Russia.

In most regions one-third or one-fourth of uezd centers met the minimum population standard for level 5. A typical guberniia supported four or five such cities of 3,000 to 10,000 population. Similar to level-6 central places, these cities served as the standard marketing places for their immediate hinterlands and as superior marketing centers for surrounding areas with level-7 markets. In addition, level-5 cities provided central commercial activities unavailable in the marketing areas of nearly level-6 central places, offering goods and facilities to a wider area.

An idealized diagram of local marketing patterns would show three uezd, in one of which the uezd city merited level-5 status while in the other two the uezd centers ranked at level 6. In this area of 150,000–200,000 persons, a great number of local fairs met, more regular commerce occurred in six level-7 markets and in the two level-6 uezd centers, and from all of these places quantities of agricultural and special handicraft products were forwarded to the level-5 city. It would not have been unusual if the level-7 markets had met 1/7, the level-6 markets 2/7, and the level-5 market 3/7. If a level-6 market had in fact met only 1/7 or a level-5 market 2/7, the days of the market would presumably have been chosen to allow merchants who traveled between the lower level central places to be present at the busiest weekly market in the highest level central place visited.

In fact, this idealized pattern was rarely approximated. There appears to have been a progression of densities of level-5 cities; the better the conditions for agriculture in a region, the higher was the proportion of uezd cities at level 5. The densest network of level-5 cities existed in the C-BE region, where more than half of all uezd cities held 3,000–10,000 inhabitants. Following the C-BE region in the proportion of administrative cities at level 5 were, in order, the L-MV region, the C-I region, and, finally, the N-NW region. Rich agricultural regions supported more cities at this level. However, an inverse relationship existed between the degree of urbanization of a region and the ratio of level-5 to level-6 settlements. The regions encompassing St. Petersburg and Moscow not only offered poorer conditions for agriculture but also were inundated with readily available processed goods and services produced on a scale larger than could be matched in level-5 cities. Under these conditions, level-5 cities were disproportionately few. The question of regional variations will be explored further in Chapter 4.

Level-5 cities can be divided between those with 5,000–10,000 persons and those with 3,000–5,000 persons. For the four regions considered here, from 32 to 44 percent of all cities at level 5 held more than 5,000 persons. Altogether, cities at level 5 averaged almost exactly 5,000 in population, roughly four times the mean population for central places at level 6. Of course, this system of levels arbitrarily imposes a boundary at certain points such as 3,000 so that a given level-6 settlement might actually have counted only one fewer person than a particular level-7 settlement. This arbitrariness is unavoidable and is reduced to a minimum for generalizations referring to hundreds of central places within a given population range.

Reference to marketing and administrative functions does not exhaust the factors contributing to urban populations although these were the principal and most regular factors for the majority of central places. Certain level-5 cities boasted specialized craft and manufacturing functions that provided large numbers of jobs in comparison to other cities of comparable size, and correspondingly relieved them of the necessity of having a full complement of level-7 and level-6 supporting settlements. This was true of both administrative and nonadministrative centers whose craftsmen served a national market. A wealthy serfowner could have aspired to convert his private settlement into a city of up to several thousand inhabitants by encouraging local crafts as well as by developing a market to compete with the one in the uezd center. More commonly, however, it was the uezd cities that acquired national significance as centers of craft production.

Level-4 cities dominated large areas in their regions. They acted as magnets that attracted intraregional trade, serving simultaneously as standard, intermediate, and central markets for increasing numbers of persons and as intraregional markets for up to one million or more inhabitants.

Level-4 cities appeared in about one-half of the guberniia of the core regions. In each case, they functioned as the administrative center for the guberniia or ranked as the largest uezd city in guberniia in which the guberniia city also supported a population of at least 10,000. Often the commercial hinterlands of these cities closely corresponded to their administrative jurisdictions as guberniia cities. Undoubtedly the selection of guberniia in the decade of reforms from 1775–1785 operated to maximize the commercial integration of areas with up to one million inhabitants. Of course, in some guberniia no level-4 city developed. The flow of resources generally passed through several level-5 cities, each of which was subordinate to a city at a higher level in another guberniia. Where transportation conditions united a guberniia, a city of 10,000–30,000 persons normally appeared, but in many cases where guberniia were bifurcated or trifurcated by various transportation systems or sparsely populated, no such city emerged.

The relatively unified guberniia in some areas approximated the following pattern: a guberniia city at level 4, several uezd cities at level 5, and about 10 uezd and non-uezd centers at level 6. For instance, of 12 administrative centers of Smolensk guberniia, Smolensk city reached a population of about 15,000, three cities numbered between 3,000 and 10,000 persons, and eight cities ranked at level 6.

Cities of 10,000 to 30,000 population in Russia operated as nodes between the local and national marketing systems. They ordinarily attracted more specialized craftsmen and a greater variety of products from distant areas of the Russian Empire and from abroad than did lower-level central places. Products destined for centers of the national market including Moscow, St. Petersburg, and the several great fairs were also funneled through these cities.

Level-3 cities were practically absent from the Russian Empire in the 1780s. Astrakhan', Riga, and probably Kiev slightly exceeded 30,000 in population, benefiting from the presence of foreign trade in the first two cases as well as by activities generated solely by the internal market. Apart from Astrakhan' near the southern border, the only level-3 city in the four core regions in 1782 was probably Saratov, which following a recent spurt had briefly surged ahead of several cities that were to overtake it in population before 1811. The ranks of level-3 cities expanded at the turn of the nineteenth century as a result of a continued increase in long-distance commerce.

Moscow at level 2 and St. Petersburg at level 1 dominated the Russian urban network, functioning as the two national administrative and marketing centers. They securely topped the pyramid of central places in Russia, far exceeding the development of other cities. The absence of any cities that remotely approached them in population signifies the dichotomy in Russia between life in these central cities and life elsewhere.

Comparative Summary

In essential respects, Russia's urban network resembled the networks of other stage G societies. Cities provided the same basic functions and displayed roughly the same composition of occupational tasks. As will be seen in the detailed comparative examination of systems of cities in Chapter 5, the distribution of central places at the various levels appears to have conformed to basic societal properties. In other respects, Russia's spatial patterns reflected distinctive conditions. Given the enormity of the task of drawing comparisons between many countries for all of the spatial patterns in social structure introduced in this chapter, this brief section explores only a few themes from the comparative perspective of China and Japan.

Comparisons of the geographical setting and of administrative divisions appear in Chapter 5, but a few additional contrasts should be noted here. Russia's huge land mass, continental setting, and conditions favoring extensive methods of farming influenced urban development in several ways. Most importantly, given available transportation technology, these factors reduced accessibility to markets and to jobs, which probably impeded urban growth, at least in comparison to Japan. At the same time, they increased the relative profitability of fairs, which developed on a far greater scale than in either China or Japan. Furthermore these factors emanating from Russia's geographical setting probably enhanced central penetration and local conformity since separate regions lacked both natural barriers and the means necessary to support a city capable of competing with Moscow or St. Petersburg. Since the same areas provided sustenance to the two central cities, it serves no useful purpose to divide Russia into two main regions as in Japan or into many regions as in China; on this comparative scale Russia properly represents a single region, consisting primarily of the core area from St. Petersburg to Astrakhan' and from Arkhangel'sk to Kursk, which in turn was bordered on several sides by peripheral areas.

The combination of vast land mass and modest population may explain the efficacy of three administrative levels (uezd, guberniia, and nation), a figure intermediate between the two levels present in Japan, where an equal population crowded onto a smaller setting consisting of several islands, and the four levels in China, which combined a considerable area with an enormous population. The new Russian administrative boundaries represented a centrally conceived, forced rationalization without parallel in the other two countries, except perhaps in the much earlier imposition of the Ch'in dynasty's territorial delineation in the third century B.C. Japan's extensive sixteenth-century overhaul may have signified an even more radical departure from past administrative divisions, but it occurred locally during more than a century of war and disorder.

Similar to China, Russia entered a seemingly unending spiral of late premodern population growth. Japan's population also had begun to rise sharply, but then suddenly growth almost ground to a halt. The causes of this abrupt turnabout in Japan, while growth was accelerating in the other two countries, merit careful study. Of course, the sparse settlement of Russia contributed to a rapid rate of sustained population growth; yet, as has already been seen, even the long-settled areas of the country supported continued population gains. At the end of the eighteenth century, Russia barely sustained the population of a large Chinese province.

The theme of stratification involves both employment and consumption, the cornerstones for the crucial mechanisms of migration and marketing. Closed classes in Russia restricted rights and activities in various ways, limiting opportunities for moving to new jobs and for utilizing the labor of others. While these restrictions may not have noticeably hampered urban growth, they affected the character of urban life. As in Japan, closed classes contributed to a separate urban life style, especially in the largest cities. Unlike Japan, however, this did not extend to the emergence of sharply segregated land use for the elite. In contrast to the dispersal of cosmopolitan values and life styles in China, in Russia even more than in Japan, an intensively centralized elite life style took root in the great national centers.

Definitions of property affected the social structure in Russia in ways similar to Europe, not East Asia. Settlements under private ownership in some cases failed to be designated as administrative centers because of the financial burden involved in their purchase. Until at least the middle of the seventeenth century, private settlements remained numerous even on the outskirts of cities, forming separate enclaves within the urban built-up area. These limitations on central jurisdiction through acceptance of private ownership rights over settlements had no parallel in China or Japan.

Under these circumstances, cities acquired different meaning in Russia than in China. A sharp rural-urban dichotomy emerged with closed classes endowed with distinctive rights and duties associated with cities. Furthermore, among Russian cities, St. Petersburg and Moscow exhibited a heightened sense of cosmopolitanism far removed from conditions in lesser cities. China's rural-urban continuum reveals no such sharp boundaries between various types of settlement and cities did not offer the prospect of preferred living conditions. Japan more closely resembled Russia in these respects, displaying a sharp rural-urban dichotomy and a distinctive aura of life in the big national centers.

⁂ 4 ⁂

REGIONAL VARIATIONS IN
URBANIZATION: RUSSIA IN THE 1780S

Unequalled in total area, the Russian Empire attracts attention because of its diversity of natural conditions, historical experiences, and ethnic backgrounds. By the eighteenth century, its reputation for heterogeneity was securely established, although the peoples of Central Asia and the Caucasus and, until the final years of the century, much of the population in the Ukraine and Belorussia as well remained outside the Empire. Among areas firmly incorporated by this time, variations in ethnicity and foreign associations ranged from the strong German imprint in the Baltic area to the urban colonies of Near Eastern traders in the lower Volga area. While the expanses of Siberia favored frontier conditions, the rich soil of the Central-Black Earth region fostered agricultural specialization, and the combination of poor soil and convenient transportation ties in the Central-Industrial region to the northeast of Moscow contributed to rural handicraft production. If we are not to ignore the impression that the whole of the Russian Empire merely represents the sum of its divergent parts, it is essential to determine what variations in urban development existed throughout the country.

Differences in the percentages of population residing in cities explicitly indicate the degree of heterogeneity of Russia's regions. These data acquire added meaning when supplemented by information on the recent history of urban growth within each guberniia, on the detailed distribution of central places at various levels, and on the exceptional features of occupational specialization and marketing present in particular uezd. This separate examination of urban networks in each region and guberniia represents a new approach to the important task of analyzing regional variations in the Russian

Empire. At the same time I disaggregate national data to make it more comprehensible for comparisons between countries.

In this chapter we continue to examine the data from 1782 introduced in the final two sections of Chapter 3.[1] Having already observed for the country as a whole estimates of how many central places should be classified at each of seven levels and what general conditions characterized settlements at each level, we now narrow the focus to the specific information available for separate localities. In addition to the comparatively full accounts and plentiful statistics given for cities in the 1780s, data presented below on urban populations in 1744 and 1762 in many areas of Russia help clarify rates of urbanization.[2]

This chapter concentrates on the four core regions of the Russian Empire and the Urals-Siberia region. Only a brief general treatment is given for the areas in the west and south included in the Baltic-Belorussia and Ukraine-South Russia regions. Sizable portions of these two regions were incorporated into the Empire late in the century; their indigenous urban histories differed from the overall Russian pattern traced in Chapter 2, and the analysis of data would present problems complex enough to require separate treatment incorporating a different set of materials. For the five regions examined, detailed treatment of individual cities is made possible by extensive archival records, substantial descriptive materials, and a large secondary literature contributed by recent Soviet scholarship.

Central-Industrial Region

Moscow dominated this region, which, as can be seen in Map 5, was practically encircled by the winding courses of the Volga and Oka rivers. Centrally situated on the Moscow river with convenient access in almost every direction to these two important waterways, Moscow monopolized the internal trade of this region and, of course, long prospered as the major center of domestic commerce in the Russian Empire. It was directly connected by water to the Oka river and by roads to the three gateway cities at level 4 (population 10,000 to 30,000): Tver' to the northwest and Iaroslavl' to the northeast both on the Volga river, and Kaluga to the southwest on the Oka river. As Table 14 shows, Moscow's population, even excluding the swell of

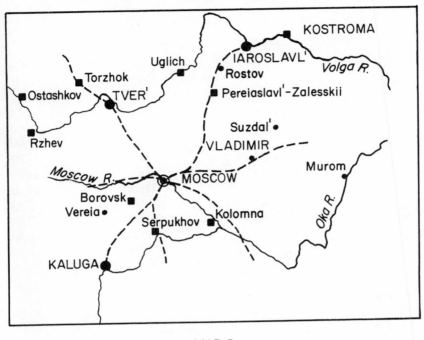

MAP 5.
C-I Region

temporary residents in winter, exceeded twice the combined population of the next ten largest cities in this region.

Designated administrative centers of guberniia comprised five of the six largest cities in the C-I region. The sixth guberniia city, Vladimir, was the only one not to be located along a major river; bulk shipments to and from Moscow bypassed this city, and other cities in its guberniia rivaled it as a marketing center. Among the uezd cities with no higher administrative importance, Torzhok, on the main route to St. Petersburg, was the most populous. Among the nonadministrative settlements, Ivanovo, a city of crafts and budding manufactures in Vladimir guberniia, came closest to ranking in the top ten cities of the region.

Overall this region experienced an almost 25-percent growth in population between 1744 and 1795, including a sharp rise of about 80 percent in Tver' guberniia. Interestingly, Vladimir, Iaroslavl', and, to a lesser extent, Moscow guberniia, all areas of intensive craft develop-

TABLE 14

Central-Industrial Region

Level	Settlements	Urban Population (millions)	Population of Top Ten Cities	
1	0		Moscow	213,000
2	1	.21	Iaroslavl'	19,000
			Kaluga	17,000
3	0		Tver'	16,000
4	3	.05	Torzhok	9,000
			Kostroma	7,000
5	28	.12	Rzhev	7,000
6	60	.04	Ostashkov	6,000
			Serpukhov	6,000
7	200		Pereiaslavl'-Zalesskii	6,000
Est. Totals	300	.43		

Number of guberniia: 6
Number of uezd: 83
Total population: 5.06 million
Percent of population urban: 8.5
Percent of urban population in levels 1–3: 49
Percent of population in administrative centers: 9.0

ment, displayed little or no population growth between 1719 and 1782. Yet, these areas showed unusual dynamism in the conversion of payments in kind or required labor days into cash payments to serfowners and in the increasing numbers of persons classified as peasants who worked as hired laborers in transportation or industry away from their home villages.

Three types of peasants predominated in the six guberniia of this region: of the total population, the number listed as serfs ranged from 59 to 78 percent; approximately another 20 percent registered as peasants formerly on monastery lands who were now treated as "economic" peasants, a subset of state peasants; and between 1 and 13 percent of the population were classified as court peasants.[3] Poor farming conditions encouraged the development of nonagricultural activities. Peasants, who for the most part owed a specified amount of cash each year, enjoyed relative freedom in choosing the means to earn this money. For example, in Moscow uezd by the 1760s almost two-thirds of the registered peasant households in villages combined nonagricultural and agricultural income-producing activities, including a considerable number of households with individuals away from home earning wage incomes.[4]

MOSCOW GUBERNIIA

This administrative entity, established during the reforms of the late 1770s, provided exceptional continuity by preserving nearly intact the boundaries of the former Moscow province.[5] Apart from Moscow, 9 uezd centers in 1744 totaled 26,000 residents, 14 uezd centers in 1782 totaled 32,000 residents, and by 1795 12 centers counted almost 35,000 residents. Using our definition of *urban*, which includes all inhabitants of cities at levels 1–5 (23,000 persons in these uezd) and one-half the population in level-6 central places (about 4,000 persons in uezd centers), the urban total outside of Moscow in 1782 numbered roughly 27,000 persons. Probably no more than one or two nonadministrative marketing centers in this guberniia ranked as high as level 6; the rest had small weekly markets meriting only a level 7 classification.

Moscow guberniia in 1782 consisted of 15 administrative centers, an additional 12 settlements with periodic markets and 57 settlements with annual fairs, roughly 5,000 villages, and close to 675,000 persons outside of the Moscow urban area.[6] The three principal cities in the guberniia after Moscow were Serpukhov, Kolomna, and Vereia, all with populations of 4,900 to 6,000. Commanding the approaches 55–65 miles to the south, southeast, and southwest of Moscow, these cities ranged in the assessment of wealth compiled for their kuptsy merchants from 220,000 to 361,000 roubles, at least ten times the figures for most other uezd centers in this guberniia.[7] With 750–900 houses per city, these level-5 places can be distinguished from the other 11 uezd centers, which ranged between a high of 486 houses and a low of fewer than 100 houses. While Serpukhov and Kolomna also emerged in the second half of the eighteenth century as centers of textile production, the sustained importance of the three cities should be attributed above all to the movement of commerce to Moscow and the related processing of agricultural and livestock products originating in the C-BE and, to a lesser extent, in the UK-S and L-MV regions. Serpukhov with a 3/7 market (meeting three times a week) and Kolomna with a 2/7 market numbered among the commercial centers, largely in the south of this guberniia, which offered visitors multiple marketing days each week. In addition to more frequent open markets, large cities in this guberniia boasted up to 400 stores, while small uezd centers could offer only 10–30 stores.

Of the remaining uezd centers, two ranked at the bottom of level 5, two were relatively sizable level-6 settlements of about 2,000 persons each, and the others were small, level-6 settlements, mostly below 1,000 in population. All seven of the uezd centers with populations ranging from about 2,000 to 6,000 numbered among the nine old uezd cities. The five new uezd centers established as part of the reforms creating the guberniia contributed a meager 2,000 persons to the urban figure of 27,000 computed above. The dropping of two of these new centers from the uezd list before the returns were in from the fifth population enumeration obviously caused little decline in the urban population calculated for administrative centers in 1795.

TVER' GUBERNIIA

The core of this guberniia were the six uezd of the former Tver' province, all of which were incorporated into the new guberniia boundaries. Among these old administrative cities were Tver', Torzhok, and Rzhev, ranking eighth, twentieth, and fortieth, respectively, in posad population among all Russian cities in 1719.[8] Together these three cities accounted for almost all of the 18,000 persons in the administrative cities of this province in 1744 and for more than 32,000 persons in 1782. Thus they approximately doubled in population during this 38-year span, and the 43-percent increase in the province's urban population from 1744 to 1762 indicates that the pace of growth was probably maintained over the entire period.

While one of the old uezd centers of the province lost its administrative role during the 1770s, two other small, level-5 uezd centers were transferred into the new Tver' guberniia, and six new administrative centers were established. This guberniia was exceptional in the large populations in some of its newly formed uezd centers. In addition to Ostashkov with more than 6,000 inhabitants, there were Vyshnyi Volochok with 3,800 and Kaliazin with 3,500 persons. Altogether, with roughly 62,000 of 930,000 guberniia residents in cities, in 1782 this area ranked second only to Moscow guberniia in urbanization within the C-I region.

Ves'egonsk, an uezd center in the northeast, counted a population of just 1,800; however, for its size, it achieved somewhat exceptional commercial stature. In addition to the usual 1/7 market, the city contained 164 stores plus 25 smithies and attracted attention for fairs in winter and summer, each of at least two weeks' duration.[9]

Kh. D. Sorina has written several articles on the major cities of Tver' guberniia. Attributing the rapid development of cities in this area to the stimulus of St. Petersburg's growth on traffic along the Volga river to Rzhev and Tver' and along the newly constructed canal from the Volga river via Torzhok and Vyshnyi Volochok, Sorina documents three types of occupational concentrations in these cities.[10] Ostashkov, which had been a prosperous private settlement known for the production of leather and metal products, remained a city of crafts. In contrast, Rzhev with a 3/7 market, two important seven-day fairs, and a daily trade in a gostinyi dvor enclosing 105 stores, represented the commercial centers of Russia.[11] Sorina classifies the other major cities in this guberniia as centers of both trade and crafts. For instance, in Tver', among males registered in the tax-paying population, traders, craftsmen, and hired laborers were distributed evenly, each ranging from 24 percent to 32 percent of the total.[12] Many craftsmen engaged in activities related to shipping. Commerce flourished in Tver', both in the city's gostinyi dvor, which held 342 shops, and at the 3/7 market.

Tver' was among three guberniia cities in this region with 16,000–19,000 persons. Similarly to Iaroslavl', it developed as a major internal port on the Volga river. Just as Iaroslavl' had flourished earlier as a center of supply for Moscow, Tver' at least doubled in population during the eighteenth century after the founding of St. Petersburg. The appearance of Tver' changed somewhat after a great fire in 1763; wooden houses on winding narrow streets were replaced to some extent in the planned reconstruction that followed. Evidence that residential buildings were larger in Tver' is that while Tver', Rzhev, and

Torzhok each accounted for 17–19 percent of the 10,500 urban houses in this guberniia, the population per house was roughly twice as high in Tver'.[13] Altogether, there were 182 stone houses plus 248 more with stone foundations among the more than 1,900 houses in Tver'.

By the turn of the nineteenth century, the city of Tver' no longer counted among the dynamic centers of population growth in Russia. Traffic to St. Petersburg began to move directly along the major waterways without stopping here. Kaluga and Iaroslavl', which were more successful in attracting manufacturing, outdistanced Tver' during the following half-century.[14]

VLADIMIR GUBERNIIA

Of the eleven provincial cities in the vast area of the old Moscow guberniia, four were incorporated into the new Vladimir guberniia. Indeed, all of the provincial cities of the old guberniia that had not become new guberniia centers by 1782, except Uglich, were absorbed into Vladimir guberniia. Yet, these had all been undistinguished as provincial cities; together with five uezd cities, in 1742 they totaled fewer than 23,000 persons and in 1762 barely 24,000 persons. Although during the following 20 years these nine cities had collectively grown by about 30 percent, the four former provincial cities as a group counted only 17,000 inhabitants.

Vladimir guberniia was unusual in several respects. Not only was it one of the least urbanized guberniia in Russia, with 3.8 percent of its population in cities, but it also was exceptional in the absence of any city of more than 6,000 persons and in the fact that the guberniia city of Vladimir was second in population by at least 1,000 persons to Pereiaslavl'-Zalesskii, one of the former provincial cities. Murom and another former provincial city, Suzdal', also ranged between 4,600 and 5,800 residents. Thus four level-5 cities, the most centrally located of which was Vladimir, each carved a hinterland in this guberniia. A fifth nonadministrative city, Ivanovo, may well have been as populous as some of these other four cities.[15]

Among the lesser cities, the former provincial center, Iur'ev-Pol'skii, and five other uezd centers each numbered 1,300 to 2,300 inhabitants. The four smallest uezd centers, all of which were newly named sites of administration, ranged in population from only 300 to 900. Altogether, the population in administrative centers adds to 34,000, and a separate calculation for the population in cities at levels 1–5 plus one-half the population in level-6 settlements reveals that roughly 32,000 persons were urban. A large population in nonadministrative centers at levels 5 and 6 almost offsets a sharp discounting of uezd center residents due to the abundance of communities with administrative functions at level 6.

Vladimir guberniia has been examined in detail by A. M. Razgon. His data for the 1780s reveal that the 888,000 persons engaged in commerce at 103 settlements in which there were fairs, markets, or both.[16] Most uezd, averaging 60,000–65,000 in population, offered from 6 to 10 locations of weekly or annual trade. The 103 settlements provided 88 fairs during the year and 73 marketing days each week. Although no large fairs existed, some settlements had two, three, or four fairs each year. The most active markets met 3/7 in Pereiaslavl'-Zalesskii and Suzdal'.

Another unusual characteristic of this guberniia was the wide development of crafts and later of manufacturing without corresponding urbanization. Razgon points out that craft production centered in nonadministrative settlements, especially in the cluster of uezd around Shiua, Suzdal', and Vladimir, where from 75 to 90 percent of the peasants owed obrok, including many engaged in textile production.[17] In this area, an exceptional number of villages and central places at levels 5–7 produced noted craft items.

IAROSLAVL' GUBERNIIA

Some 6 percent of the 750,000 persons registered in Iaroslavl' guberniia in 1782 resided in the guberniia city and the 12 uezd centers. If we count as urban only half the population in level-6 centers, this figure drops to roughly 5 percent. The core of the guberniia consisted of most of the former Iaroslavl' province, whose four cities had held 18,000–19,000 persons in 1744 and 1762. If the relative posad populations are an accurate indicator, then roughly 14,000 of this total had resided in the city of Iaroslavl'. By 1782, Iaroslavl's population had risen to 19,000.

Also incorporated into the new guberniia were the former provincial city of Uglich and two uezd cities, one of which was Rostov.

Together Iaroslavl', Uglich, and Rostov accounted for 60 percent of the homes in the administrative cities of the guberniia and roughly two-thirds of their population. The six new uezd centers included four cities with more than 2,000 residents, each of which had enjoyed substantial commerce prior to its formal designation as an uezd center, and two small settlements with fewer than 1,000 persons.

The cities of this guberniia can be usefully compared in terms of their stores, markets, fairs, and manufacturing enterprises. Iaroslavl' with 770 stores and a 3/7 market dominated the area's commerce.[18] Located on the Volga river, it was involved in the movement of goods between the N-NW, the C-I, and the L-MV regions. The city's eighteenth-century prosperity based in part on the shipment of grain and other goods bound for St. Petersburg differed somewhat from its earlier substantial development linked to Moscow and Arkhangel'sk. By the turn of the nineteenth century, the increased manufacturing of textiles and, secondarily, of livestock products and metals again made it possible for Iaroslavl' to gain steadily in population. Second in population was Uglich with 297 stores. Although the volume of production reached only about a fifth of that in the guberniia center, this city relied more exclusively on manufacturing and crafts. In contrast, Rostov prospered as a trading center. Its 570 stores operated daily, but the highlight of the year was the spring fair lasting two to three weeks and enjoying national importance greater than that of any other fair in the C-I region. Not mentioned in the records of the 1740s, this fair emerged as an important gathering by the 1760s and acquired national significance by the 1780s. G. L. Vartanov states that no comparable rapid growth of a fair occurred in Russia during this period, attributing Rostov's success to the growing regional specialization in phases of textile production both in cities and in rural settlements of Iaroslavl' and nearby guberniia.[19]

Lesser cities in Iaroslavl' guberniia for the most part had unusually high ratios of stores to population, in many cases ranging from 1:20 to 1:10.[20] In addition, substantial annual gatherings existed among the 56 settlements in the guberniia with fairs. Throughout most of September big fairs were in progress in Poshekhon'e uezd city and in the 2/7 marketing center of Velikoe selo, 20 miles from Rostov uezd city.[21]

KOSTROMA GUBERNIIA

Both in the percentage of population in cities and in the total urban population, Kostroma, located well to the northeast of Moscow, ranks as the least urbanized guberniia in the C-I region and one of the least urbanized in all of Russia. Formed primarily from the two provinces of Kostroma and Galich, the latter formerly a part of the northern Arkhangel'sk guberniia, this guberniia also acquired three uezd centers from other provinces. Kostroma province, consisting of four uezd, represented about 40 percent of the population of the new guberniia. These four uezd centers held more than 8,900 residents in 1744 and over 9,900 in 1762. Actually well over half of this total population must have lived in Kostroma city, which in 1782 counted almost 7,200 residents. Galich province, with 6,600 to 6,800 persons in administrative centers in 1744 and 1762, respectively (a little more than 2.5 percent of the total population), contributed three old administrative centers. By 1782 they totaled 7,250 inhabitants. With Kostroma and Galich the only level-5 cities, this guberniia of 815,000 persons counted almost 31,000 persons in administrative centers, resulting in an actual urban population according to the definition used here of roughly 3 percent.

Conditions for agriculture in Kostroma guberniia were poor, and commerce remained insubstantial with the exception of textile-related trade conducted chiefly at the more than 30 fairs during the year.[22] One of the two fairs of interregional significance took place in Kineshma uezd city for 12 or 13 days in September, attracting merchants from such major centers as Kostroma, Iaroslavl', Nizhnii Novgorod, and Moscow.[23] Most of the uezd cities had 1/7 periodic markets, while the markets in Kostroma and one or two other cities met more frequently at 2/7. In both Luk and Sudislavl' uezd, five marketing settlements, most located 10–20 miles from the uezd city, existed apart from the administrative center.

KALUGA GUBERNIIA

In this guberniia, 40,000 of almost 800,000 persons resided in administrative centers, including more than 17,000 persons in Kaluga, 5,500 persons in Borovsk, and 3,000 persons in Kozel'sk. None of the other ten uezd centers counted as many as 2,000 residents.

Within the old boundaries of Kaluga province, there had been nine uezd centers. Together, those centers accounted for 21,600 of the provincial total of 441,000 persons in 1744 and 22,900 of 472,000 persons in 1762. In 1782, when eight of these uezd centers were incorporated into the new guberniia, their population totaled somewhat more than 29,000. The addition of Borovsk as an uezd city boosted the guberniia's urban population. Iu. R. Klokman describes how this center of grain and hemp trade was shifted from adjoining Moscow guberniia when no satisfactory settlement could be found for a twelfth uezd center in Kaluga guberniia.[24]

Kaluga city developed as a diversified center with considerable textile production, a variety of other crafts, and a large commerce in grain. As trade between the C-BE region and Moscow expanded rapidly in the mid-eighteenth century, this city undoubtedly increased in population, accounting for much of the rise from 21,600 to 29,000 in administrative centers over a 38-year period. Its 3/7 market, 670 stores, and more than 3,500 homes all signified a sizable city.[25] Like other level-4 and large level-5 cities, it did not have much need for an annual fair and, indeed, was one of two administrative centers in the uezd without a single fair.

The varied scale of fairs is well documented for this guberniia. Typical of the tens of small rural fairs in the guberniia were the six fairs in four settlements (sela) of Likhvin uezd.[26] All specialized in the accumulation of hemp for outside merchants, but in each case the volume of sells never reached 36,000 pounds. In contrast, the volume of turnover at the uezd city's fair measured at least twice that of the next fair. In turn, this fair ranked only intermediate among those in the guberniia, being easily dwarfed by the week-long July fair in Meshchevsk uezd city.

Of the six guberniia in this region, Kaluga trailed only Tver' in population growth. Accessible to the C-BE, C-I, and N-NW regions, it shared with Tver' guberniia the function of a crossroads between the two central cities of Russia and its richest granary able to supply their vast needs.

Central-Black Earth Region

This region lacked a dominant center such as Moscow. Indeed, its agricultural products, including large quantities of grain, flowed mainly from south to north bound for Moscow and, to a lesser extent, for St. Petersburg. Although no city in the C-BE region exceeded 30,000 in population, the number of cities at levels 4 and 5 as seen in Table 15 far surpassed the figures for the C-1 region despite the similarity in total population. They helped boost the urban portion

TABLE 15

Central-Black Earth Region

Level	Settlements	Urban Population (millions)	Population of Top Ten Cities	
1	0		Tula	25,000
			Kursk	19,000
2	0		Orel	17,000
3	0		Voronezh	13,000
			Bolkhov	11,000
4	7	.11	Ostrogozhsk	11,000
5	47	.24	Elets	11,000
			Tambov	9,000
6	30	.02	Putivl'	8,000
7	200		Korocha	8,000
Est. Totals	285	.37		

Number of guberniia: 6
Number of uezd: 81
Total population: 5.4 million
Percent of population urban: 6.9
Percent of urban population in levels 1–3: 0
Percent of population in administrative centers: 7.1

of this area in 1782 to almost 7 percent. The seven cities with 10,000 to 30,000 inhabitants each influenced a modest hinterland along the various routes to the north; no single city could have exerted a wide impact beyond the boundaries of one or two guberniia.

The three largest cities, together constituting roughly one-sixth of the region's urban population, were guberniia centers situated in the western part of the region. Foremost was Tula, about 115 miles directly south of Moscow on the road to Kiev. As seen in Map 6, this

MAP 6.
C-BE Region

city occupied a focal position between the main rivers in the direction toward which the goods of the region were being transported. The other two major cities, Kursk and Orel, together with Kaluga in the C-I region downstream on the Oka river, virtually formed a straight line along which goods from the Ukraine and the C-BE region moved north. Among the other three guberniia cities, only Riazan' with fewer than 7,000 residents failed to win a place in the top ten cities. While no nonadministrative central place ranked even among the twenty or thirty largest cities of the region, three uezd centers, each with roughly 11,000 inhabitants, surpassed the populations of all but the four largest guberniia centers.

In addition to their degree of urbanization, the guberniia of this region can be distinguished according to rates of population growth and forms of peasant obligation. The total regional population rose sharply between 1744 and 1795, climbing by more than two million

to nearly six million.[27] Growth was most rapid in Voronezh guberniia, where a mere 313,000 persons had almost tripled to 897,000.
In contrast, guberniia in the north and west experienced less rapid
growth, as had generally been true since the time of the first enumeration in 1719. Earlier secured from raids launched by nomadic bands
to the south and located closer to the central cities of the Empire, the
areas of Orel, Kursk, Tula, and Riazan' guberniia started with larger
populations.

A similar geographical split occurred in the forms of peasant obligation. Serfs in Tula, Riazan', and Orel guberniia constituted from
62 to 77 percent of the total population, while in the other guberniia
they accounted for just 36 to 45 percent. Despite some recently established large serf estates, Voronezh guberniia possessed the highest
percentage of state peasants, including many classified as *odnodvortsy*,
descendents of the former service categories of the population. While
the obligations of odnodvortsy came to resemble those of other state
peasants, persons in this category preserved the privilege of owning
serfs. A few possessed as many as 15 or 20 serfs, although most had
none.[28] In this region, most serfs owed barshchina labor services,
especially in Kursk and Tula guberniia, where this form predominated almost to the exclusion of obrok.[29] Thus, much of the marketed surplus originated from the landholdings of serfowners directly
engaged in commerce.

OREL GUBERNIIA

Orel guberniia was formed from three provinces, Orel, Sevsk, and
Elets, of the old Belgorod and Voronezh guberniia. Each province
contributed two to five uezd cities, while four new uezd centers were
added. The population of the three provinces, which had risen from
1.3 million to a little over 1.4 million during the years between the
second and third enumerations, comprised 78,000 in administrative
centers in 1744 and 86,000 in 1762. The new guberniia incorporated
most large cities, including all three provincial centers.

In 1782 Orel guberniia was the home of 965,000 persons, of whom
72,000 resided in administrative centers. Since the four new uezd centers accounted for just 2,600 persons, almost all of the urban residents
lived in cities taken from the three provinces. The populations of

Orel, Bolkhov, and Mtsensk, all from Orel province, totaled 34,000. Because Belev city, which had been transferred to Tula guberniia, had almost 5,800 residents, this former province obviously represented a major center of urban growth after 1762, adding roughly 12,000 persons to a previous total of 29,000 in these four cities plus two small uezd centers. Karachev, Sevsk, and three other cities from the former Sevsk province totaled almost 20,000 persons in 1782; had this province not lost two level-5 cities to Kursk guberniia, it would have counted more than 35,000 urban residents in 1782, far more than the 24,000 in 1762. Finally, Elets province contributed two cities, Elets and Livny, together almost 16,000 in population. If we include the cities of this province that were yielded to other guberniia, we find that some increase in administrative centers occurred after 1762, but it was smaller than in the other two provinces. In the area of Orel guberniia as a whole, the rate of urban growth clearly exceeded the rate of increase in the total population.

As a port on the Oka river, Orel had served as a principal transit point for the shipment of grain and other agricultural products from at least the end of the seventeenth century. While several cities in its guberniia in 1782 counted between 1,000 and 2,000 houses, Orel's share included almost 2,400 of the more than 11,500 houses in administrative centers.[30] Except for about 2 percent of the houses in this city and less than 1 percent of the houses in the uezd cities, construction was of wood. Stone houses remained a rarity until the nineteenth century.

In a study of the location of fairs during the first half of the nineteenth century, M. K. Rozhkova found that large fairs were especially numerous in areas with grain surpluses; 14 of the 64 fairs in 1817 with turnovers of more than 1 million roubles were located in the C-BE region.[31] Both then and in the late eighteenth century the Svinskaia fair, located two miles from the city of Briansk in western Orel guberniia, ranked as one of the great gatherings of Russia. It met for ten days in August, serving trade between the Ukraine and the C-BE, C-I, and N-NW regions. The importance of this fair for interregional exchange is evident from the large volumes of goods shipped directly from the July Makar'evskaia fair in the L-MV region.

KURSK GUBERNIIA

More than 80 percent of the population of Kursk guberniia inhabited areas formerly within Belgorod province, a frontier area of the seventeenth century in which most of the 20 uezd centers functioned as fortresses lacking commercial activity.[32] Only 7 of these 20 centers were retained as uezd cities in 1782, but they were clearly the most populous. The overall population of these 7 cities now numbered more than 50,000 as opposed to a total population of 30,000 in all 20 uezd centers in 1762. Another 13,000 urban dwellers joined the guberniia urban total with the inclusion of Putivl' and Rylsk, formerly of Sevsk province. Among the least populous of the administrative centers in 1782 were the 6 newly designated uezd centers. Altogether 80,000 of the guberniia's 1,032,000 inhabitants resided in administrative centers.

With the reorganization of 1775–1781, Kursk replaced Belgorod as the principal administrative city. Belgorod had served as the center of a line of fortifications, but by the early eighteenth century many of the fortress uezd centers had lost their defensive character and walls and towers were allowed to fall into disrepair. At the same time, Kursk, located further to the north, was developing as the point of accumulation of goods from this area en route north. Between the first and second enumerations, the city had risen from fourteenth to tenth among Russian cities in the size of the posad population.[33] In the 1780s Kursk outrivaled other cities in this guberniia with more than 2,100 houses, followed by Belgorod with 1,600 and Putivl' with more than 1,100 houses.[34]

Markets and fairs were numerous in Kursk guberniia. All of the uezd centers had periodic markets, including more than half with frequencies of 2/7 or 3/7. Moreover, in the uezd cities alone, 33 fairs met annually. Many nonadministrative settlements also received the right to hold multiple fairs, in a few cases five or more annually.

V. I. Nedosekin has described the fairs of Kursk and Voronezh guberniia.[35] The network of fairs was expanding here in the second half of the eighteenth century, enabling more of the peasants' production to reach market. Especially typical of this area was the concentration of fairs set up by serfowners seeking a supplementary source of income. According to Nedosekin, fairs did not turn into institutions of intercity exchange, but instead supplemented regular trade in large settlements by creating consecutive gatherings in weakly settled locations.

The largest annual gathering in the guberniia was the Korrenaia fair, fewer than 20 miles from Kursk city. Its turnover grew rapidly during the eighteenth century, making it, along with the Svinskaia fair, a great center for trade between the Ukraine and Russia. Within about 30 years, to the 1780s, the turnover at this two-week fair rose by 500 percent to approximately 3 or 4 million roubles annually.[36]

The city of Kursk expanded in an essentially unplanned fashion until the 1780s. Many stores were located in the center of the city in two gostinyi dvor and later in a third stone building added during the 1790s with 193 additional stores. Streets were lined with many wooden stores, including 120 for meat, 12 for fish, 73 for grain, 69 for leather products, 77 for metal products, and 148 for textiles and related materials.[37] Streets were not laid out in a regular pattern, and much of the city was divided into slobody clustered around churches, a pattern reminiscent of Moscow a century earlier. However, after a major fire in 1781, Catherine II approved a city plan calling for more stone construction and straight streets. As a result, the number of wooden houses decreased, the number of stone buildings doubled within 15 years, and the city was newly divided into quarters.

TAMBOV GUBERNIIA

In 1782, of the 887,000 persons registered in 13 uezd, 58,000 resided in administrative centers. This represented about 6.5 percent of the population in Tambov guberniia.

Typical of this region, Tambov guberniia had few uezd centers with populations of fewer than 3,000, and few nonadministrative marketing settlements prospered enough to rank at level 6. Here we find that the urban population in levels 1–5 plus half of the population in level 6 closely approximates the total in administrative centers.

In many uezd, two or four level-7 settlements existed along with the uezd city ranked at level 5; level-6 central places were rare. An exception was Tambov uezd, in which a large level-6 settlement some 18 miles from Tambov with more than 2,600 residents straddled the road to Saratov. Other large nonadministrative settlements in existence prior to the late 1770s, such as Lipetsk and Korsanov, gained recognition as uezd centers by 1782.

Tambov and Shatsk provinces contributed the most to the new guberniia. Together they provided six administrative centers, although they had previously contained 17 uezd. Since each province in 1762 had held about 530,000 persons of which 5.1–5.4 percent resided in administrative centers, it is likely that some rise occurred in the population of those cities that entered the guberniia.

Smaller than Orel or Kursk, Tambov was credited with 1,600 houses,[38] and a population of 9,200 in 1782. About 100 miles away, Shatsk, the second city of the guberniia, had 5,900 residents in 1,000 homes. Similar to other old uezd centers in the area, it bore the legacy of its earlier importance as a fortress; administrative offices and expensive homes were concentrated in the part of the city known as the fort.[39] No longer, however, were garrisons large or fortifications well maintained. As frontiers had shifted far to the south, the cities of this region lost their military character.

Lebedian' uezd city was famous for two of the largest specialized fairs in the guberniia.[40] In addition to two other relatively small gatherings of 3 and 7 days each, this city sported two fairs each lasting 3 weeks, which attracted dvoriane and merchants from the C-I and C-BE regions interested in fine horses.

Borisoglebsk offers an example of an uezd city with just under 1,900 residents, a fairly large 3-day fair in July, and 37 shops.[41] Within its uezd, which measured roughly 75 by 30 miles, were close to 55,000 persons, who had an opportunity to trade at two periodic markets in addition to the market in the uezd center.

VORONEZH GUBERNIIA

A part of the area comprised by this guberniia came from the former Voronezh province, in which as many as 11–13 percent of the population had resided in administrative centers. This high percentage can be partially attributed to frontier conditions in which most of the 19 uezd fortress centers had little surrounding rural population. By 1782, however, most of the fortresses with little commerce had lost their standing as uezd centers, and rural settlement had become denser. Nonetheless, the 8.5 percent of the guberniia population in administrative centers remained the highest figure in this region.

In 1782, the 15 administrative centers of Voronezh guberniia had a total population of nearly 68,000. Only six of these settlements can be traced back to old uezd centers. As in other guberniia of this region, many new uezd centers had been recognized in the reforms after 1775. Most of these new cities had relatively large populations, including seven in Voronezh guberniia that ranked at level 5, ranging in population from 3,100 to 7,400. The two largest cities were the old administrative centers of Voronezh with almost 12,700 persons and Ostrogozhsk with nearly 11,200 persons. Since only three of the fifteen administrative centers fell short of 3,000 in population, the urban total in this guberniia practically equaled the figure for all residents of uezd centers.

As many Russian cities, Voronezh continually experienced devastating fires, notably in 1672, 1703, 1748, and 1773. The fire of 1748 burned down more than 1,000 houses, and the one in 1773 destroyed at least 280 houses. Following the 1773 fire, a new city plan was prepared, requiring the reconstruction of the city over a larger area.[42] The city's perimeter now reached 6–7 miles, encompassing about 70 streets. A new gostinyi dvor built in 1779 enclosed 255 stone stores. Further construction before the end of the century included a two-story stone mansion for the governor and five two-story buildings along the main street, which housed public functions.

TULA GUBERNIIA

Half of the urban population in this guberniia was located in Tula, a city which in some respects resembled Iaroslavl' on the opposite side of Moscow. First, Tula had long claimed a large population. Similar to Iaroslavl', it was not a setting of much recent growth. From the urban data on Tula province in 1744 and 1762, I judge that Tula's population numbered approximately 25,000 throughout this period. With nearly 4,600 houses, barely 3 percent of which were constructed of stone, this city continued to be considerably larger than Iaroslavl'. Second, Tula also combined considerable industrial production with prosperous trade. In comparison to the 10 factories and 57 plants in Iaroslavl', Tula had 62 factories and 192 plants.[43] In addition, there were 432 blacksmith shops. Having developed rapidly during the reign of Peter the Great as a center of the armaments industry, Tula became noted for its metal crafts and weapons factories. In 1782 about 45 percent of the registered male population was employed in weapons production.

The other 11 uezd centers averaged about 2,500 persons, ranging from 5,900 in Belev and 4,800 in Venev to barely 800 in Krapivna and Novosil'. Whereas Tula had two monasteries or nunneries, all 11 of these cities together had only one, and there was also one located in a nonadministrative settlement. And while in Tula stood 26 churches of which 25 were built of stone, in the other uezd centers 60 churches stood, of which 45 were built of stone. In the entire guberniia about 850 churches existed, some 42 percent of which were constructed of stone. With 106 streets, Tula exceeded by roughly ten times several level-6 centers for which figures are available. Of course, the rest of the guberniia could not match Tula in factories and plants; altogether only 21 of these were scattered outside of the guberniia city. Tula also exceeded 50 percent of the houses and stores in the guberniia's twelve administrative centers.

This guberniia consisted of old uezd centers with one exception: Bogoroditsk, with its nearly 2,600 residents, had been purchased from a private owner during the administrative reforms because of its location at the center of a desired new uezd and its already sizable craft and commercial activity.[44] Among the small level-6 uezd centers, many had previously served as fortresses in the once sparsely settled southern parts of the guberniia. They did not benefit from the lively grain trade on the Oka river as did several larger cities including Belev.

About half the uezd centers had markets with frequencies of 2/7. Most had one or two fairs, and some had as many as three or four. According to G. L. Vartanov's classification of fairs in uezd centers into three levels, of the ten fairs in this guberniia, five ranked at the middle level of activity. As many as three ranked at the top, a clear contrast with the figures for five guberniia of the C-I region, excluding Tver', which totaled 27 fairs with slight activity, only 9 fairs in the middle range, and 8 fairs in the most active range.[45] Typical of an area with large agricultural production, this guberniia gave birth to substantial fairs.

RIAZAN' GUBERNIIA

Similar to Tula guberniia, this area straddled the customary line dividing Russia into industrial and black-earth zones. Unlike Tula, however, no single large city dominated the guberniia. Riazan' was a small guberniia city with only 6,900 of the 55,000 residents in all administrative centers. Mikhailov, Pronsk, Skopin, Zaraisk, Kasimov, and Sapozhok rivaled or even exceeded its population. While three or four of these uezd centers may have been unusual in the composition of the urban population, having an exceptional number of persons registered as soldier-cultivators who might actually have lived outside the city, Skopin and Zaraisk deserve mention as major commercial centers, each having a registered population of kuptsy and meshchane in excess of 2,000.[46]

The area of Riazan' guberniia, reaching a maximum width of about 180 miles and a length of close to 135 miles, was customarily divided into three sides. According to the *Geographical Dictionary*, these three sides differed in the way the population lived, the rivers flowed, and the land was utilized.[47] To the southeast, the first side near Tambov consisted of five uezd and parts of two others. Lacking forest areas, it was known as the steppe, and produced large amounts of grain as well as horses for the fair at nearby Lebedian' in Tambov guberniia. Centers of the grain trade here included Skopin, Ranenburg, and the selo of Ukholov in Sapozhok uezd. Of the total guberniia population of 869,000 this part contained almost one-third.

The second side of the guberniia, located between the two main rivers passing through the area and encompassing four uezd plus parts of two others, was called the Riazan' side and included, in addition to the guberniia city, Zaraisk, Mikhailov and Pronsk, all with more than 5,000 registered residents. This was a narrow swath about 50 miles wide, but more than 150 miles long, and was the most populous of the three parts. Grain was marketed here in uezd cities and in sela, but not in great quantities compared to the steppe area. Dvoriane received profits also from many varieties of fruits and berries, which were sold to kuptsy for shipment out of the area, especially to Moscow.

The third side of Riazan' guberniia, located on the opposite bank of the Oka river reaching to Vladimir guberniia, included three uezd cities and part of a fourth uezd. The soil here was sandy or marshy and not good for grain. In the forests and by the lakes, settlements specialized in wood crafts, including dishware and sleighs.

With 6.3 percent of the guberniia population in administrative centers and roughly the same percentage classified as urban, this area was second only to Tula guberniia, with 6.0 percent, as the least urbanized of the six guberniia of the C-BE region. As in the case of Tula, proximity to Moscow was greatest here, increasing the opportunities for a big city's goods to penetrate local markets and more importantly for local goods to be sent to a vast urban market. Goods gathered in various level-5 cities in Riazan' guberniia could be sent directly to Moscow without passing through any city at a higher level.

North-Northwest Region

Whereas the C-I and C-BE regions formed the nucleus of the Russian state, as they had for the previous four or five centuries, the N-NW region harbored the most important outposts of foreign trade and strategically the most valuable frontiers. Novgorod, Pskov, Smolensk, Arkhangel'sk, and finally St. Petersburg operated as successive urban enclaves through which trade and contact with western and northern Europe were channeled. For the most part, these cities, situated in sparsely populated, grain deficient areas, developed in relative isolation from but highly dependent on the more central regions around Moscow.

As Map 7 shows, vast expanses separated many of this region's principal cities. Trade routes appeared as spokes, leading in radial fashion out from the center toward the sea. For more than a century while Arkhangel'sk captured much of the foreign trade, no single city in this vast region influenced a wide hinterland. However, after the establishment of St. Petersburg as the national capital and the completion of canals linking the city to the Volga river, the distribu-

MAP 7.
N-NW Region

tion of population among the top ten cities in this region, as shown
in Table 16, came to approximate that of the C-I region. By 1782
St. Petersburg had surpassed Moscow in population and had become
an even more dominant force over its surrounding area, which was
less populous and agriculturally poorer than the C-I region. The fact
that 63 percent of the urban population in the N-NW region resided in St. Petersburg suggests the great reliance on supplies from
outside the region.

The five largest cities in this region were all guberniia centers. Only

TABLE 16

North-Northwest Region

Level	Settlements	Urban Population (millions)	Population of Top Ten Cities	
1	1	.30	St. Petersburg	297,000
2	0		Arkhangel'sk	15,000
			Smolensk	15,000
3	0		Novgorod	11,000
4	5	.06	Vologda	10,000
			Kronstadt	10,000
5	16	.09	Viaz'ma	9,000
6	40	.03	Ustiug Velikii	8,000
			Pskov	7,000
7	100		Toropets	7,000
Est. Totals	160	.48		

Number of guberniia: 7
Number of uezd: 69
Total population: 3.67 million
Percent of population urban: 13.0
Percent of urban population in levels 1–3: 63
Percent of population in administrative centers: 13.9

the Kronstadt naval complex on the island protecting St. Petersburg was able to reach 10,000 in population without offering guberniia administrative functions. Indeed, Kronstadt ranks as the largest non-administrative city in the core areas of the Russian Empire. The two smallest of the seven guberniia centers were Pskov, which was ninth among the cities of this region, and Petrozavodsk, with somewhat more than 5,000 inhabitants.

During the second half of the eighteenth century, this region displayed greater diversity than the C-I or C-BE regions. In some respects, it is useful to divide the N-NW area into three components: 1) the extremely sparsely populated northernmost guberniia of Arkhangel'sk, Vologda, and Olonets; 2) the smaller and more accessible but still grain-deficient northwestern guberniia of St. Petersburg,

Novgorod, and Pskov; and 3) Smolensk, the most populous guberniia located in the west. The northern guberniia generally witnessed the slowest population growth; only Vologda guberniia
reached the regional average between 1744 and 1795. The northwestern guberniia grew more rapidly, highlighted by the extraordinary
growth in St. Petersburg guberniia. Not only did its major city alone
account for an increase of roughly 300,000 in Russia's urban population during the eighteenth century, the rural population of this
guberniia gained at least 550,000 persons in a half-century reaching
a total of more than 700,000. Smolensk guberniia shared this rapid
pace, growing by about 400,000 persons from 1744 to 1795.

Forms of peasant obligation tended to follow these geographical
divisions.[48] While serfs remained rare in the north, somewhat over
half of the rural population belonged to private owners in the three
northwestern guberniia and a peak of 80 percent was reached in
Smolensk. Separate guberniia exhibited unusual distributions, particularly Novgorod's 33 percent of the total population "economic"
peasants, Arkhangel'sk's 22 percent court peasants, and Olonets' 75
percent state peasants. Overall, the pattern in this region supports
the view that the better the conditions for agriculture, the higher the
percentage of serfs.

SMOLENSK GUBERNIIA

In 1782 nearly 47,000 of 903,000 persons in this guberniia inhabited
the 12 administrative centers, i.e., 5.2 percent of the total population.
About three-quarters of this urban total lived in the five old administrative cities, including nearly 15,000 in Smolensk, 9,000 in Viaz'ma,
and almost 5,000 in Dorogobuzh. The seven newly recognized uezd
centers, all ranking at level 6, failed to reach the size of even the
smallest of the old cities. Together, these 12 cities counted about
8,900 houses, of which nearly 30 percent stood in Smolensk.

Smolensk, like many guberniia in Russia, consisted of tiny settlements; indeed, at least 11,000 (some of which may have been vacant)
can be identified for the late eighteenth century.[49] Somewhat later,
in 1857, G. T. Riabkov has shown that more than 2,900 settlements
counted fewer than 25 persons each (mostly only one or two house-

holds), nearly 6,000 settlements numbered 25-100 persons, and just 19 percent of the settlements exceeded a minimum of 100 persons.[50]

Riabkov has also presented information on markets and fairs in this guberniia. He notes that all uezd centers had periodic markets, most of which met 2/7 or 3/7, while many sela had 1/7 or 2/7 markets.[51] Along rivers, certain sela maintained commercial sites consisting of stores, carts, barges, and boats, which in good weather could attract up to 2,000 persons on marketing day. Fairs spread relatively early in Smolensk guberniia. A list of 35 guberniia in the mid-eighteenth century placed Smolensk fourth in the quantity of fairs with 74, following Voronezh and two guberniia in the Ukraine and Belorussia. The recorded number doubled to 159 in 1855, and Riabkov indicates that a basis exists for arguing that the actual figures should have been much higher. The fairs in uezd centers met 1-4 times per year and lasted from three days to two weeks.

ST. PETERSBURG GUBERNIIA

Established in 1780, this guberniia inherited the boundaries of the former guberniia of the same name. Seven previously existing administrative centers, three new centers, and the naval fortress of Kronstadt comprised 328,000 of the 652,000 persons in the guberniia in 1782 or 50.3 percent of the total population, a figure unrivaled in all of Russia. Of course, 90 percent of the total in cities lived in the capital of Russia and an additional 10,000 lived in the island city of Kronstadt, leaving a residue of only 18,000 persons in the nine uezd centers. The Baltic port of Narva with 5,600 persons and the lake port of Shlissel'burg with 3,900 were the largest of these other centers.

The major commercial and craft needs of this rapidly growing area were almost entirely satisfied in St. Petersburg, while new uezd centers and some of the old ones as well failed to achieve much prosperity. For instance, Gdov with a population of fewer than 600 lacked a periodic market and possessed only a single fair.[52] Like other old administrative centers in the northwest, many of these uezd centers previously functioned as fortresses near the western border, without having ever established themselves as local commercial nodes.

Probably the only major fairs in this guberniia occurred in Narva and Novaia Ladoga.[53] As at the time of Swedish control before Peter I's military successes, two fairs in Narva dealt with export trade in lumber, hemp, and grain and opened for two weeks each in February and June. Novaia Ladoga had been founded in 1704 and grew to a population of nearly 1,800, based on its position as a center of the fish trade on the huge Ladoga lake and as a port connected to a canal used for traffic from the C-I region to St. Petersburg. Each year a fair met for one week beginning August 15 in the gostinyi dvor, a structure about 1,300 feet in perimeter that enclosed 69 stores.

The growth of St. Petersburg had a tremendous impact on patterns of trade not only in this region but also in nearly all of Russia. The city required construction materials and grain in large quantities. By the 1720s it rivaled Moscow in its demands for grain, and demand continued to grow rapidly. Yet from the 1740s to the first decade of the nineteenth century, the value of grain imports was exceeded by the even more rapidly rising value of other agricultural products, including hemp, flax, and lard, much of which was exported. Data on the value of goods shipped to St. Petersburg show that the city quickly approached Moscow's importance in dominating the national market.[54]

NOVGOROD GUBERNIIA

The old Novgorod province was reduced in size to serve as the core of this guberniia, losing uezd to Olonets, St. Petersburg, and Pskov guberniia and keeping just three administrative centers— Novgorod, Staraia Russa, and Tikhvin. The new guberniia also was granted two of the four uezd centers in the old Belozero province, and at the same time five new uezd centers were established.

The two provinces incorporated into Novgorod had previously been little urbanized. The average uezd in Novgorod in 1744 and 1762 and in Belozero in 1744 was just over 3 percent urban; all uezd centers combined in Novgorod for a total population of 55,000. Although Belozero rose to nearly 5 percent in uezd centers by 1762, the average uezd center still counted fewer than 3,000 residents.

By 1782, 44,000 of 581,000 persons in the new Novgorod guberniia resided in ten administrative centers. What accounts for this sudden urban increase to 7.6 percent? To some extent, it was due to the addition of sizable new uezd centers, including Valdai with more than 4,000 persons and Borovichi with nearly 3,500. Part of the increase should also be attributed to the loss of areas with disproportionately large rural populations to other guberniia. Finally, a third factor is the rise in population of up to 40 percent that accompanied commercial expansion in the three cities formerly of Novgorod province.

During the period of Mongol rule in much of the rest of Russia, Novgorod had been separately governed, serving as an entrepot for the Hanseatic league of cities in northern Europe. Even after the city came under the firm control of the authorities in Moscow, it continued for a time as a major center of foreign trade, declining sharply only during the late sixteenth century. Novgorod remained, along with Pskov, one of two major cities of the northwest and a center of metal-working crafts with a recorded population of roughly 7,000 in the 1670s.[55] Then during the eighteenth century the city acquired a new role on the trade routes from various parts of the Russian Empire to St. Petersburg and other Baltic ports. Cattle were herded through Novgorod in the summer and fall, while meat, fish, butter, and other edibles and such major export products as flax and hemp, were transported from here to St. Petersburg during the winter. Already by 1714, according to B. B. Kafengauz, the city had wide ties with many areas of Russia and especially active trade as a supplier of St. Petersburg.[56]

Novgorod remained a well-known religious center of Russia. Until church lands were confiscated in the 1760s, more than a third of the peasants in the guberniia worked for the church, and the city of Novgorod boasted 62 churches, 58 of which were built of stone.[57] In addition there were 17 public buildings (12 of stone) and more than 1,300 houses (46 of stone). The city's population numbered about 11,500 in 1782.

Staraia Russa, 75 miles to the south, ranked second in the guberniia with more than 5,500 residents. It continued to be a center of salt mining, but had diversified somewhat by the 1780s, when of 246 craftsmen there were 46 tailors, 35 shipbuilders, 34 carpenters, 35 shoemakers, 21 blacksmiths, and 12 bricklayers or stonemasons.[58] Flax was accumulated for transshipment to St. Petersburg. Among the city's structures were 16 churches, 9 built of stone, and about 1,100 houses.

Tikhvin, Valdai, Borovichi, and Ustiuzhna-Zhelezopol'skaia were the other level-5 cities.[59] Containing 8 churches and 800 houses, Tikhvin straddled the road from Vologda to St. Petersburg. Its large fair opened shortly after Easter. In the city were 18 tailors, 25 shipbuilders, and 69 blacksmiths. Valdai, on the road between Moscow and St. Petersburg about 100 miles from Novgorod, functioned as a post station; it was more than twice as long as it was wide. Three fairs in the city ranged from three to six days in duration. Three fairs lasting up to one week long also met in Borovichi, while 21 fairs met within its uezd. Ustiuzhna-Zhelezopol'skaia, with about 6,000 persons and 17 or 18 churches, had been especially noted for its metal crafts since the second half of the sixteenth century. Indeed, the word *zhelezo* means iron in Russian.

PSKOV GUBERNIIA

Supporting approximately the same total population as Novgorod guberniia, Pskov guberniia in 1782 trailed considerably in urbanization. Just 4.7 percent of 587,000 persons resided in the 10 uezd centers. Of these 28,000 persons, the cities of Pskov and Toropets each counted about one-fourth. Velikie Luki and Opochka were smaller level-5 cities, while the other six uezd centers included two newly designated places with roughly 400 persons each and four older centers, none of which exceeded 1,800 persons.

Prior to the formation of Pskov guberniia, this territory consisted of Pskov and Velikie Luki provinces and a small part of Novgorod province. Pskov province had been a border area before 1772 and supported the exceptionally high average of one uezd center for every 16,000–18,000 persons in 1744 and 1762. For the most part these were fortresses with little commercial significance, and the province was among the least urbanized in Russia. By 1782 only five of the

15 former uezd centers in this province were preserved, with two of these transferred to St. Petersburg guberniia. In contrast, all three of the uezd centers in Velikie Luki province persisted and, indeed, showed substantial population growth, gaining nearly 5,000 persons from 1762 to reach a total of more than 12,000 inhabitants. The two uezd centers formerly in Novgorod province and the one newly designated center together contributed fewer than 2,400 residents.

Pskov guberniia specialized in flax production for export. Not only was the number of serfs (over 70 percent) high, four-fifths of these owed barshchina, providing labor for their owners. To the extent that serfowners sent local produce directly to easily accessible Baltic ports, little benefit accrued to cities in this guberniia.

The history of the rise and fall of Pskov and the city's continuation as a center of the northwest area resembles that of Novgorod, which almost always overshadowed Pskov. Similar to Novgorod guberniia, this area had once been a center of craft production, but by the 1780s little industry remained except leather production in Velikie Luki and Toropets and some metal-working shops in Toropets. Altogether there were 1,374 houses in Toropets, a city in which 480 to 580 houses had burned down in each of the fires of 1738, 1742, and 1758.[60]

OLONETS GUBERNIIA

The area of this guberniia brought little in the way of urban population from the old Novgorod and Belozero provinces from which it was detached. The two old uezd centers for the guberniia's 206,000 persons in 1782 were Olonets and Kargopol', each with populations of roughly 2,500. Furthermore, of five newly designated uezd centers, only one much exceeded 1,000 in population, i.e., Vyterga with nearly 1,900. Yet, in the population data given following the enumeration of 1782 this guberniia supported a total urban population of almost precisely 15,000, a not inconsequential 7.2 percent of the total population. The explanation for this sudden spurt in urbanization lies in the founding of a new city in 1777. Petrozavodsk became the guberniia city by 1784, replacing Olonets. Constructed as an arsenal for St. Petersburg, Petrozavodsk's prosperity resulted from its special importance in metal-working. Partly because of its recent origin, the city's skyline was highlighted by a number of two-story stone buildings.[61]

The small population of uezd in this guberniia was compounded by the abnormally great distances between their administrative centers in this inhospitable northern area. After the founding of Petrozavodsk, Olonets declined in population, but continued to be a secondary commercial center of up to 50 registered craftsmen and 68 stores. Kargopol' had only 52 stores, as well as 617 houses and 20 churches, but was probably a newer looking city having been rebuilt with straight streets following a fire in 1765. In the vast area of this guberniia, fairs served an important function, with two of the largest gatherings lasting one week each in Olonets city.[62] Many of the fairs here met in the long months of winter when travel by sleigh became possible.

VOLOGDA GUBERNIIA

Because of the immense area in this guberniia, which extended about 750 miles from southwest to northeast, it was divided into two sections. The center of one section with five uezd was Vologda, the guberniia city. The other section was centered in Ustiug Velikii, more than 270 miles to the northeast. Together, these two former provincial cities totaled 18,000 in population, 60 percent of the figure in all 12 administrative centers. The third city, Tot'ma, contributed 2,700 residents.

Vologda and Ustiug Velikii were frequently devastated by fires.[63] Yet, in the latter city, even following large conflagrations of 1772 and 1782, only 30 of 1,500 dwellings were constructed of stone.

Many small fairs were sprinkled across this guberniia of 572,000 inhabitants. In Vel'sk uezd, three settlements had annual fairs, and the uezd center, with about 700 residents, supported three small fairs each year. The guberniia's biggest fair probably was one that lasted 5–7 days during the winter in a rural settlement and attracted merchants from Iaroslavl', Kostroma, and Galich as well as from the main guberniia cities.[64] The major trading point was Vologda, with a daily market, except on holidays, supplemented by a 3/7 market in the active winter season to which peasants brought grain, firewood, straw, and wooden crafts and at which they bought goods available in the city.

ARKHANGEL'SK GUBERNIIA

This was one of the least populous and most desolate areas of the Russian Empire, stretching along the Arctic Ocean. The population of 170,000 in 1782 at best slightly exceeded the population of the old Arkhangel'sk province in 1744 and 1762. The urban population reached somewhat over 10 percent of the total, due primarily to the 15,000 inhabitants of the guberniia city. None of the six other uezd centers exceeded 2,000 in population, and most did not even reach 1,000.

Arkhangel'sk developed as a seaport during the sixteenth and seventeenth centuries. Although it was quickly surpassed during the eighteenth century by St. Petersburg, the city continued to share in the growing foreign trade. From May to October, a continuous fair operated as goods arrived by river from further south in Russia and by sea from northern and western Europe. A garrison of more than 2,500 soldiers contributed substantially to the city's population.

At a small number of winter fairs in this guberniia merchants bought peasant crafts. The largest fair at Vazhskaia Blagoveshchenskaia has been mentioned in Chapter 3. Merchants from several guberniia were prominent at this March gathering.

Lower and Middle Volga Region

The various areas along the Volga river have been compared by N. B. Golikova.[65] The upper Volga area within the C-I region was densely settled, but the soil was not fertile and many settlements were noted for specialized craft production and as sources of migrant labor to the big cities. In contrast, the middle Volga area remained somewhat sparsely settled as late as the 1720s (except for parts in the north) despite the rich soil over much of this area. Minority populations present in the southern and southeastern portions of the middle Volga area preserved a frontier character; however, along the river, where vast quantities of goods flowed, exceptionally bustling cities appeared. The lower Volga was less suitable to agriculture and supported few peasants. Non-Russian nomads occupied much of the area, while Russians concentrated in the cities, engaging in trade, crafts, and transportation. Similarly to the middle Volga area, populous cities developed along the river, as can be visualized in Map 8.

MAP 8.
L-MV Region

Considerable population growth occurred in the L-MV region during the second half of the eighteenth century. Between 1744 and 1795 the population rose by two-thirds. The lower Volga area experienced the most rapid growth, led by Saratov guberniia's jump from 182,000 to 762,000 inhabitants. As the most southerly of the areas in this region with good land for farming, Saratov guberniia attracted a great influx of people when it became militarily secure during the eighteenth century.

The Volga river basin preserved some diversity in peasant ownership.[66] In Nizhnii Novgorod guberniia to the north, in the rich agricultural area of Penza guberniia to the west, and to a lesser extent in Saratov and Simbirsk guberniia, serfs predominated. In contrast, Kazan' guberniia with a large non-Russian population was populated primarily by state peasants, and Astrakhan' guberniia had practically no persons registered as peasants.

The five largest cities of the L-MV region, as listed in Table 17, were all guberniia centers located along the Volga river. Together

TABLE 17

Lower and Middle Volga Region

Level	Settlements	Urban Population (millions)	Population of Top Ten Cities	
1	0		Saratov	31,000
2	0		Astrakhan'	30,000
			Kazan'	22,000
3	2	.06	Simbirsk	10,000
4	1	.02	Nizhnii Novgorod	9,000
			Penza	8,000
5	24	.13	Vol'sk	8,000
6	45	.03	Petrovsk	8,000
			Syzran'	6,000
7	200		Saransk	6,000
Est. Totals	270	.25		

Number of guberniia: 6
Number of uezd: 68
Total population: 3.8 million
Percent of population urban: 6.5
Percent of urban population in levels 1–3: 24
Percent of population in administrative cities: 7.5

they totaled more than 100,000 in population, roughly 40 percent of the urban population of the region. Since two other cities along the Volga river exceeded 6,000 in population and there were many smaller river ports as well, it is probable that more than 50 percent of the urban population in these six guberniia lived along the Volga river. The sixth guberniia center, Penza, and the region's eighth city, Petrovsk, were the largest settlements not situated on the Volga, but they also were located along major rivers.

NIZHNII NOVGOROD GUBERNIIA

Roughly 35,000 of this guberniia's population of 816,000 in 1782 resided in 13 administrative centers. Although barely 22,000 of this total were located in the four cities at level 5, the addition of several level-6 and at least one level-5 nonadministrative centers brought to nearly 35,000 the urban population as tabulated here. Nizhnii Novgorod, comprised 9,000 or more of this total.

Nizhnii Novgorod guberniia consisted of two uezd centers from the former province of the same name, one center from Arzamas province, one center from Sviiazhsk province, and nine newly designated administrative centers. The two cities from Nizhnii Novgorod province contributed more than 12,000 population, a slight increase over their population in the middle of the century. Some increase was also evident for Arzamas, which had nearly 5,600 residents in 1782 versus 4,600–4,700 in 1744 and 1762. All but one of the new uezd centers supported populations of fewer than 1,800 persons. Altogether about 6,500 houses stood in administrative centers, including almost 2,000 in the guberniia city.

Iu. R. Klokman has described the commercial and craft activities in cities of this guberniia, pointing out that many of the crafts were related to shipping needs.[67] More than 3,000 ships with up to 80,000 boatmen annually passed through Nizhnii Novgorod and nearby Volga cities.[68] Among cities not located along the Volga river, Arzamas was noted for its soap and leather enterprises, and the nonadministrative city of Pavlovo with as many as 1,000 houses (including at least 20 constructed in stone) specialized in metalworking, producing large quantities of knives, forks, and locks.[69]

This unusually specialized local craft production had a ready outlet at the Makar'evskaia fair, the most important annual gathering point for commerce in the Russian Empire. Makar'ev, a newly named uezd center with fewer than 800 residents, had long flourished during the summer when merchants gathered to do business at its 829 stores. Of course, during the rest of the year the guberniia's commerce focused on the daily trade in Nizhnii Novgorod supplemented by a 2/7 market for nearby peasants. Other major cities operated 2/7 markets, while most uezd centers had 1/7 markets.

PENZA GUBERNIIA

Consisting of nine uezd centers from three former provinces and four newly established uezd centers, Penza guberniia was formed at the end of 1780. Many of these uezd centers had originally been founded as fortress cities during the seventeenth century, but already by the end of that century the border had moved further south, reducing their military significance. By the mid-eighteenth century, the population of these cities consisted mainly of kuptsy, meshchane, and especially the imprecise category of state peasants (including the former service population) and, in a few uezd centers, court peasants. I. A. Bulygin presents a table in which the approximate population for all 13 uezd centers is given for the 3rd, 4th, and 5th enumerations, omitting dvoriane and clergy.[70] A continuous rise in population is evident, beginning with a total of fewer than 44,000 in 1762, climbing to more than 49,000 in 1782 and finally reaching 57,000 persons in 1795. The strata of kuptsy and meshchane, officially registered in crafts and commerce, increased relatively rapidly in most cities. Also the number of household personnel rose quickly as many dvoriane resettled from villages into the administrative centers.

The city of Penza was supplied agricultural goods from rural areas in the guberniia via local markets and fairs, craft items from urban artisans, and textiles and foreign products through big cities and large fairs, particularly the Makar'evskaia fair, the Rostov fair in the C-I region, and the largest fair in this guberniia, the Lomovskaia fair in Nizhnii Lomov uezd center. This latter fair lasted for 6 weeks in June and July, when 300 stores opened and 8,000 buyers appeared. Craft production within the guberniia centered in Penza and Saransk, where leather and soap plants were most plentiful. Penza predominated in trade; its kuptsy in 1787 were credited with 154,000 roubles in capital, while those in Saransk were worth 67,000 roubles, and those in all the other uezd centers combined for a total of 57,000. I. A. Bulygin explains these data by pointing out that in most uezd centers only a local market in agricultural products functioned, while Penza merchants engaged in the large-scale movement of grain to the central regions of Russia.[71]

Along with several guberniia in the C-BE region, Penza was among Russia's leading sources of commercial grain. During the eighteenth century, grain exports rose sharply as did the production of alcoholic beverages and other products that depended on agricultural raw materials and on firewood. Much of the production for a distant market was directly under serfowners, whose holdings, especially in the south of this guberniia, expanded continually.

At 13 uezd centers, 42 other marketing settlements, and about 17 additional settlements with fairs, large amounts of grain were purchased by local officials and sent to storehouses in St. Petersburg.[72] Merchants also took advantage of the exceptional water transportation along the Volga river in the north, the Oka river in the west, and the Don river in the south, shipping grain to St. Petersburg, Moscow, Saratov, Astrakhan', and other destinations.

According to Bulygin, in 1782 the administrative centers of Penza guberniia comprised approximately 7.5 percent of the total population of 655,000.[73] With more than 8,000 residents, Penza was the largest city. Figures on the number of houses per administrative center correspond closely to these urban data; Penza with 1,697 and Saransk with 1,252 houses constituted 17–18 and 13 percent, respectively, of the roughly 9,600 houses in the 13 administrative centers.[74]

KAZAN' GUBERNIIA

Prior to the reforms of 1781, the uezd of this area had varied greatly in population. The two uezd of the old Kazan' province had shared a population of 545,000 in 1744 and then 641,000 in 1762, thus resembling old Penza uezd with 350,000 inhabitants. Other uezd in neighboring provinces counted as few as 20,000–25,000 inhabitants, not much larger than such small uezd as Narovchat, which at the time of its incorporation into Penza guberniia barely totaled 12,000 residents.[75]

Following the administrative reforms in 1782, the 13 uezd of the new Kazan' guberniia shared a more evenly distributed population of 767,000. The population within the 13 administrative centers numbered more than 40,000, of which nearly 22,000 lived in Kazan' city.

Encompassing almost 3,100 houses and a gostinyi dvor with 777 stores,[76] Kazan' prospered as a point of interchange between European Russia, Central Asia, and Siberia. The city also gained fame as a craft center for the production of soap, leather, and other products. Similar to other large Volga ports, its population included a large garrison, in this case more than 2,500 soldiers and officers.

Kazan' city was roughly six times as populous as the next largest cities of the guberniia, the small level-5 centers of Koz'modem'iansk and Cheboksary. Most other uezd centers supported much smaller populations, ranging from 700 to 1,300.

SIMBIRSK GUBERNIIA

The population figures for this guberniia in 1782 resemble those of Kazan' guberniia. In both cases, 5.3 percent of the total population of 743,000 inhabitants resided in 13 administrative centers. Simbirsk's figures trailed slightly; 39,000 lived in these 13 centers.

Perhaps because this guberniia stretched further along the Volga river instead of eastwardly through sparsely settled lands, no single city dominated this area as Kazan' dominated its guberniia. Simbirsk, with 1,400 houses, contained about 21 percent of all houses in the uezd centers and 23–24 percent of their population. Syzran' ranked second with 1,310 houses and 15–16 percent of the population in administrative centers. Three other cities ranged in population between 3,000 and 4,400, and two cities approached 2,500.

Unlike the overwhelming state peasant population of Kazan' guberniia, serfs constituted about half the population of this guberniia. Grain marketed in increasing quantities by both serfs and their owners and fish caught in the Volga river fetched profits when shipped north to other regions. Similar to Kazan' guberniia, there existed outlying areas settled principally by ethnic minorities, while the cities became almost exclusively Russian.[77]

SARATOV GUBERNIIA

While the total population of this guberniia tripled between 1744 and 1782, the urban population also rose rapidly. By 1782, Saratov reached 31,000 inhabitants (including a garrison of more than 3,000 soldiers and officers), Vol'sk and Petrovsk were second with nearly

11,000, and Kuznetsk was fourth with about 5,600. Although these figures may include some state peasants registered in cities but living in rural areas, it seems likely that the ten centers of this guberniia contained well over 10 percent of the total of 581,000.

The development of Saratov through the first half of the eighteenth century is described by E. N. Kusheva.[78] The city, which began as a fortress on the Volga river in the late sixteenth century, gradually had become a commercial center. Walled in 1674 with eight wooden towers and three gates, Saratov was attacked three times between 1693 and 1717, but in each case avoided capture. By the mid-eighteenth century, the fortifications had become unnecessary, the population had scattered beyond the old wall, the moat had disappeared, and the walls had been leveled.

Saratov gained rapidly in population during the eighteenth century, serving as a transshipment center where goods were reloaded from boats on the Volga river to the winter land route to Moscow. Central Asian and Near Eastern products, salt, and fish moved to Moscow, while products from the C-I and C-BE regions passed through Saratov en route to Astrakhan' and foreign destinations. Until the mid-eighteenth century, trade with members of the Kalmyk population in this area had also been substantial, but it quickly lost significance. As the guberniia was being rapidly colonized by serfs and serfowners, the city emerged as the center of an agricultural region.

ASTRAKHAN' GUBERNIIA

While areas further to the north had already experienced considerable colonization, the population of Astrakhan' guberniia at the mouth of the Volga river had not yet surpassed 200,000 by 1782. An abnormally large percentage of the population was urban. In Astrakhan' city, the registered population numbered more than 30,000, in addition to many uncounted temporary residents. Similarly to other cities along the Volga river, this city maintained a large garrison, which totaled 2,853 men. Figures for 1782 are also available for several cities in the Caucasus area recently brought into the Russian Empire and sometimes included in this guberniia. If these cities were incorporated in our totals, the total population in administrative centers might well have reached 50,000–60,000. Excluding them, a figure of roughly 35,000 is correct, since there were few administrative centers and only Astrakhan' was populous.

As late as the first quarter of the eighteenth century, the Astrakhan' area consisted of settlements along the Volga river, whose Russian populations engaged principally in trade, fishing, salt mining, crafts, and some vegetable gardening. Scattered clusters of nomadic peoples brought horses, cattle, and skins to the markets organized by the Russians and purchased in return finished products and grain. Few persons engaged in agriculture, and the area was not divided into uezd.

Astrakhan' city had been conquered in 1558 after the lower Volga region was annexed by Russia. As the gateway to the East, it attracted imports from Persia, Bukhara, India, and other distant lands. At the mouth of the Volga river near the bank of the Caspian Sea, its closest ties within Russia were to the Makar'evskaia fair, Moscow, and cities along the Volga river. Grain, lumber, wood products, textiles, metals, and handicraft items flowed downriver while imported goods, fish, and salt moved upriver.

N. B. Golikova's description of land use in Astrakhan' is one of the most complete available for any city in the Russian Empire. The city was divided into three parts: 1) the Kreml', 2) the Beloi gorod, and 3) the Zemlianoi gorod. Enclosed by a stone wall, the Kreml' dated from the late sixteenth century. By 1700, administrative and religious structures as well as private residences crowded into its small area. The large courtyard of the principal church authority, the three-story palace of the *voevoda* or chief official, the magazine for the local garrison, a monastery, and several other compounds all formed separate walled areas within the Kreml'. Snuggled between these walled enclosures stood 155 courtyards, each containing wooden *izba* or houses, many with their own barns and other attached structures. These residences belonged to persons of nearly all social strata. Only in 1721 did the governor of the newly formed guberniia order that all residences and earthen churches be removed to other parts of the city.[79]

The Beloi gorod measured three times the area of the Kreml', reaching a length of almost 2,000 feet and a width of 1,500 feet—

roughly the area of a small uezd center. During the second quarter of the seventeenth century, a wall enclosed this area; passageways were provided through seven of the twelve towers. By the early eighteenth century, various administrative buildings and granaries stood within this wall. Similar to the Kitai gorod outside the Kremlin in Moscow, this area also attracted the most trade, centered in three gostinyi dvor built or rebuilt around the beginning of the eighteenth century (known as the Russian, Indian, and Armenian gostinyi dvor), and nine riady or trading rows with 303 stores in 1707. In the same year, this area comprised 1,160 residential courtyards, most measuring under 2,000 square feet and many having two or three izba crowded together inside. Again we can observe diverse strata and occupations among the population, but, as in the Kreml', few non-Russians resided here.

The largest section of Astrakhan' was the Zemlianoi gorod. Built during the second half of the seventeenth century for the protection of an increasing number of slobody, its wooden wall enclosed more than five times the area of the Beloi gorod. Among these scattered built-up areas were the walled compounds of monasteries and of distinct ethnic minorities. For instance, an Armenian sloboda numbered among the many compounds that were locked at night. Golikova indicates that by the early eighteenth century sharp boundaries were disappearing between the sloboda. By 1707 the Zemlianoi gorod was almost entirely built-up with an estimated 4,000–4,500 courtyards.

Golikova also describes some built-up areas beyond the Zemlianoi gorod scattered amidst gardens, orchards, and vineyards. Altogether she estimates that the city numbered at least 6,500 to 7,000 households.[80]

Urals and Siberia Region

This vast, extremely sparsely settled area occupied the entire Eurasian land mass east of the core regions. The three guberniia in the Urals area bordered the L-MV and N-NW regions, offering goods to cities as far apart as Arkhangel'sk and Astrakhan'. During the eighteenth century, these guberniia were increasingly brought into the network of large-scale trade linking the core areas of Russia; their mines and granaries supplied much-valued products. The population of the Urals rose by two-thirds from 1719 to 1744, and then more than doubled during the next half century, reaching nearly 2.6 million. By the 1780s, Orenburg to the south, as seen in Map 9, had

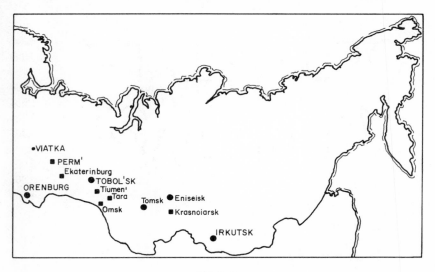

MAP 9.
U-S Region

overtaken Viatka and Perm' as the fastest growing guberniia. In Siberia, the population did not grow quite as rapidly. While in 1719 about 482,000 persons inhabited Siberia as opposed to 770,000 in the Urals area, by 1782 the population of Siberia had dropped below half of that in the Urals area.[81] Nonetheless, Siberia also experienced rapid growth, especially along the major trading route in the south. Altogether in a period of 76 years the population of this entire region of six guberniia had more than tripled.

The top ten cities comprised roughly 55 percent of the U-S region's urban population. Included on this list in Table 18 are the large Siberian guberniia centers of Tobol'sk and Irkutsk and the city of Tomsk, later designated as a guberniia center. Also on the list are Orenburg and Ekaterinburg, the two largest cities in the Urals region although neither assumed the functions of a guberniia center. In both cases the chief administration functions had been awarded to cities more centrally located. Perm', the administrative city of the

TABLE 18

Urals and Siberia Region

Level	Settlements	Urban Population (millions)	Population of Top Ten Cities	
1	0		Tobol'sk	20,000
2	0		Orenburg	16,000
			Irkutsk	12,000
3	0		Tomsk	11,000
4	5	.07	Eniseisk	10,000
			Ekaterinburg	9,000
5	18	.10	Tara	9,000
6	40	.03	Tiumen'	8,000
			Perm'	8,000
7	100		Krasnoiarsk	8,000
Est. Totals	160	.20		

Number of guberniia: 5
Number of uezd: 76
Total population: 3.3 million
Percent of population urban: 6.0
Percent of urban population in levels 1–3: 0
Percent of population in administrative centers: 6.6

guberniia in which Ekaterinburg was located, ranked among the ten largest cities, but Ufa, in what was customarily called Orenburg guberniia, supported a population of only 4,000, not much larger than the neighboring small guberniia center of Viatka. Most uezd centers within the U-S region remained tiny; probably as many as 30–35 of the 70–80 administrative centers failed to sustain populations of as many as 1,000 residents.

State peasants predominated in the population of the U-S region. In Siberian guberniia, three-fourths to seven-eighths of the population belonged to this category. While the figures were somewhat lower in the Urals, only in Orenburg guberniia, which was second to Astrakhan' in the high percentage of non-Russians exempt from the podat' tax obligations, were fewer than half classified as state peasants.

The period from 1680 to 1720 saw a shift in the development of the Urals region in a concentrated effort to set up mines and metal plants and also due to changes in transportation routes. Previously dominant cities in the north of the Urals such as Solikamsk and Verkhotur'e slowed in development or even declined, while cities to the south grew rapidly. One reason was a series of shifts in foreign trade, including the rise of St. Petersburg as opposed to Arkhangel'sk; the rise of overland inter-Asian trade; and the expansion of commerce with China through southern Siberia. A second factor was the colonization of arable land in the southern part of the Urals and in southern Siberia. Giving official recognition to these trends, a new southern route from Moscow to Siberia was designated in 1731.

VIATKA GUBERNIIA

Throughout the eighteenth century, the area of Viatka guberniia was one of the least urbanized parts of the Russian Empire. The former Viatka province, which served as the core of the new guberniia, supported only 2 percent of its population in six uezd centers. Roughly half the population of the new guberniia came from territory formerly in other provinces, but these lands near the central Volga region also remained sparsely urbanized. As a result, only 22,000 of the 829,000 residents of Viatka guberniia in 1782 registered in the 13 uezd centers. This represented 2.6 percent of the population, the lowest figure in the Russian Empire. The guberniia center at Viatka was the only level-5 city, barely exceeding 3,800 residents. Among the other 12 administrative centers, eight fell short of 1,000 residents. This guberniia deserves special attention as an example of weak urbanization.

In an article entitled, "Economic development of Viatka guberniia at the end of the XVIIIth century," A. V. Emmausskii argues that, despite the unimpressive urban concentrations in this out-of-the-way guberniia, it followed the same path of economic development as the rest of Russia.[82] Craft production on a considerable scale occurred in at least 71 enterprises: among them 12 iron-producing factories, 19 lard firms, 14 lumber yards, 7 leather shops, and 6 distilleries. Flour mills had multiplied in rural areas, reaching a total of 2,794 in the 14,461 settlements within the guberniia. Merchants traded in stores, periodic markets, and fairs. Some tens of undistinguished one-day fairs catered to local peasants, attracting merchants from neighboring uezd centers. Up to 18 more substantial fairs made an impact on commerce within the guberniia as a whole. More than half of these lively fairs were located in administrative centers, cities which often boasted two or three fairs annually. At the pinnacle of the annual commercial cycle stood four fairs, all in nonadministrative settlements, luring merchants from nearby guberniia. Chief among these was the gathering at Alekseevskaia in Kotel'nits uezd. Lasting for 20 days in March, this fair drew merchants from cities in several regions and was said to have attained a national significance approaching that of the great Irbit fair in Perm' guberniia. Periodic markets met in all but one uezd center of this guberniia. Many opened weekly on Sunday, but the most active markets met 2/7 or 3/7, often on Tuesday and/or Saturday as well as on Sunday.

In 1782 Russians comprised roughly 82 percent of the population in the 13 uezd of Viatka guberniia, with the remainder consisting of various ethnic minorities concentrated in the south and southeast. Approximately equal in population, the uezd varied greatly in area, in population density, and in the percentage of the total land under cultivation. Grain prices were lowest in the central and western parts of the guberniia. A substantial surplus of grain was regularly provided from these areas with a high percentage of land under cultivation. Prices gradually rose along the river routes leading to the Volga, but even here there was little desire to sell grain when higher prices could be obtained downriver. The highest grain prices occurred in isolated uezd centers where the supply was inadequate to meet local needs.

The three cities with 2,300–2,500 residents and Viatka are separately identified as the principal markets in this guberniia along with two nonadministrative centers in which mining and metallurgy had been developed as state enterprises.[83] The small population in Viatka city may be attributed to the fact that it was not well situated to function as an accumulation point for grain shipments to other guberniia, and its market was limited primarily to consumers within the guberniia. Weak development of the city's crafts resulted from the insignificant supplies of raw materials to the city's market.[84] Similarly, the low level of urbanization throughout the guberniia is related to the out-flow of raw materials and grain to cities in other guberniia.

P. N. Luppov argues that Viatka (called Khlynov before the re-forms of 1775–1781) declined in population from a peak of about 4,500–5,000, which had been maintained through much of the sev-enteeth century.[85] The earlier population level depended on a con-siderable grain trade with areas to the north, especially with the city of Arkhangel'sk. Subsequently this city declined to fewer than 1,000 residents in 1717 due to the general depression in the north following both the founding of St. Petersburg and the shift southward of trade routes to Siberia. While Luppov also asserts that Viatka's decline can be traced to the rising exactions on urban residents to pay for Peter I's wartime policies, this factor would presumably have been present in other cities and would not account for a long-term decline in population.

PERM' GUBERNIIA

In 1782 slightly more than 6 percent of the 788,000 inhabitants of this guberniia registered in the 15 administrative centers. The first four cities each counted populations of more than 5,500, two other cities exceeded 3,000, and three uezd centers fell short of 1,000. Many nonadministrative settlements also ranked at levels 5 and 6, places which had developed as mining and metallurgy centers during the eighteenth century.[86]

Similar to Orenburg guberniia, the area of Perm' was divided into two parts, one under the guberniia city and the other under the gu-berniia's largest city, Ekaterinburg. Both Perm' and Ekaterinburg had recently been founded. At first, Ekaterinburg developed rapidly as the administrative center for all the plants and factories in the Urals area.[87] Previously the site of a nonadministrative settlement with a metal-working plant and acquiring rising importance as a transshipment center for iron and copper, Perm' became the gu-berniia city in 1780 and soon rivaled Ekaterinburg in population.

One of the largest fairs in the Russian Empire was at Irbit in Orenburg guberniia. The location of great fairs in level-6 settlements can be puzzling to the observer who expects to find commerce concentrated in major cities. Some insight into the rationale for the choice of this site is provided by L. E. Iofa, reviewing the history of Irbit.[88] First, Iofa notes that Irbit was a neutral point between the two major cities of Ekaterinburg and Tiumen' in Siberia, whose merchants sought the fair for themselves. Second, he observes that Irbit was well situated to facilitate connections with other fairs. Siberian merchants faced the problem of making their way back to Eniseisk before the roads became impassable with the spring thaw. If the fair had been located further into the Urals area such as at Ekaterinburg, the trip would have been too far for these merchants. Consequently, a fair set up in Ekaterinburg never flourished as a rival to the Irbit fair. Also important was the timing of the Makar'evskaia fair to which goods were forwarded from Irbit and from which goods arrived en route to Siberia. Traffic from the Urals to the central areas of Russia traveled mainly by water in summer, while goods to Siberia moved by sled in winter. The beginning of the 4- to 6-week Irbit fair was shifted from early January to February in order to allow adequate time for Chinese goods acquired at the east Siberian Kiakhta fair to arrive while still permitting both Siberian merchants to return in winter and Russian merchants to reach the Volga river in early summer. Despite the tremendous volume of trade in its annual fair, Irbit was not a large uezd center. In 1775 its population numbered fewer than 1,600.

ORENBURG GUBERNIIA

Located in the southern Urals area, this guberniia's population totaled 600,000 in 1782, up from 281,000 in 1744. Intensive colonization was already noticeable in the 1730s; agricultural zones appeared, and 23 fortresses were built approximately 12–15 miles apart, forming what was known as the Orenburg line.[89] The city of Orenburg, founded in 1735 as one of these fortresses, was relocated in 1739 and grew quickly, making the transition from a primarily military population to a more normal composition of urban strata. Inside the fortress at Orenburg, as in the fortresses of Troitsk and Petropavlovsk, gostinyi dvor were erected. By the early 1750s the replacement of wooden stores in the gostinyi dvor with those of stone construction signified the growing prosperity of Orenburg. The city had become a main trading point, even enjoying barter with traders from Kazakhstan and other points in Central Asia.

Of the total population of 38,000 in 13 administrative centers, 16,000 lived in Orenburg and only 4,000 in the new guberniia center of Ufa. According to Iofa, Orenburg had reached its peak in the 1770s.[90] Other central places within the guberniia were to experience relatively rapid population gains in the next decades, but not this city. Whereas 13 settlements with 450 or more houses existed at the beginning of the 1770s, thirty years later this category had grown to 29 settlements.

Two of the three big fairs in the Urals area were located in Orenburg guberniia. While neither had as great national significance as the Irbit fair, both the Orenburg and Troitskaia (at Troitsk) fairs boasted large volumes of foreign trade and of commerce in metal products originating in the Urals area. Goods not sold at the Irbit fair often were transported to these two summer fairs, where much of the trade between the Russian Empire and Central Asia was conducted. Orenburg's big stone gostinyi dvor housed daily trade in its more than 150 stores and warehouses. In addition, summer bartering was done at a special location with 344 stores and 148 warehouses. Caravans arrived from Bukhara, Turkistan, and even as far as India —in general from places for which the Orenburg and Troitskaia fairs were more accessible than was Astrakhan', also noted for trade with Central and South Asia.

SIBERIAN GUBERNIIA

Although the total population of Siberia barely exceeded that of most guberniia in the core area of the Russian Empire, it was divided into Tobol'sk and Irkutsk guberniia and, for much of the eighteenth and nineteenth centuries, also into a third guberniia centered either in Kolyvansk or Tomsk. More than 30 administrative centers together totaled at least 125,000 inhabitants in 1782. Overall, approximately 11.5 percent of the population of this vast area resided in these administrative centers. While many of these were tiny uezd centers in vast, largely unsettled areas, the 10–15 largest cities, with more than 5,000 persons each, included at least 100,000 inhabitants.

The early uezd centers in Siberia all originated as fortresses with administrative functions; some remained in this state, while others acquired trading functions and in some cases developed a complex of trading and craft activities similar to those found in sizable cities within the core regions of Russia.[91] By the late seventeenth century, level-4 and 5 cities had emerged along the main routes of colonization in areas suitable for agriculture, while in areas of sparse settlement and poor agriculture, tiny uezd centers persisted.

West Siberia was settled before east Siberia. By the 1620s, west Siberia already formed a large agricultural zone with widespread trade. A dense network of cities was appearing. Corresponding development in east Siberia occurred only at the end of the seventeenth century, centering on the two cities of Irkutsk and Eniseisk. Initial colonization in search of valuable furs attracted a disproportionately male population, but by the early eighteenth century even in east Siberia the development of agriculture and crafts led to a reduction in the ratio of males to females.[92]

Between the first and fourth enumerations, the west Siberian city of Tiumen' experienced substantial changes, which have been documented by M. M. Gromyko.[93] The number of households nearly doubled from 982 to 1,856, and the archival records show a male population of just over 4,000 in 1782. At the earlier date, about half of all households were in some way identified with military service, many being classified as families of retired soldiers or of the service population. Subsequently, as in many Siberian cities, the military function fell into decline, while commerce and crafts prospered. By 1775 two specialized groupings of craft professions had emerged in Tiumen' with production for distant markets; leather and wood products together employed more than 70 percent of the 813 registered craftsmen in the city. During a period of 60 years the posad population of Tiumen' had risen from 6.5 to 48 percent of the total population, while the military-service strata had declined sharply.

Tiumen' enjoyed close commercial ties with many cities of Siberia and with the Irbit fair, to which merchants journeyed after the big January fair in Tiumen'. Many other fairs and periodic markets in Tiumen' uezd forwarded goods to Tiumen' city.

Most Siberian cities were constructed almost entirely of wood. For example, in Turinsk, an uezd center with at least 2,000 residents in 1782, only two stone churches interrupted the domination of wooden buildings. Even the defensive barrier enclosing this settlement, which had only recently become militarily secure, was built of wood. Of western Siberian cities, only Tobol'sk possessed a stone kreml' inside its boundaries. It also had Siberia's best stone gostinyi dvor, constructed on two floors. However, 8 of 14 churches in the city were built of wood as were more than 3,100 houses.[94]

Nearly all of the large-scale trade in east Siberia took place at Irkutsk, Eniseisk, Krasnoiarsk, and the fair at Kiakhta on the Chinese border. More than 8 percent of Russia's foreign trade was conducted in Kiakhta, where Siberian furs were exchanged for Chinese silks and other textiles. There were at least 20 other fairs of note east of Eniseisk in the eighteenth century. One of the most important of these was in Iakutsk uezd center, located in the Far East. Also in Verkhneudinsk, some 185 miles from Irkutsk, there were month-long fairs in both winter and summer. The exchange in these places, in Kiakhta, and in other locations was primarily under the control of Irkutsk merchants. More than Eniseisk and Krasnoiarsk, Irkutsk operated as the gateway to the distant reaches of the east.

THE LEFT-BANK UKRAINE AND THE SOUTH RUSSIA (UK-S) REGION, AND BELORUSSIA AND THE BALTIC (B-B) REGION

During the seventeenth and eighteenth centuries, areas in the west and south of the Russian Empire were successively annexed from the declining military powers of Poland and the Ottoman Empire, and from the smaller Crimean and Cossack military bands. The left-bank section of the Ukraine, annexed in 1648–1654, was both populous and urban by the standards of other parts of the Russian Empire. Although trade ties quickly developed between this area and places in Russia, not until 1750 did these ties expand rapidly. According to I. G. Shul'ga, between 1750 and 1800 this area in the Ukraine became an active part of the national market of the Russian Empire.[95] Agricultural products now moved in large quantities to Moscow, St. Petersburg, and Riga, and to C-BE cities such as Tula. The left-bank section of the Ukraine, consisting of the four guberniia of Khar'kov, Novgorod Severskii, Kiev, and Chernigov, with a total population in 1782 of roughly 3.1 million, had become integrated into a single commercial network.

The right-bank section of the Ukraine, annexed during the 1790s, is omitted from this discussion. Its development during the 140 years of political separation does not appear to have diverged much from that of the left-bank, and it was quickly incorporated into the same basic trading networks with some differences due to greater distance from the central cities of Russia and closer proximity to foreign countries.

The area of Russia just north of the Black Sea, which unlike the Ukraine remained sparsely settled and without notable cities, was annexed in several stages during the eighteenth century. Beginning in the 1770s, colonization became active, particularly through the immigration of Ukrainians and Moldavians.[96] At the end of the century, some recently founded cities were beginning to increase rapidly in population, and commercial ties were developing with the C-BE region. In 1782, the population of South Russia, still barely 1.1 million, probably slightly exceeded the urban percentage over the entire country.

Belorussia entered the Russian Empire in two stages through the partitions of Poland. First, in the 1770s, a little less than one-third of the area of Belorussia was annexed, including the guberniia of Mogilev and Polotsk, which were designated during the administrative reforms. In 1782, the population for this area reached almost 1.3 million. In 1790 the central and western parts of Belorussia were likewise annexed. By 1795 the total area of roughly 150,000 square miles contributed just over 4 million of the 37 million persons in the Russian Empire.

The Baltic area entered the Russian Empire under Peter I. During the 1780s it consisted of the guberniia of Lifliandiia, Estlandiia, and Vyborg. All of these administrative units were small, and together totaled somewhat more than 900,000 inhabitants, about the figure for a single guberniia in other areas of the Russian Empire.

The data in Table 19 pertain to all of the above areas within the Russian Empire during the 1780s. Of the more than 6.4 million persons in the UK-S and B-B regions, almost half resided in the left-bank

TABLE 19

Ukraine-South Russia and Belorussia-Baltic Regions

Level	Settlements	Urban Population (millions)	Population of Top Ten Cities	
1	0		Riga	35,000
			Kiev	30,000
2	0		Revel'	17,000
3	2	.06	Nezhin	12,000
			Mogilev	12,000
4	7	.09	Vitebsk	11,000
5	80	.40	Akhtyrsk	11,000
			Khar'kov	10,000
6	80	.06	Sumy	10,000
7	300		Minsk	10,000
Est. Totals	470	.60		

Number of guberniia: 11
Number of uezd: 121
Total population: 6.43 million
Percent of population urban: 9.3
Percent of urban population in levels 1–3: 10
Percent of population in administrative centers: 9.2

area of the Ukraine. Within this area, approximately 290,000 persons lived in cities. Khar'kov guberniia was probably the most urban unit, counting more than 100,000 urban residents of a total population of about 805,000. Although no single city exceeded 11,000 in population, Khar'kov, Akhtyrsk, and Sumy all numbered about 10,000 persons and the number of uezd and nonadministrative settlements with a minimum of 3,000 residents was probably as high as 15. Kiev and Chernigov guberniia were 8–9 percent urban.

Kiev was the largest city in the Ukraine, comprising up to 4,000 houses and 500 stores, excluding suburban areas.[97] Nezhin was the only level-4 city in Chernigov guberniia, but five cities supported populations of 5,000–10,000. The least urbanized Ukrainian guberniia was Novgorod Severskii, with only 50,000 of almost 750,000 persons in administrative centers.

Throughout the Ukraine, there were many populous nonadministrative settlements, and almost all uezd centers ranked at level 5, often with populations of 5,000–10,000. Thus, unlike other regions of the Russian Empire, the population in administrative centers actually represents a slight underestimation of the urban population as defined here. By either measure, the Ukraine exceeded by roughly one percent the national urban percentage.

Many settlements in the Ukraine and other western areas of the Russian Empire were labeled *mestechki* during the sixteenth and the first half of the seventeenth centuries when they were under Polish rule. Altogether in Belorussia by the mid-seventeenth century there were at least 350 administrative centers and mestechki, and in the Ukraine there were roughly 1,000 settlements in both categories.[98] More mestechki were added by the late eighteenth century, including as many as 80 or 90 in Belorussia. Usually, mestechki formed around the household of a local lord, who secured the right to hold a fair or a market at the center of his estate. Unlike administrative centers, which normally had populations of at least 1,500, mestechki generally ranged in population between 200 and 1,500. Residents of mestechki customarily lacked the rights granted to the population of administrative centers, and many engaged in agriculture. Most of these settlements do not qualify as central places since they lacked periodic markets. Some even lacked fairs. In settlements that did have fairs, the number of annual gatherings was increasing throughout the Ukraine. Whereas one to three and occasionally as many as five fairs had been common in the seventeenth century, many places had acquired six to eight fairs and some cities even offered as many as twelve fairs by the late eighteenth century.[99]

The Ukraine had long lacked a strong political authority, and correspondingly its urban network was fragmented. The largest seventeenth-century cities had been Kiev and L'vov (in the right-bank section) with 15,000–20,000 persons. The data for the late eighteenth century reveal a population overwhelmingly concentrated in level-5 cities.

Information from 1818–1820 indicates that fairs were more widespread in the Ukraine than in other regions of the Russian Empire.[100] Of the 64 fairs in the country with a turnover of at least one million roubles, 26 met annually in the Ukraine. While the average number of fairs for 40 guberniia hovered around 100, at least two guberniia in the Ukraine each exceeded 400 fairs, and altogether as many as 2,000 of the 4,000 fairs in the Russian Empire may have been located in the Ukraine and the newly settled area adjoining it in south Russia. Many of the large fairs in the left-bank section served the export of cattle and livestock products to other regions and the import of finished craft items from the C-I region. Above all, fairs in the Ukraine were points of accumulation for cattle, grain, and alcoholic beverages, and peasant craft products for shipment to distant markets. Much of the grain in this area was distilled into alcohol, which was easier to transport over long distances.

Apart from the Ukraine, each of the other three areas in the great arc from the Baltic Sea to the Sea of Azov supported between 90,000 and 110,000 persons in cities. In the Baltic area, more than half of the total population in cities clustered in Riga and Revel'. These ports increased substantially in population as the urban total of the region more than doubled between 1744 and 1782, while the area's total population rose by less than 50 percent. In the area of south Russia, no one city had begun to dominate as Odessa would after 1800. Only in the 1790s did foreign trade through the Black Sea begin to develop. Belorussia had a distribution of cities more typical of the Russian Empire; two cities ranked at level 4, totaling 24,000 persons, 13 cities at level 5 totaling 61,000 persons, and there were 20–25 level-6 central places.

A doctoral dissertation by A. M. Karpachev studies the development of cities in Belorussia from 1650 to 1800, devoting separate chapters to many aspects that are poorly documented in other published sources, such as the agricultural activities of urban residents.[101] Particularly noteworthy about this dissertation is its extensive use of statistical materials on all aspects of urban life and on some aspects of rural life as well.

Serfs predominated in Belorussia. Karpachev states that 26 owners possessed one-third of all serfs, a concentration probably unequaled in Russian guberniia. Crafts were organized as estate activities with serf labor; near the end of the eighteenth century, almost all of the 9,000 craft enterprises recorded for this area were operated by serfowners. Mills and breweries predominated. Lumber-related crafts, which were also numerous, made more use of hired labor.

From the mid-seventeenth to the early eighteenth centuries, the cities of Belorussia suffered through a series of wars. The total population fell, rose, and finally fell again to a low point around 1720. During the next half-century the area's population more than doubled, and many cities regained earlier population levels.

As in the Ukraine, two types of settlements were recognized in Belorussia as distinct from ordinary villages. In 1791 there were 438 of these administrative centers and mestechki. Karpachev calculates that only 39 of this number qualify as cities, containing a minimum of 300 houses. Together, these 39 settlements comprised 21,000 houses in 1791 and 126,000 persons. Of these 39 cities, 28 possessed certain rights of self-government. The remaining 399 of the 438 settlements were mestechki, of which 38 had self-government provisions. These settlements averaged about 630 persons. As late as 1800, barely half of the mestechki offered fairs, an indication that most places in this category probably lacked markets as well. Large mestechki had 200–300 houses, while some tiny ones had fewer than 20 or even 10 houses.

Summary

Different regions of the Russian Empire inherited diverse patterns of land ownership and peasant obligation, of urban land use and function, reflecting agricultural and transportation conditions and the duration of the area's subservience to the tsarist government. Among the measures available to distinguish one rural area from another are: 1) the amount and rate of population growth; 2) the percentage of the population registered as serfs, state peasants, or other less numerous categories as court and "economic" peasants; 3) the percentage of serfs on obrok or barshchina; 4) the distribution by size of serf estates; 5) the quality and amount of arable land per capita; and 6) the proportion of peasants engaged in nonagricultural activities. Many of these measures have been introduced in the discussion of separate guberniia and regions in this chapter. Similarly, to distinguish one urban area from another one can make use of available information on: 1) the percentage of an area's population registered in the posad; 2) the amount of wealth credited to kuptsy and meshchane; 3) the number of factories and shops; and 4) the relative importance of the city's commerce, crafts and military preparedness. This and similar types of information have been incorporated into the discussion of urban networks for examination in this chapter.

None of these measures, however, provides a systematic and relatively comprehensive standard for drawing comparisons between areas that is meaningful on a world setting. In this chapter, therefore, these measures have served only a supplementary role, while primary attention has focused on urban population data. For each core area guberniia and each proposed region, I have estimated the percentage of the population in cities during the 1780s and its distribution among central places at various levels. Utilizing these data, I have sought to make precise variations among areas, relating them to the other measures of urban and rural conditions.

Generally, the geographical pattern of urban distribution in 1782 reflected longstanding differences between areas. The overall impression from data for 1744 and 1762 is one of considerable stability in the relative urban ranking of areas as the percentage of the population residing in cities rose gradually.

The core regions of Russia appear remarkably uniform between 1744 and 1782. Only in St. Petersburg guberniia and Olonets guberniia in the N-NW region, where new administrative centers were recently founded, did urban growth probably far exceed population growth. To a lesser extent, in Tver' guberniia, where traffic along the Volga river entered a new canal system en route to St. Petersburg, and in a few rapidly settled southern guberniia of the C-BE and L-MV regions urban growth also proceeded briskly.

This overall uniformity reflected widespread urban growth. In most guberniia, the urban population rose even more rapidly than the total population; that is, by more than 30 percent in the C-I region and by even larger percentages elsewhere. No evidence was found of any area with net urban decline or with a marked drop in the urban percentage. We must conclude that the portion of the population in cities within the core areas of Russia was rising gradually as a result of increments contributed by several regions. The total urban population in these four regions rose from roughly 1.0 million in 1744 to between 1.5 and 1.6 million in 1782.

Between 1744 and 1782 only the C-BE region may have experienced some decline in the percentage of population in cities. During the first half of the century its southern areas had maintained a frontier character with fortress cities and a small agricultural population. By 1782 the agricultural population of this part of the region had risen, reducing the urban percentage in some areas. In increasing amounts, exports from throughout the C-BE region flowed to cities in other regions. The absence of any cities in excess of 30,000 population suggests the large outflow to the top levels of the urban pyramid from the lower levels within the C-BE.

The L-MV region had been considerably less urban than the C-BE region in 1744, but by 1782 the gap had narrowed appreciably. This area's urban percentage climbed to 6.5, while the C-BE's figure slipped to 6.9 percent. During the first half of the century, the L-MV was still weakly integrated into a national market, although considerable traffic already moved along the Volga river. With rapid colonization, this region quickly came to resemble the C-BE region as a major source of exports to cities in other regions. The presence of Astrakhan' and Saratov with populations of 30,000–35,000 contrasts with the absence of level-3 cities in the C-BE urban network, but these cities, in fact, were not much bigger than level-4 cities such as Tula, and the C-BE region was well ahead in the number of cities at level 4.

The C-I region experienced some increase in its urban percentage during the decades before 1782, reaching 8.5 percent. Moscow recovered from some drop in population during the first decades of St. Petersburg's growth and attracted increasing supplies from outside as seen by the high of 49 percent in cities at levels 1–3 in this region. A large proportion of urban residents in cities of this size indicates dependence on outside goods.

The most substantial urbanization continued in the N-NW region as it had since the beginning of the century, primarily as a result of St. Petersburg's development. By 1782, 63 percent of the urban population in this region resided in St. Petersburg, and 13 percent of the region's residents lived in cities.

In Tables 14 through 19, data are presented for the urban percentage of the population in each of the regions of the Russian Empire, with the UK-S and B-B regions grouped together. The most urbanized region was the N-NW with 13.0 percent of its population in cities. Second among the core areas of the Empire was the C-I region with 8.5 percent of its population in cities. Both of these regions had a high percentage of their urban residents in cities at levels 1–3, indicating dependence on supplies from other regions. In contrast, the C-BE region with 6.9 percent of its population in cities supported no cities of this size, and the L-MV region, with 6.5 percent of its population classified as urban, sustained the low figure of 24 percent of all urban residents in cities at levels 1–3. The high urban percentages in the regions around St. Petersburg and Moscow should be attributed to support received primarily from the C-BE and secondarily from the L-MV region. Together, these four regions formed a single urban network including about 8.3 percent of their population. On the fringes of this network were the U-S region, which with 6.0 percent of its population in cities was too sparsely settled to support a city of as many as 30,000 inhabitants, and the UK-S and B-B regions, which exceeded the national average with 9.3 percent urban and at the same time provided some support to large cities in other regions. The low percentage of the total urban population in large cities in these regions may reflect the small scale of their separate populations and their relative autonomy.

Ranking guberniia according to the percentage of population in cities reveals a clustering between 5 and 8 percent. Especially in the core areas of Russia, most guberniia conformed to this range. Lower figures of 2–4 percent were obtained for a swath of northeast Russia extending from Vladimir, Vologda, and Kostroma guberniia to Viatka and other parts of the Urals area. Canceling the effect of these low figures were the much higher percentages of 12 to 15 in several outlying guberniia: Lifliandiia and Khar'kov to the west and Saratov and Tobol'sk to the southeast and east. Three guberniia far surpassed the figures for other areas: St. Petersburg and Moscow containing 50 and 28 percent, respectively, of their guberniia populations were joined by Astrakhan' with 31 percent of the much smaller population in its sparsely settled area.

Among the five regions examined in detail, the seven-level hierarchy of central places reveals important similarities between the U-S and N-NW regions. These areas supported the fewest level-7 marketing settlements per capita and the highest ratios of level-6 to level-7 and of level-4 to level-5 central places. Guberniia in these regions consisted of only 20 or 30 central places each, almost half of which were uezd centers. Their common pattern represents the sparsely settled, agriculturally poor, large guberniia in the north and east of the Russian Empire.

For the other three regions, many similarities can be identified. Each guberniia averaged roughly 50 central places, and the ratio of residents in level-4 to level-5 cities measured slightly below one-third. The C-BE region deviated from the ratio of three or four times as many persons in level-5 as in level-6 centers, claiming an extraordinarily high ratio of 12:1. This figure reflected the prevalence of relatively large uezd centers and the near absence of large nonadministrative marketing settlements. The L-MV region also differed from the general pattern in the great number of level-7 periodic markets relative to its total population. A typical uezd in this region counted as many as four central places. Together, these three regions, constituting two-thirds of the population in the five regions examined closely, represent the prevalent pattern of urban distribution in Russia.

A special problem exists in the treatment of Russian regions. In China and Japan, where cities hundreds of miles apart at levels 1 and 2 resemble the spatial distribution of St. Petersburg and Moscow, it is possible to identify distinct regions with at least 15 million persons as the specific hinterlands of each city. The two countries can therefore be neatly divided into separate regions, each centering on one or two major cities. The two central cities of Russia seem to have had no such clearly delimited supporting areas. Large volumes of goods from the C-BE and L-MV regions were transported to both cities, not exclusively to one. Even parts of the N-NW and C-I regions contributed a high proportion of their products to the central city in the other region. An important factor in the overlapping of areas of support was the circuitous course of the Volga river, which looped through three regions and, in addition, offered ready access through major tributaries to traffic originating in the C-BE and U-S regions. Moscow's central location gave it an initial advantage, but with the completion in the early eighteenth century of canals from the Volga river to St. Petersburg, the city facing the Baltic became nearly as accessible despite its more distant location from most of Russia. Normally no advantage was obtained by sending goods first to Moscow then to St. Petersburg; rather, at certain points along the Volga river and other major routes, the quantities of goods headed for either destination were channeled into separate paths. Furthermore, all of the major fairs of Russia and particularly the Makar'-evskaia fair were located in places that were convenient for the movement of goods to both cities. Probably one of the principal explanations for the preservation and growth of national fairs into the nineteenth century is the lack of separate hinterlands for the two great cities of Russia.

For the most part, these five regions bore striking similarities. Their range of urbanization varied only between 6 and 13 percent, with the regions that exceeded the national average clearly dependent on the least urbanized regions for supplies. At least one nationally significant fair emerged in each region with the possible exception of the N-NW area with its seaport orientation. Periodic markets and small-scale handicraft production for the market appeared in rural areas of every region. The same basic components of the urban population were registered in cities everywhere. While St. Petersburg's huge contribution uplifted the urban percentage of the N-NW region above figures elsewhere, the turnover of fairs in the Ukraine far exceeded that of other regions, the dense cluster of specialized craft communities in the C-I region had no parallel elsewhere, a disproportionate number of soldiers were stationed in L-MV cities to guard transport along the Volga, and other particular regional variations have been noted in this chapter. The general impression is of similar urban networks, at least in the five regions examined closely.

❊ 5 ❊

URBAN NETWORKS OF ADVANCED
PREMODERN (STAGE G)
SOCIETIES

A stage G society is defined as a nonmodernized society unexposed to substantial contacts with any relatively modernized society and in which all seven levels of central places are present or a truncated network of central places is present which, if the scale of the society were larger, would presumably have consisted of all seven levels. This definition excludes all modernized or modernizing societies, all colonies and major trading partners of modernizing societies, and all premodern societies that lacked the complete network of seven levels unless that deficiency can be attributed to the insufficient scale of the society. Among those societies that had reached stage G in their development were Russia from the early eighteenth to the early nineteenth century, China from the mid-sixteenth to the mid-nineteenth century, Japan from the early seventeenth to the mid-nineteenth century, England from the late sixteenth to the mid-eighteenth century, and France from about 1600 to the late eighteenth century. Of course, all of these dates are subject to verification, and the identification of these examples as stage G societies is based on data presently available to the author of this study.

Comparison of stage G societies serves several purposes. First, it enables us to view the spatial aspects of Russian social structure and the urban data presented in Chapters 3 and 4 in a broad perspective. The notion of Russian backwardness can now be reassessed in terms of specific conditions, time periods, and countries and through a framework of premodern development in which measurement of the rate of change becomes possible. Second, in the light of the comparisons made in Chapter 2, it is now possible to consider in a systematic way in what respects stage G societies differed from societies at earlier stages of premodern development. With this information, we can reconsider world history in an effort to determine how many societies at what stages of development existed century by century. Third, an entirely new step can be taken in the application of the urban networks approach. On the basis of data from five countries in diverse parts of the world, areas of geographical integration can be specified with their characteristic populations. The evolution of stages of societies may be conceived in terms of these ever-expanding integrative zones. Based on these comparisons, the relationships between urban networks, urbanization, commercialization, land use, stratification, and centralization are briefly explored in this chapter. Finally a new area for future inquiry based on this approach to periodization is anticipated. Modernization originated in European stage G societies. In responding as latecomers to the problems of achieving rapid modernization, Russia, China, and Japan all built upon the foundations previously achieved as stage G societies. Thus, comparison of stage G societies leads to the study of preconditions for modernization. It is hoped that identification of similarities and differences between societies at this advanced stage of premodern development will serve as a starting point for the study of rates of modernization in various nineteenth- and twentieth-century countries.

Before proceeding to these comparative tasks, it is necessary to present information on England and France as stage G societies. Earlier, we examined the urban networks of Japan at the turn of the nineteenth century and of China roughly in the 1830s, and now the corresponding Russian patterns for the 1780s have also been studied. By focusing our attention on the two Western European countries at earlier times, we can exclude the impact of initial modernization and also make use of the best available data. The specific dates chosen here for detailed analysis of urban networks are the 1680s for England and the 1760s for France.

The English and French Urban Networks

Along with Japan, England and France are the most thoroughly studied countries with respect to the histories of individual cities and local areas. Nevertheless, there exists no single synthesizing work on the premodern cities of either country, and there is no general comparative study with each other or with any other country dealing with urban or internal marketing history. Despite the voluminous materials on separate English counties and the impressive quantitative studies of the 'demographic and economic history of certain French provinces, this brief section represents the first highly generalized account of the urban networks of late premodern England and France.

The data used in compiling the estimates in Table 20 are drawn from many sources. The number of central places corresponds to

TABLE 20

The English Urban Network in the 1680s

Level	Settlements	Urban Population (millions)
1	1	.53
2	0	
3	0	
4	7	.10
5	75	.37
6	255	.12
7	460	
Total	800	1.12

Population of England and Wales: 5.5 million
Percentage of population in cities: 20–21
Percentage of urban population in levels 1–3: 47

Alan Everitt's count of markets for Tudor and Stuart England and to Gregory King's tabulation of towns in the 1690s.[1] A total of 801 cities and market towns was also given by J. Adams during the 1680s.[2] The distribution of central places at levels 1–5 is based on an extrapolation from population data given in separate local studies. Similarly, the breakdown of central places with fewer than 3,000 inhabitants into levels 6 and 7 is based on an extrapolation from detailed descriptions of the populations, marketing activities and occupational structures of settlements in individual counties. The most detailed information on the urban networks of nine counties and Wales, together accounting for roughly 40 percent of all central places in the country, is presented in Table 21.[3]

TABLE 21

The Urban Networks of 9 English Counties and Wales

	Number of Settlements			
Level	Devon	Lancashire-Cheshire	Worcestershire	Lincolnshire
1				
2				
3				
4	1	0	0	0
5	4	5	1	3
6	16	15	4	12
7	24	24	6	22
Total	45	44	11	37

	Number of Settlements			
Level	Suffolk-Norfolk	Essex	Kent	Wales
1				
2				
3				
4	1	0	0	0
5	4	2	6	4
6	15	10	10	19
7	44	15	17	31
Total	64	27	33	54

By the 1680s, almost half of the urban population of England re-sided in London. The spectacular growth of this city after 1500 and especially after 1600 greatly exceeded the rate of increase of the national population. With fewer than 100,000 residents in 1500, London made up only 2 or at most 3 percent of the national population, and its 170,000 residents in 1600 still totaled barely 4 percent of the national figure. But by the 1680s, London's population of roughly 530,000 had reached nearly 10 percent of the 5.5 million persons in

England and Wales. London's dramatic rise in the seventeenth century paralleled the even more spectacular seventeenth-century rise of Edo (Tokyo) and the eighteenth-century growth of St. Petersburg, in all three cases following the emergence of a stage G society.

E. A. Wrigley has analyzed the tremendous impact on English society caused by London's population spurt after 1650.[4] He points to a demonstration effect that permeated much of England, causing economic, demographic, and other social changes. Peter Clark and Paul Slack describe London's growth during the sixteenth and seventeenth centuries as a takeover by the national community that shifted the balance of English urbanism away from medium-sized cities.[5] A severe reorientation of communities accompanied the rise of London.

The division of English central places into five levels has previously been proposed by W. G. Hoskins for the sixteenth century.[6] His hierarchy consists of London, regional capitals, county towns, towns without administrative functions but having big markets, and ordinary marketing settlements. Correspondingly, Hoskins divides these central places into population levels: twelve to fourteen regional cities had populations of 5,000–10,000, and Norwich had 12,000 persons in 1524; many county towns had 3,000–4,000 residents although most had populations of fewer than 2,000; big market towns numbered 200–300 households and smaller market towns generally had far fewer than 200 households.

Alan Everitt focuses on three levels of central places.[7] His figure of 60 county towns by the 1560s with populations of close to 6,000–7,000 encompasses all the cities at both levels 4 and 5 as presented here with the exception of the smallest level-5 settlements. The number of county towns exceeds the number of counties, since some counties, including five large ones mentioned by Everitt in the southeast, had two, rival towns. He also divides marketing settlements into out-of-the-way places with 300 or 400 persons and larger markets that served greater concentrations of population and often held 600 to 1,000 residents. Everitt states that most of the 40 counties had roughly half-a-dozen such major centers, suggesting a total number of what I call level-6 central places that corresponds closely to the 255 given in Table 20.

Gregory King's classification of central places should also be noted.

He calculated that as many as 650 of the approximately 800 settlements had no more than about 200 houses, while roughly 130 towns had between 300 and 500 houses.[8] Using King's data, but arguing that in fact some of King's middle category of 130 towns had many more houses, Clark and Slack divide cities into three levels: the six or seven major cities plus London (corresponds to levels 1–4 given here); 120 intermediate cities that met four criteria; and more than 650 marketing towns. Their four criteria embraced not only a peculiar concentration of population and a specialized economic function, but also a sophisticated political superstructure and a community impact beyond the immediate limits of the town.

Table 22 and Map 10 provide a breakdown of England into regions. With the exception of Wales, in which there were no level-4 or major level-5 cities, each region delineated here enclosed 117–187 central places and four or five main cities. Only in the southeast dominated by London did fewer than four cities emerge which exceeded 7,000 in population.

As J. Adams' list of central places shows, throughout England only a small number of settlements had 2/7 or 3/7 markets as opposed to the ubiquitous weekly markets.[9] The markets with greater frequencies served as superior centers of trade for surrounding 1/7 markets, although in England as in Russia hierarchical relationships even existed among weekly markets; some 1/7 markets also ranked as superior trading centers. The rarity of 2/7 and 3/7 markets is seen in Lincolnshire, where just 3 of 37 central places had markets that met more frequently than once a week. As one would expect, these three centers were relatively far apart, permitting them to serve as centers for standard markets throughout much of the county. Just outside the northern and southeastern borders of the county were located the major cities of Hull and King's Lynn, which undoubtedly attracted considerable commerce from Lincolnshire. Moreover, the city of Lincoln, which had only a 1/7 market, was probably a superior marketing point in the west of the county.

J. H. C. Patten's doctoral dissertation is the fullest examination of the urban network in a subregion of England. He chose East Anglia, consisting of Norfolk and Suffolk counties, which together constituted about 5½ percent of the population of England and Wales and,

TABLE 22

England's Regions and Main Cities

Region	Counties	Number of Markets	Main Cities
North	Northumberland, Cumberland, Durham, Westmorland, Yorkshire, Lancashire, Cheshire	137	Newcastle York Hull Leeds Chester
Midlands	Nottingham, Leicestershire, Rutland, Northampton, Warwickshire, Stafford, Worcestershire, Shropshire, Hereford-shire, Derbyshire, Monmouth	131	Birmingham Worcester Coventry Leicester Nottingham
Southwest	Dorset, Wiltshire, Gloucester, Somerset, Devon, Cornwall	187	Bristol Exeter Plymouth Salisbury
Southeast	Buckinghamshire, Bedfordshire, Hertford, Oxford, Berkshire, Hampshire, Middlesex, Surrey, Essex, Kent, Sussex	186	London Colchester Canterbury
East	Suffolk, Norfolk, Lincolnshire, Cambridgeshire, Huntingdonshire	117	Norwich Yarmouth King's Lynn Ipswich Cambridge

as seen in Table 21, roughly 8 percent of all central places. The area was unusual in having four cities with at least 8,000 inhabitants each (Ipswich had 7,900 residents in 1670 and presumably reached 8,000 by the 1680s), approximately 20–25 percent of all cities that exceeded this minimum in England and Wales.

Patten constructed scalograms showing the number and structure of occupations present in 44 marketing and three other settlements in East Anglia.[10] His analysis shows a gradual transition from settlements with numerous types of occupations characteristic of urban areas to those with few occupations as in villages. The criterion for

MAP 10.
England's Regions and Major Cities

urbanity is the ordered association of occupations and services, which closely paralleled the population of settlements. For the most part Patten is differentiating among what are here called level-6 and 7 central places. On this list from East Anglia there were about forty such settlements, each providing basic crafts and services for a local area or a slightly wider area. Patten distinguishes between settlements at the bottom of the scalogram in which there were six or seven types of occupations and only 300 residents and those higher on the scalogram with more than twenty occupations and roughly 1,000 residents. The four large level-5 cities each had between 82 and 136 occupations in the 1670s and life in the substantial center of Norwich was enriched by more than 250 occupations.

An advanced phase in the development of stage G societies is signaled by the decline of periodic markets. This decline began in some areas of Russia after 1800, and following a century of little change in the number of markets also began in Japan after 1800. In England it is likely that this phase began about a century earlier. Patten refers to the decline of largely agricultural markets in the face of competition from neighbors better equipped with diverse occupations and services.[11] He notes the elimination of one market by the early eighteenth century and of several others by the 1730s. Everitt refers to the same process in Leicestershire, pointing out that, stage by stage, the city of Leicester attracted trade from two nearby lesser markets until these places died out as centers of commerce.[12] Similarly to Japan, the number of markets had apparently remained stationary before it began to drop around 1700.

The decline of periodic marketing was related to the spread of shops. Corresponding to a great increase in inland traffic all over England during the seventeenth century, cities became more open to outside influences, even in a literal sense as town walls fell into disuse and passageways were sometimes cut through them for more convenient transportation. The shift away from trade confined to markets that had been under way for centuries accelerated with the construction of large numbers of retail as well as craft shops. By the early eighteenth century, the number of shops in a county reached several hundreds, with large villages and marketing centers having many shops each.[13] To the extent that these shops were directly supplied from major marketing centers, the need for numerous local markets was reduced.

Fairs were present along with markets in many settlements. In the relatively poor area of Lancashire and Cheshire during a long period from the twelfth to the sixteenth centuries there are recorded 34 locations with relatively major markets, many of which had several annual fairs; 27 locations with minor markets and normally just one fair each year; about 10 locations with minor markets and no fairs; and 6 locations with fairs but no markets.[14] According to Everitt, it is incorrect to conclude that the prosperity of fairs peaked in the sixteenth century, giving way to an age of markets.[15] In fact, fairs, markets, and retail shops expanded together in the sixteenth and seventeenth centuries, although some fairs lost international clientele. While markets in England normally served an area with a radius of about 10 miles, local fairs served areas extending 10 to 30 miles, and the two or three important fairs in most regions served areas 30 to 75 miles distant. Stourbridge fair in Cambridge topped the list of national fairs serving an even larger hinterland. Most fairs complemented rather than competed with markets, serving as specialized points of exchange for particular types of goods such as livestock, and, unlike the national fairs in Russia, the volume of exchange was trivial in comparison to the great trade in the national administrative center. In scale and function, English fairs appear to have resembled fairs in China.

Before discussing the French urban network, we should consider some of the similarities and differences between the English and Russian networks and observe some parallels between England and Japan. The widespread presence of periodic markets linked with administrative centers many of which had superior markets, the existence of a clear hierarchy of central places extending from level 7 to level 1, and the persistence of various types of fairs were typical of both England in the 1680s and Russia in the 1780s. In addition, retail shops were spreading rapidly and periodic markets were about to be eclipsed in certain areas of both countries. During the century after England entered stage G, the proportion of population in cities rose by about one-half, exceeding 20 percent by the 1680s.[16] The increase was probably not quite as high in Russia, but the rise to more than 8 percent in the 1780s represented a growth of at least one-third from the proportion in cities at the beginning of the century. In this respect, England and Japan were more similar, since in slightly more than a century after it became a stage G society, Japan's urban figure jumped from 10 to 17 percent. While in Russia the total population in cities at levels 1–3 rose by about 250 percent during this period, in Japan and England the rise during the course of two centuries exceeded 600 percent.

Populations of French settlements are listed in two multivolume works similar in format to the *Geographical Dictionary* published in St. Petersburg at the beginning of the nineteenth century and used here for data on the Russian urban network. Both of these French works, entitled *Dictionnaire de la France*, which date from 1726 and 1771, give marketing frequencies, dates of fairs, and physical descriptions for some central places as well as noting the population for almost every settlement.[17] The data used in the compilation of Table 23

TABLE 23

The French Urban Network in the 1760s

Level	Settlements	Urban Population (millions)
1	1	.58
2	0	
3	15	.90
4	48	.70
5	230	1.15
6	700	.35
7	1200	
Total	2200	3.7

Population of France: 23 million
Percentage of population in cities: 16
Percentage of urban population in levels 1–3: 40

are primarily from the 1771 *Dictionnaire de la France* although the 1726 work has been used for estimates in instances where figures for the latter date are absent or unexpectedly high or low. Separate figures for many of the large cities at various points during the eighteenth century published by Roger Mols, Etienne Helin, and Pierre Goubert have also been used to modify the 1771 figures.[18] In addition, by determining the relationships between the 96 departments in 1798 and the 32 provinces that were the most important units of France before the Revolution, I have compared the figures used here with the data on the total population in cities with a minimum of 5,000 population given by Marcel Reinhard.[19] Further information on the French urban network has been drawn from separate studies of provinces, local areas, and cities.

Relying on figures presented by others, Charles Tilly estimates "that about 4 percent of the French population at the time of the Revolution was in cities of 50,000 or more, and about 7.5 percent in cities of 20,000 or more."[20] These estimates correspond closely to the figures in Table 23 showing 6.4 percent in cities of 30,000 or more and 9.5 percent in cities of 10,000 or more. Tilly also repeats estimates by Marcel Reinhard giving "the number in settlements of 2,000 or more at the end of the old regime as 4 million of the 26 million total population."[21] This results in a figure of 15–16 percent in such settlements. Reinhard's cutoff point of 2,000 is roughly the same as that of the definition of urban used here, which includes all those in central places of more than 3,000 population plus one-half of the population in level-6 central places, and, correspondingly, his total is about the same proportion of the French population as the 16 percent calculated in Table 23.

The *Dictionnaire de la France* of 1771 divides settlements into various levels. The largest cities were designated as cities of the first, second, or third order, generally corresponding to populations of at least 25,000, with approximately 80,000 required to be classified as the first order. Smaller cities were differentiated into "villes considerables," "villes," and "petites villes." Among those settlements that had not gained official recognition as villes were many "bourgs," which frequently also had marketing activities and occasionally had populations of more than 3,000.

The number of central places and the distribution of settlements at levels 6 and 7 can be estimated separately for each province using data in the *Dictionnaire de la France*. There is also more extensive information on low-level central places in certain areas of France, some of which has been interpreted by recent French scholarship. Pierre Goubert describes in detail a complex of 39 central places centering on Beauvais in the north.[22] Two studies of Languedoc province in the southeast also report extensively on marketing patterns and provide a basis for estimating that there were about 12,000 persons per central place in this area, close to the figure of 10,000–11,000 that can be derived for all of France from Table 23.[23] Examination of a 1764 source for Rouen généralité in the northwest indicates that 60–70 settlements qualified as central places, including probably all 30 of the villes and more than one-quarter of the 122 bourgs in the area.[24] Altogether, in areas representing roughly 10 percent of the population of France, there were somewhat more than 200 central places. On the basis of this fairly accurate sample and rough figures obtained for each of the provinces of France, I have estimated that the total number of central places was 2,200.

In Table 24 and Map 11, France is divided into seven regions, ranging in population from 1.6 million to 5.2 million. The principal urban areas are the north and the southeast. Paris, with 16 percent of the urban population of France, was located in the north. The population of this city had been slowly increasing, approximately keeping pace with the growth in the national population, holding 2.5–3.0 percent of the total. Also within this region were the textile-producing centers near the border with the Low Countries. Foremost among these was Lille, a city of at least 60,000 persons. Both provinces of Picardie and Champagne were about 14 or 15 percent urban; in the former, the dominant cities were Amiens at level 3 and Abbeville at level 4, while Champagne was divided into the marketing spheres of at least four and, perhaps, as many as five cities at level 4.

The other exceptionally urbanized region was the southeast. Containing only 11 or 12 percent of the population of France, this region held more than one-quarter of all cities at level 3. Together, Marseille, Toulouse, Montpellier, and Nîmes totaled roughly 270,000 persons, almost half the population of Paris in a region which had just one-half the population of the north.

Other regions ranged between 11 and 15 percent in cities. Only

TABLE 24

The Urbanization of France's Regions

Region	Provinces	Population (millions)	Urban Pop. (millions)	Urban Percent
N	Ile-de-France, Champagne, Picardy, Flanders, Artois, Boulonois	4.4	1.1	25
NW	Normandy, Brittany, Maine, Anjou, Poitou	5.2	.72	14
NE	Alsace, Lorraine	1.6	.24	15
C	Orléanais, Touraine, Berry, Nivernais, Bourbonnais, Marche, Limousin, Auvergne	3.3	.38	11–12
E	Franche-Comté, Burgundy, Lyonnais, Dauphiné	2.7	.35	13
SE	Provence, Languedoc, Roussillon	2.6	.55	21
SW	Saintonge, Guyenne, Gascony, Béarn	3.6	.32	9

in the southwest did fewer than 10 percent of the total population reside in cities according to these preliminary estimates.

It is apparent from Map 11 that for three of the five less urbanized regions of France there was only one city at level 3. In the northeast there were two cities, but these did not greatly exceed 30,000 each in population and together did not quite equal the population of Bordeaux and fell considerably short of the 110,000 persons in Lyon. Only in the northwest did the number of cities at level 3 match the southeast, but this region held twice the population of the southeast.

Almost all of the level-3 cities in France were located along large, navigable rivers, including the Seine, the Loire, the Gironde, the Rhône, and the Rhine. Typically these cities served hinterlands of a million or more persons and also provided the major outlets for foreign trade. The location of most of these cities near the country's borders shows the outward orientation of French commerce as part

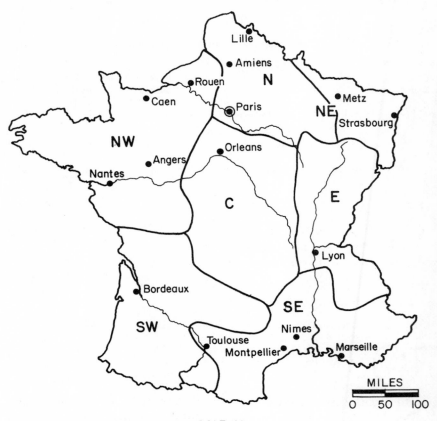

MAP 11.
France's Regions and Cities at Levels 1-3

of a larger European network. It also indicates that some of the interregional trade within France was carried on the Mediterranean Sea
and the Atlantic Ocean. The construction of two major canals by the
early eighteenth century connecting the Atlantic and the Mediterranean through Toulouse and Bordeaux and joining the Loire and
Seine rivers near Orléans and Paris increased the volume of interregional transport.

Divisions of France were more complex than those in any of the
other countries chosen for comparison. Separate boundaries delineated religious, judicial, military, and financial administrative units. In
addition, France was divided into provinces, most dating back many
hundreds of years. Of all these units, the province was the most

durable and is the most convenient for the study of regional patterns. Within provinces, the élection most closely approximates the local administrative entity elsewhere such as the uezd. Indeed, in the French geographical dictionaries, the élections and provinces are given most prominence, and in every case the cities are described in which the fiscal administration of these units was centered.

The capitals of provinces often served as the administrative centers of généralités, the superior fiscal unit in most areas divided into 5–12 élections. Populous provinces such as Normandy were divided into more than one généralité while several tiny provinces were engulfed by the généralités of neighboring provinces. Unlike provinces, which varied markedly in population, généralités usually had from 400,000 to 800,000 inhabitants.

Many French provinces were separated into lower and upper sections, each with its own capital city. Most of the level-4 cities of France acted as capitals of provinces or généralités or as the capitals of these sections within provinces. The average region with 4 or 5 provinces had seven cities of 10,000–30,000 population.

Most level-5 cities were the seats of élections. In Tours province, for instance, the cities of Amboise and Chinon each had 4,600–4,700 residents, and Loches was credited with 3,000 residents. All of these cities were the centers of élections. Within Anjou province in the généralité of Tours were 6 élections, whose cities ranged in population from Angers, with 36,000, to Montreuil-Bellay, with 1,500. Frequently there were fewer parishes and correspondingly a smaller population in élections whose cities were relatively unpopulated, e.g., only 56 of the 644 parishes in Anjou were found in the élection of Montreuil-Bellay. In contrast, the élection of the nearby provincial city of Poitiers had 257 parishes. Altogether, the 1,865 parishes that averaged several hundreds of persons in the généralité of Rouen were distributed into 12 élections, ranging from 61 to 225 parishes each. Understandably, other things being equal, the larger the population of the areas administered, the larger the population of the administrative seat.

Markets and fairs abounded in France. Marketing frequencies of 1/7, 2/7, and 3/7 characterized settlements with populations comparable to corresponding marketing centers in Russia. In all or nearly all provinces, central places displaying each of these frequencies were present, and 2/7 and 3/7 patterns were successively less common. Abel Poitrineau writes that the life of the bourg centered on the once or twice a week market and on the annual fairs.[25] A special building called *une halle* served as the location of the market. In Paris les Halles were the pinnacle of French commercial activity much as the gostinyi dvor was in Moscow.

The decline in periodic markets in France appears to have begun by about 1730. In the Toulouse area, Georges Frêche notes that several markets ended during the middle decades of the eighteenth century as commerce became increasingly concentrated.[26] Yet, he also adds that new markets were still appearing where improved transportation made areas more accessible.

Throughout France, the number of fairs continued to increase. Many settlements with a few fairs were granted the right to hold more frequent fairs, and it became more common for cities to hold monthly fairs especially for trade in livestock. Describing lower Auvergne province, Poitrineau counts an increase in fairs from 344 to 407 between 1743 and 1777.[27] If the per capita distribution of fairs in this area had prevailed throughout France, then there would have been between 15,000 and 20,000 fairs. This figure does not refer to the number of settlements with fairs, but to the number of fairs per year. In France fairs generally lasted for one day, occasionally for several days, and rarely for a week or longer. There were probably fewer long fairs than in Russia, and there were certainly more settlements with multiple fairs than in late eighteenth-century Russia.

Some of the most famous interregional and international fairs in world history took place in France. During the twelfth through fourteenth centuries, the fairs in several cities of Champagne province were reputed to be the principal meeting place of Western Europe from Italy and Spain to the Low Countries, England, and Germany. During the following two centuries the fairs of Lyon achieved exceptional fame. Although there were no French fairs with comparable reputations during the eighteenth century, a clear hierarchy of fairs continued to function with 5 to 10 fairs of interregional significance for trade in livestock or industrial goods.[28] Some of these fairs were in major cities such as Paris, Bordeaux, and Caen, but others were not. Perhaps, the two most widely noted fairs were at Beaucaire and Guibray, inconsequential settlements, serving inter-regional trade with southeast and northwest France, respectively.

The growth of French cities at least kept pace with the rise in national population during the eighteenth century, but the percentage of the French population in cities was not rising markedly. Certain ports grew rapidly while many cities showed little population change, suggesting that increased foreign trade and particularly trade with French colonies was a major factor in the dynamics of eighteenth century cities. The principal period of increase in the urban percentage throughout France was the sixteenth and seventeenth centuries. According to J. C. Russell, in the early fourteenth century, France was one of the least urbanized areas of Western Europe. The top ten cities in each of its three complete regions together included 440,000 of the total population of almost 10 million.[29] At this time, the urban percentage in France was probably somewhat below 10. Similarly to England, France experienced a phase of decentralization in the late fourteenth and fifteenth centuries that was not marked by any increase in the percentage of population in cities, and this was followed by accelerated urbanization. The rapid development of Paris during the sixteenth and seventeenth centuries must have accompanied the general increase in urbanization to almost 16 percent as a stage G society was established and matured in France.

Among these five countries France was most similar to Japan in its urban network. In both of these countries, the urban population came to approximately 16 percent of the total population. Moreover, of the seven regions in each country, two ranged between 20 and 25 percent urban, while the others were between 9 and 15 percent urban. Paris and the other major cities of north France served as a counterpart to Edo in the Kantō region, and the many cities of the coastal southeast region in France appear in this context equivalent to Osaka, Kyoto, and other major centers of the Kinki region. Aggregate figures for both countries indicate that the closest resemblance was at levels 3–5. Inhabited by roughly three-quarters as many persons as Japan, France had almost precisely three-quarters as many cities at each of these levels. In contrast, at levels 1 and 2 France was far behind, with fewer than one-third the population of Edo, Osaka, and Kyoto. This deficit was in large part compensated for by the fact that French level-3 cities were more populous than Japanese counterparts and France had many more level-6 central places. Despite its smaller population, France had about 400 more central places than Japan.

The Universe of Premodern Societies

There have been tens of thousands, perhaps even hundreds of thousands, of societies in the world. Few of them have existed in modern times and even of these only a tiny number have been modernized. From the perspective of world history, the vast majority of societies have been nonmodernized.[30] Indeed, prior to the second half of the eighteenth century, not only did all societies remain nonmodernized, none was even yet exposed to contact with modernized societies. The universe of premodern societies consists of all societies before 1750, all societies except for England and perhaps a few other Western European cases before 1800, and a gradually dwindling number of societies in the nineteenth century, with only some holdouts in remote areas persisting into the twentieth century. Premodern societies predominate in history.

Among premodern societies, many have been short-lived. Either their members have been wiped out in a disaster or they have been assimilated by other societies. Some societies incorporated into an empire cannot be identified with a distinct network of settlements since they were served by the central places of the dominant society. Frequently these were stage A nonagricultural societies located in mountainous, desert, or frontier areas under the administrative jurisdiction of the population of a society at a more advanced stage. Other premodern societies evolved from stage to stage, preserving territorial continuity and the legacy of previous stages. The five countries selected for comparative treatment in this book all fit this last category, each having experienced six or seven types of premodern societies as reflected in the stages of their urban networks.

As the world's population has been rising over thousands of years, the average size of societies has been increasing. The number of separate societies probably fell into decline well before the development of modern communications during the nineteenth century. Fewer societies expanded to occupy more settled territory. The more advanced the stage of a society, the more populous it was likely to have been. Stage A societies remained small, generally with only some tens of thousands of persons sparsely distributed as were the various American Indian tribes. At the other extreme among premodern cases, stage G societies were apt to have populations in the millions, and, where urban networks were complete, populations ranged as high as tens or hundreds of millions. In comparing urban development, it is important to know the scale of societies as well as their stages.

Estimates of the world's population over 3,000 years and of the distribution of that population at selected intervals in societies at stages A through G are presented in Graphs 3 and 4.[31] For almost the entire 3,000 years, a single society, China, comprised more than half of the world's population in the most advanced stage of society existing at the time. In contrast, the steadily diminishing percentage of the world's population in stage A societies continued to be distributed among thousands or even tens of thousands of small-scale entities. While the population in stage A societies had been declining to probably fewer than 10 percent of the nearly 1 billion inhabitants of the world in 1800, the proportion of all societies represented by the stage A type continued to exceed 90.

A tremendous growth in world population after 1500 accompanied the emergence of stage G societies. At the same time, stage G societies signified an increase in urbanization. In every instance, these societies appear to have been more urbanized than previous societies on the same territory. The simultaneous growth of population and of cities meant that a large percentage of all premodern urban residents were found during the period 1550 to 1800 in stage G societies. In Japan roughly 60 percent of all urban residents before 1800 lived in cities during the brief span between 1600 and 1800. In the Russian Empire, close to 45 percent of urban residents before 1800 can be attributed to the final century, and as many as 30 percent lived in cities during just the second half of the eighteenth century. In China, with its much longer history of cities and more gradual urban de-

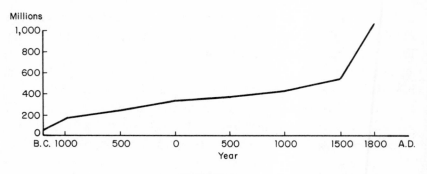

GRAPH 3.
The Premodern World Population

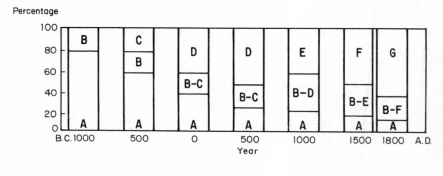

GRAPH 4.
Distribution of World Population in Societies at Stages A-G

velopment, about 25 percent of all urban residents before 1800 inhabited cities from the second half of the sixteenth century when the stage G phase of development was entered.

Stage G societies reigned as the elite of premodern societies. They were the most populous and the most urbanized. A close look at the societies of the world around 1800 will permit a more exact statement of the relative position of stage G societies before we proceed to compare five societies of this type.

In Table 25, the world's population has been divided according to country, with a distinction made between those countries integrated into a single administrative unit and decentralized congeries of

TABLE 25

Estimates of World Population by Countries in 1800

Country	Population (millions)	
	Relatively centralized	Relatively decentralized
China	300	
India		195
Russian Empire	39	
Japan	30	
France	26	
Austria-Hungary		20–25
Ottoman Empire	20–25	
Germany		20–25
Great Britain	16	
Italy		14
Indonesia		13
Spain	10	
Korea	7	
United States	5	
Persia	5	
Others	15–20	230
Total	500	475

states which in some cases do not merit being classified together as a single country. Half of the world's population resided in centralized China and decentralized India. Two-thirds of the world's total lived in countries with a minimum of 20 million inhabitants, and three-quarters of the total lived in the 15 countries identified as having populations in excess of 5 million.[32] The focus of our comparisons is the Russian Empire (4 percent of the world's population), East Asia (35 percent of the world's population), and Western Europe (11 percent of the world's population). Together, these three zones with an estimated population of 480–485 million represented one-half of the world in 1800. They included the four largest centralized countries and nine of the thirteen largest entities referred to here as countries.

The dominance of these three zones is even more evident in their urban records. Together they encompassed approximately two-thirds of the world's population in urban settlements.[33] In other words, this half of the world was on the average twice as urban as the other half. In 1800 their collective urban population reached considerably more than 40 million, perhaps approaching or exceeding 45 million. Scattered through the rest of the world were fewer urban residents and correspondingly fewer great cities.

It is apparent from Table 26 that considerably more than half and probably as many as two-thirds of the world's great cities in 1800 were located in these three zones. Of up to 70 cities with more than 100,000 inhabitants, approximately 24 were in China (see the note at the end of the table indicating that these Chinese data refer to the 1830s), 5 were in Japan, 1 was in Korea, 2 were in the Russian Empire, and 15 were in Western Europe.

Approximately one-quarter of the world's urban population in 1800 (with some upward adjustment in urban figures necessary for Chinese data from a few decades later) resided in these 65–70 cities.[34] This group, representing the world's largest cities, encompassed a total of roughly 16–17 million residents. The next group of cities, with 30,000 to 100,000 residents, was decidedly more numerous. In this range there numbered roughly 86 cities in China, 18 in Japan, and 70 in Western Europe in addition to the 4 in the Russian Empire. Altogether there were probably at least 280 cities within this population range, contributing 13–14 million to the world's urban total. Cities at level 4 with 10,000 to 30,000 population numbered 200 in China, 60 in Japan, and at least 200 in Western Europe in addition to the 28 in the Russian Empire. Throughout the world there may have been 700 or 800 cities at this level, registering a combined population of 10–12 million. From the above estimates we see that probably close to 40 million persons inhabited more than 1,000 cities with a minimum of 10,000 residents.

Most cities did not reach these population levels. Within these three zones there were about 2,500 cities with populations between 3,000 and 10,000. This would suggest a minimum of 4,000 level-5 cities in the world, registering a total population of roughly 20 million. According to the definition of urban used here, one-half of the

TABLE 26

The World's Largest Cities in 1800[a]

A. 500,000–1,000,000 or more	D. 100,000–200,000
1. Edo (Tokyo)	32. Tientsin
2. Peking	33. Lisbon
3. London	34. Calcutta
4. Soochow	35. Murshidabad
5. Wuhan	36. Benares
6. Nanking	37. Amarapura
7. Canton	38. Bombay
8. Istanbul	39. Rome
9. Paris	40. Madrid
10. Hangchow	41. Berlin
	42. Milan
B. 300,000–500,000	43. Palermo
11. Foochow	44. Venice
12. Chungking	45. Baghdad
13. Chengtu	46. Yang-chou
14. Naples	47. Tsi-ning
15. Osaka	48. Kanazawa
16. Kyoto	49. Nagoya
17. St. Petersburg	50. Chen-chiang
18. Lucknow	51. Lyon
19. Sian	52. Tabriz
	53. Lin-ch'ing
C. 200,000–300,000	54. T'ai-yuan
20. Cairo	55. Wu-hu
21. Ch'ang-sha	56. Ch'ang-chou
22. Nan-ch'ang	57. Hsiang-t'an
23. Ching te-chen	58. Hamburg
24. Vienna	59. Warsaw
25. Moscow	60. Mexico City
26. Patna	61. Dacca
27. Amsterdam	62. Ahmadabad
28. Seoul	63. Surat
29. Fo-shan	64. Delhi
30. K'ai-feng	65. Madras
31. Hyderabad	66. Smyrna

[a] Three cautions should be kept in mind in using this list of cities. First, the list is likely to be incomplete for areas of the world not examined in this study. Second, the ordering of cities becomes less certain the further we go down the list. Third, the data on China refer to the 1830s when the national population had already climbed to about 400 million and correspondingly the urban total had risen.

population in level-6 centers also must be counted as urban. This probably adds about ten percent to the roughly 60 million already calculated in urban settlements. These estimates conservatively total to at least 60 and more likely 65 million city dwellers in 5,000 fully urban settlements and roughly 12,000 semi-urban level-6 centers.

From the preceding discussion, it should be clear that the societies chosen for comparisons with stage G Russian society ranked as large-scale, centralized, and exceptional centers of urbanization. These four societies occupied parts of the two zones in the world that dominated as the centers of development of stage G societies— East Asia and Western Europe. France and England, comprising somewhat less than one-third of the population of Western Europe, and China and Japan, constituting all of East Asia except for relatively small Korea, represented together with the Russian Empire at least 40 percent of the world's population in 1800.

Comparisons of Urban Networks in Five Countries

China, England, France, Japan, and the Russian Empire, in the decades chosen for comparative study, each contained from 800 to 31,500 central places and from 1.1 to 24 million urban residents as previously calculated in tables for each of these countries. The figures for the number of central places at the various levels for all of these countries are juxtaposed in Table 27 and cumulative percentages are contrasted in Graphs 5 and 6. Using the totals for all central places, two indices provide a preliminary basis for comparisons. The first index offers a calculation of the average population per central place. Ranging from about 7,000 to 17,000 persons, this average was lowest for England followed by France and was highest for Japan and the Russian Empire. This comparison signifies that the smallest concentrations of population gave rise to central places in the Western European countries, while the largest average populations per central place prevailed in the most densely settled country, Japan, and the least densely settled country, the Russian Empire. The second calculation gives the average urban population per central place, most of which were, of course, at level 7 and therefore not urban although they formed part of the marketing hierarchy supporting urban populations. In this respect, China registered the smallest av-

TABLE 27

Comparative Distribution of Central Places in 5 Stage G Societies

Level	Number of central places					Percentage of central places					Percentage of urban population in central places				
	E	F	R	J	C	E	F	R	J	C	E	F	R	J	C
1	1	1	1	1	1	0	0	0	0	0	47	16	13	18	4
2	0	0	1	2	9	0	0	0	0	0	0	0	9	15	20
3	0	15	4	20	100	0	1	0	1	0	0	24	6	18	28
4	7	48	28	60	200	1	2	2	3	1	8	19	18	18	14
5	75	230	210	250	1100	9	10	13	17	3	33	31	46	27	22
6	255	700	300	400	6000	32	32	18	22	19	11	9	10	4	12
7	460	1200	1100	1000	24000	58	55	67	56	76	—	—	—	—	—
Total	800	2200	1650	1750	31500										

Urban percentage

E	20–21
F	16
R	8–9
J	17–18
C	6–7

E = England and Wales (population: 5.5 million)
F = France (population: 23 million)
R = Russian Empire (population: 28 million)
J = Japan (population: 30 million)
C = China (population: 400 million)

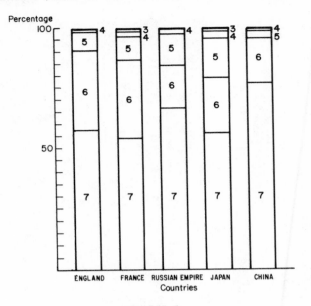

GRAPH 5.

Cumulative Percent of Central Places in 5 Countries

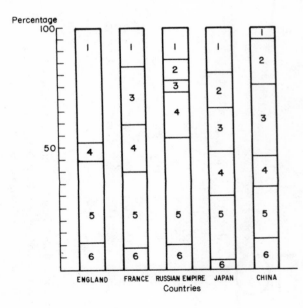

GRAPH 6.

Cumulative Percent of Urban Population in 5 Countries

erage with only 800, while Japan represents the other extreme with an average of roughly 3,000 persons for each settlement at levels 1–7. These figures provide one measure of the efficiency of the urban hierarchy, with Japan requiring the fewest settlements per capita to support its urban residents. England, France, and the Russian Empire appear quite similar in this respect, varying only from about 1,400 to 1,700 city dwellers per central place.

The efficiency of the urban hierarchy can be calculated in at least two additional ways: first by omitting level-7 settlements in order to determine the average urban population per urban and semi-urban location and second by omitting the semi-urban level-6 places as well in order to calculate the average number of urban residents per full-fledged city. The averages for each country using each of the three methods of calculation are presented in Table 28. In the calculation

TABLE 28

Measures of the Efficiency of the Urban Hierarchy

	Urban population	Urban population	Urban population
	Total of central places	Central places at levels 1–6	Central places at levels 1–5
England	1,400	3,200	13,000
France	1,700	3,700	13,000
Russian Empire	1,400	4,200	9,400
Japan	3,000	6,400	16,000
China	800	3,200	17,000

based on levels 1–6, Japan continues to show the highest population per central place, the Russian Empire stands second, and China has caught up to England. However, the ordering of countries changes sharply in the averages of urban population based on cities at levels 1–5. Now Russia, with its predominance of relatively small cities at level 5, exhibits the smallest average, while China, with disproportionately few level-5 centers, tops the list with an average of 17,000.

England's high figure of more than 20 percent urban reflected a large concentration of central places at levels 1 to 5 in relation to the national population (one for every 66,000 persons as opposed to one for every 80,000–110,000 in France, Japan and Russia and only one for every 280,000 or more persons in China). The Russian urban percentage was much lower than the figures for Japan and France because of the prevalence of level-5 cities, while the Chinese percentage would have been even lower than it was if not for the abundance of large cities among central places at levels 1 to 5.

Comparisons of the distribution of central places at various adjoining levels provide more specific indicators of the ways in which the urban network fits together in these five countries. The ratio of level-7 to level-6 settlements serves as a guide to the efficiency of resource movement at the most local level, the smaller this ratio, the greater the number of semi-urban places supported by a given number of standard marketing settlements. In these countries, the ratio ranged between 4:1 and less than 2:1. England and France stood out with ratios below 2:1, Japan followed at 2.5:1 and China trailed at 4:1.

A second ratio measures the number of level-6 places for each level-5 center. In this regard, greater efficiency characterized the Japanese and Russian networks with ratios of less than 1.6:1, while China ranked last with a figure of about 5.5:1. Ranging between roughly 1.4:1 and 5.5:1, this ratio shows greater variation than the preceding ratio between centers at levels 7 and 6. In both cases, the largest number of lower level places gave rise to the smallest number of higher level centers in China.

One final ratio between settlements at adjoining levels should suffice for this approach to comparing the distribution of central places. For each level-4 city in these countries, there could be counted between 4.2 level-5 centers (in Japan) and 10.7 level-5 centers (in England). While France and China were not far behind the Japanese level, the Russian Empire trailed considerably with a ratio of 7.5:1. Unlike England, Russia was of sufficient scale to support as many level-4 centers in proportion to its level-5 centers as in the other countries. This ratio exposes an inefficient link in Russia's urban network.

All three of these ratios can be visualized from the rounded off figures given in Table 27 for the percentage of central places at each of the seven levels. From these calculations, we learn that at level 6

England and France were exceptionally developed; at level 5 Japan and Russia stood out in development; and at level 4 France, Japan, and China all revealed similar urban concentration in relation to the central places at the level just below. Considered in terms of the countries that were lagging at specific levels, these ratios show China well behind at levels 5 and 6, while England and Russia were under-represented at level 4.

Identical conclusions can be reached from the figures in Table 27 on the percentage of the urban population in central places at the various levels. Comparing the distribution at levels 5 and 6, we see that Japan and Russia had ratios of 6.8:1 and 4.6:1, respectively, while the Chinese ratio reached only 1.8:1. A given number of residents in level-6 centers gave rise to a much smaller population in level-5 cities in China than in these other countries. The comparison of levels 4 and 5 shows England and Russia trailing.

In light of the above comparisons, we can consider the unusual qualities of each country's urban network separately, beginning with the Russian network. One of the most striking characteristics of Russia's urban network is the enormous concentration of urban residents in level-5 cities in relation to all settlements above and below. In contrast, level-4 and particularly level-3 cities were weakly represented considering the number of central places and urban residents at the level just below. Nevertheless, despite its weak base at levels 3 and 4, the Russian Empire proved quite successful in supporting as much as 22 percent of its urban population in cities at levels 1 and 2. In brief, this country, with relatively few central places for its total population and quite a high percentage of all central places at level 7, supported a high ratio of urban population per central place, and over two-thirds of these city dwellers resided in places at levels 1, 2, and 5.

Japan's urban network resembled the Russian network in the large average population per central place and in the high ratio of level-5 to level-6 settlements. Unlike Russia, at no level was the Japanese efficiency ratio markedly low. Japan surpassed China and Russia in getting resources from level 7 to level 6; along with Russia it was in the lead in moving resources from level 6 to level 5; and along with China it both supported the largest level-4 population in relation to the population in level-5 settlements and counted the unusually high figure of more than 50 percent of urban residents in cities at levels 1–3. Except for England, which because of its small scale was weakly developed at levels 2–4, Japan showed the highest percentage of city dwellers in national centers at levels 1 and 2. With 21 percent of all central places at levels 1–5, Japan easily exceeded the other countries including Russia with 15 percent, France with 13 percent, England with 10 percent, and China with only 4 percent. In any overall measure of efficiency, Japan's urban network must rank at or near the top.

Undoubtedly the least efficient network for moving resources from the lowest to the highest levels existed in China. Although China's ratio of total population to central places ranked midway between England and France on one end and Japan and the Russian Empire on the other, level-7 standard markets constituted a disproportionate share of the total. Level-5 cities were scarce relative to the total number of central places, and the urban population of China was concentrated fairly heavily in higher level cities. This indicates a certain efficiency in moving resources up the urban ladder from level 5 that was lacking at lower levels.

One of the distinguishing features of England and France in these five-country comparisons was the large number of level-6 centers present for a given number of level-7 settlements. Indeed, the urban networks of these two Western European countries were remarkably similar at levels 5–7, and the differences between them at higher levels may be attributed to the smaller scale of England, allowing London to appropriate functions normally assumed not only by cities at level 3 but also for much of England and Wales at level 4. Neither England nor France sustained a population sufficient to require the presence of a level-2 city before the urban network reached completion. Setting aside differences between these two countries resulting from problems of scale, their overall networks appear more similar than any other pair studied. England did reveal greater concentration of resources at the top of the hierarchy, however, and also required smaller hinterland populations per central place at levels 5–7.

The meaning of these comparisons should be explored in many ways, taking full consideration of such factors as transportation conditions, population densities, and regional variations within countries.

Yet, based on the high degree of consistency between regions found in the examination of networks within separate areas of countries and on other information pertaining to spatial aspects of social structure, I am prepared to hypothesize that none of the explanations of different distributions in networks pointing to natural endowments, crop selection, or technological innovations as the principal factor is correct. Instead, I hypothesize that characteristic urban patterns must be explained in terms of gradually evolving networks with a momentum to fill in spaces and expand integrated units in accord with existing conditions although also subject to modification through new administrative divisions of the country, revised systems of taxation, rents, and land ownership, and newly established commercial organizations that altered the flow of resources into cities. Further comparative study should be directed at determining how differences in the number of central places at various levels originated. In the absence of such a study, we must confine our attention to what these differences may have signified for various types of centralization.

First, why do countries vary in the total number of central places per capita? My initial explanation is that the smaller the average population in the hinterland of each central place, the greater the participation of individual rural households in marketing activities was likely to have been. In turn, this level of participation presumably related inversely to the degree to which labor was utilized by interfamilial groupings without remuneration through wage payments and inversely to the level of taxation in kind and rent payments in kind to absentee landlords. The highest averages of population per central place, which were registered in Japan and Russia, accordingly may have related to the considerable taxation in kind in the former country and to the system of serf labor in the latter. In like manner, the lowest averages, found in England and France, could have reflected decidedly different conditions of taxation and labor utilization. Presumably China's intermediate position resulted from a lower level of taxation, especially payments in kind, than in Japan and the predominance of small peasant proprietors actively involved in commerce although marketing less than rural inhabitants in Western Europe.

Second, what accounts for variations in the ratio of the number of places at levels 1–6 to the number at level 7? In this case any explanation must take into account the movement upwards of resources that have already passed into the hands of merchants or administrators. Having 42–45 percent of all central places at levels 1–6, England, France, and Japan can be contrasted to Russia with 33 percent and China with only 24 percent of central places that did not function solely as standard markets. These figures, which provide a ranking of countries roughly in accord with that obtained from the overall national urban percentages, reflect the centralizing forces in the society. My tentative explanation here is that, where the percentage of central places at level 6 was high, commercial forms of local centralization appear to have been advanced. Large amounts of marketed goods forwarded commercially probably gave rise to the high figures for England and France, while conversely the low figure for China indicated a considerable circulation of goods limited to the confines of a single market without finding its way up the urban hierarchy. This conclusion regarding China is consistent with what is known about the rural concentration of the Chinese elite and the low level of taxation.

A corresponding hypothesis (as in other comparisons of stage G societies, based on the second set of definitions of the seven levels) for level-5 central places would be: the higher the percentage of the urban population in cities at this level as opposed to level-6 places, the greater the development of local administrative centralization. Japan and Russia stood out with 68–75 percent as many central places at level 5 as at level 6, which contrasts sharply to figures of 18 to 33 percent elsewhere. In both countries large numbers of new local administrative centers had been designated during or after the transition to stage G societies, and major reforms were directed at increasing revenues in these cities. Moreover, closely regulated merchants operating from administrative centers monopolized certain facets of local commerce. Compensating for the weak development of level-6 centers in relation to England and France, these two countries, largely through deliberate efforts at social engineering, had greatly strengthened local administration.

Beyond the local area, intermediate possibilities existed for high degrees of resource concentration below the national centers at levels 1 and 2. The third question is what accounts for a high percentage of the urban population in levels 3 and 4. It was in France and China that the urban percentages subsumed by these two levels were highest. In these countries, relatively populous regional centers, especially ones at level 3, remained quite autonomous in the accumulation of resources, not funneling large amounts into national centers. This may have been related to the weakness of mechanisms for concentrating tax resources and to the dispersed pattern of distribution of the country's elite.

In retrospect, from this approach to channeling resources up the urban hierarchy, England and Japan appear unusually developed with respect to cities at levels 1 and 2. With only 0.6 and 3.1 percent, respectively, of the world's population, these countries supported two of the world's three largest cities, and Japan also counted two other cities in the top twenty of 1800 (with Chinese data referring to the 1830s). It is even possible that earlier in the eighteenth century as many as three Japanese cities should be ranked in the select top ten. China and Russia followed in urban concentration at levels 1 and 2, while France trailed sharply with only 16 percent of its urban population in cities of this rank. The fourth question concerns what accounts for differences at this level. Among the factors to explore in considering this divergence is the possibility that merchant groupings in England and Japan were more hierarchically organized on a national basis and that elite consumption patterns relied heavily in these two countries on goods obtained only from the national centers.

In summary, using this narrow notion of centralization, which refers to the mobilization of resources on which urban populations were sustained, England appears advanced in individual commercial participation, local commercial centralization, and national centralization. France shares the first two traits but replaces national with regional centralization. Japan appears advanced in both local administrative and national centralization. Russia resembles Japan in local administrative centralization, and China stands out as weakly centralized except at the regional level. These generalizations are noted in Table 29.

Having examined basic differences in urban networks, we may now return to similarities in an effort to understand better what

TABLE 29

Countries Overrepresented at Various Levels of the Urban Network

Level	Country	Designation
1 & 2	England and Japan	National centralization
3 & 4	China and France	Regional centralization
5	Japan and Russia	Local administrative centralization
6	England and France	Local commercial centralization
7	England and France	Individual commercial participation

causes characteristic distributions of central places. First we will consider separately cities that are classified as administrative centers. Second we will explore the set of integrated areas ranging from local to national markets.

Among the central places in all five countries can be distinguished centers at various levels in an administrative hierarchy. In each country at least 80 percent of urban populations consisted of residents of cities with administrative functions. Especially in Russia and Japan, where more than 90 percent of city dwellers were in cities of this type, recent reforms had speeded the development of administrative centers. Of course, in all of these countries cities in the administrative hierarchy also occupied rungs on the ladder of marketing activities. Large urban populations reflected relatively high positions in the marketing hierarchy supported by subordinate periodic marketing centers without administrative functions and by other administrative centers as well. Keeping in mind this close interdependence of administrative and marketing functions, we can focus our comparisons on the administrative patterns of the five countries.

In each country, a basic unit of local administration can be identified. The uezd in Russia had its counterparts in the English county, the Chinese hsien, and, in a less exact way, the Japanese han and the French éléction. To a remarkable extent, the number of these basic units present in each country turns out to have been a function of the national population. There were about 1,600 local administrative units in China, 376 in France, 301 in core areas of Russia, 255 in Japan, and 40 in England. Actually China was relatively underrepresented since these 1,600 units registered an average population of

250,000 by the 1830s; however if we keep in mind that the Chinese population had numbered between 80 and 150 million during most of the previous millennium when hsien were largely confirmed in their boundaries, then these administrative units likewise appear as areas with 50,000 to 100,000 inhabitants. Japan also gives the impression of having been underrepresented by administrative units, but since more than one-quarter of the national population resided in areas not divided into han, the mean population per administrative unit, in fact, did not exceed 100,000. Indeed, at the time the boundaries of most han were demarcated, the average population probably numbered close to 60,000. Furthermore, in areas of Japan directly under central administration, separate units of administration were often designated with populations of roughly 60,000 to 70,000. English counties also correspond to this pattern. They fully emerged at a time when the national population was climbing from below two to more than three million. By the 1680s they averaged nearly 110,000 persons, if we calculate by excluding London from the population divided between counties. Finally élections and comparable units in France shared a population averaging roughly 60,000 by the 1760s, up slightly from the beginning of the century.

These observations concerning the prevalence of local administrative units of a similar size should be qualified with an awareness that averages conceal varying distributions in the five countries. The deliberate effort to equalize populations of uezd in the 1770s meant that these basic units in Russia showed relatively slight deviation from national averages. In contrast, Chinese hsien ranged from fewer than 50,000 to more than one million persons, and most Japanese han held populations of just 10,000 to 50,000 while a small number of han counted more than 500,000 residents. Despite these qualifications, the frequency of local units ranging in population from about 50,000 to somewhat more than 100,000 suggests that some benefit was obtained in premodern societies, at least those at stage G, from choosing units on this order. In the light of these similarities, one wonders if the excessive population in hsien starting in the late eighteenth century did not contribute to the breakdown in China's local administration that has often been noted for the nineteenth century.

Recurrent similarities in population figures also characterized superior administrative units in three of these countries. Following the government reforms of 1775–1785 in Russia, the newly designated guberniia became the superior administrative unit. It had no counterpart in England (understandable because of the small national population) or in Japan, in which a hierarchy of feudal loyalties and a system of alternate residences affecting the lords of all han served as a remarkably efficient bridge between local and central administration. However, comparable units can be identified in China and France. In China, hsien or equivalent units were generally grouped into fu, of which there were roughly 180. In France, the 32 provinces provide the closest parallel amid a complex pattern of units serving a variety of administrative functions. At this administrative level, the number of units per country again corresponds quite closely to what one would expect from national population figures, with the qualification again that Chinese population growth by the nineteenth century caused fu to far exceed the 700,000 to 900,000 inhabitants probably once common in these units as in the corresponding units elsewhere.

Mention should also be made of the 18 sheng or provinces, which provided China with an even higher administrative unit, embracing populations that had originally averaged close to 10 million. By 1830 these units averaged more than 20 million inhabitants. A unit at the level of the sheng obviously proved unnecessary in countries with populations of no more than a few tens of millions.

From these comparisons, a composite view of administrative units below the national level can be constructed. In a relatively small country whose population numbered in the millions, a single local administrative unit sufficed, encompassing about 60,000 to 100,000 residents. In turn, larger countries with populations in the tens of millions added a second superior administrative unit that embraced roughly some 700,000 to 900,000 residents. Finally the world's only centralized country with a population well in excess of 100 million supported a third administrative unit, which during long periods of relatively efficient administration contained populations averaging approximately 10 million.

Additional similarities in the distribution of the urban population at various administrative levels can be discerned from Table 30. First

TABLE 30

Percentages of Total Urban Population in Administrative Centers

| | Ranks of Administrative Centers | | |
	National & Regional	Intermediate	Local
China	30	21	35
Japan	35	—	55–60
Russia (core areas)	31	25	38
England	46	—	35–40
France	16	33	40–45

we observe that, in cities with highest administrative functions, some 30 to 35 percent of the national urban population generally was concentrated. Russia's two capitals, Japan's three national centers, and China's two capitals plus 18 sheng seats embraced between 30 and 35 percent of the total urban population within their respective countries. While London's proportion of England's urban total exceeded this level, it absorbed most of the population that would normally have been found in intermediate administrative centers. Only the French case clearly does not fit the expected pattern. Paris contributed only 16 percent of the national urban population, and France had no other national centers. Part of this weakness at the highest administrative levels in France was compensated for by the relatively strong showing of provincial cities, exceeding the percentage of urban residents associated with intermediate cities elsewhere. A possible explanation for France's poor showing in national centers may have been the general weakness of the national administration. Indeed, transport in France was impeded by a host of local tolls along rivers and at entrances to towns. Similar barriers to trade had been largely removed by central authorities in the other countries.

In order to systematize comparisons of the development of levels of central places in relation to the populations of their hinterlands, we should consider a third hierarchical pattern in premodern societies. So far seven levels of central places have been proposed, and seven stages of societies have been suggested in which increasing numbers of levels were present. Frequent reference has been made to the hypothesis that, as more levels of central places emerge and a more developed societal stage is reached, wider areas with larger populations become integrated first administratively and then commercially. It follows that a hierarchy of areas of integration parallels the hierarchy of central places. The examination of this hierarchy for stage G societies will be useful in clarifying the manner in which administrative and marketing units overlap.

Settlements at levels 5, 6, and 7 have been frequently referred to as serving local areas. Correspondingly we can designate three areas of local integration. The smallest of these local units is the standard marketing area (area VII), in most cases centering on a level-7 settlement but in some cases absorbed into the hinterland of a higher level settlement.[35] Generally, some ten to forty settlements would be integrated into this basic unit of rural interaction. The actual number of settlements differed from country to country, and within each country varied partly as a function of population density, transportation availability, type of terrain, and other factors. Subtracting the urban population from the national population, we find that the average number of persons in a standard marketing area ranged from about 5,550 in England and 8,800 in France to 11,900 in China, 13,800 in Japan, and 15,600 in Russia. Since Russian rural settlements were the least populous, it is clear that considerably more settlements constituted standard marketing areas there. Rural settlements were probably larger in China and Japan than in England and France, and correspondingly the populations of standard marketing areas were noticeably greater in the East Asian countries.

Together, these countries with a total population of almost 490 million encompassed roughly 38,000 standard marketing areas. All societies at stages E–G were likewise endowed with integrative units of this kind. If we generalize to a world of one billion persons (400 million in China plus 600 million in other societies at stages E–G around the turn of the nineteenth century), then we should envision almost 80,000 area VIIs as the basic units of local integration beyond the rural settlement. As Table 31 indicates, each standard marketing area of roughly 10,000–15,000 persons comprised roughly .001 percent of this idealized world.

TABLE 31

Areas of Integration in a World of Stage G Societies

Area	Designation	Examples	Population range (millions)	Percentage of world population
Ia	Largest society	China	400	40
Ib	Region of largest society	Chinese region	55–110	8
II	Very large administrative unit	Chinese sheng, France, Japan, Russia	15–40	2–3
III	Large administrative unit	England or region of France, Japan, Russia	2–6	.5
IV	Intermediate administrative unit	Region of England, French province, guberniia, fu	.5–1	.1
V	Standard admin. unit or central mark. area		.06–.12	.01–.02
VI	Intermediate marketing area		.02–.05	.005
VII	Standard marketing area		.005–.015	.001

The second smallest unit into which settlements are grouped is the intermediate marketing area. There appear to have been two basic patterns of these local units. First there was the pattern most prevalent in China, but also evident to a lesser degree in the other countries. This pattern was characterized by standard marketing areas separately centered on level-7 central places, which in turn were incorporated into the greater hinterlands of one or more level-6 central places. Accordingly a level-6 marketing center served a hinterland containing one to five (in China usually three or four) subordinate level-7 centers. Frequently standard markets were dependent on two or three intermediate markets and a given level-6 center might have as many as six level-7 centers at least partially dependent on it. The alternate pattern, most prevalent in England, France, and Japan but also evident in Russia and China, was characterized by level-6 central places lacking support from lower level markets while directly serving their own standard and intermediate marketing areas. In both patterns intermediate marketing areas (area VI) centered on level-6 settlements.

Altogether there were about 10,000 intermediate marketing areas in these five countries, each serving an average of somewhat fewer than 46,000 persons after subtracting for residents of higher-level cities. In China, where these areas generally encompassed parts of at least three or four standard marketing areas, they averaged over 50,000 persons, while in England they averaged fewer than 14,000, and in France fewer than 20,000 persons. Russian areas were almost as populous as Chinese areas, averaging close to 48,000 persons, and Japanese areas numbered about 32,000 in average population. In Table 31 we see that a world of 1 billion persons in societies of stages F–G would have consisted of about 20,000 of these units.

The largest of the three local units was the central marketing area. Characteristically, this area centered on a level-5 city, which combined administrative and marketing functions. In these five countries there were more than 1,900 level-5 cities. In addition, all 400 central places at higher levels served simultaneously as nodes of central marketing areas. Again subtracting urban populations in higher-level cities from the national population, we find about 200,000 persons in the average central marketing area. This average is deceptive because the figure for China reached almost 280,000, while in the other countries it ranged from slightly over 110,000 in the Russian Empire to 59,000 in England and Wales. The order of these five countries with respect to the average population in a central marketing area was the inverse of the order of these countries in overall urbanization. England and China were at opposite poles, while Japan and France were almost even.

Integration at the level of the central marketing unit as at the level of the intermediate marketing unit was achieved in stage F societies. On this basis, new potentialities existed for local centralization through administrative measures. Local administration could now be based on commercially integrated areas, providing governments with new opportunities for mobilizing resources. Reorganization of the fiscal system, of commercial associations, of the distribution of production to the elite, and of the places of administration could make possible an increased flow of goods from local areas.

In most places the central marketing unit corresponded to the standard administrative unit, i.e., the uezd, the county, the éléction, the hsien, or the han. Cities at level 5 were normally the points at which the central government actively intervened to shape local conditions. Although for many purposes it is important to distinguish between central marketing units and local administrative units, for the purpose of generalizing about the basic areas of the world we can refer to both of these units as area V. These areas would each have represented from .020–.035 percent of the world population of 1 billion. If, however, we regard Chinese administrative units as excessive in population by the 1830s and consider a population of 100,000 to be representative of standard administrative units, then each of these areas would have been equivalent to .01–.02 of the world's population. In England and Japan, there were more level-5 cities (centers of central marketing units) than local administrative centers, however; in Russia there were fewer than half as many level-5 cities as uezd; and in France there were fewer than two-thirds as many level-5 cities as éléction.

Integration beyond the local area took place at the level of the intermediate administrative unit. In these five countries, there were about 400 cities at levels 1–4. Theoretically, in a world of 1 billion where such units were universal, there would have been about 800 cities of this size. The population in the average area served by each of these cities was slightly more than the .1 percent of the world population total registered in Table 31.

English regions, French provinces, and Russian guberniia all had populations that were in the general range of 500,000–1,000,000 associated with intermediate administrative units. In Japan, however, there was no administrative unit at this level, and in China by the 1830s fu had substantially larger populations than did the intermediate administrative units in the other three countries. If we take the average fu population prior to the population spurt from the late eighteenth century, then we can use the narrower population range of 500,000 to 1,000,000, as we used a narrow range based on earlier populations for hsien in generalizing about area V.

While area IV refers to intermediate administrative units, area III signifies large administrative units. England and Wales constituted an area of this type as did the regions of France, Japan, and the Russian Empire. An area with a population of 2–6 million generally gave rise to one or more level-3 cities, but in the case of England, where this area was not integrated into any larger unit, a single level-1 city developed without any supporting centers at levels 2 or 3. It is likely that stage F societies were already capable of supporting the commercial integration of areas of this size. England became a single integrated area at a time when larger countries still lacked a national market.

The largest countries in the world in 1800, other than China and India, qualify as area IIs. Comprising about 2–3 percent of the world's population, they could support a full network of seven levels of central places or, as in France, could still be small enough to bypass level 2. The equivalent to these areas in China were the 18 sheng, most of which were in the population range of 15–40 million.

Among the five countries examined, only China had areas with even larger populations than 40 million. The symbol Ib refers to the regions of China, all but one of which had populations of 55 or more million, and the symbol Ia stands for all of China.

Applications of the Urban Networks Approach

The most basic use of this approach is as a systematic method of periodization. By identifying seven levels of central places and specifying seven stages of premodern history in terms of the number and types of levels present, this system makes possible the assignment of each premodern country at any point in history to a single societal type. For the first time this makes available a typology including all premodern societies that states unambiguously which characteristics qualify a country for assignment to a given societal type. At the same time, this approach to the development of central places satisfies a second requirement of a system of periodization; it identifies an ordered sequence of societal types. Accompanying the sequential advance through stages of history, successively enlarged areas of integration appeared. It is these areas of integration that make understandable the trend of evolutionary societal development.

Evidence from China, Japan, and Russia together with preliminary information on England and France support the hypothesis that the basic pattern of social change in premodern countries is directional, cumulative, and immanent within existing conditions. In no case have I documented a reversal from a more to a less developed stage and, with the rare exception of colonization or borrowing from stage D societies, foreign diffusion in these countries did not make possible skipping any of the stages of development. Evolution internal to each country gave rise to widened areas of integration focused on central places. This maturation of urban networks marked the inexorable course of social change lasting between 1,000 and 3,500 or more years in these countries.

The seven stages of evolution in premodern countries reflect seven basic patterns of organizing space through the integration of administrative and commercial activities. In stage A societies regular integrative functions remain confined to individual settlements. Eventually an important barrier is passed when the first urban societies emerge at stage B. These societies are characterized by higher levels of integration, taking the form of the regular movement of goods primarily through administrative measures from rural areas to separate, relatively isolated cities. A tributary relationship can be said to have existed, whereby residents of surrounding areas owed a lord and his subordinates in the city regular payments of goods and services. Subsequently the area of integration based primarily on administrative measures widens to encompass two levels of cities, including both local centers and state capitals. Finally on the foundation of these societies at stage C the vastly expanded boundaries of an imperial stage D society are reached. The greatest of the empires realized populations of nearly 100 million, counting up to four levels of administrative centers and sustaining local commerce within closely regulated markets located in these cities. As these empires either collapsed or gradually evolved, the old patterns of administrative centralization loosened and new patterns of commercial centralization began to develop. The first phases of commercial centralization have deceptively left the impression of a step backward away from city growth and state control. Based on the evidence from these countries, I would suggest that it is more correct to interpret these phases as a universal retooling essential for proceeding toward new heights of centralization. First, area VII integration creates the opportunity for mass participation in commerce; then area VI integration bridges the gap between administrative centers and local markets; and finally successively wider areas of commercial linkage utilize the existing skeleton of the long-evolving administrative hierarchy. Whereas stage D societies nurture an embryonic national market confined chiefly to luxury products and stage F societies sustain an intermediate form of adolescent national marketing involving certain necessities, only in stage G societies do mature, integrated national markets prevail. Precisely this pattern of expanding integration identified in the histories of the five countries examined gives meaning to the notion of a single underlying evolutionary path of development.

Presumably the urban networks approach is only one of many possible systems of periodization that would meet the criterion of classifying all premodern countries century by century as specific types of societies at successive stages of development. In the absence of attempts to devise alternative approaches, it is premature to consider how other systems of periodization might compare with the one adopted here. For the moment, it should be sufficient to point to the superiority of the urban networks approach in comparison to the Marxist and tripartite viewpoints as described in Chapter 1. This superiority lies in greater clarity, precision, quantification, and other features that establish a firm basis for drawing explicit comparisons between societies. Whereas the rough tools for comparison of these old viewpoints confuse the relative positions of the five countries examined here, this new system of periodization enables us to determine the exact course of urban change.

In the final analysis, the value of any approach to periodization is determined by the range of attributes of the social structure that can be explained within the framework of development designated by the approach. The urban networks approach explains, in the first place, differences between distributions of central places. In seeking now to determine what other aspects of societies can be explained in terms of this approach, we must make a preliminary attempt to answer three questions: 1) what are the interdependencies between stages of urban networks and other societal characteristics? 2) what characteristics of societies at a single stage of development vary as a function of the presence of different levels of central places (stages D–F) or as a function of different distributions of numbers of central places at various levels (stage G)? and 3) what variations among countries relate to the rate of prior movement from one stage of development to the next?

We can first consider in what ways the maturation of an urban network may have affected other aspects of social structure. The direct impact of successively more complex systems of settlements would conceivably have been revealed in increasing percentages of a country's population in cities. Thus, the first variable to examine is urbanization. There is no necessary reason why urbanization should increase as urban networks become more complex in stages B–G, but it seems rather straightforward to argue that more levels of central places and wider areas of integration would be reflected in higher urban percentages. In like manner, a variety of other urban features may well have reflected stages of urban network development. Expanded areas of integration revealing the accumulation of resources from a larger population could easily have been mirrored in more diverse urban functions including greater occupational specialization and greater dispersal of merchant and artisan activities. Accordingly, the occupational structure and land use patterns of cities would change with the stages of development. In the terminology of urban sociology, cities at separate levels in countries at distinct stages of history as designated in the urban networks approach should be distinguishable with respect to areal growth processes, land use factors, internal social stratification and mobility, and the dynamics of population growth.

Indirectly changing urban networks should also have exerted an impact on rural conditions. As areas of commercial integration widened, opportunities probably expanded for production destined for an impersonal market, for the use of labor in nonagricultural by-employments, and for migration into cities. In terminology appropriate for rural sociology, villages in the hinterlands of central places at separate levels in countries at distinct stages of history should be distinguishable with respect to agricultural specialization, labor utilization, and patterns of out-migration and mobility.

Most importantly, processes with a national scope might be expected to have varied in accord with distinct stages of history as designated in terms of urban networks. Among the processes already introduced in this book, urbanization, commercialization, and centralization can be readily discussed in the context of changing urban networks.

While the evidence from the five countries examined suggests that the degree of development of the urban network clearly represents the increasing complexity of premodern countries and that it is likely that many features of social structure varied largely as a function of the stage of development so determined, there is no reason to argue that knowledge of urban networks is sufficient to predict exact urban, rural, or national conditions. Variations in terrain, in available natural resources, and in the accessibility of cheap transportation are among the many other factors that undoubtedly influenced urban land use, occupational distributions, and other social structural characteristics. Moreover, long-standing perceptions of how cities should be ordered, legal requirements for land ownership, and explicit attempts at social engineering by government authorities continually affected social conditions. Nonetheless, our awareness that numerous causal factors are present does not reduce the desirability of explaining as much as possible initially with a single variable. By defining the stages of history solely in terms of central place attributes, I make very little true by definition. Consequently the relationships between variables can be tested without any element of circularity. For many features of urban and rural life, I believe that the tests will show that a certain degree of development of the urban network is a necessary although not sufficient condition. Of course, identification of the necessary condition invariably facilitates study of the sufficient conditions as well.

To clarify this reference to necessary and sufficient conditions, let us consider the relationship between urban networks and urbanization. In each of the five countries studied, the percentage of population in cities rose as the country advanced from one stage of development to the next. In China, this increase in the percentage of population in cities proceeded exceedingly slowly, at least in stages E–G. In contrast, the growth in urban percentages during these final stages within England and Japan occurred very rapidly by premodern standards. Especially after stage G societies had emerged, a substantial increase occurred in the urbanization of Japan and England and to a lesser extent in France and Russia as well. Perhaps, the absence of a similar spurt in the proportion of city dwellers in China's population means that this country remained at an early substage of stage G while the other four countries passed on to a more developed substage. Nevertheless, even if the general pattern of rising urbanization can be explained by stages and, perhaps, substages of urban network maturation, the degree of urbanization in each country certainly did not vary solely as a function of the stage of development. In short, the single variable of stages based on urban network development tells us a great deal about urbanization, but is not a sufficient explanation for variations in urban percentages.

Explanations of premodern urbanization ought to invoke at least two other variables: the degree of availability of water transportation and the ratio of foreign trade to domestic trade. To some extent both of these variables reflect the exigencies of the geographical setting. Benefiting from bountiful waterways, England as a stage F society probably supported a higher percentage of its population in cities than did China or Russia as stage G societies. Presumably in all stages of premodern urban history, England and Japan supported higher urban percentages than had other countries. As islands with long seacoasts and ports accessible to large hinterlands, these countries enjoyed reduced transportation costs. Finally this geographical advantage probably became most pronounced in stage G as the amount of local resources sent from area to area expanded appreciably following the development of a full-fledged national market. Countries with superior waterways experienced marked urban growth, while other countries kept roughly the same urban percentage. The contrast between Japan and China is sharp in this respect. Making relatively little use of sea transportation and lacking navigable long-distance water routes to back up the east-west artery on the Yangtze river and the partial north-south artery on the Grand Canal, China did not experience a visible rise in the percentage of persons in cities. A strikingly different effect was experienced in Japan, where almost all major cities bordered or were just upriver from the seacoast; the urban percentage probably doubled after a national market emerged. Russia's urban percentage continued to rise after the completion of a national market, but its transportation network resembled that of China more than those of Japan and England. Although the Volga river, with its tributaries and adjacent canals, gave Russia a single, integrative river system perhaps unequaled elsewhere, rivers remained frozen during part of the year, and ice-bound seacoasts were practically useless for domestic trade. Given these conditions, Russia's eighteenth-century urbanization does not appear so inconsiderable compared to the earlier development of English and Japanese cities.

England and France stand out in the impact of foreign trade on the urban network. In contrast, the influence of foreign trade was practically nil in Japan, and in China it was minuscule, confined primarily to the southeast coast. England was a small-scale society by the standards of the other four, and foreign trade could more easily have had a substantial effect on cities. London served two commercial arenas apart from the British Isles. First, it was the center of a rapidly expanding trade with distant parts of the globe, including the colonies in the British Empire. In some respects, London was a level-1 city not only for England and Wales but for countries thousands of miles away as well. Second, London continued to serve as part of the long-evolving European trading sphere. What is regarded as internal trade in China was the equivalent of international trade within Europe. The goods of England were exchanged for those of other countries in Western Europe including France. Nevertheless, foreign trade was probably not a major factor in shaping the urban network or influencing the level of urbanization in England. After all, the value of internal trade in the 1740s is reported as several times that of external commerce.[36]

Foreign trade probably had some impact on the urban populations of a small number of Russian cities, but it contributed little to overall levels of urbanization. In this respect, Russia was intermediate between the Western European countries, which traded extensively, and the East Asian countries, in which foreign trade was only a tiny fraction of domestic trade.

Of these three factors, the most basic one for explaining the differences between urban percentages in the five countries is the stage of societal development. It establishes a foundation on which the importance of other explanatory variables can be interpreted, most significantly the availability of water transportation for domestic commerce. With this geographic advantage, a country could more readily mobilize resources.

In addition to urbanization, a second major variable that is closely associated with the development of urban networks is commercialization. Stores, periodic markets, and fairs are all present in stage G societies. We have already observed in Russia the appearance of periodic markets signaling the development of a stage E society, the integration of marketing settlements into a network of central places marking the emergence of a stage F society, and the formation of a national market heralding the evolution of a stage G society. During these same stages, numerous fairs appeared and stores spread along the streets of cities. Various indicators of increased and more efficient commerce have been identified. Throughout the world, as societies advanced from stage to stage, commercialization appears to have proceeded in a similar manner.

Three additional examples of countries in which markets and fairs were appearing are Korea, India, and Portugal. In the Korean case, we have evidence that markets were beginning to develop around 1400–1425 as officials were requesting permission to establish periodic markets outside of administrative cities.[37] By 1500 such periodic markets existed in almost all administrative units within Chŏlla province, and by 1600 they were in almost all of the administrative units of four of the eight Korean provinces. The sudden growth of Seoul from 80,000 to 200,000 persons during the years 1660 to 1720 probably indicates the formation of a national market. By the end of the seventeenth century, Korea was probably a stage G society and commercialization was continuing. By the first decade of the nineteenth century, the total population had tripled to 7.5 million, and there were 1,061 periodic or daily marketing centers, with almost every local administrative unit having at least 3 or 4.

In India small rural markets were present at least by the fourteenth century and became especially numerous during the fifteenth and sixteenth centuries.[38] Apparently by the second half of the sixteenth century and, perhaps, considerably earlier, networks of weekly markets existed, mostly meeting once a week as opposed to the 2/10 markets in Korea. As in Russia and the Western European countries, substantial local markets in India generally had frequencies of twice a week. By the time of active colonization, India was either a stage F or a stage G society.

Detailed records of the founding dates for fairs have been preserved for Portugal.[39] The first fairs appeared in the mid-twelfth century and were followed by a proliferation of fairs during the thirteenth century, although in southern Portugal this process continued well into the fourteenth century. The fact that few fairs were founded after this period suggests that commercial consolidation characteristic of stage F societies was occurring in Portugal. This may well have given way to a stage G society as it did elsewhere in Western Europe by the early seventeenth century.

The rise and consolidation of periodic markets and fairs has left a record of commercialization that can be documented for many societies. Among stage G societies, we have noticed the spread of stores especially in large cities, reducing the reliance on periodic markets and fairs, and the decline of some level-7 markets as goods were sent directly to higher-level central places and village stores began to appear. Since stage G societies all had complete urban networks, we have looked for signs that some were more advanced than others in these indicators of commercialization as in other respects such as continued urbanization. The clearest sign that points to an advanced substage of stage G so far is the decline in periodic marketing that occurred in at least one or more regions of four of the five countries under study. Using this indicator of commercial development, I have tentatively concluded that England at the turn of the eighteenth century was several decades ahead of France and roughly one century ahead of Japan and Russia, with China trailing considerably further behind.

While certain indicators of commercialization, by definition, signify particular stages of the advancement of urban networks and other indicators appear to have changed as a direct response to widening urban integrative areas, the concept of commercialization also conveys the impression of a percentage of total production marketed. Similar to the degree of urbanization, the marketing percentage could have been influenced by many variables. Levels of taxation, forms of land ownership, and methods of transportation must be included among these variables. Again we should conclude that the stage of development as measured by central place formation provides necessary but insufficient information for explaining prevailing states of commercialization.

In addition to the study of the relation of various aspects of social structure to the stages of development designated by the urban networks approach, the second essential methodology proposed in this chapter is the comparison of distributions of central places in societies at the same stage. Societies at stages E and F appear either feudal or centralized depending on the precise levels of cities present. In this respect, China, which boasted levels 4 and 5, incorporated lower-level marketing settlements into existing administrative units without a disintegration of central power, while all of the other countries with weaker foundations at the intermediate levels of the network experienced a period of feudal patterns.

Variations in centralization among stage G societies were examined in the previous section of this chapter. Corresponding to arguments already given for the determinants of other societal conditions, the potentialities for centralization of resources into urban centers are likely to have risen in each succeeding stage of urban network growth. It has been shown that stage G societies utilized these potentialities in varying ways. Conditions corresponding to the stage of urban integration did not suffice to ensure that a high degree of centralization would be realized.

The issue of centralization is complicated by the many levels involved. China has generally been portrayed as highly centralized, and its declining administrative efficiency in the nineteenth century can be convincingly attributed to overcentralization, if we mean by this that local administrators had inadequate resources to respond to developing problems. The concept of the distribution of power is rooted in locating decision-making authority at the various levels of the administrative hierarchy. Indeed, the central government in

Peking had long enjoyed wide powers, and its capacity to exercise those powers effectively for centuries limited the appeal of reforms that would have enlarged the government's actual control over increasing quantities of goods and services. By the eighteenth century, the Chinese bureaucracy contained few officials relative to the total population, and taxes were slight compared to Japan. From the earlier comparisons of distributions of central places at the seven levels, China's weakness in resource mobilization stands out most acutely at levels 5 and 6, suggesting that centralization in local administrative centers did not take advantage of expanded commerce in level-7 marketing places. In this light, the notion of overcentralization suggests considerable development of the urban network at the top, but not in the middle of the hierarchy. Perhaps the continued ability to meet the requirements at the national level and to maintain a high degree of peace and prosperity for premodern times accompanied by the preserved wisdom of tenets favoring a rural land-based elite militated against the emergence of conditions that would have led to a massive reorganization of Chinese administrative or commercial patterns.

In contrast, the Japanese and Russian cases reveal explicit attempts to mobilize resources, including the large-scale reorganization of administrative patterns and the reconstruction of elite strata. By the eighteenth century, these countries realized exceptional centralization at local and national levels, seen in the percentages of all urban residents at levels 1, 2, and 5. Newly imposed centralized conditions were premised on relatively high levels of commercialization.

The presence of a rural-urban dichotomy is related to the amount of centralization. In four of the five countries studied, there was a sharp dichotomy between the population figures and life styles of one or more national centers and those of other cities and rural settlements. Only in China where the national administrative centers of Peking and Nanking were rivaled by many large cities with populations approaching one million and there was a gradual gradation between cities at various population levels did no dichotomy exist. In the other cases the difference between the population of national centers and other cities was substantial. The difference between London's population and that of the next largest city of England was nearly 30:1; the difference for France between Paris and Lyon was more than 5:1; the difference for Japan between Edo and the first city after the other national centers of Osaka and Kyoto was at least 8:1; and the ratio between St. Petersburg and the largest city other than Moscow was also at least 8:1. All of these four countries had what in modern times would be called primate cities, which stood apart from the rest of the society's settlements. Furthermore, in each case, the dichotomy between one or more central cities and other settlements widened during the stage G phase. It seems that the conditions of stage G created the opportunity for greater centralization and that four of the five countries examined made significant use of this opportunity.

Without pursuing the matter further here, I would conclude that not only did few aspects of the social structure of premodern societies vary at random to the development of urban networks but that there is every likelihood that, by using this approach, sets of powerful interdependencies can be identified between numerous indicators of social change. As a system of periodization, this approach first provides a methodology for ascertaining the similarities between countries and then establishes a framework for explaining differences. Starting with social processes with wide implications such as urbanization, commercialization, and centralization, we will be in a position to consider other ways that people interact which are related to the development of settlement patterns. Changing urban networks acting through such intermediaries as rising rates of internal migration to and from cities, new patterns of social and occupational mobility, and the growth of marketing had a pervasive impact in ways that remain to be further explored.

Obviously not every social characteristic changes as a direct function of the stage of the urban network. Just as modernization occurs through the transformation of existing societal forms and not independently of them, so too does the far more gradual premodern social development fail to obliterate what precedes it. Especially in countries where the urban network emerged rapidly, we would expect pre-existing social forms to have preserved more vitality in shaping the course of development. Although this was not always the case, as we witness in China where the relatively gradual pace of change contributed to complacency about the need to reform long-standing patterns, the preservation of feudal loyalties in Japan and of serfdom in Russia provide examples of the gradual modification of earlier patterns under the stimulus of rapid development.

In applying this approach to comparing premodern societies, the rate of change over long periods of time should not be ignored. One of the interesting findings is that Japan and Russia passed from stage to stage at a consistently rapid pace, while the Chinese lead dissipated through a steady but gradual development. Short-term vigorous leaders, reform movements, invasions, and plagues scarcely deflected the rates of movement from stage to stage that characterized these countries. By the mid-eighteenth century among these five countries at stage G in their urban development, England and France had now pulled into the lead followed by Japan and then Russia with China falling quickly behind. These relative positions in urban development represented the culminations of long histories of remarkably consistent rates of change.

From these comparisons of the long-run course of urban development, one additional application of the urban networks approach should be anticipated. Since the ranking of these five countries in the eighteenth century coincides with the order in which they completed the transformation toward modernization, does it not seem reasonable to examine the premodern period in search of preconditions for modernization? This is exactly what the Marxist system of periodization calls for in its insistence that the roots and sprouts of the subsequent stage of development are nourished in the environment of each preceding stage. Without necessarily accepting the conclusion that modernization would have soon appeared in every country that was relatively developed by the premodern standards of the eighteenth century, we still should consider the relevance of changes in urban networks for the origins of modernization and, even more importantly, for the development of capabilities to achieve rapid modernization as a latecomer to the process.

Certainly one of the most important applications of a system of periodization should be to discern the preconditions of modernization in premodern societies and correspondingly to predict the pace of modernization that would follow once close contact was established with the firstcomers to modernization. Building on the structure of comparisons between five countries carried out in this study, I intend next to extend comparisons of China, Japan, and Russia to the early phases of modernization.

❊ 6 ❊

CONCLUSIONS

Traditions of social science writings linger on long after the appearance of necessary conditions for replacing them with more useful methodologies. Existing treatments of periodization and notions of eighteenth-century Russian backwardness are survivals from a distant past that have long merited new scrutiny. These themes have attracted widespread attention without receiving substantial clarification. No matter how frequently it is repeated that before 1800 Russia remained a backward society by premodern standards and that stages of history reflect increasing levels of complexity in human interaction, the meaning of these statements has remained vague or distorted.

The essential interdependence of these themes is evident from the fact that Russia's relative position in development can only be determined by a comparative approach to the periodization of premodern countries and that data from countries such as Russia are required in the formation of any approach to periodization. In this book these two themes merge. Using the urban networks approach to periodization, we have seen in a comparative perspective the course of Russia's development century by century, focusing in greatest detail on the late eighteenth century. Simultaneously the information presented on Russia added to data on East Asian and Western European countries has established a foundation for generalizations about historical stages, especially the most developed stage of premodern history. Findings from single country studies, explicit and systematic comparisons between five countries, and the further elaboration of the urban networks approach combine to give a new outlook on the themes of periodization and Russian backwardness.

In the precise terms of the urban networks approach, Russia's relative backwardness is confirmed for a period of nearly 1,000 years to the end of the eighteenth century. By the standard of the number of levels of central places present, Russia revealed less developed forms of integrated spatial organization than did any of the other four countries examined until the early eighteenth century. Even after that date, although Russia shared with the other countries the general attributes of a stage G (advanced premodern) society, it clearly continued to rank behind England, France, and Japan in most measures of efficiency in funneling resources up the hierarchy of central places. Yet, while Russia continued to lag behind these countries, it was generally narrowing the gap separating it from countries with more advanced urban networks. Russia's rate of movement from stage to stage of premodern history exceeded that of any other country, even somewhat surpassing the brisk pace maintained in Japan. Moreover, by the late eighteenth century, the Russian network at various levels revealed greater efficiency than did China's network, suggesting that Russia had followed in the footsteps of its predecessors—England, France, and Japan—in passing China with respect to this basic dynamic of social change. Information on the decline of periodic marketing further indicates that Russia may have been approaching Japan's peak of premodern development by the early nineteenth century. In brief, the concept of Russian backwardness must be tempered by our new awareness that this unusually dynamic premodern country had by the late eighteenth century surpassed the state of development reached anywhere in the world prior to the seventeenth century and joined the ranks of a small number of countries as relatively urbanized, advanced premodern societies.

Eighteenth-century Russian cities are ordinarily contrasted negatively with Western European cities. Organizationally Russian cities lacked the vitality of self-governing commercial agencies; physically they were wooden and disorderly without much monumental architecture; and occupationally they comprised large numbers of serfs bound in various ways to their villages. Were these signs of backwardness? Not necessarily. Each of these characteristics varied quite independently of the stages of development.

The absence of self-government reflects the early achievement of high levels of centralization by the standards of the time and perhaps also reflects other historical circumstances. China and Japan also lacked the forms of self-government visible in certain Western European countries. We should not assume that alternate forms of government cannot accompany high levels of premodern societal advancement. The commercialization of a country is more clearly seen in relation to the evolution of urban networks than to the existence of particular forms of merchant organization.

The desirability of permanence in construction also does not appear to be related directly to the rate of societal development. Russia and to an even greater extent China and Japan had few monuments. Moreover, high densities of population can be achieved in one- and two-story wooden dwellings enclosed in courtyards as well as in four- or five-story apartment houses. Population densities were exceptionally high in East Asian cities without high-rise buildings. Whether construction is of stone or of wood, basic changes in urban land use can still be detected corresponding to the stages of development of the urban network. The spread of stores within cities and the extension of built-up areas along rivers are universal indicators of development as opposed to the variations in the use of materials and methods of construction.

Finally we should reassess the assumption that serfdom slowed development before 1800. The study of the consequences of serfdom must be made more specific with regard to the stage of development and other characteristics of societies. Similar in some ways to the oft-disparaged feudal loyalties of Tokugawa Japan, serfdom may have been an important factor in mobilizing resources and in speeding the progression of a stage G society. Despite the existence of serfdom for nearly half the population of the Russian Empire, restrictions on internal migration into cities do not seem to have been a limiting factor in urbanization.

As Russia came into contact with modernizing societies, the old rates of development appeared unimpressive. When the tortoise started racing the hare rather than other tortoises, the comparative perspective was suddenly radically altered. During the second half of the nineteenth century Russia began to be successful in rapid modernization. Most interest in this success has focused on the policies that accompanied it. We still know little about the basis from which modern change took place. If, Russia was, indeed, relatively advanced as a stage G society (in comparison with societies outside of Western Europe and Japan), had experienced rapid development by the standards of premodern societies, and also had certain special features such as a high level of local administrative centralization for a premodern society, then Russia may well have started with a considerable advantage. Further study is now needed of the relationship between premodern stages of development and the process of modernization.

By replacing existing comparative statements about Russian premodern development with a detailed assessment of the state of that country's development on the eve of initial modernization, this book may set in motion new efforts to place Russian history in comparative perspective. Current conceptions of Russia's place in comparative historic development must be revised if we are to rid ourselves of what I believe should properly be referred to as the myth of Russian backwardness. As this approach to periodization has shown, Russia should rightfully be classified among the advanced premodern societies in urban and most likely other measures of development.

The major goal of this book has been to generalize about premodern periodization. In my previous comparative study of premodern urban development, the selection of only two countries, China and Japan, limited the foundation for generalizations pertaining to countries in all parts of the world and at various phases of development. Now the sample has been expanded to five countries, all populous and relatively centralized and together embracing some 37 million urban inhabitants, an impressive figure when the entire world in 1800 probably registered only 60–65 million urban inhabitants.

Based on the data drawn from the histories of China, Japan, the Russian Empire, England, and France, seven stages of premodern development have been identified. Signifying the expanded integration of settlements first through essentially administrative and then through primarily commercial means of centralization, these stages represent an ordered, cumulative evolution from simple to complex forms of interaction. The identification of historic stages is of great importance for comparisons of societies before 1800 and, indeed, for efforts to generalize about the majority of persons and societies that have existed in this world. At present the long-persisting Marxist and tripartite approaches to periodization continue to be widely utilized despite their numerous shortcomings. Their replacement by a sounder approach to periodization should spur studies that bridge the disciplines of sociology and history.

Contrary to attitudes frequently expressed about the inherent shortcomings of evolutionary approaches to social change, the urban networks approach provides a means of ordering empirical data. It offers a series of testable generalizations drawn from the concrete and the historical. The urban networks approach is based on the ideal of explaining as much as possible in the most parsimonious way, using the fewest possible variables. No pretense is made that every social characteristic can be predicted by knowing the stage of a country's development according to the maturation of levels of central places, but the argument is made that the most powerful explanatory variables are likely to be associated with stages of development. Various measures of urbanization, commercialization, centralization, and stratification have been shown to have reflected stages of central place development. Unlike other systems of periodization, this approach builds on precise definitions, quantified statements, and unambiguous methods of classification. As such, it establishes a framework for systematic, explicit comparisons between the social structures of all premodern countries.

In addition to setting forth this revised framework for analysis, this book has represented the first effort to apply the framework through generalizations pertaining to the entire universe of premodern societies and in a more concerted fashion to the galaxy of stage G societies. A first step has been taken to specify the percentage of the world's population at various points in history in societies at each stage of development. Lists of the world's largest countries and cities in 1800 place in perspective the scale and urbanization of the five countries examined. In turn, evidence has been presented to show why conclusions drawn from these five countries should have more universal application.

The Russian case has served as a pivot around which comparisons of countries to the east and west have turned. On the basis of these comparisons, late premodern England and France appear remarkably similar, although English patterns did reflect a smaller and nationally more centralized scale. Also on the basis of these comparisons, conclusions previously given for China and Japan have been confirmed. It is clear that in most respects the late premodern societies in these East Asian countries differed sharply, even in comparison to countries located in other parts of the world. Yet, all of these differences have been demonstrated against the background of a series of underlying similarities in societies at a single stage of development. As a method of comparing societies, the urban networks approach has made possible the identification of similarities on the basis of which differences can be analyzed. Other premodern countries should now be studied in terms of this approach, and additional variables should be considered in an effort to find the limits of the explanatory powers of this system of periodization.

First set of propositions: Uniformities of premodern societies

1. Premodern societies were predominantly rural; with the possible exception of one or more very small-scale societies, the percentage of the population residing in cities did not exceed 20–21.
2. Premodern cities were generally small; with the exception over thousands of years of perhaps 8–12 cities in very large-scale societies no cities approached a population of one million. Cities of fewer than 10,000 people predominated everywhere.
3. The two principal functions that distinguished relatively large places from other settlements were commercial and administrative.
4. Based on the significance of their commercial or administrative functions, all premodern settlements can be classified according to seven levels of central places.
5. The shifting number of levels present and the order in which new levels appeared proceeded according to discernible regularities.

    a. Initial central places were at level 2.

    b. The combination of levels 1 and 5 or 2 and 5 provided the nucleus of early urbanism.

c. Once level-7 central places appeared, they persisted and were followed within a few centuries by the emergence of level-6 places.

d. With the coexistence of cities at levels 1 and 2, urban networks were complete.

Second set of propositions: Types of premodern societies

1. Determination of the number and types of levels of central places present century by century makes possible a consistent comparative system of measurement of societal development.
2. Premodern societies can be classified according to seven stages of development, each characterized by a different settlement pattern.
3. The seven stages signify a sequential pattern of growing complexity in commercial and administrative interactions among settlements.

    a. The later the stage of the society, the more likely it was to be larger in scale than previous societies on the same territory.

    b. Stages B, C, and D represent administrative centralization, with commerce of secondary importance.

    c. Stages E, F, and G represent commercial centralization with administrative functions secondary in accounting for the size of urban centers.

    d. The later the stage of a society, the higher its percentage of people in cities was likely to be in comparison to previous societies on the same territory.

Third set of propositions: Characteristics of advanced premodern societies

1. Among societies with a complete (or incomplete presumably owing to the small-scale of the society) network of central places, the distribution of settlements exhibits a pyramidal shape, with large numbers of central places at lower levels (7 and 6) supporting successively smaller numbers at higher levels.
2. Ratios of the number of central places in adjoining levels measure the efficiency of moving goods up the hierarchy of settlements, suggesting variations among countries in administrative

and commercial centralization on national, regional, local and inter-village levels.

3. At least seven areas of integration can be identified (each with a distinct population range), which were ordered into marketing or administrative units of successively larger scale.

4. Substages of stage G (advanced premodern societies) can be discerned, pointing to differences in urbanization, commercialization and centralization, all of which deserve further examination for their impact on preconditions of modernization.

5. On the basis of data on urban networks, the capacity for subsequent modernization can be predicted; the results obtained so far suggest that Russia resembled Japan and, to some extent, England and France as opposed to China's distinctively less efficient pattern of settlements on the eve of initial modernization.

GLOSSARY

Frequently used terms referring to Russia and other countries
(Russian terms are used here consistently in either singular or plural)

Barshchina:	Obligatory labor owed by the serf to the owner
Boiars:	Nobles; persons of highest social stratum before Peter I
Bourg:	French settlement; often with marketing activities
Chasty:	Precincts: administrative sections of Russian cities
Desiatina:	Unit of land measurement: 1 desiatina = 2.7 acres
Detinets:	Inner fortified section of ancient Russian city; kreml'
Dvoriane:	Gentry; persons of highest social stratum after Peter I
Dvory:	Households; often separate self-supporting units
Éléction:	Administrative unit of France
Fu:	Administrative unit of China; prefecture
Généralité:	Administrative unit of France
Gostinyi dvor:	A large building with numerous shops
Guberniia:	Administrative unit of Russia from early 18th century
les Halles:	A large covered market in France
Han:	Administrative unit of Japan; domain or fief
Hsien:	Administrative unit of China: district or county
Iarmarki:	Fairs; annual commercial gatherings
Izby:	Houses; often huts or shacks
Kreml':	Kremlin; inner fortress in city
Kuptsy:	Merchants; officially recognized urban stratum
Kvartaly:	Quarters or wards: small administrative sections of cities
Meshchane:	Townsmen; officially recognized urban stratum
Mestechki:	Settlements in the west of the Russian Empire once endowed with some urban privileges
Obrok:	Obligatory payment owed by the serf to the owner

GLOSSARY

Pereulki:	Small or minor streets
Podat':	Tax; categories of population owing tax
Pomest'ia:	Landed estates; originally rewarded for service but during 18th century turned into full private property
Posad:	Section of city; center of trade and crafts just outside the fortress; also used for certain urban strata
Raznochintsy:	Persons not belonging to any recognized strata
Riady:	Rows of shops; often specialized in a certain product
Sazhen':	Unit of measurement; 1 sazhen' = 2.13 meters
Sborniki:	Collections of articles on a single theme
Sela (sing. selo):	Peasant settlements; often relatively large local centers
Sheng:	Administrative unit of China: a province
Slobody (sing. sloboda):	Suburbs or other settlements with a non-serf population
Sobor:	Cathedral
Strel'tsy:	Members of military-service population of 16th and 17th century Russia
Tiaglo:	A unit for measuring the capacity to meet tax obligations
Torgi (torzhki):	Markets; weekly commercial gatherings
Tsekhovye liudy:	Guildsmen; persons organized into artisan guilds
Uezd:	Administrative unit of Russia; district or county
Uklad:	A type of societal formation; refers to stage of development of social structure
Ulitsy:	Main streets
Ulozhenie:	Code of laws
Ville:	French city
Voevoda:	Official; the main administrator in a Russian city to the 18th century
Votchiny:	Hereditary landed estates; distinct from pomest'ia until 18th century

NOTES

NOTES TO INTRODUCTION

1. Data to support this figure are presented in Chapters 3 and 4. For sources of inaccurately low estimates of Russia's urban population, see my article, "Comparative Approaches to Urbanization: Russia, 1750–1800," in Michael Hamm, ed., *The City in Russian History* (Lexington, Ky., forthcoming).

2. Examples of references to Russia as a backward country prior to 1800 can be found in Nicholas V. Riasanovsky, *A History of Russia* (New York, 1963), 315; Jerome Blum, *Lord and Peasant in Russia* (New York, 1969), 611; and Iu. R. Klokman, *Sotsial'no-ekonomicheskaia istoriia russkogo goroda: vtoraia polovina XVIII veka* (Moscow, 1967), 316. Among the many sources that emphasize the long-run negative impact of Mongol rule on Russian development are George Vernadsky, *A History of Russia* (New Haven, 1961), 78–80; and A. M. Sakharov, *Goroda severo-vostochnoi Rusi XIV–XV vekov* (Moscow, 1959), 225. P. A. Khromov, *Ocherki ekonomiki feodalizma v Rossii* (Moscow, 1957), 17, notes that Russia, without ports on the Black and Baltic Seas, was distant from international trade routes that allowed economic growth. Limits on Russian development due to serfdom, the absence of merchant self-government, and other urban policies are practically universally mentioned as in Marc Raeff, *Imperial Russia, 1682–1825* (New York, 1971), 98, and 114–22; and N. E. Nosov, "Russkii gorod: russkoe kupechestvo v XVI stoletii," *Issledovaniia po sotsial'no-politicheskoi istorii Rossii* (Leningrad, 1971), 168.

3. See *The Modernization of Japan and Russia* (New York, forthcoming), written by Cyril E. Black, Marius B. Jansen, Herbert S. Levine, Marion J. Levy, Jr., Henry Rosovsky, Gilbert Rozman, Henry D. Smith, II, and S. Frederick Starr.

4. For a critique of the self-government approach, see Rozman, "Comparative Approaches to Urbanization: Russia, 1750–1800."

5. S. N. Eisenstadt, *The Political Systems of Empires: The Rise and Fall of the Historical Bureaucratic Societies* (New York, 1969); and Karl A. Wittfogel, *Oriental Despotism: A Comparative Study of Total Power* (New Haven, 1963).

6. Rushton Coulborn, ed., *Feudalism in History* (Princeton, 1956). For an interesting discussion of problems in using the concept of feudalism, see John W. Hall, "Feudalism in Japan—A Reassessment," in John W. Hall and Marius

B. Jansen, *Studies in the Institutional History of Early Modern Japan* (Princeton, 1968), 15–51.

7. George H. Nadel, "Periodization," *International Encyclopedia of Social Sciences,* 11 (1968), 581–84.

8. A comparison of the philosophies of history presented by Polybius and Ssu-ma Ch'ien is found in N. I. Konrad, "History of World Social Science," *Soviet Sociology* (Spring 1967), 54–88.

9. The practice of dividing the history of societies into distinct types acquired popularity during the nineteenth century, with separate typologies offered by such leading sociologists as Auguste Comte and Émile Durkheim.

10. In the United States, recent works relating sociology and history include Werner J. Cahnman and Alvin Boskoff, *Sociology and History* (New York, 1964); and Richard Hofstadter and Seymour Martin Lipset, eds., *Sociology and History: Methods* (New York, 1968). In the Soviet Union, recent titles include P. N. Fedoseev and G. P. Frantsov, "Sotsiologiia i istoriia," *Sotsiologiia v SSSR,* I (1966); *Istoriia i sotsiologiia* (Moscow, 1964); and L. M. Drobizheva, *Istoriia i sotsiologiia* (Moscow, 1971).

11. *Problemy vozniknoveniia feodalizma u narodov SSSR* (Moscow, 1969); and A. P. Novosel'tsev, V. T. Pashuto, and L. V. Cherepnin, *Puti razvitiia feodalizma* (Moscow, 1972).

12. Robert A. Nisbet, *Social Change and History* (Oxford, 1969).

13. See, for instance, Richard P. Appelbaum, *Theories of Social Change* (Chicago, 1970); Szymon Chodak, *Societal Development: Five Approaches with Conclusions from Comparative Analysis* (New York, 1973); and Guy E. Swanson, *Social Change* (Glenview, Ill., 1971).

14. Brian J. L. Berry and Allen Pred, *Central Place Studies: A Bibliography of Theory and Applications* (Philadelphia, 1961).

15. G. William Skinner, "Marketing and Social Structure in Rural China," *Journal of Asian Studies* 24: 1, 2, 3 (1964–65).

16. J. C. Russell, *Medieval Regions and Their Cities* (London, 1972); C. T. Smith, *An Historical Geography of Western Europe* (London, 1967); and E. A. J. Johnson, *The Organization of Space in Developing Countries* (Cambridge, Mass., 1970).

17. See, for instance, Paul Wheatley, "The Concept of Urbanism," Peter J. Ucko, et al., eds., *Man, Settlement and Urbanism* (London, 1972), 617.

NOTES TO CHAPTER 1

1. For a review of the initial postwar Soviet debate on periodization, see Konstantin Shteppa, *Russian Historians and the Soviet State* (New Brunswick, 1962), 242–75; and for the openly conflicting viewpoints of many of the leading historians of the 1960s, see *Perekhod ot feodalizma k kapitalizmu v Rossii* (Moscow, 1969). Interestingly, E. M. Zhukov starts off the discussion section of the volume by asserting that the problem of the transition from feudalism to capitalism is on the border of the subjects of history and sociology (page 104).

2. The comparative study of so-called Asiatic despotism is an approach

which, in my opinion, has not proven useful in stimulating research or in integrating knowledge about historic societies. For a Soviet review of the use of this concept by foreign Marxists, see Iu. V. Kachanovskii, "Diskussiia ob aziatskom sposobe proizvodstva na stranitsakh zarubezhnoi marksistskoi pechati," *Problemy dokapitalisticheskikh obshchestv v stranakh Vostoka* (Moscow, 1971), 45–94.

3. This discussion is reviewed by Leo Yaresh, "The Problem of Periodization," C. E. Black, ed., *Rewriting Russian History: Soviet Interpretations of Russia's Past* (New York, 1956), 52–58.

4. For a brief account of Marx's historical epochs as a basis for comparative analysis, see R. Stephen Warner, "The Methodology of Marx's Comparative Analysis of Modes of Production," in Ivan Vallier, ed., *Comparative Methods in Sociology: Essays on Trends and Applications* (Berkeley, 1971), 49–74.

5. An introduction to the Soviet interpretation of feudal society is given in B. F. Porshnev, *Feodalizm i narodnye massy* (Moscow, 1964), 23–24.

6. L. V. Cherepnin, "Rus': spornye voprosy istorii feodal'noi zemel'noi sobstvennosti v IX–XV vv.," in A. P. Novosel'tsev, V. T. Pashuto, and L. V. Cherepnin, *Puti razvitiia feodalizma*, 144.

7. An overview of differences of opinion on the periodization of these centuries is provided in *Perekhod ot feodalizma k kapitalizmu*, 8–17.

8. One of the most striking examples of an idiosyncratic opinion is provided by D. P. Makovskii, *Razvitie tovarno-denezhnykh otnoshenii v sel'skom khoziaistve russkogo gosudarstva v XVI veke* (Smolensk, 1963), who argues, without introducing much evidence, that Russia was ahead of Europe in important respects during the sixteenth century but then declined during the next two centuries.

9. L. V. Cherepnin in *Puti razvitiia feodalizma*, 250–51.

10. For two views on the Mongol impact, see L. V. Cherepnin, *Obrazovanie russkogo tsentralizovannogo gosudarstva v XIV–XV vekakh* (Moscow, 1960); and A. M. Sakharov, *Obrazovanie i razvitie rossiiskogo gosudarstva v XIV–XVII vv.* (Moscow, 1969).

11. The initial signs of capitalism are variously referred to as "sprouts of capitalism" or the process of the "primary accumulation of capital." Karl Marx's reference to the primary accumulation of capital in the fourteenth and fifteenth centuries and further remarks about economic development in Italy at this time can be found in A. D. Rolova, "Osnovnye cherty ekonomicheskogo razvitiia Italii v XVI–XVII vv.," *Vozniknovenie kapitalizma v promyshlennosti i sel'skom khoziaistve stran Evropy, Azii i Ameriki* (Moscow, 1968), 54. The birth of capitalism in Russia as opposed to Western Europe is most thoroughly debated in *Perekhod ot feodalizma k kapitalizmu v Rossii*, 18-36, and in separate discussions that occupy most of the book. For example, see the comments of I. A. Bulygin, 259.

12. Soviet historians suggest many indicators of the stage of development of feudal society as measured by commerce. For instance, M. K. Rozhkova describes fairs as a typical form of trade in the period of *developed* feudalism. In less developed feudalism fairs are not yet significant, while with the emergence of capitalism after the appearance of the capitalist uklad, fairs soon lose sig-

nificance as trading centers and are supplanted by trade in stores. With this formulation, we can use information presented by Rozhkova and others concerning the dates when fairs were appearing, flourishing, and then declining as one basis for determining the periodization of Russian society in relation to that of other societies. See M. K. Rozhkova, "K voprosu o znachenii iarmarok vo vnutrennei torgovle doreformennoi Rossii (pervaia polovina XIX v.)," *Istoricheskie zapiski* 54 (1955), 298.

13. *Perekhod ot feodalizma k kapitalizmu*, 35. See also "Osnovnye etapy genezisa kapitalizma v Rossii," in V. K. Iatsunskii, *Sotsial'no-ekonomicheskaia istoriia Rossii XVIII–XIX vv.* (Moscow, 1973), 71–115.

14. A relatively full discussion of subdivisions of feudalism in Russia to 1800 and the factors interrupting the smooth development from one subdivision to another is presented in *Istoriia SSSR: s drevneishchikh vremen do nashikh dnei*, II and III (Moscow, 1966).

15. The urban explanation for unnecessarily protracted feudalism is given by Iu. R. Klokman, who describes governmental reforms related to cities as occurring "very slowly," points to the weakness of urban self-government as a consequence of the "long domination of serfdom," and refers to policies of autocracy that "slowed the economic growth of cities, and this, in its turn, complicated the development of the urban system of the country as a whole." See his *Sotsial'no-ekonomicheskaia istoriia russkogo goroda*, 320–31. On the retarding effects of serfdom, see A. L. Shapiro, ed., *Agrarnaia istoriia severo-zapada Rosii: vtoraia polovina XV– nachalo XVI v.* (Leningrad, 1971), 372–73. Here it is stated that although the Mongol occupation slowed the development of Russia and was a cause of her backwardness, by the end of the fifteenth century the ruinous consequences of the Mongols had been overcome and agriculture was on the threshold of two possible forms of development. If there had been no serfdom, i.e., if Russian agriculture had followed the other course, Shapiro argues that there is no doubt but that Russia would have experienced a faster transition to capitalism.

16. N. I. Pavlenko makes this observation in *Perekhod ot feodalizma k kapitalizmu v Rossii*, 111.

17. Ibid.

18. Ibid., 182.

19. Ibid., 266–67.

20. Ibid., 192.

21. For example, see N. B. Golikova, "Ocherki po istorii naseleniia gorodov Nizhnego Povolzh'ia v kontse XVII– pervoi chetverti XVIII v." (a doctoral dissertation submitted to Moscow State University, Department of the History of the USSR, Section of Feudalism, 1970), 5–6. She repeats one of the recommendations of the 1965 conference from which derived the volume, *Perekhod ot feodalizma k kapitalizmu v Rossii*, calling for "wider study of the history of the city and of the city population of Russia by means of local studies as well as general monographs." Golikova argues that while pre-Revolutionary bourgeois studies of Soviet cities were one-sided, Soviet research on cities has been insufficient, with most research concentrating on serfs to the exclusion of cities. To the extent that cities have been studied, they have been located

mainly in the central, west, and north of Russia and most attention has been given to the posad population. Cities in other areas and other categories of the urban population have been neglected.

22. This quotation is mentioned by many Soviet authors. See, for instance, Klokman, *Ocherki sotsial'no-ekonomicheskoi istorii gorodov severo-zapada Rossii v seredine XVIII v.* (Moscow, 1960), 4.

23. A. M. Karpachev, "Sotsial'no-ekonomicheskoe razvitie gorodov Belorussii vo vtoroi polovine XVII–XVIII v." (a doctoral dissertation submitted to the Academy of Sciences of the Belorussian Soviet Socialist Republic, Department of Social Sciences, 1969), 1.

24. Klokman, *Ocherki sotsial'no-ekonomicheskoi istorii gorodov severo-zapada Rossii v seredine XVIII v.*, 15.

25. Ibid., 3.

26. *Perekhod ot feodalizma k kapitalizmu*, 183; and *Goroda feodal'noi Rossii* (Moscow, 1966), 88.

27. A recent effort to relate the discussion of the formation of the national market to the periodization of Russian history can be found in Iu. A. Tikhonov, "Problema formirovaniia vserossiiskogo rynka v sovremennoi sovetskoi istoriografii," *Aktual'nye problemy istorii Rossii epokhi feodalizma* (Moscow, 1970), 200–23.

28. The meaning of these subdivisions for the economic development of Europe is reviewed by Richard M. Hartwell, "Economic Growth in England before the Industrial Revolution: Some Methodological Issues," *The Journal of Economic History* 20:1 (March 1969), 13–31. For a history of Europe which often focuses on networks of central places during these periods, see C. T. Smith, *An Historical Geography of Western Europe*.

29. See Hisayuki Miyakawa, "An Outline of the Naitō Hypothesis and Its Effects on Japanese Studies of China," *Far Eastern Quarterly* 14:4 (August 1955), 533–52. For a series of articles on the periodization of Chinese history, see also John Meskill, ed., *The Pattern of Chinese History: Cycles, Development, or Stagnation?* (Lexington, Mass., 1965).

30. Albert Feuerwerker, ed., *History in Communist China* (Cambridge, Mass., 1968); and R. V. Viatkin and N. P. Svistunova, eds., *Istoricheskaiia nauka v KNR* (Moscow, 1971).

31. E. P. Stuzhina, "Problemy ekonomicheskoi i sotsial'noi struktury goroda i remeslennogo proizvodstva Kitaia XI–XIII vv. v sovremennoi istoriografii," *Istoriografiia stran Vostoka* (Moscow, 1969), 343–76.

32. I. G. Pozdniakov, "Progressivnaia iaponskaia istoriografiia o kharaktere feodalizma v Iaponii," *Narody Azii i Afriki* (1962:3), 167–77.

33. H. Pirenne, *Medieval Cities: Their Origins and the Revival of Trade* (Princeton, 1952); and Denis Twitchett, "The T'ang Market System," *Asia Major* (1966), 202–48.

34. See, for instance, Fu I-ling, *Ming Ch'ing shih-tai shang-jen chi shang-yeh tzu-pen* (Peking, 1956).

35. Soviet sources argue that bourgeois historians of Russian cities ignore the evolution of crafts and commerce while focusing on the absence of urban self-government. They contrast this neglect with the contributions of Soviet

scholarship. For instance, see F. Ia. Polianskii, *Gorodskoe remeslo i manufaktura v Rossii XVIII v.* (Moscow, 1960), 7–8. Polianskii points to Rybakov's study of crafts in Russian cities during the Kievan period, to Smirnov's study of the development of the posad in the sixteenth and seventeenth centuries, and to Zaozerskaia's study of the appearance of capitalist relations in small industries in the early eighteenth century as providing evidence of the evolutionary path of urban change.

36. B. F. Porshnev, *Feodalizm i narodnye massy*, 91.

37. Max Weber, *The City* (Glencoe, 1958).

38. E. P. Stuzhina, *Kitaiskoe remeslo v XVI–XVIII vv.* (Moscow, 1970), 19–24.

39. These levels were first given in *Urban Networks in Ch'ing China and Tokugawa Japan.*

40. See Arthur F. Wright, "Symbolism and Function: Reflections on Ch'ang-an and Other Great Cities," *Journal of Asian Studies* 24: 4 (August 1965), 667–79.

NOTES TO CHAPTER 2

1. Coincidentally this division into four periods corresponds closely to the six periods chosen for the development of Russian cities by K. A. Nevolin, "Obshchii spisok russkikh gorodov," *Polnoe sobranie sochinenii*, VI (St. Petersburg, 1859), 25–95. Nevolin's six periods are: 1) 862–1015, 2) 1015–1238, 3) 1238–1462, 4) 1462–1689, 5) 1689–1762 and 6) 1762– . If the second and third periods are combined and the sixth period is excluded as too late for the scope of this chapter, then Nevolin's periods are within a few decades of those chosen here.

2. *Urban Networks in Ch'ing China and Tokugawa Japan*, chapter 1.

3. M. N. Tikhomirov, *Drevnerusskie goroda* (Moscow, 1956), 9-16.

4. For a brief explanation of the causes of the appearance of early Russian cities that emphasizes the prior development of agriculture and crafts, see A. L. Khoroshkevich in *Goroda feodal'noi Rossii*, 44. A more detailed account of the state of development of the Eastern Slavs during the sixth to eighth centuries can be found in *Problemy vozniknoveniia feodalizma u narodov SSSR*, 28–70.

5. According to Tikhomirov, built-up areas outside the fortress appeared in most cities only in the eleventh century. Rarely did they exist before the late tenth century. See *Drevnerusskie goroda*, 43–51.

6. A list of the main cities of this early period is given in ibid., 17.

7. See I. I. Liapushkin, "Slaviane Vostochnoi Evropy nakanune obrazovaniia drevnerusskogo gosudarstva (VII– pervaia polovina IX v.)," *Materialy i issledovaniia po arkheologii SSSR* 152 (Leningrad, 1968), 164.

8. M. N. Tikhomirov contrasts small cities tied only to nearby agricultural areas located within about 20 miles to large cities joined to more distant areas by main trade routes. See *Drevnerusskie goroda*, 63 and 96–101. The oft-repeated Soviet position is that foreign trade was not the primary factor in the development of Russian cities, nor were these cities principally a creation of Varangians who were securing the trade routes from Scandinavia to Constanti-

nople. See *Drevnerusskie goroda*, 12–16, and also A. L. Khoroshkevich's criticism of V. O. Kliuchevsky's views in *Goroda feodal'noi Rossii*, 37.

9. Frequently mentioned sources of these population data are V. I. Urlanis, *Rost naseleniia v Evrope* (Moscow, 1941), 84–88; and M. N. Tikhomirov, *Drevnerusskie goroda*, 140.

10. Ibid., 43.

11. Ibid., 139–40. These cities are described separately in Part II of Tikhomirov's book and are designated in block letters on the map on pp. 432–33.

12. Ibid., 167–75.

13. G. P. Latysheva and M. G. Rabinovich, *Moskva i moskovskii krai v proshlom* (Moscow, 1973), 49.

14. For an archaeological study on the construction of a second line of fortifications in Moscow, see M. G. Rabinovich, *O drevnei Moskve* (Moscow, 1964), 35–36, 51–59. The early wall around the posad in Suzdal' is mentioned by A. M. Sakharov, *Goroda severo-vostochnoi Rusi XIV–XV vekov*, 41.

15. L. V. Cherepnin in *Puti razvitiia feodalizma*, 159–63.

16. For instance, see the introduction to Volume II of *Istoriia SSSR*, where it is argued that the Tatars interrupted the process of unification of scattered lands, that many parts of the later Russian Empire lost historic ties with each other, that the Russian state was weakened to the point that it could be attacked with damaging consequences by aggressors from the west, and that Russia received the Tatar blow, serving as a shield for Western civilization. Thus Russia was sacrificed while Europe was saved and could experience rapid development. A. M. Sakharov carries this argument further, asserting that cities in ancient Russia had been as developed as in other European countries at the time, but that, by the fifteenth century, Russian cities had fallen very much behind and because of the continued threat of Tatars until the seventeenth or eighteenth century bourgeois elements could emerge only slowly in Russia. See *Obrazovanie i razvitie rossiiskogo gosudarstva v XIV–XVII vv.*, 28–33.

17. Much evidence for this conclusion is provided in Chapter Three of L. V. Cherepnin, *Obrazovanie russkogo tsentralizovannogo gosudarstva v XIV–XV vekakh*, 297–454.

18. A. M. Sakharov, *Goroda severo-vostochnoi Rusi XIV–XV vekov*, 23–24.

19. The competition for control over networks of cities can be pieced together from the histories of separate cities such as Tikhomirov. *Drevniaia Moskva (XII–XV vv.)* (Moscow, 1947); and *Istoriia goroda Gor'kogo* (Gor'kii, 1971).

20. These generalizations about population figures are based largely on data given in Sakharov, *Goroda severo-vostochnoi Rusi XIV–XV vekov*.

21. The rapid growth of Moscow's population is described in Sakharov, *Obrazovanie i razvitie rossiiskogo gosudarstva v XIV–XVII vv.*, 44–60.

22. The early history of the Kremlin is described in Tikhomirov, *Drevniaia Moskva (XII–XV vv.)*, 148–61.

23. See A. L. Shapiro, ed., *Agrarnaia istoriia severo-zapada Rossii*, 329–36.

24. Sakharov, *Goroda severo-vostochnoi Rusi XIV–XV vekov*, 146–50, and 177.

25. S. V. Bakhrushin, *Nauchnye trudy*, I (Moscow, 1952), 25–54.

26. Sakharov, *Goroda severo-vostochnoi Rusi XIV–XV vekov*, 128. Also see data on the first half of the sixteenth century in A. I. Kopanev, "Naselenie russkogo gosudarstva v XVI v.," *Istoricheskie zapiski* 64 (1959), 239–41.

27. See Cherepnin, "O formakh ob'edinenii remeslennikov v russkikh gorodakh XIV–XV vv.," N. V. Ustiugov, ed., *Voprosy sotsial'no-ekonomicheskoi istorii i istochnikovedeniia perioda feodalizma v Rossii* (Moscow, 1961), 19–24; and also Cherepnin, *Obrazovanie russkogo tsentralizovannogo gosudarstva v XIV–XV vekakh*, 366–67.

28. Cherepnin in *Goroda feodal'noi Rossii*, 105, argues that a number of studies have shown that the rise of cities as craft and trade centers and the strengthening of economic ties between them created the objective preconditions for the formation of a politically unified country.

29. A. I. Kopanev, "Naselenie russkogo gosudarstva v XVI v.," 235 and 246.

30. Ia. E. Vodarskii, *Naselenie Rossii za 400 let (XVI– nachalo XX vv.)* (Moscow, 1973), 27; and A. I. Kopanev, "Naselenie russkogo gosudarstva v XVI v.," 233–34, 245–46 and 254.

31. See V. Grekov, "Khoziaistvennii krizis v moskovskom gosudarstve v 70–80–kh godakh XVI v.," *Voprosy istorii* (1945:1), 6–21.

32. The most complete accounts of separate cities of Russia to 1750 have been compiled for the sixteenth and the first half of the seventeenth centuries. See N. D. Chechulin, *Goroda moskovskogo gosudarstva v 16 veke* (St. Petersburg, 1889); P. P. Smirnov, *Goroda moskovskogo gosudarstva v pervoi polovine XVII veke* (Kiev, 1917); and M. N. Tikhomirov, *Rossiia v 16 stoletii* (Moscow, 1962).

33. This process of changing Russian-nomadic relations in the Astrakhan' area is described by N. B. Golikova, "Ocherki po istorii naseleniia gorodov Nizhnego Povolzh'ia," 24.

34. V. T. Pashuto in *Goroda feodal'noi Rossii*, 95–97, divides cities into two categories, private and public, and further divides private cities into those under a prince, a religious organization, or a boiar.

35. P. P. Smirnov, *Posadskie liudi i ikh klassovaia bor'ba do serediny XVII veka*, I and II (Moscow, 1947). Smirnov argues that, in the fourteenth and fifteenth centuries, land ownership in Russian cities was highly fragmented. Princes gave away separate areas of cities, and individuals in these areas frequently worked for and were dependent on the local owner. During the sixteenth and seventeenth centuries, however, control over all areas of the city was consolidated. In the process, rights were granted to the broad population of posad residents, who increasingly worked for an impersonal market. Corresponding to the decline in rural areas of lords owning large votchiny with low productivity who were being replaced by small-scale lords with new methods of organization, in cities owners of large areas of urban land and numerous dependents were being superseded by a rising number of persons in trade and craft activities who owed responsibility to a single ruler. Further remarks on the decline of private urban possessions can be found in *Goroda feodal'noi Rossii*, 43–44, 57, and 187 in articles written by A. L. Khoroshkevich, Iu. R. Klokman, and M. Ia. Volkov.

36. N. E. Nosov, "Russkii gorod i russkoe kupechestvo v XVI stoletii," 159. Also see E. V. Chistiakova, "Moskva v seredine 30-kh godov XVII v.," *Novoe o proshlom nashei strany* (Moscow, 1967), 301–09.

37. For data on urban population during the sixteenth century, see Nosov, "Russkii gorod i russkoe kupechestvo v XVI stoletii," 157–59.

38. See also V. K. Iatsunskii in *Goroda feodal'noi Rossii*, who relying on P. P. Smirnov's data for 1650 gives a total of 226 cities of which 160 had posad, but this list omits non-uezd centers with trade and craft activities.

39. On Moscow as a trade and craft center at this time, see S. V. Bakhrushkin, *Nauchnye trudy*, I, 157–87.

40. G. P. Latysheva and M. G. Rabinovich, *Moskva i moskovskii krai v proshlom*, 143.

41. S. B. Veselovskii, *Selo i derevnia v severo-vostochnoi Rusi XIV–XVI vv.* (Moscow, 1936), 24–26. Also see an article on early periodic markets and fairs by S. V. Bakhrushkin, *Nauchnye trudy*, I, 188–203.

42. K. N. Serbina in *Goroda feodal'noi Rossii*, 135–43, presents information on marketing settlements during the sixteenth century, pointing to the existence of more than 100 trade and craft settlements in addition to administrative cities in the 34 uezd for which data were found. Most of these 100 settlements belonged to monasteries, while the others were privately owned by boiars, princes, and the court.

43. N. I. Kostomarov', *Ocherki torgovli moskovskogo gosudarstva v XVI i XVII stoletiiakh* (St. Petersburg, 1862), 134–38.

44. See K. N. Serbina, *Ocherki iz sotsial'no-ekonomicheskoi istorii russkogo goroda: tikhvinskii posad v XVI–XVIII vv.* (Moscow, 1951), 14–18. Also a description of one periodic marketing center is given by N. A. Baklanova, "Torgi i promysly Vasil'surska v XVII veke," *Istoricheskie zapiski* 40 (1952), 283–87.

45. Much of the evidence on the expansion of commerce comes from separate studies of the increasing trade contacts of a single city. One of the most important is A. I. Merzon and Iu. A. Tikhonov, *Rynok Ustiuga Velikogo XVII veka* (Moscow, 1960).

46. A. L. Shapiro, "Ob imushchestvennom neravenstve i sotsial'nom rassloenii russkogo krest'ianstva v epokhy feodalizma," *Voprosy genezisa kapitalizma v Rossii* (Leningrad, 1960), 126–32.

47. A. L. Khoroshkevich, "Obrazovanie edinogo rossiiskogo gosudarstva," *Istoriia SSSR*, II, 105–41.

48. Iu. A. Tikhonov, "Rossiia v pervoi polovine XVII v.," *Istoriia SSSR*, II, 297–334.

49. See Bakhrushkin, *Nauchnye trudy*, I, 38–43, on the new commercial locations. A. L. Khoroshkevich in *Goroda feodal'noi Rossii*, 42, points to Tikhomirov's information on the switch from work for orders to work for the market in Moscow—a transition that occurred later in other cities.

50. A. A. Zimin, "Sostav russkikh gorodov XVI v.," *Istoricheskie zapiski* 52 (1955), 336–47; and Zimin, "Ukreplenie rossiiskogo gosudarstva narody Povolzh'ia i Priural'ia v XVI v.," *Istoriia SSSR*, II, 142–209.

51. One of the most complete studies of land use in a seventeenth century city is provided by K. N. Serbina, *Ocherki iz sotsial'no-ekonomicheskoi istorii russkogo goroda*, 44–53.

52. By 1650 Moscow had taken roughly the appearance it was to have until the early nineteenth century. The Kremlin was developed as the center of court and administrative functions. The nearby Kitai gorod including Red Square was the commercial center with specialized rows of shops for each major type of good and with one or more gostinyi dvor for large-scale and long-distance trade. Trade was also developing in the other walled parts of the city, but the dispersal of trade in the Beloi gorod outside the Kitai gorod occurred primarily in the second half of the seventeenth century. See M. V. Dovnar'-Zapol'skii, *Torgovlia i promyshlennost' Moskvy XVI–XVII vv.* (Moscow, 1910), 41–51.

53. An introduction to the English economy between 1350 and 1500 is provided by Peter King, *The Development of the English Economy to 1750* (London, 1971), 160–63 and 219–53. A detailed study of a single area of France is given by Étienne Fournial, *Les villes et l'économie d'échange en Forez aux XIIIe et XIVe siècles* (Paris, 1967). For an overview of Western Europe at this time see C. T. Smith, *An Historical Geography of Western Europe*, 364–84.

54. See Alan Everitt, "The Marketing of Agricultural Produce," Joan Thirsk, ed., *The Agrarian History of England and Wales*, IV: *1500–1640* (Cambridge, 1967), 469.

55. Iu. R. Klokman (*Goroda feodal'noi Rossii*, 55) emphasizes the changing character of the Russian city during the seventeenth and eighteenth centuries corresponding to the development of commercial production, industry, and trade and the further widening of the differentiation of labor. Cities acquired more significance as economic centers of surrounding areas and an increasing role in what Klokman refers to as the economic and social life of the country.

56. On the consolidation of serfdom see V. I. Koretskii, "K istorii formirovaniia krepostnogo prava v Rossii," *Voprosy istorii* (1964:6), 77–96. On the bureaucratization of the state administration see N. F. Demidova, "Biurokratizatsiia gosudarstvennogo apparata absoliutizma v XVII–XVIII vv.," *Absoliutizm v Rossii* (Moscow, 1964), 206–42. On the reforms of Peter I see Marc Raeff, ed., *Peter the Great: Reformer or Revolutionary* (Boston, 1966).

57. The financial policies of the period are examined by S. M. Troitskii, "Finansovaia politika russkogo absoliutizma vo vtoroi polovine XVII i XVIII vv.," *Absoliutizm v Rossii*, 281–319.

58. Sharp regional differences existed in the percentage of commercially active urban residents registered in the posad population. In the second half of the seventeenth century about 650 of the 1,000 households in Pskov were listed in the posad population and they owned 85 percent of the city's stores as opposed to 9 percent of the stores that belonged to members of the clergy who comprised 5 percent of the city population and to 6 percent of the stores which belonged to persons from the category of soldiers and service population. See E. V. Chistiakova, "Pskovskii torg v seredine XVII v.," *Istoricheskie zapiski* 34 (1950), 199–204. More typical of cities in the south and east was Astrakhan', where only 27 percent of stores belonged to registered local posad residents,

10 percent to persons registered in posad elsewhere, and 63 percent to persons in other strata. See N. B. Golikova, "*Ocherki po istorii naseleniia gorodov Nizhnego Povolzh'ia,*" 16.

59. M. Ia. Volkov (*Goroda feodal'noi Rossii*, 189–95) indicates that in the 1660s–1680s the posad population won a number of concessions, including a reduction in the tax burden and greater self-government and that additional changes in the rules affecting the posad were made during practically every decade, resulting by the 1720s in the registration of some of the former service population in the posad. Volkhov notes, however, that there were still many in cities who remained outside of the posad category.

60. Iu. R. Klokman, "Gorod v zakonodatel'stve russkogo absoliutizma vo vtoroi polovine XVII–XVIII v.," *Absoliutizm v Rossii*, 320–54.

61. G. P. Latysheva and M. G. Rabinovich, *Moskva i moskovskii krai v proshlom*, 173–74. On stratification in this period see Ia. E. Vodarskii, *Naselenie Rossii za 400 let (XVI– nachalo XX vv.)* 34–41.

62. On the reforms in administrative divisions see Iu. Got'e, *Istoriia oblastnogo upravleniia v Rossii ot Petra I do Ekateriny II* (Moscow, 1913 and 1941).

63. Ia. E. Vodarskii, "Chislennost' i razmeshchenie posadskogo naseleniia v Rossii vo vtoroi polovine XVII v.," in *Goroda feodal'noi Rossii*, 279.

64. An overview of development during the second half of the seventeenth century is given by A. A. Preobrazhenskii, "Sotsial'no-ekonomicheskoe razvitie russkogo gosudarstva 40-e gody– konets XVII v.," *Istoriia SSSR*, III, 15–33. A comparable overview for the eighteenth century is provided by N. I. Pavlenko, "Khoziaistvennyi pod'em," *Istoriia SSSR*, III, 192–224.

65. See N. L. Rubinshtein, "Nekotorye voprosy formirovaniia rynka rabochei sily v Rossii XVIII veka," *Voprosy istorii* (February 1952), 74–101.

66. For a review of social differentiation in cities during the seventeenth and early eighteenth centuries, see M. Ia. Volkov in *Goroda feodal'noi Rossii*, 182–85.

67. B. B. Kafengauz, *Ocherki vnutrennego rynka Rossii pervoi poloviny XVIII veka* (Moscow, 1958), 3. In addition to Kafengauz's book on marketing see an article by A. A. Preobrazhenskii and Iu. A. Tikhonov, "Itogi izucheniia nachal'nogo etapa skladyvaniia vserossiiskogo rynka (XVII v.)," *Istoriia SSSR* (1960), 80–109.

68. B. B. Kafengauz, "Khlebnaia torgovlia Moskvy v 30-kh godakh XVIII stoletiia," *Voprosy istorii* (1947:9), 105–12; *Ocherki vnutrennego rynka Rossii pervoi poloviny XVIII v.*, 191–261; and "Geografiia vnutrennei torgovli i ekonomicheskaia spetsializatsiia raionov Rossii v 20-kh godakh XVIII veka," *Voprosy geografii* 20 (1950), 163–202; and E. N. Kusheva, "Torgovlia Moskvy v 30–40-kh godakh XVIII v.," *Istoricheskie zapiski* 23 (1947), 44–104.

69. V. M. Vazhinskii (*Goroda feodal'noi Rossii*, 298–307) describes the rapid growth of commercial ties between cities in the Central-Black Earth region and those in the Central-Industrial region during the third quarter of the eighteenth century.

70. This fair is described by B. B. Kafengauz, *Ocherki vnutrennego rynka Rossii pervoi poloviny XVIII veka*, 114–90.

71. On Siberia see O. N. Vilkov, *Remeslo i torgovlia zapadnoi Sibiri v XVII veke* (Moscow, 1967); and A. N. Kopylov in *Goroda feodal'noi Rossii*, 334–42.

72. See E. I. Zaozerskaia, *Razvitie legkoi promyshlennosti v Moskve v pervoi chetverti XVIII v.* (Moscow, 1953), and *U istokov krupnogo proizvodstva v russkoi promyshlennosti XVI–XVII vekov* (Moscow, 1970). She argues that the seventeenth century was a time of substantial development of simple small-scale craft production and of the birth of large-scale production especially in textiles. This pattern of development was continued during the beginning of the eighteenth century when, according to Zaozerskaia, there was a basic change in the light industry of Moscow as the city attracted growing amounts of raw materials from outside.

73. A. M. Razgon, "Promyshlennye i torgovye slobody i sela vladimirskoi gubernii vo vtoroi polovine XVIII v.," *Istoricheskie zapiski* 32 (1950), 135.

74. L. L. Murav'eva, *Derevenskaia promyshlennost' tsentral'noi Rossii: vtoroi poloviny XVII v.* (Moscow, 1971), 37.

75. G. D. Kapustina in *Goroda feodal'noi Rossii*, 375.

76. See my article, "Comparative Approaches to Urbanization: Russia 1750–1800."

77. Ia. E. Vodarskii in *Goroda feodal'noi Rossii*, 280.

78. See F. Ia. Polianskii, *Gorodskoe remeslo i manufaktura v Rossii XVIII v.*, 26–29. Polianskii mentions that in addition to the 189 cities with posad at the time of the first enumeration (1719 not 1722), there were about 80 uezd centers that lacked posad. Among cities with posad, 103 are labeled by Polianskii as already formed, having at least 500 males. By the time of the second enumeration in 1742, the total number of cities with posad had risen to 202, of which 112 qualified as having at least 500 males. To his credit, Polianskii adds that the posad population does not fully reflect the economic significance of cities and is not necessarily an accurate indication of actual population.

79. N. B. Golikova, "Ocherki po istorii naseleniia gorodov Nizhnego Povolzh'ia," 50–81.

80. See Ia. E. Vodarskii in *Goroda feodal'noi Rossii*, 279, for the seventeenth century figures. The most detailed study of the posad population and the regulations affecting them during the period of the first, second, and third enumerations from 1719 to 1762 is the well-known book by A. A. Kizevetter, *Posadskaia obshchina v Rossii XVIII st.* (Moscow, 1903).

81. N. B. Golikova points out that in addition to the posad population there was often a large service population in Russian cities, which might include craftsmen on a fixed wage and a grain stipend who were registered with a government body, farmhands working in state orchards and vineyards, or fishermen working for the state. In most cities the largest component of the service population were the strel'tsy and other categories attached to the garrison. Although they were required to take part in military expeditions and to serve guard duty, they were also called upon to serve the state in such varied ways as in the repair of fortifications, in the construction of public buildings, in the supply of firewood, hay and other provisions, and in the transportation of various goods. In theory, these responsibilities to serve local administrators

were unlimited; yet members of the service population, in fact, were also part of the private work force, engaging in such activities as hired labor, commerce, and gardening. During the early eighteenth century as new taxes were imposed on members of this strata, old stipends and rights were withdrawn, and they became scarcely different from other elements of the urban population, including the posad category. See N. B. Golikova, "Ocherki po istorii naseleniia gorodov Nizhnego Povolzh'ia," avtoreferat, 9–14, and related sections in the full dissertation.

82. See Mason Hammond, *The City in the Ancient World* (Cambridge, Mass., 1972).

83. Norman J. G. Pounds, "The Urbanization of the Classical World," *Annals of the Association of American Geographers* 59 (March 1969), 135–57.

84. In ibid., 153–54, the cities of Gaul and Britain are divided into levels. Cities at each level are described in terms of their area, their marketing functions, and their populations.

85. Peter King, *The Development of the English Economy to 1750*, 45–51.

86. Marguerite Boulet-Sautel, "La formation de la ville médiévale dans les régions du centre de la France," in Société Jean Bodin, *La Ville*, II (part 2) (Brussels, 1955), 357–70.

87. See J. C. Russell, *Medieval Regions and Their Cities*, 87–96, 112–29, 146–65.

88. Alan Everitt ("The Marketing of Agricultural Produce," 466–67) points out that most markets were formed in a 200-year period following the Norman conquest but that some markets existed even before the late eleventh century. Eleventh-century English markets are mentioned by Alan Rogers, *A History of Lincolnshire* (London, 1970), 30–32. For information on early French markets and fairs see Félix Bourquelot, *Études sur les foires de Champagne* (Brionne, 1970), 6–17.

89. Russell, *Medieval Regions and Their Cities*, chapter one.

90. On the history of markets, fairs and charters in a particular area of England, see W. G. Hoskins, *Devon* (London, 1964), 57–62, 105–112.

91. Peter Clark and Paul Slack, eds., *Crisis and Order in English Towns 1500–1700* (Toronto, 1972), 10.

92. Dorothy Davis, *Fairs, Shops and Supermarkets: A History of English Shopping* (Toronto, 1966), 71.

NOTES TO CHAPTER 3

1. Russia's proximity to and extensive interaction with the early modernizing societies meant that in some respects its transition from a premodern to a modernized society began, albeit quite slowly, by the early nineteenth century, as much as 50 years before the transition of other major latecomers to modernization such as China and Japan. For this reason the treatment of Russia here is confined to the years before 1800 although in most respects the country probably continued to evolve in accord with the internal dynamics present in the premodern phase. It should be noted that for some purposes, as for the study of modernization in Japan and Russia, comparisons are more usefully

drawn using the 1860s as a cutoff, since the full-scale transition in Russia began only at that time.

2. Many of the changes under way throughout much of the eighteenth century are mentioned in *Istoriia SSSR*, III, 424; and in S. M. Troitskii, *Finansovaia politika russkogo absoliutizma v XVIII veke* (Moscow, 1966), 88. Even the build-up of mining and metallurgy, usually associated with wartime needs and Peter I's leadership, occurred in large part during the middle of the century. L. E. Iofa in *Goroda Urala*, I (Moscow, 1951), 158-59, calculates that the number of plants in the Urals area rose from 40 in 1734 to 114 in 1767.

3. V. K. Iatsunskii (*Goroda feodal'noi Rossii*, 84) notes that P. P. Smirnov calculated that, during the entire eighteenth century, 315 settlements were founded as cities. Iatsunskii explains this large figure as, above all, a consequence of granting official urban status to trade and craft settlements, raising doubt as to whether it is correct to equate the foundation of cities with the recognition of existing settlements as administrative centers. He correctly implies that some of the new official cities resulting from the reforms of 1775-1785 should be counted as cities even prior to these dates, which is the practice I have followed in rejecting a purely administrative definition of cities.

4. Iu. R. Klokman, *Ocherki sotsial'no-ekonomicheskoi istorii gorodov severo-zapada Rossii v seredine XVIII v.*, 13.

5. N. L. Rubinshtein, "Russkaia iarmarka XVIII veka," *Uchenye zapiski* (of Moscow Oblast' Pedagogical Institute) 1 (1939), 5-29.

6. G. L. Vartanov, "Kupechestvo i torguiushchee krest'ianstvo tsentral'noi chasti Evropeiskoi Rossii," *Uchenye zapiski* (of Leningrad State Pedagogical Institute) 229 (1962), 161-96.

7. A. M. Razgon, "Promyshlennye i torgovye slobody," 133-72.

8. See N. L. Rubinshtein, "Vneshniaia torgovlia Rossii i russkoe kupechestvo vo vtoroi polovine XVIII v.," *Istoricheskie zapiski* 54 (1955), 355; and F. Ia. Polianskii, *Gorodskoe remeslo i manufaktura v Rossii XVIII v.*, 50.

9. N. A. Rubinshtein, *Sel'skoe khoziaistvo Rossii vo vtoroi polovine XVIII v.* (Moscow, 1957), 330-33, 422-32.

10. For instance, see N. L. Rubinshtein, "Nekotorye voprosy formirovaniia rynka rabochei sily v Rossii XVIII veka," 74-101.

11. Some writers choose to emphasize either the positive or negative forces during this period. A. L. Shapiro stresses the barriers to development, focusing on the presence of serfdom as a factor preventing the accumulation of wealth by peasants and therefore slowing the differentiation of the population. See his article, "Razvitie rynochnykh otnoshenii i krepostnichestvo v russkoi derevne pervoi poloviny XVIII v.," *Ezhegodnik po agrarnoi istorii Vostochnoi Evropy. 1961* (Riga, 1963), 207-17. In contrast, G. L. Vartanov emphasizes the factors favoring development, describing the second half of the eighteenth century as a period when Russian productive forces made a big step forward. Basic to this advance was an increase in the area under cultivation, a rise in population, and an increase in the number of manufacturing enterprises. Commercial production developed in all fields of the economy and on this basis a wide unfolding of trade ties occurred in the national market. Vartanov adds that the tempo of economic development quickened from the 1770s as exports tripled over 30

years and even more success was realized in internal trade. See G. L. Vartanov, "Kupechestvo gorodov moskovskoi gubernii vo vtoroi polovine XVIII veka" (avtoreferat of candidate's dissertation submitted to the Leningrad State Pedagogical Institute, Department of the History of the USSR, 1967), 3.

12. I. A. Bulygin, *Polozhenie krest'ian i tovarnoe proizvodstvo v Rossii: vtoraia polovina XVIII veka* (Moscow, 1966), 5.

13. P. G. Ryndziunskii, "Novye goroda Rossii kontsa 18 v.," in *Problemy obshchestvenno-politicheskoi istorii Rossii i slavianskikh stran* (Moscow, 1963), 359–61.

14. Got'e, *Istoriia oblastnogo upravleniia v Rossii ot Petra I do Ekateriny II*, I, 116.

15. See Vartanov, "Kupechestvo i torguiushchee krest'ianstvo," 161–96.

16. These changes are described in detail in Klokman, *Sotsial'no-ekonomicheskaia istoriia russkogo goroda*, 100–09, 122–206.

17. Ryndziunskii ("Novye goroda Rossii kontsa 18 v.," 359–70) argues that, during these reforms, uezd centers with little economic development were most likely to be eliminated. Bulygin (*Goroda feodal'noi Rossii*, 490) indicates that this consideration operated even earlier; the new uezd centers of 1775–1785 were frequently chosen from among already active marketing settlements. For instance, the governor-general of Vladimir, Tambov, and Penza in 1780 cited the fact that various settlements had weekly markets as a sign of their suitability for becoming uezd cities. Bulygin asserts that this provides evidence that the first consideration in the choice of new cities was the presence in the settlement of a periodic market. Presumably further development of marketing activities permitted preservation of the uezd designation in 1796 and 1803.

18. See Klokman, *Sotsial'no-ekonomicheskaia istoriia russkogo goroda*, 202. Also see V. F. Zheludkov, "Vvedenie gubernskoi reformy 1775 goda," *Uchenye zapiski* (of Leningrad State Pedagogical Institute) 229 (1962), 197–226.

19. V. M. Kabuzan, *Narodonaselenie Rossii v XVIII– pervoi polovine XIX v. (po materialam revizii)* (Moscow, 1963), 107–223.

20. Other divisions of all or parts of the Russian Empire into regions can be found in N. A. Rubinshtein, *Sel'skoe khoziaistvo Rossii vo vtoroi polovine XVIII v.*, 21–23; V. M. Kabuzan, *Izmeneniia v razmeshchenii naseleniia Rossii v XVIII– pervoi polovine XIX v. (po materialam revizii)* (Moscow, 1971); and Iu. R. Klokman, *Sotsial'no-ekonomicheskaia istoriia russkogo goroda*, 122–206.

21. See A. V. Emmausskii, "Ekonomicheskoe razvitie viatskoi gubernii v kontse XVIII veka," *Uchenye zapiski* (of Kirov State Pedagogical Institute) 19 (1965), 4.

22. The writings of V. M. Kabuzan include two major books cited in notes 19 and 20 on the population of Russia and on changes in the distribution of that population during the years of the ten enumerations from 1719 to 1857. In addition, two articles of his that deserve special mention are "Nekotorye materialy dlia izucheniia istoricheskoi geografii Rossii XVIII– nachala XIX v.," *Problemy istochnikovedeniia*, XI (Moscow, 1963), 159–95; and an article jointly authored with S. M. Troitskii, "Izmeneniia v chislennosti, udel'nom vese i razmeshchenii dvorianstva v Rossii v 1782–1858 gg.," *Istoriia SSSR* (1971:4), 153–68. In addition, Kabuzan has an important unpublished article on urban

populations, which has been referred to by V. K. Iatsunskii in *Goroda feodal'noi Rossii*, 87–88.

23. V. M. Kabuzan, *Izmeneniia v razmeshchenii naseleniia Rossii*, 10.

24. Ibid., 27–28, 31, 37.

25. Ibid., 12–13.

26. See V. F. Zheludkov, "Vvedenie gubernskoi reformy 1775 goda," 209–10.

27. One source of data on uezd populations is A. Shchekatov, ed., *Geograficheskii slovar' rossiiskogo gosudarstva* (hereafter called *Geographical Dictionary*) (Moscow, 1801–08).

28. Ibid., I, 116–19, 192–93, 580–85.

29. Iu. A. Tikhonov, "Krest'ianskoe khoziaistvo tsentral'noi Rossii pervoi chetverti XVIII v.," *Istoriia SSSR* (1971:4), 169–78.

30. See the *Geographical Dictionary* for data on the number of households per uezd.

31. On Russian peasant households in the early twentieth century, see Teodor Shanin, *The Awkward Class: Political Sociology of Peasantry in a Developing Society: Russia 1910–1925* (Oxford, 1972), 28–32, 64–71. Far less information is currently available on peasant households in premodern Russia. Apparently during the second half of the eighteenth century some reduction occurred in the average size of peasant households as multi-family units decreased. See G. T. Riabkov, "Krest'ianskoe khoziaistvo v kontse XVIII– pervoi polovine XIX veka (po materialam smolenskoi gubernii): k istorii genezisa kapitalizma v sel'skom khoziaistve" (avtoreferat of doctoral dissertation submitted to the Academy of Sciences of the USSR, 1970), 31.

32. N. A. Rubinshtein, *Sel'skoe khoziaistvo Rossii vo vtoroi polovine XVIII v.*, 149–51.

33. For the data on which this discussion is based see Kabuzan, *Izmeneniia v razmeshchenii naseleniia Rossii*, 95–106.

34. The conflicting figures for urban population given elsewhere are discussed in my article, "Comparative Approaches to Urbanization: Russia, 1750–1800."

35. On the legal position of the urban population, see P. G. Ryndziunskii, *Gorodskoe grazhdanstvo doreformennoi Rossii* (Moscow, 1958), 40–51; and Klokman, *Sotsial'no-ekonomicheskaia istoriia russkogo goroda*, 54–121.

36. The most important archival source used to obtain data from the fourth enumeration of 1782 is the *Tsentral'nyi Gosudarstvennyi Arkhiv Drevnikh Aktov* (*TsGADA*), fund 248, opis' 58, books 4338–4341.

37. On the legal aspects of peasant movement into cities, see Ryndziunskii, *Gorodskoe grazhdanstvo doreformennoi Rossii*, 52–61. For a general treatment of the rural population see E. I. Indova, *Agrarnyi stroi v Rossii v XVIII v.* (Moscow, 1966). Information on peasants' nonagricultural activities and migration to cities is given by N. A. Rubinshtein, *Sel'skoe khoziaistvo Rossii vo vtoroi polovine XVIII v.*, 302–16.

38. For the population and geographical distribution of dvoriane see Kabuzan and Troitskii, "Izmeneniia v chislennosti, udel'nom vese i razmeshchenii

dvorianstva v Rossii v 1782–1858 gg.," 153–68. Archival sources list the population of dvoriane per city.

39. An example of archival data on clergy is found in *TsGADA*, fund 248, opis' 58, book 4340, pages 418–87. In Iaroslavl' guberniia, the number of clergy totaled almost 15,000, including 648 in the guberniia city and 1,287 in the uezd centers.

40. A. G. Rashin, "Dinamika chislennosti i protsessy formirovaniia gorodskogo naseleniia Rossii v XIX– nachale XX vv.," *Istoricheskie zapiski* 34 (1950), 60–65.

41. Troitskii, "Finansovaia politika russkogo absoliutizma vo vtoroi polovine XVII i XVIII vv.," 304–19. See also Troitskii, *Finansovaia politika russkogo absoliutizma v XVIII veke.*

42. See A. I. Kopanev, *Naselenie Peterburga v pervoi polovine XIX veka* (Moscow, 1957), 108–09.

43. N. I. Pavlenko, "K voprosu ob evoliutsii dvorianstva v XVII–XVIII vv.," *Voprosy genezisa kapitalizma v Rossii* (Leningrad, 1960), 54–75; and Kabuzan and Troitskii, "Izmeneniia v chislennosti, udel'nom vese i razmeshchenii dvorianstva v Rossii v 1782–1858 gg.," 153–68.

44. Ibid., 158.

45. *Geographical Dictionary*, III, 169–73.

46. Ibid., VI, 74–77.

47. Bulygin, *Polozhenie krest'ian i tovarnoe proizvodstvo v Rossii*, 24–25, 31–32.

48. E. I. Indova, *Krepostnoe khoziaistvo v nachale XIX veka: po materialam votchinnogo arkhiva Vorontsovykh* (Moscow, 1955), 24–26.

49. G. T. Riabkov, "Krest'ianskoe khoziaistvo v kontse XVIII– pervoi polovine XIX veka," 16–17.

50. N. M. Shepukova, "Ob izmenenii razmerov dushevladeniia pomeshchikov Evropeiskoi Rossii v pervoi chetverti XVIII– pervoi polovine XIX v.," *Ezhegodnik po agrarnoi istorii Vostochnoi Evropy. 1963* (Vilnius, 1964), 388–419.

51. See ibid., 393. For additional information see I. D. Koval'chenko, *Russkoe krepostnoe krest'ianstvo v pervoi polovine XIX v.* (Moscow, 1967).

52. L. V. Milov, *Issledovanie ob 'ekonomicheskikh primecheniiakh' k general'nomu mezhevaniiu (k istorii russkogo krest'ianstva i sel'skogo khoziaistva vtoroi poloviny XVIII v.)* (Moscow, 1965), 20–21, 225, 269–70. Also see V. I. Semevskii, *Krest'iane v tsarstvovanie imperatritsy Ekateriny II*, I (St. Petersburg, 1903), 24–37; and N. A. Rubinshtein, *Sel'skoe khoziaistvo Rossii vo vtoroi polovine XVIII v.*, 164–65.

53. See G. T. Riabkov, "Krest'ianskoe khoziaistvo v kontse XVIII– pervoi polovine XIX veka," 15–27; I. D. Koval'chenko, "O tovarnosti zemledeliia v Rossii v pervoi polovine XIX v.," *Ezhegodnik po agrarnoi istorii Vostochnoi Evropy. 1963* (Vilnius, 1964), 467–86; and Michael Confino, *Domaines et seigneurs en Russe vers la fin du XVIIIe siècle* (Paris, 1963).

54. N. F. Demidova, "Biurokratizatsiia gosudarstvennogo apparata absoliutizma v XVII–XVIII vv.," *Absoliutizm v Rossii* (Moscow, 1964), 240;

S. M. Troitskii, "Sotsial'nyi sostav i chislennost' biurokratii Rossii v seredine XVIII v.," *Istoricheskie zapiski* 89 (Moscow, 1972); and Walter Pintner, "The Social Characteristics of the Early 19th Century Russian Bureaucracy," *Slavic Review* 29:3 (Sept. 1970), 430–43.

55. Kopanev, *Naselenie Peterburga v pervoi polovine XIX veka*, 113.

56. Pintner, "The Social Characteristics of the Early 19th Century Russian Bureaucracy," 434.

57. V. N. Iakovtsevskii, *Kupecheskii kapital v feodal'no-krepostnicheskoi Rossii* (Moscow, 1953), 51–60. See also G. L. Vartanov, "Moskovskoe i inogorodnoe kupechestvo vo vtoroi polovine XVIII v.," *Uchenye zapiski* (of Leningrad State Pedagogical Institute) 278 (1965), 272–90.

58. Kopanev, *Naselenie Peterburga v pervoi polovine XIX veka*, 103.

59. See Iakovtsevskii, *Kupecheskii kapital v feodal'no-krepostnicheskoi Rossii*, 45; and *Ocherki istorii SSSR (period feodalizma: Rossiia vo vtoroi polovine XVIII v.)* (Moscow, 1956), 135.

60. Kopanev, *Naselenie Peterburga v pervoi polovine XIX veka*, 103.

61. Kizevetter (*Posadskaia obshchina v Rossii XVIII st.*, 48–63) makes clear that the mobility of registered posad residents was generally restricted. For travel beyond a certain distance (often about 20 miles) from their city or, perhaps, outside the boundaries of their uezd a passport was required. However, as long as posad members kept their original place of registration and paid taxes there, they generally were permitted to live elsewhere. Transfer of registration proved somewhat easier for posad members moving to the U-S region. For an account in English of the rules affecting the posad population, see M. Hittle, "The City in Muscovite and Early Imperial Russia" (a doctoral dissertation submitted to the Department of History at Harvard University, 1971).

62. See Bulygin, *Polozhenie krest'ian i tovarnoe proizvodstvo v Rossii*, 58–65.

63. Vartanov, "Kupechestvo i torguiushchee krest'ianstvo tsentral'noi chasti Evropeiskoi Rossii vo vtoroi polovine XVIII veka."

64. Latysheva and Rabinovich, *Moskva i moskovskii krai v proshlom*, 173.

65. The geographical distribution of posad residents can be found in Kizevetter, *Posadskaia obshchina v Rossii XVIII veka*, 118–19.

66. I have drawn similar tables for China and Japan in *Urban Networks in Ch'ing China and Tokugawa Japan*, 86.

67. Kopanev, *Naselenie Peterburga v pervoi polovine XIX veka*, 87, 110–12.

68. Kondrashenkov in *Goroda feodal'noi Rossii*, 508.

69. On wages of boatmen during the 1790s see N. L. Rubinshtein, "Nekotorye voprosy formirovaniia rynka rabochei sily v Rossii XVIII veka," 93–101. On budgets of serfowners and peasants see Bulygin, *Polozhenie krest'ian i tovarnoe proizvodstvo v Rossii*.

70. Riabkov, "Smolenskii rynok v kontse XVIII– pervoi polovine XIX veka," 56–57.

71. For some of the functions of Russian fairs, see N. L. Rubinshtein, "Russkaia iarmarka XVIII veka," 7–8.

72. Khromov, *Ocherki ekonomiki feodalizma v Rossii*, 224.

73. M. K. Rozhkov, "Torgovlia," in M. K. Rozhkov, ed., *Ocherki ekonomicheskoi istorii Rossii pervoi polovine XIX veka* (Moscow, 1959), 249–50.

74. G. L. Vartanov, "Gorodskie iarmarki tsentral'noi chasti Evropeiskoi Rossii vo vtoroi polovine XVIII v.," *Uchenye zapiski* (of Leningrad State Pedagogical Institute) 194 (1958), 145–46.

75. M. K. Rozhkova, "K voprosu o znachenii iarmarok vo vnutrennei torgovle doreformennoi Rossii (pervaia polovina XIX v.)," 305. See also I. G. Shul'ga, "Razvitie torgovli na levoberezhnoi Ukraine vo vtoroi polovine XVIII v.," *Voprosy genezisa kapitalizma v Rossii*, 157–69; and I. G. Shul'ga, "K voprosu o razvitii vserossiiskogo rynka vo vtoroi polovine XVIII veka (po materialam levoberezhnoi Ukrainy)," *Voprosy istorii* (1958:10), 34–45.

76. M. Chulkov, "Slovar' uchrezhdennykh v Rossii iarmarok i torgov," *Novyi i polnyi geograficheskii slovar' rossiiskogo gosudarstva,* IV (1788); and M. Chulkov, *Istoricheskoe opisanie rossiiskoi kommertsii,* IV:6 (1789).

77. N. L. Rubinshtein, "Russkaia iarmarka XVIII veka," 12.

78. See Vartanov, "Kupechestvo gorodov moskovskoi gubernii vo vtoroi polovine XVIII veka," 5. He asserts that in the C-I region the basic network of fairs and markets appeared during the period from the 1760s to the 1780s.

79. M. K. Rozhkova, "K voprosu o znachenii iarmarok," 298.

80. Ibid., 306–08.

81. Vartanov, "Gorodskie iarmarki," 150–51.

82. *Geographical Dictionary,* IV, 11–12.

83. Razgon, "Promyshlennye i torgovye slobody," 152–54.

84. *Istoricheskoe i topograficheskoe opisanie gorodov moskovskoi gubernii,* 83–368.

85. Razgon, "Promyshlennye i torgovye slobody," 155–56.

86. *Geographical Dictionary,* III, 953–54.

87. Ibid., IV, 329–32.

88. N. L. Rubinshtein, "Russkaia iarmarka XVIII veka," 7.

89. *Geographical Dictionary,* II, 258 and 266.

90. Ibid., III, 591–95.

91. Ibid., IV, 418–19.

92. Ibid., I, 1281–84.

93. *Istoriia SSSR,* III, 420.

94. Kafengauz, *Ocherki vnutrennego rynka Rossii pervoi poloviny XVIII v.* See also *Ocherki Istorii SSSR,* III, 121–50; and Kafengauz, "Geografiia vnutrennei torgovli i ekonomicheskaia spetsializatsiia raionov Rossii v 20-kh godakh XVIII veka," 163–202.

95. On the Irbit fair, see Iofa, *Goroda Urala,* I, 130–36, 195–200.

96. On the Vazhskaia Blagoveshchenskaia fair, see Kafengauz, *Ocherki vnutrennego rynka Rossii pervoi poloviny XVIII v.,* 262–86.

97. On the Makar'evskaia fair, also see ibid., 114–90.

98. On the Korennaia fair, see V. I. Samsonov, "Kurskaia korennaia iarmarka," *Uchenye zapiski* (of Kursk State Pedagogical Institute) 2 (1949), 96–131.

99. "Plany gorodov," *Polnoe sobranie zakonov,* I (St. Petersburg, 1859).

100. For example, I. I. Ditiatin', *Ustroistvo i upravlenie gorodov Rossii,* I

(St. Petersburg, 1875); and Kizevetter, *Posadskaia obshchina v Rossii XVIII st.*

101. Klokman, *Sotsial'no-ekonomicheskaia istoriia russkogo goroda*, 3; Polianskii, *Gorodskoe remeslo i manufaktura v Rossii XVIII v.*, 151; and Ryndziunskii, *Gorodskoe grazhdanstvo doreformennoi Rossii*, 14–17.

102. *Geographical Dictionary*, III, 477–79; IV, 618; V, 1233–35.

103. Razgon, "Promyshlennye i torgovye slobody," 135–55.

104. *Geographical Dictionary*, III, 944 and VI, 790–91.

105. Ibid., II, 594–98; and *Istoricheskoe i topograficheskoe opisanie gorodov moskovskoi gubernii*, 182–201.

106. Ibid., 221–40.

107. These numbers for stores are found in the *Geographical Dictionary*, III, 1055–56, and IV, 456–59. Estimates of this ratio are given also by Klokman, *Sotsial'no-ekonomicheskaia istoriia russkogo goroda*, 40–41.

108. *Geographical Dictionary*, I, 465–67.

109. *Istoricheskoe i topograficheskoe opisanie gorodov moskovskoi gubernii*, 134–46, 241–60, 261–79.

110. See L. V. Milov, "O tak nazyvaemykh agrarnykh gorodakh Rossii XVIII veka," *Voprosy istorii* (1968:6), 54–64.

111. *Geographical Dictionary*, II, 681; IV, 984–86.

112. Ibid., I, 325–27; and *Istoricheskoe opisanie gorodov moskovskoi gubernii*.

113. *Geographical Dictionary*, IV, 1048–53.

114. Ibid., III, 1027–30.

115. Ibid., VI, 406–23.

116. Ibid., IV, 1030–33.

117. Ibid., II, 580–84; V, 30–38. For a detailed discussion of the location of trade in cities see Karpachev, "Sotsial'no-ekonomicheskoe razvitie gorodov Belorussii," 504–613. Karpachev notes that by the 1640s in major cities of Belorussia stores had already appeared outside of the market squares. In addition to central all-purpose marketing squares, other squares had emerged as sites of specialized trade such as clusters of meat stores. Cities with a large number of stores generally had *riadi*, with stores, often grouped by type of good, facing each other in two rows. Salt or fish riadi were common. In some riadi, stores were of the same size, but more often they varied. For instance, in Pinsk in 1783, of the 93 stores in the marketplace, some measured only one-half the normal size; so it is more correct to calculate the total as 75 stores. Mogilev, a city of more than 9,000 persons in the 1780s, had 238 stores, 135 in seven riadi and 20 in the front parts of merchants' homes. Shklov, with only 2,400 inhabitants, counted 190 stores, of which 120 were located in a stone gostinyi dvor.

118. *Geographical Dictionary*, IV, 718.

119. Ibid., IV, 1345–48.

120. Ibid., III, 85–127; VI, 382–403.

121. Ibid., III, 1006–27; VI, 139–53.

122. Golikova, "Ocherki po istorii naseleniia gorodov Nizhnego Povolzh'ia," 50–51.

123. *Geographical Dictionary*, VI, 386–403.

124. Ibid., I, 267–82.

125. Golikova, "Ocherki po istorii naseleniia gorodov Nizhnego Povolzh'ia," 62–68.

126. *Geographical Dictionary*, V, 667.

127. Ibid., V, 624–52.

128. P. V. Sytin, *Istoriia planirovki i zastroiki Moskvy*, II (Moscow, 1954), 200–201.

129. *Geographical Dictionary*, IV, 337–93; V, 624–705.

130. For the number of stores in the city divided by location see *Istoricheskoe i topograficheskoe opisanie gorodov moskovskoi gubernii*, 20–82; and Sytin, *Istoriia planirovki i zastroiki Moskvy*, 201.

131. Ibid., 362–63.

132. See Ryndziunskii's article in *Goroda feodal'noi Rossii*, 71.

133. Sytin, *Istoriia planirovki i zastroiki Moskvy*, 562–63; and Sytin, *Iz istorii moskovskikh ulits* (Moscow, 1952), 79–160.

134. Sytin, *Istoriia planirovki i zastroiki Moskvy*, 81–84, 366–67.

135. Ibid., 200, 486–90.

136. See the *Geographical Dictionary*, IV, 365; *Istoricheskoe i topograficheskoe opisanie gorodov moskovskoi gubernii*, 3; and *Ocherki istorii SSSR*, IV, 151–52. A somewhat lower estimate of 300,000 winter residents around 1795 is quoted by Sytin, *Istoriia planirovki i zastroiki Moskvy*, 198.

137. Ibid., 7.

138. Ibid., 491.

139. *Geographical Dictionary*, IV, 337–93.

140. Ibid., II, 603–606.

141. Sytin, *Istoriia planirovki i zastroiki Moskvy*, 197.

142. Ibid., 19, 367.

143. *Geographical Dictionary*, V, 624–58.

144. Kopanev, *Naselenie Peterburga v pervoi polovine XIX veka*, 1–11.

145. Ivan Kirilov, *Tsvetushchee sostoianie vserossiiskogo gosudarstva* (Moscow, 1831), 90–92.

146. References to the places of origin for merchants at local markets and fairs can be found throughout the *Geographical Dictionary*.

147. *Istoricheskoe i topograficheskoe opisanie gorodov moskovskoi gubernii*; Razgon, "Promyshlennye i torgovye slobody"; and Bulygin, *Polozhenie krest'ian i tovarnoe proizvodstvo v Rossii*.

148. Razgon, "Promyshlennye i torgovye slobody," 135.

149. Khromov, *Ocherki ekonomiki feodalizma v Rossii*, 217.

150. *Geographical Dictionary*, IV, 564–66.

NOTES TO CHAPTER 4

1. Data on the administrative units in the Russian Empire, their populations, their urban populations, and the composition of the social strata present are the basic information used in this chapter. Much of this quantitative information can be found in the writings of V. M. Kabuzan. Urban data from

1782 are taken in large part from the previously cited *TsGADA* records in Moscow.

2. The archival records of *TsGADA*, fund 248, opis' 58 also contain sections with data from the third enumeration of 1744. Other archival materials, including the records of the Tsentral'nyi gosudarstvennyi voenno-istoricheskii arkhiv (*TsGVIA*), fund VUA, provide extensive data from the fourth enumeration.

3. Kabuzan, *Izmeneniia v razmeshchenii naseleniia Rossii*, 95–97.

4. S. I. Volkov, *Krest'iane dvortsovykh vladenii Podmoskov'ia: v seredine XVIII v.* (Moscow, 1959), 46. See also N. A. Rubinshtein, *Sel'skoe khoziaistvo Rossii vo vtoroi polovine XVIII v.*, 111.

5. Klokman, *Sotsial'no-ekonomicheskaia istoriia russkogo goroda*, 143, 164–65. Throughout this chapter, I have relied upon Klokman's descriptions of administrative reorganization.

6. These data are from the *Geographical Dictionary* and the *Istoricheskoe i topograficheskoe opisanie gorodov moskovskoi gubernii*, 83–368.

7. Ibid., 101–368.

8. Kizevetter, *Posadskaia obshchina v Rossii XVIII st.*, 88–99.

9. *Geographical Dictionary*, I, 859–61.

10. Kh. D. Sorina, "Ocherk sotsial'no-ekonomicheskoi istorii g. Tveri v 50–60–kh godakh XVIII v.," *Uchenye zapiski* (of Kalinin State Pedagogical Institute) 26a (1962), 88–89.

11. *Geographical Dictionary*, V, 30–38.

12. Sorina, "Ocherk sotsial'no-ekonomicheskoi istorii g. Tveri v 50–60–kh godakh XVIII v.," 94–95. See also Sorina, "K voprosu o protsesse sotsial'nogo rassloeniia goroda v sviazi s formirovaniem kapitalisticheskikh otnoshenii v Rossii (g. Tver')," *Uchenye zapiski* (of Kalinin State Pedagogical Institute) 38 (1964), 281–300.

13. Data on the number of houses are given for the cities of this guberniia separately listed in the *Geographical Dictionary*.

14. See Rashin, "Dinamika chislennosti i protsessy formirovaniia gorodskogo naseleniia Rossii v XIX– nachale XX vv.," 36–37.

15. Iatsunskii (*Goroda feodal'noi Rossii*, 87) indicates that Ivanovo counted 5,000 permanent residents in 1808, excluding a large number of temporary residents. Also see K. N. Shchepetov, *Krepostnoe pravo v votchinakh Sheremetovykh (1708–1885)* (Moscow, 1947), 348–53.

16. Razgon, "Promyshlennye i torgovye slobody," 152–54.

17. Ibid., 155–56.

18. *Geographical Dictionary*, VII, 385–94; and Klokman, *Sotsial'no-ekonomicheskaia istoriia russkogo goroda*, 224.

19. Vartanov, "Gorodskie iarmarki tsentral'noi chasti Evropeiskoi Rossii vo vtoroi polovine XVIII v.," 157–65.

20. Data on stores are given in the *Geographical Dictionary* separately for administrative cities.

21. Ibid., I, 782–83 and IV, 1276–79.

22. Vartanov, "Gorodskie iarmarki," 146 and 150.

23. *Geographical Dictionary*, III, 465.

24. Klokman, *Sotsial'no-ekonomicheskaia istoriia russkogo goroda*, 145–46.

25. *Geographical Dictionary*, III, 157–69.

26. Vartanov, "Gorodskie iarmarki," 154–55.

27. Kabuzan, *Izmeneniia v razmeshchenii naseleniia Rossii*, 59–118.

28. *Ocherki istorii voronezhskogo kraia*, I (Voronezh, 1961), 128.

29. On the rural population and production of this region see N. A. Rubin-shtein, *Sel'skoe khoziaistvo Rossii vo vtoroi polovine XVIII v.*, 221–28, 374–80, 401–11; and Confino, *Domaines et seigneurs en Russe vers la fin du XVIIIe siècle*, 184–94.

30. *Geographical Dictionary*, IV, 877–83.

31. Rozhkova, "K voprosu o znachenii iarmarok," 299.

32. See V. P. Zagorovskii, "Belgorodskaia cherta" (avtoreferat of a dissertation submitted to Voronezh State University, 1969); and A. Umrikhina, *K voprosu o sotsial'no-ekonomicheskom razvitii belgorodskogo kraia vo vtoroi polovine XVIII veka* (Belgorod, 1971).

33. Kizevetter, *Posadskaia obshchina v Rossii XVIII st.*, 88–111.

34. *Geographical Dictionary*, I, 646–51; III, 1006–27; IV, 1345–48.

35. V. I. Nedosekin, "Sotsial'no-ekonomicheskoe razvitie chernozemnogo tsentra Rossii vo vtoroi polovine XVIII veka" (avtoreferat of a dissertation submitted to Moscow State Pedagogical Institute, 1968), 28–29.

36. Samsonov, "Kurskaia korennaia iarmarka," 96–131.

37. See *Kursk: ocherki iz istorii goroda* (Kursk, 1957), 46–81.

38. *Geographical Dictionary*, VI, 57–64.

39. Ibid., VII, 216–19.

40. Ibid., III, 1082–84.

41. Ibid., I, 522–25.

42. Ibid., I, 1036–1149.

43. Ibid., VI, 382–403.

44. Klokman, *Sotsial'no-ekonomicheskaia istoriia russkogo goroda*, 150.

45. Vartanov, "Gorodskie iarmarki," 150.

46. *TsGADA*, fund 248, book 4339, pages 449–520.

47. *Geographical Dictionary*, V, 468–81.

48. Kabuzan, *Izmeneniia v razmeshchenii naseleniia Rossii*, 59–118.

49. *Geographical Dictionary*, V, 1036–41.

50. Riabkov, "Krest'ianskoe khoziaistvo v kontse XVIII– pervoi polovine XIX veka," 15–16.

51. Riabkov, "Smolenskii rynok v kontse XVIII– pervoi polovine XIX veka," 55–61.

52. *Geographical Dictionary*, II, 27–28.

53. Ibid., III, 1055–56; and Klokman, *Ocherki sotsial'no-ekonomicheskoi istorii gorodov severo-zapada Rossii v seredine XVIII v.*, 67–68.

54. See A. L. Shapiro in *Goroda feodal'noi Rossii*, 386–96.

55. See P. A. Kolesnikov and Iu. A. Tikhonov in ibid., 144–52, 309.

56. B. B. Kafengauz, "Torgovlia Novgoroda Velikogo i osnovanie Peterburga," *Ocherki vnutrennego rynka Rossii pervoi poloviny XVIII v.*, 32–113.

57. *Geographical Dictionary*, IV, 684–702.

58. Ibid., V, 1166–69.

59. For information on all of these cities, see Klokman, *Ocherki sotsial'no-ekonomicheskoi istorii gorodov severo-zapada Rossii v seredine XVIII v.*, as well as the entries for them in the *Geographical Dictionary*.

60. *Geographical Dictionary*, VI, 314–17.

61. Ibid., IV, 1118–24.

62. Ibid., IV, 834. On Olonets city see also Klokman, *Ocherki sotsial'no-ekonomicheskoi istorii gorodov severo-zapada Rossii v seredine XVIII v.*, 62–66.

63. *Geographical Dictionary*, I, 768–80, 974–1014.

64. Ibid., I, 784–89.

65. N. B. Golikova, *Naemnyi trud v gorodakh Povolzh'ia v pervoi chetverti XVIII veka* (Moscow, 1965), 19–20.

66. Kabuzan, *Izmeneniia v razmeshchenii naseleniia Rossii*, 59, 71, 95.

67. Klokman, *Sotsial'no-ekonomicheskaia istoriia russkogo goroda*, 266–80.

68. M. D. Kurmacheva in *Goroda feodal'noi Rossii*, 464, 470.

69. *Geographical Dictionary*, IV, 984–86.

70. I. A. Bulygin, *Goroda feodal'noi Rossii*, 488–89.

71. Ibid., 495–97.

72. Bulygin, *Polozhenie krest'ian i tovarnoe proizvodstvo v Rossii*.

73. Ibid., 75–76.

74. *Geographical Dictionary*, IV, 1030–33 and V, 732–51.

75. See Klokman, *Sotsial'no-ekonomicheskaia istoriia russkogo goroda*; and Bulygin, *Polozhenie krest'ian i tovarnoe proizvodstvo v Rossii*, 20.

76. *Geographical Dictionary*, III, 85–127.

77. Klokman, *Sotsial'no-ekonomicheskaia istoriia russkogo goroda*, 187.

78. E. N. Kusheva, "Saratov v pervoi polovine XVIII v.," *Problemy sotsial'no-ekonomicheskoi istorii Rossii* (Moscow, 1971), 26–51.

79. Golikova, "Ocherki po istorii naseleniia gorodov Nizhnego Povolzh'ia," 52–56.

80. Ibid., 56–81.

81. Kabuzan, *Izmeneniia v razmeshchenii naseleniia Rossii*, 63, 75, 99, 107, 111.

82. A. V. Emmausskii, "Ekonomicheskoe razvitie viatskoi gubernii v kontse XVIII veka," 3–24.

83. Ibid., 22–23.

84. See A. I. Komissarenko in *Goroda feodal'noi Rossii*, 455.

85. P. N. Luppov, *Istoriia goroda Viatki* (Kirov, 1958), 91–98, 125.

86. A. S. Cherkasova, "Gornozavodskie tsentry srednego Urala v XVIII v." (avtoreferat of doctoral dissertation submitted to Perm' State University, 1966), 5–15. Cherkasova points out that by the mid-nineteenth century when only 12 administrative centers in the central Urals had more than 3,000 residents, at least 40 other settlements with big factories, regular trade and fairs also exceeded a minimum of 3,000 residents.

87. Iofa, *Goroda Urala*, I, 191.

88. Ibid., I, 130–36. On the Irbit' fair, also see A. I. Andrushchenko in *Goroda feodal'noi Rossii*, 473–78.

89. N. G. Appolova in *Goroda feodal'noi Rossii*, 457.

90. Iofa, *Goroda Urala*, I, 207.

91. A. N. Kopylov in *Goroda feodal'noi Rossii*, 334–35.

92. See Vilkov, *Remeslo i torgovlia Zapadnoi Sibiri v XVII veke; Istoriia Sibiri*, II; and V. A. Aleksandrov, *Russkoe naselenie Sibiri XVII– nachala XVIII v. (eniseiskii krai)* (Moscow, 1964).

93. M. M. Gromyko, *Zapadnaia Sibir' v XVIII veke* (Novosibirsk, 1965), 55–56, 68; and *Istoriia Sibiri*, II, 263.

94. Ibid., II, 273–81.

95. I. G. Shul'ga, "K voprosu o razvitii vserossiiskogo rynka vo vtoroi polovine XVIII veka (po materialam levoberezhnoi Ukrainy)," 35–45.

96. See V. M. Kabuzan, "Zaselenie severnogo Prichernomor'ia (Novorossii) v XVIII– pervoi polovine XIX veka (1719–1858 gg.)" (avtoreferat of doctoral dissertation submitted to the Academy of Sciences, Institute of History, 1969).

97. *Geographical Dictionary*, III, 518–32.

98. See E. Iu. Kopysskii, *Ekonomicheskoe razvitie gorodov Belorussii XVI– XVII vv.* (Minsk, 1966), 24–32.

99. E. S. Kompan and V. A. Markina in *Goroda feodal'noi Rossii*, 350–62.

100. Rozhkova, "K voprosu o znachenii iarmarok," 299–300.

101. Karpachev, "Sotsial'no-ekonomicheskoe razvitie gorodov Belorussii."

NOTES TO CHAPTER 5

1. Alan Everitt, "The Marketing of Agricultural Produce," 466–592. Gregory King's classification of towns is given in Clark and Slack, eds., *Crisis and Order in English Towns 1500–1700*, 4–5.

2. J. Adams, *Alphabetical Table of Cities* (1680s).

3. The data used in compiling Table 21 are primarily from the following sources: W. G. Hoskins, *Devon*; T. W. Freeman, H. B. Rodgers and R. H. Kinvig, *Lancashire, Cheshire and the Isle of Man* (London, 1966); Alan D. Dyer, *The City of Worcester in the Sixteenth Century* (Leicester, 1973); J. W. E. Hill, *Tudor and Stuart Lincoln* (Cambridge, 1956); Alan Rogers, ed., *The Making of Stamford* (Hertfordshire, 1965); J. H. C. Patten, "The Urban Structure of East Anglia in the Sixteenth and Seventeenth Centuries" (a doctoral dissertation submitted to the University of Cambridge, 1972); A. F. J. Brown, *Essex at Work 1700–1815* (Chelmsford, 1969); C. W. Chalkin, *Seventeenth Century Kent* (London, 1965); and Harold Carter, *The Towns of Wales* (Cardiff, 1966).

4. E. A. Wrigley, "A Simple Model of London's Importance in Changing English Society and Economy 1650–1750," *Past and Present* 37 (July 1967).

5. Clark and Slack, eds., *Crisis and Order in English Towns 1500–1700*, 40–41.

6. W. G. Hoskins, "An Elizabethan Provincial Town, Leicester," in J. H. Plumb, ed., *Studies in Social History* (London, 1955), 35–39.

7. Alan Everitt, "The Marketing of Agricultural Produce," 476–79.

8. Clark and Slack, eds., *Crisis and Order in English Towns 1500–1700*, 4–5.

9. J. Adams, *Alphabetical Table of Cities*.

10. Patten, "The Urban Structure of East Anglia in the Sixteenth and Seventeenth Centuries," 132–250. See also his article, "Village and Town: An Occupational Study," *The Agricultural History Review* 20 (1972), 1–16.

11. Patten, "The Urban Structure of East Anglia in the Sixteenth and Seventeenth Centuries," 199–203, 241.

12. A. M. Everitt, "Leicester and Its Markets: The Seventeenth Century," in A. E. Brown, ed., *The Growth of Leicester* (Leicester, 1970), 39.

13. Brown, *Essex at Work 1700–1815*, 62–63.

14. Freeman, Rodgers, and Kinvig, *Lancashire, Cheshire and the Isle of Man*, 44.

15. A. M. Everitt, "The Marketing of Agricultural Produce," 533–43.

16. According to Peter Clark and Paul Slack, there was nearly a doubling of the percentage of the English population in towns of 1,000 or more persons between 1500 and 1700. See *Crisis and Order in English Towns 1500–1700*, 6.

17. Claude Saugrain, *Dictionnaire de la France*, I–III (Paris, 1726); and *Dictionnaire de la France*, I–VI (Paris, 1771).

18. Roger Mols, *Introduction à la démographie histoire des villes d'Europe du XIVe au XVIIIe siècle*, II; Etienne Hélin, *La démographie de Liège aux XVIIe et XVIIIe siècles*, 238–58; and Pierre Goubert, *Beauvais et le Beauvaisis de 1600 à 1730* (Paris, 1960), 255.

19. Marcel Reinhard, *Étude de la population pendant la Révolution et l'empire* (Paris, 1961), 48–49.

20. Charles Tilly, *The Vendée* (New York, 1967), 23.

21. Ibid.

22. Pierre Goubert, *Beauvais et le Beauvaisis de 1600 à 1730*.

23. See Georges Frêche, "Études statistiques sur le commerce céréalier de la France Méridionale au XVIIIe siècle," *Révue d'histoire économique et sociale* 49 (1971:1), 5–43; and Pierre Rascol, *Les paysans de l'Albigeois à la fin de l'ancien régime* (Aurillac, 1961).

24. M. Dumoulin, *La géographie du Royaume de France*, II (Paris, 1764).

25. Abel Poitrineau, *La vie rurale en Basse-Auvergne au XVIIIe siècle (1726–1789)*, I (Paris, 1965), 675.

26. See Georges Frêche, "Études statistiques sur le commerce céréalier de la France Méridionale au XVIIIe siècle," 37–43.

27. Abel Poitrineau, *La vie rurale en Basse-Auvergne au XVIIIe siècle (1726–1789)*, 461.

28. See Félix Bourquelot, *Études sur les foires de Champagne*, I, 34.

29. J. C. Russell, *Medieval Regions and Their Cities*, 87–96, 146–59.

30. The distinction between relatively modernized and relatively nonmodernized societies is given by Marion J. Levy, Jr., *Modernization and the Structure of Societies* (Princeton, 1966).

31. Data on the history of the world's population can be found in Marcel Reinhard and André Armengaud, *Histoire générale de la population mondiale* (Paris, 1961), 9–222; and Glenn T. Trewartha, *A Geography of Population: World Patterns* (New York, 1969).

32. Population statistics for 1800 are from John P. Durand, "The Modern

Expansion of World Population," *Proceedings of the American Philosophical Society*, 111:3 (June 1967), 136–41.

33. Urban populations for 1800 are based primarily on data presented in *Urban Networks in Ch'ing China and Tokugawa Japan*; in Etienne Hélin, *La démographie de Liège aux XVIIe et XVIIIe siècles* (Brussels, 1963), 238–58; in Roger Mols, *Introduction à la démographie histoire des villes d'Europe du XIVe au XVIIIe siècle*, II (Louvain, 1954) and in separate studies of individual countries or cities.

34. Sources used in drawing up this ranking of the largest cities in 1800 include the writings on China, Japan, and Europe cited in the previous note plus Iu. V. Vanin, *Ekonomicheskoe razvitie Korei v XVII–XVIII vekakh* (Moscow, 1968); A. I. Chicherov, *India: Economic Development in the 16th–18th Centuries* (Moscow, 1971); and Fredy Bémont, *Les villes de l'Iran* (Paris, 1969). Cities of India and southeast Asia are mainly classified according to the population estimates given by Tertius Chandler and Gerald Fox, *3,000 Years of Urban Growth* (New York, 1974). These authors give estimates for the number of cities in 1800 at various population levels which generally approximate the ones independently developed here.

35. See G. William Skinner, "Marketing and Social Structure in Rural China," *Journal of Asian Studies* 24: 1, 2, 3 (1964–65).

36. Peter Mathias, *The First Industrial Nation* (New York, 1969), 18.

37. Vanin, *Ekonomicheskoe razvitie Korei v XVII–XVIII vekakh*, 174–212.

38. A. I. Chicherov, *India: Economic Development in the 16th–18th Centuries* (Moscow, 1971), 95–102.

39. Virginia Rau, *Subsidios para o estudo das feiras medievais portuguesas* (Lisbon, 1943), 38–39.

SELECTED BIBLIOGRAPHY

Adams, J., *Alphabetical Table of Cities* (1680s).

Aleksandrov, V. A., *Russkoe naselenie Sibiri XVII– nachala XVIII v. (eniseiskii krai)* (Moscow, 1964).

Appelbaum, Richard P., *Theories of Social Change* (Chicago, 1970).

Arima Tatsuo, *Roshia kōgyōshi kenkyū* (Tokyo, 1973).

Bakhrushin, S. V., *Nauchnye trudy*, I (Moscow, 1952).

Baklanova, N. A., "Torgi i promysly Vasil'surska v XVII veke," *Istoricheskie zapiski* 40 (1952), 283–87.

———. *Torgovo-promyshlennaia deiatel'nost' kalmykovykh vo vtoroi polovine XVII v.: k istorii formirovaniia russkoi burzhuazii* (Moscow, 1959).

Bémont, Fredy, *Les villes de l'Iran* (Paris, 1969).

Berry, Brian J. L., and Pred, Allen, *Central Place Studies: A Bibliography of Theory and Applications* (Philadelphia, 1961).

Black, Cyril E., Jansen, Marius B., Levine, Herbert S., Levy, Jr., Marion J., Rosovsky, Henry, Rozman, Gilbert, Smith, II, Henry D. and Starr, S. Frederick, *The Modernization of Japan and Russia* (New York, forthcoming).

Blackwell, William L., *The Beginnings of Russian Industrialization 1800–1860* (Princeton, 1968).

Blum, Jerome, *Lord and Peasant in Russia* (New York, 1969).

Bogoiavlenskii, C. K., *Nekotorye statisticheskie dannie po istorii russkogo goroda XVII st.* (Moscow, 1848).

Boulet-Sautel, Marguerite, "La formation de la ville médiévale dans les régions du centre de la France," in Soçiété Jean Bodin, *La Ville*, II (part 2) (Brussels, 1955), 357–70.

Bourquelot, Félix, *Études sur les foires de Champagne* (Brionne, 1970).

Brown, A. F. J., *Essex at Work 1700–1815* (Chelmsford, 1969).

Bulygin, I. A., *Polozhenie krest'ian i tovarnoe proizvodstvo v Rossii: vtoraia polovina XVIII veka* (Moscow, 1966).

Cahnman, Werner J. and Boskoff, Alvin, *Sociology and History* (New York, 1964).

Carter, Harold, *The Towns of Wales* (Cardiff, 1966).

Chalkin, C. W., *Seventeenth Century Kent* (London, 1965).

Chandler, Tertius and Fox, Gerald, *3,000 Years of Urban Growth* (New York, 1974).

Chechulin, N. D., *Goroda moskovskogo gosudarstva v 16 veke* (St. Petersburg, 1889).

Cherepnin, L. V., "O formakh ob'edinenii remeslennikov v russkikh gorodakh XIV–XV vv." N. V. Ustiugov, ed., *Voprosy sotsial'no-ekonomicheskoi istorii i istochnikovedeniia perioda feodalizma v Rossii* (Moscow, 1961), 19–24.

———. *Obrazovanie russkogo tsentralizovannogo gosudarstva v XIV–XV vekakh* (Moscow, 1960).

———. "Rus': spornye voprosy istorii feodal'noi zemel'noi sobstvennosti v IX–XV vv." in A. P. Novosel'tsev, V. T. Pashuto and L. V. Cherepnin, *Puti razvitiia feodalizma* (Moscow, 1972).

Cherevan', A. S., "Ocherki istorii sotsial'no-ekonomicheskogo i pravavogo polozheniia gos. krest'ian Urala i Evropeiskogo Severa Rossii do reformy P. D. Kiseleva" (avtoreferat of doctoral dissertation submitted to Kiev State University, 1968).

Cherkasova, A. S., "Gornozavodskie tsentry srednego Urala v XVIII v." (avtoreferat of doctoral dissertation submitted to Perm' State University, 1966).

Chicherov, A. I., *India: Economic Development in the 16th–18th Centuries* (Moscow, 1971).

Chistiakova, E. V., "Moskva v seredine 30-kh godov XVII v.," in *Novoe o proshlom nashei strany* (Moscow, 1967), 301–09.

———. "Pskovskii torg v seredine XVII v.," *Istoricheskie zapiski* 34 (1950), 198–235.

———. "Remeslo i torgovlia na voronezhskom posade v seredine XVII v.," *Trudy voronezhskogo gosudarstvennogo universiteta* 25 (1954), 46–62.

Chodak, Szymon, *Societal Development: Five Approaches with Conclusions from Comparative Analysis* (New York, 1973).

Chulkov, M., *Istoricheskoe opisanie rossiiskoi kommertsii*, IV:6 (1789).

———. "Slovar' uchrezhdennykh v Rossii iarmarok i torgov," *Novyi i polnyi geograficheskii slovar' rossiiskogo gosudarstva*, IV (1788).

Clark, Peter and Slack, Paul, eds., *Crisis and Order in English Towns 1500-1700* (Toronto, 1972).

Confino, Michael, *Domaines et seigneurs en Russe vers la fin du XVIIIe siècle* (Paris, 1963).

Coulborn, Rushton, ed., *Feudalism in History* (Princeton, 1956).

Davis, Dorothy, *Fairs, Shops and Supermarkets: A History of English Shopping* (Toronto, 1966).

Demidova, N. F., "Biurokratizatsiia gosudarstvennogo apparata absoliutizma v XVII-XVIII vv.," *Absoliutizm v Rossii* (Moscow, 1964), 206-42.

Dictionnaire de la France, I-VI (Paris, 1771).

Ditiatin', I. I., *Ustroistvo i upravlenie gorodov Rossii* (St. Petersburg, 1875).

Dovnar'-Zapol'skii, M. V., *Torgovlia i promyshlennost' Moskvy XVI-XVII vv.* (Moscow, 1910).

Drobizheva, L. M., *Istoriia i sotsiologiia* (Moscow, 1971).

Dumoulin, M., *La géographie du Royaume de France*, II (Paris, 1764).

Durand, John S., "The Modern Expansion of World Population," *Population Problems, Proceedings of the American Philosophical Society*, III:3 (June 1967), 136-59.

Dyer, Alan D., *The City of Worcester in the Sixteenth Century* (Leicester, 1973).

Eisenstadt, S. N., *The Political Systems of Empires: The Rise and Fall of the Historical Bureaucratic Societies* (New York, 1969).

Emmausskii, A. V., "Ekonomicheskoe razvitie viatskoi gubernii v kontse XVIII veka," *Uchenye zapiski* (of Kirov State Pedagogical Institute) 19 (1965), 3-24.

Everitt, Alan, "Leicester and its Markets: The Seventeenth Century," A. E. Brown, ed., *The Growth of Leicester* (Leicester, 1970).

———. "The Marketing of Agricultural Produce," Joan Thirsk, ed., *The Agrarian History of England and Wales*, IV: *1500-1640* (Cambridge, 1967), 466-592.

Fedoseev, P. N. and Frantsov, G. P., "Sotsiologiia i istoriia," *Sotsiologiia v SSSR*, I (1966).

Feuerwerker, Albert, ed., *History in Communist China* (Cambridge, Mass., 1968).

Fournial, Étienne, *Les villes et l'économie d'échange en Forez aux XIIIe et XIVe siècles* (Paris, 1967).

Frêche, Georges, "Études statistiques sur le commerce céréalier de la

France Méridionale au XVIIIe siècle," *Revue d'histoire économique et sociale* 49 (1971:1), 5–43.

Freeman, T. W., Rodgers, H. B. and Kinvig, R. H., *Lancashire, Cheshire and the Isle of Man* (London, 1966).

Fu I-ling, *Ming Ch'ing shih-tai shang-jen chi shang-yeh tzu-pen* (Peking, 1956).

Fuhrmann, Joseph T., *The Origins of Capitalism in Russia: Industry and Progress in the Sixteenth and Seventeenth Centuries* (Chicago, 1972).

German, Karl, *Statisticheskie issledovaniia otnositel'no rossiiskoi imperii*, I (St. Petersburg, 1819).

Golikova, N. B., *Naemnyi trud v gorodakh Povolzh'ia v pervoi chetverti XVIII veka* (Moscow, 1965).

———. "Ocherki po istorii naseleniia gorodov Nizhnego Povolzh'ia v kontse XVII– pervoi chetverti XVIII v." (a doctoral dissertation submitted to Moscow State University, Department of the History of the USSR, Section of Feudalism, 1970).

Goroda feodal'noi Rossii (Moscow, 1966).

Gorodskie poseleniia v rossiiskoi imperii (St. Petersburg, 1860).

Got'e, Iu., *Istoriia oblastnogo upravleniia v Rossii ot Petra I do Ekateriny II* (Moscow, 1913 and 1941).

Goubert, Pierre, *Beauvais et le Beauvaisis de 1600 à 1730* (Paris, 1960).

Grekov, V., "Khoziaistvennii krizis v moskovskom gosudarstve v 70–80-kh godakh XVI v.," *Voprosy istorii* (1945:1), 6–21.

Gromyko, M. M., *Zapadnaia Sibir' v XVIII veke* (Novosibirsk, 1965).

Hall, John W., "Feudalism in Japan—A Reassessment," in John W. Hall and Marius B. Jansen, *Studies in the Institutional History of Early Modern Japan* (Princeton, 1968), 15–51.

Hammond, Mason, *The City in the Ancient World* (Cambridge, Mass., 1972).

Hartwell, Richard M., "Economic Growth in England before the Industrial Revolution: Some Methodological Issues," *The Journal of Economic History* 20:1 (March, 1969), 13–31.

Hélin, Étienne, *La démographie de Liège aux XVIIe et XVIIIe siècles* (Brussels, 1963).

Hill, J. W. E., *Tudor and Stuart Lincoln* (Cambridge, 1956).

Hittle, M., "The City in Muscovite and Early Imperial Russia" (a doctoral dissertation submitted to the department of history at Harvard University, 1971).

Hofstadter, Richard and Lipset, Seymour Martin, eds., *Sociology and History: Methods* (New York, 1968).

Hoskins, W. G., "An Elizabethan Provincial Town, Leicester," J. H. Plumb, ed., *Studies in Social History* (London, 1955).

——. *Devon* (London, 1964).

Iakovtsevskii, V. N., *Kupecheskii kapital v feodal'no-krepostnicheskoi Rossii* (Moscow, 1953).

Iatsunskii, V. K., "Osnovnye momenty istorii sel'skokhoziaistvennogo proizvodstva v Rossii s XVI v. do 1917 g.," *Ezhegodnik po agrarnoi istorii Vostochnoi Evropy. 1964* (Kishinev, 1966), 44–64.

——. *Sotsial'no-ekonomicheskaia istoriia Rossii XVIII–XIX vv.* (Moscow, 1973).

Indova, E. I., *Agrarnyi stroi v Rossii v XVIII v.* (Moscow, 1966).

——. *Dvortsovoe khoziaistvo v Rossii: pervaia polovina XVIII veka* (Moscow, 1964).

——. *Krepostnoe khoziaistvo v nachale XIX veka: po materialam votchinnogo arkhiva Vorontsovykh* (Moscow, 1955).

Iofa, L. E., *Goroda Urala*, I (Moscow, 1951).

Isaev, G. S., *Rol' tekstil'noi promyshlennosti v genezise i razvitii kapitalizma v Rossii 1760–1860* (Leningrad, 1970).

Istoricheskoe i topograficheskoe opisanie gorodov moskovskoi gubernii (Moscow, 1787).

Istoriia goroda Gor'kogo (Gor'kii, 1971).

Istoriia gorodov i sel USSR (Kiev, 1967).

Istoriia i sotsiologiia (Moscow, 1964).

Istoriia Kieva, I (Kiev, 1963).

Istoriia Moskvy, II (period feodalizma XVIII v.) (Moscow, 1953).

Istoriia Sibiri, II (Leningrad, 1968).

Istoriia SSSR: s drevneishchikh vremen do nashikh dnei, II and III (Moscow, 1966).

Johnson, E. A. J., *The Organization of Space in Developing Countries* (Cambridge, Mass., 1970).

Kabuzan, V. M., *Izmeneniia v razmeshchenii naseleniia Rossii v XVIII– pervoi polovine XIX v. (po materialam revizii)* (Moscow, 1971).

——. *Narodonaselenie Rossii v XVIII– pervoi polovine XIX v. (po materialam revizii)* (Moscow, 1963).

——. "Nekotorye materialy dlia izucheniia istoricheskoi geografii Rossii XVIII– nachala XIX v.," *Problemy istochnikovedeniia*, XI (Moscow, 1963).

——. "Zaselenie severnogo Prichernomor'ia (Novorossii) v XVIII– pervoi polovine XIX veka (1719–1858 gg.)" (avtoreferat of doctoral dissertation submitted to the Academy of Sciences, Institute of History, 1969).

Kabuzan, V. M. and Troitskii, S. M., "Izmeneniia v chislennosti, udel'nom vese i razmeshchenii dvorianstva v Rossii v 1782–1858 gg.," *Istoriia SSSR* (1971:4), 153–68.

Kachanovskii, Iu. V., "Diskussiia ob aziatskom sposobe proizvodstva na stranitsakh zarubezhnoi marksistskoi pechati," *Problemy dokapitalisticheskikh obshchestv v stranakh Vostoka* (Moscow, 1971), 45–94.

Kafengauz, B. B., "Geografiia vnutrennei torgovli i ekonomicheskaia spetsializatsiia raionov Rossii v 20-kh godakh XVIII veka," *Voprosy geografii* 20 (1950), 163–202.

———. "Khlebnaia torgovlia Moskvy v 30-kh godakh XVIII stoletiia," *Voprosy istorii* (1947:9), 105–12.

———. *Ocherki vnutrennego rynka Rossii pervoi poloviny XVIII veka* (Moscow, 1958).

Kapustina, G. D., "Iz istorii remeslennogo uchenichestva v Moskve v nachale XVIII v.," N. V. Ustiugov, ed., *Voprosy sotsial'no-ekonomicheskoi istorii i istochnikovedeniia perioda feodalizma v Rossii* (Moscow, 1961).

Karpachev, A. M., "Sotsial'no-ekonomicheskoe razvitie gorodov Belorussii vo vtoroi polovine XVII–XVIII v." (a doctoral dissertation submitted to the Academy of Sciences of the Belorussian Soviet Socialist Republic, Department of Social Sciences, 1969).

Kaufmann-Rochard, Jacqueline, *Origines d'une bourgeoisie russe XVIe et XVIIe siècles: marchands de Moscovie* (Paris, 1969).

Khromov, P. A., *Ocherki ekonomiki feodalizma v Rossii* (Moscow, 1957).

King, Peter, *The Development of the English Economy to 1750* (London, 1971).

Kirilov, Ivan, *Tsvetushchee sostoianie vserossiiskogo gosudarstva* (Moscow, 1831).

Kizevetter, A. A., *Posadskaia obshchina v Rossii XVIII st.* (Moscow, 1903).

Klokman, Iu. R., "Gorod v zakonodatel'stve russkogo absoliutizma vo vtoroi polovine XVII–XVIII v.," *Absoliutizm v Rossii* (Moscow, 1964), 320–54.

———. *Ocherki sotsial'no-ekonomicheskoi istorii gorodov severo-zapada Rossii v seredine XVIII v.* (Moscow, 1960).

———. *Sotsial'no-ekonomicheskaia istoriia russkogo goroda: vtoraia polovina XVIII veka* (Moscow, 1967).

———. "Uchrezhdenie gorodov v iaroslavskoi gubernii po oblastnoi reforme 1775 g.," *Problemy obshchestvenno-politicheskoi istorii Rossii i slavianskikh stran* (Moscow, 1963).

Konrad, N. I., "History of World Social Science," *Soviet Sociology* (Spring 1967), 54–88.

Kopanev, A. I., "Naselenie russkogo gosudarstva v XVI v.," *Istoricheskie zapiski* 64 (1959), 233–54.

———. *Naselenie Peterburga v pervoi polovine XIX veka* (Moscow, 1957).

Kopysskii, E. Iu., *Ekonomicheskoe razvitie gorodov Belorussii vo vtoroi polovine XVI–XVII vv.* (Minsk, 1966).

Koretskii, V. I., "K istorii formirovaniia krepostnogo prava v Rossii," *Voprosy istorii* (1964:6), 77–96.

Kostomarov', N. I., *Ocherki torgovli moskovskogo gosudarstva v XVI i XVII stoletiiakh* (St. Petersburg, 1862).

Koval'chenko, I. D., "O tovarnosti zemledeliia v Rossii v pervoi polovine XIX v.," *Ezhegodnik po agrarnoi istorii Vostochnoi Evropy. 1963* (Vilnius, 1964).

———. *Russkoe krepostnoe krest'ianstvo v pervoi polovine XIX v.* (Moscow, 1967).

Kursk: ocherki iz istorii goroda (Kursk, 1957).

Kusheva, E. N., "Saratov v pervoi polovine XVIII v.," *Problemy sotsial'no-ekonomicheskoi istorii Rossii* (Moscow, 1971), 26–51.

———. "Torgovlia Moskvy v 30–40-kh godakh XVIII v.," *Istoricheskie zapiski* 23 (1947), 44–104.

Latysheva, G. P. and Rabinovich, M. G., *Moskva i moskovskii krai v proshlom* (Moscow, 1973).

Levy, Marion J., *Modernization and the Structure of Societies* (Princeton, 1966).

Liapushkin, I. I., "Slaviane Vostochnoi Evropy nakanune obrazovaniia drevnerusskogo gosudarstva (VII– pervaia polovina IX v.)," *Materialy i issledovaniia po arkheologii SSSR* 152 (Leningrad, 1968).

Luppov, P. N., *Istoriia goroda Viatki* (Kirov, 1958).

Makovskii, D. P., *Razvitie tovarno-denezhnykh otnoshenii v sel'skom khoziaistve russkogo gosudarstva v XVI veke* (Smolensk, 1963).

Mathias, Peter, *The First Industrial Nation* (New York, 1969).

Merzon, A. I. and Tikhonov, Iu. A., *Rynok Ustiuga Velikogo XVII veka* (Moscow, 1960).

Meskill, John, ed., *The Pattern of Chinese History: Cycles, Development, or Stagnation?* (Lexington, Mass., 1965).

Milov, L. V., *Issledovanie ob 'ekonomicheskikh primecheniiakh' k general'nomu mezhevaniiu (k istorii russkogo krest'ianstva i sel'skogo khoziaistva vtoroi poloviny XVIII v.)* (Moscow, 1965).

Milov, L. V., "O tak nazyvaemykh agrarnykh gorodakh Rossii XVIII veka," *Voprosy istorii* (1968:6), 54–64.

Mitiaev, K. G., "Oboroty i torgovye sviazi smolenskogo rynka v 70-kh godakh XVII vekakh," *Istoricheskie zapiski* 13 (1942), 54–83.

Miyakawa Hisayuki, "An Outline of the Naitō Hypothesis and its Effects on Japanese Studies of China," *Far Eastern Quarterly* 14:4 (August 1955), 533–52.

Mols, Roger, *Introduction à la démographie histoire des villes d'Europe du XIVe au XVIIIe siècle*, II (Louvain, 1954).

Murav'eva, L. L., *Derevenskaia promyshlennost' tsentral'noi Rossii: vtoroi poloviny XVII v.* (Moscow, 1971).

Nadel, George H., "Periodization," *International Encyclopedia of Social Sciences*, 11 (1968), 581–84.

Nedosekin, V. I., "Sotsial'no-ekonomicheskoe razvitie chernozemnogo tsentra Rossii vo vtoroi polovine XVIII veka" (avtoreferat of a dissertation submitted to Moscow State Pedagogical Institute, 1968).

Neresova, E. A., "Ekonomicheskoe sostoianie kostromskoi provintsii moskovskoi gubernii po khoziaistvennym anketam 1760-kh godov," *Istoricheskie zapiski* 40 (1952), 154–85.

Nevolin, K. A., "Obshchii spisok russkikh gorodov," *Polnoe sobranie sochinenii*, VI (St. Petersburg, 1859), 25–95.

Nisbet, Robert A., *Social Change and History* (Oxford, 1969).

Nosov, N. E., "Russkii gorod: russkoe kupechestvo v XVI stoletii," *Issledovaniia po sotsial'no-politicheskoi istorii Rossii* (Leningrad, 1971).

Ocherki istorii Leningrada, I (period feodalizma 1703–1861 gg.) (Leningrad, 1955).

Ocherki istorii SSSR (period feodalizma: Rossiia v pervoi polovine XVIII v.) (Moscow, 1954).

Ocherki istorii SSSR (period feodalizma: Rossiia vo vtoroi polovine XVIII v.) (Moscow, 1956).

Ocherki istorii voronezhskogo kraia, I (Voronezh, 1961).

Patten, J. H. C., "The Urban Structure of East Anglia in the Sixteenth and Seventeenth Centuries" (a doctoral dissertation submitted to the University of Cambridge, 1972).

———. "Village and Town: An Occupational Study," *The Agricultural History Review* 20 (1972), 1–16.

Pavlenko, N. I., "K voprosu ob evoliutsii dvorianstva v XVII–XVIII vv.," *Voprosy genezisa kapitalizma v Rossii* (Leningrad, 1960).

Perekhod ot feodalizma k kapitalizmu v Rossii (Moscow, 1969).

Pintner, Walter, "The Social Characteristics of the Early 19th Century Russian Bureaucracy," *Slavic Review* 29:3 (Sept. 1970), 430–43.

Pirenne, H., *Medieval Cities: Their Origins and the Revival of Trade* (Princeton, 1952).

Poitrineau, Abel, *La vie rurale en Basse-Auvergne au XVIIIe siècle* (1726–1789), I (Paris, 1965).

Polianskii, F. Ia., *Gorodskoe remeslo i manufaktura v Rossii XVIII v.* (Moscow, 1960).

Polnoe sobranie zakonov, I (St. Petersburg, 1859).

Porshnev, B. F., *Feodalizm i narodnye massy* (Moscow, 1964).

Pounds, Norman J. G., "The Urbanization of the Classical World," *Annals of the Association of American Geographers* 59 (March 1969), 135–57.

Pozdniakov, I. G., "Progressivnaia iaponskaia istoriografiia o kharaktere feodalizma v Iaponii," *Narody Azii i Afriki* (1962:3), 167–77.

Preobrazhenskii, A. A. and Tikhonov, Iu. A., "Itogi izucheniia nachal'nogo etapa skladyvaniia vserossiiskogo rynka (XVII v.)," *Istoriia SSSR* (1960), 80–109.

Privalova, N. I., "Torgi gor. Kasimova v seredine XVII veka," *Istoricheskie zapiski* 21 (1947), 105–33.

Problemy vozniknoveniia feodalizma u narodov SSSR (Moscow, 1969).

Rabinovich, M. G., *O drevnei Moskve* (Moscow, 1964).

Raeff, Marc, *Imperial Russia, 1682–1825* (New York, 1971).

———, ed., *Peter the Great: Reformer or Revolutionary* (Boston, 1966).

Rakhmatullin, M. A., "Khlebnyi rynok i tseny v Rossii v pervoi polovine XIX v.," *Problemy genezisa kapitalizma* (Moscow, 1970), 334–412.

Rascol, Pierre, *Les paysans de l'Albigeois à la fin de l'ancien régime* (Aurillac, 1961).

Rashin, A. G., "Dinamika chislennosti i protsessy formirovaniia gorodskogo naseleniia Rossii v XIX– nachale XX vv.," *Istoricheskie zapiski* 34 (1950), 32–81.

———. *Naselenie Rossii za 100 let (1811–1913 gg.)* (Moscow, 1956).

Rau, Virginia, *Subsidios para o estudo das feiras medievais portuguesas* (Lisbon, 1943).

Razgon, A. M., "Promyshlennye i torgovye slobody i sela vladimirskoi gubernii vo vtoroi polovine XVIII v.," *Istoricheskie zapiski* 32 (1950).

Reinhard, Marcel, *Étude de la population pendant la Révolution et l'empire* (Paris, 1961).

——— and Armengaud, André, *Histoire générale de la population mondiale* (Paris, 1961).

Riabkov, G. T., "Krest'ianskoe khoziaistvo v kontse XVIII– pervoi polovine XIX veka (po materialam smolenskoi gubernii): k istorii genezisa kapitalizma v sel'skom khoziaistve" (avtoreferat of doctoral dissertation submitted to the Academy of Sciences of the USSR, 1970).

———. "Smolenskii rynok v kontse XVIII– pervoi polovine XIX veka," *Uchenye zapiski* (of Smolensk State Pedagogical Institute) 4:1 (1957), 55–61.

Riasanovsky, Nicholas V., *A History of Russia* (New York, 1963).

Rogers, Alan, *A History of Lincolnshire* (London, 1970).

———. *The Making of Stamford* (Hertfordshire, 1965).

Rolova, A. D., "Osnovnye cherty ekonomicheskogo razvitiia Italii v XVI–XVII vv.," *Vozniknovenie kapitalizma v promyshlennosti i sel'skom khoziaistve stran Evropy, Azii i Ameriki* (Moscow, 1968), 50–97.

Rozhkov, M. K., ed., *Ocherki ekonomicheskoi istorii Rossii pervoi polovine XIX veka* (Moscow, 1959).

Rozhkova, M. K., "K voprosu o znachenii iarmarok vo vnutrennei torgovle doreformennoi Rossii (pervaia polovina XIX v.)," *Istoricheskie zapiski* 54 (1955), 298–314.

Rozman, Gilbert, "Comparative Approaches to Urbanization: Russia, 1750–1800," Michael Hamm, ed., *The City in Russian History* (Lexington, Ky., forthcoming).

———. *Urban Networks in Ch'ing China and Tokugawa Japan* (Princeton, 1973).

Rubinshtein, N. A., *Sel'skoe khoziaistvo Rossii vo vtoroi polovine XVIII v.* (Moscow, 1957).

Rubinshtein, N. L., "Nekotorye voprosy formirovaniia rynka rabochei sily v Rossii XVIII veka," *Voprosy istorii* (February 1952), 74–101.

———. "Russkaia iarmarka XVIII veka," *Uchenye zapiski* (of Moscow Oblast' Pedagogical Institute) 1 (1939), 5–29.

———. "Territorial'noe razdelenie truda i razvitie vserossiiskogo rynka," *Iz istorii rabochego klassa i revoliutsionnogo dvizheniia* (Moscow, 1958).

———. "Vneshniaia torgovlia Rossii i russkoe kupechestvo vo vtoroi polovine XVIII v.," *Istoricheskie zapiski* 54 (1955), 343–61.

Russell, J. C., *Medieval Regions and Their Cities* (London, 1972).

Rybakov, I. F., "Nekotorye voprosy genezisa kapitalisticheskogo goroda v Rossii," *Voprosy genezisa kapitalizma v Rossii* (Leningrad, 1960), 229–39.

Ryndziunskii, P. G., *Gorodskoe grazhdanstvo doreformennoi Rossii* (Moscow, 1958).

———. "Novye goroda Rossii kontsa 18 v.," *Problemy obshchestvenno-politicheskoi istorii Rossii i slavianskikh stran* (Moscow, 1963), 359–70.

Sakharov, A. M., *Goroda severo-vostochnoi Rusi XIV–XV vekov* (Moscow, 1959).

———. *Obrazovanie i razvitie rossiiskogo gosudarstva v XIV–XVII vv.* (Moscow, 1969).

Samsonov, V. I., "Kurskaia korennaia iarmarka," *Uchenye zapiski* (of Kursk State Pedagogical Institute) 2 (1949), 96–131.

Saugrain, Claude, *Dictionnaire de la France*, I–III (Paris, 1726).

Semevskii, V. I., *Krest'iane v tsarstvovanie imperatritsy Ekateriny II*, I (St. Petersburg, 1903).

Serbiṇa, K. N., *Krest'ianskaia zhelezodelatel'naia promyshlennost' severo-zapadnoi Rossii XVI– pervoi poloviny XIX v.* (Leningrad, 1971).

———. *Ocherki iz sotsial'no-ekonomicheskoi istorii russkogo goroda: tikhvinskii posad v XVI–XVIII vv.* (Moscow, 1951).

Shanin, Teodor, *The Awkward Class: Political Sociology of Peasantry in a Developing Society: Russia 1910–1925* (Oxford, 1972).

Shapiro, A. L., ed., *Agrarnaia istoriia severo-zapada Rossii: vtoraia polovina XV– nachalo XVI v.* (Leningrad, 1971).

———. "Ob imushchestvennom neravenstve i sotsial'nom rassloenii russkogo krest'ianstva v epokhy feodalizma," *Voprosy genezisa kapitalizma v Rossii* (Leningrad, 1960).

———. "Razvitie rynochnykh otnoshenii i krepostnichestvo v russkoi derevne pervoi poloviny XVIII v.," *Ezhegodnik po agrarnoi istorii Vostochnoi Evropy. 1961* (Riga, 1963), 207–17.

Shchetatov, A., ed., *Geograficheskii slovar' rossiiskogo gosudarstva*, I–VII (Moscow, 1801–08).

Shchepetov, K. N., *Krepostnoe pravo v votchinakh Sheremetovykh (1708–1885)* (Moscow, 1947).

Shepukova, N. M., "K voprosu o chislennosti barshchinnykh i obrochnykh pomeshchichikh krest'ian Evropeiskoi Rossii vo vtoroi polovine XVIII veka," *Ezhegodnik po agrarnoi istorii Vostochnoi Evropy. 1964* (Kishinev, 1966), 400–08.

———. "Ob izmenenii razmerov dushevladeniia pomeshchikov Evropeiskoi Rossii v pervoi chetverti XVIII– pervoi polovine XIX v.," *Ezhegodnik po agrarnoi istorii Vostochnoi Evropy. 1963* (Vilnius, 1964).

Shteppa, Konstantin, *Russian Historians and the Soviet State* (New Brunswick, 1962).

Shul'ga, I. G., "Razvitie torgovli na levoberezhnoi Ukraine vo vtoroi polovine XVIII v.," *Voprosy genezisa kapitalizma v Rossii* (Leningrad, 1960), 157–69.

Shul'ga, I. G., "K voprosu o razvitii vserossiiskogo rynka vo vtoroi polovine XVIII veka (po materialam levoberezhnoi Ukrainy)," *Voprosy istorii* (1958:10), 35-45.

Skinner, G. William, "Marketing and Social Structure in Rural China," *Journal of Asian Studies* 24: 1, 2, 3 (1964-65).

Sliusarskii, A. G., *Sotsial'no-ekonomicheskoe razvitie slobozhanshchiny XVII-XVIII vv.* (Khar'kov, 1964).

Smirnov, P. P., *Goroda moskovskogo gosudarstva v pervoi polovine XVII veke* (Kiev, 1917).

———. *Posadskie liudi i ikh klassovaia bor'ba do serediny XVII veka*, I and II (Moscow, 1947).

Smith, C. T., *An Historical Geography of Western Europe* (London, 1967).

Sorina, Kh. D., "K voprosu o protsesse sotsial'nogo rassloeniia goroda v sviazi s formirovaniem kapitalisticheskikh otnoshenii v Rossii (g. Tver')," *Uchenye zapiski* (of Kalinin State Pedagogical Institute) 38 (1964), 281-300.

———. "Ocherk sotsial'no-ekonomicheskoi istorii g. Tveri v 50-60-kh godakh XVIII v.," *Uchenye zapiski* (of Kalinin State Pedagogical Institute) 26a (1962), 88-117.

———. "Ocherk sotsial'no-ekonomicheskoi istorii g. Vyshnego Volochka vo II polovine XVIII i nachale XIX vv.," *Uchenye zapiski* (of Kalinin State Pedagogical Institute) 35 (1963), 122-36.

———. "Rzhev: torgovo-posrednicheskii gorod na verkhnei volge vo vtoroi polovine XVIII- pervoi polovine XIX veka," *Uchenye zapiski* 62 (of Kalinin State Pedagogical Institute), 130-50.

Storch, Heinrich, *Statistische Ubersicht der Statthalterschaften des Russischen Reichs* (Riga, 1795).

Strumilin, S. G., "K voprosu o genezise kapitalizma v Rossii," *Voprosy istorii* (Sept. 1961), 56-69.

———. *Ocherki ekonomicheskoi istorii Rossii i SSSR* (Moscow, 1966).

Stuzhina, E. P., *Kitaiskoe remeslo v XVI-XVIII vv.* (Moscow, 1970).

———. "Problemy ekonomicheskoi i sotsial'noi struktury goroda i remeslennogo proizvodstva Kitaia XI-XIII vv. v sovremennoi istoriografii," *Istoriografiia stran Vostoka* (Moscow, 1969), 343-76.

Swanson, Guy E., *Social Change* (Glenview, Ill., 1971).

Sytin, P. V., *Istoriia planirovki i zastroiki Moskvy*, II (Moscow, 1954).

———. *Iz istorii moskovskikh ulitsy* (Moscow, 1952).

Tikhomirov, M. N., *Drevnerusskie goroda* (Moscow, 1956).

———. *Drevniaia Moskva (XII-XV vv.)* (Moscow, 1947).

———. *Rossiia v 16 stoletii* (Moscow, 1962).

Tikhonov, Iu. A., "Krest'ianskoe khoziaistvo tsentral'noi Rossii pervoi chetverti XVIII v.," *Istoriia SSSR* (1971:4), 169–78.

———. "Problema formirovaniia vserossiiskogo rynka v sovremennoi sovestskoi istoriografii," *Aktual'nye problemy istorii Rossii epokhi feodalizma* (Moscow, 1970), 200–23.

Tilly, Charles, *The Vendée* (New York, 1967).

Trewartha, Glenn T., *A Geography of Population: World Patterns* (New York, 1969).

Troitskii, S. M., *Finansovaia politika russkogo absoliutizma v XVIII veke* (Moscow, 1966).

———. "Finansovaia politika russkogo absoliutizma vo vtoroi polovine XVII i XVIII vv." *Absoliutizm v Rossii* (Moscow, 1964), 281–319.

———. "Sotsial'nyi sostav i chislennost' biurokratii Rossii v seredine XVIII v.," *Istoricheskie zapiski* 89 (Moscow, 1972).

Tverskaia, D. I., *Moskva vtoroi poloviny XVII veka: tsentr skladyvaiushchevosia vserossiiskogo rynka* (Trudy Gosudarstvennogo Istoricheskogo Muzeia 34) (Moscow, 1959).

Twitchett, Denis, "The T'ang Market System," *Asia Major* (1966), 202–48.

Umrikhina, A., *K voprosu o sotsial'no-ekonomicheskom razvitii belgorodskogo kraia vo vtoroi polovine XVIII veka* (Belgorod, 1971).

Urlanis, V. I., *Rost naseleniia v Evrope* (Moscow, 1941).

Vanin, Iu. V., *Ekonomicheskoe razvitie Korei v XVII–XVIII vekakh* (Moscow, 1968).

Vartanov, G. L., "Gorodskie iarmarki tsentral'noi chasti Evropeiskoi Rossii vo vtoroi polovine XVIII v.," *Uchenye zapiski* (of Leningrad State Pedagogical Institute) 194 (1958), 137–68.

———. "Kupechestvo gorodov moskovskoi gubernii vo vtoroi polovine XVIII veka" (avtoreferat of candidate's dissertation submitted to the Leningrad State Pedagogical Institute, Department of the History of the USSR, 1967).

———. "Kupechestvo i torguiushchee krest'ianstvo tsentral'noi chasti Evropeiskoi Rossii," *Uchenye zapiski* (of Leningrad State Pedagogical Institute) 229 (1962), 161–96.

———. "Moskovskoe i inogorodnoe kupechestvo vo vtoroi polovine XVIII v.," *Uchenye zapiski* (of Leningrad State Pedagogical Institute) 278 (1965), 272–90.

Vernadsky, George, *A History of Russia* (New York, 1961).

Veselovskii, S. B., *Selo i derevnia v severo-vostochnoi Rusi XIV–XVI vv.* (Moscow, 1936).

Viatkin, R. V. and Svistunova, N. P., eds., *Istoricheskaia nauka v KNR* (Moscow, 1971).

Vilkov, O. N., *Remeslo i torgovlia zapadnoi Sibiri v XVII veke* (Moscow, 1967).

Vodarskii, Ia. E., *Naselenie Rossii za 400 let (XVI- nachalo XX vv.)* (Moscow, 1973).

Volkov, S. I., *Krest'iane dvortsovykh vladenii Podmoskov'ia: v seredine XVIII v.* (Moscow, 1959).

Warner, R. Stephen, "The Methodology of Marx's Comparative Analysis of Modes of Production," Ivan Vallier, ed., *Comparative Methods in Sociology: Essays on Trends and Applications* (Berkeley, 1971).

Weber, Max, *The City* (Glencoe, 1958).

Wheatley, Paul, "The Concept of Urbanism," Peter J. Ucko, Ruth Tringham and G. W. Dimbleby, eds., *Man, Settlement and Urbanism* (London, 1972), 601–37.

Wittfogel, Karl A., *Oriental Despotism: A Comparative Study of Total Power* (New Haven, 1963).

Wright, Arthur F., "Symbolism and Function: Reflections on Ch'ang-an and Other Great Cities," *Journal of Asian Studies* 24 (August 1965), 667–79.

Wrigley, E. A., "A Simple Model of London's Importance in the Changing English Society and Economy 1650–1750," *Past and Present* 37 (1967), 44–70.

Yaresh, Leo, "The Problem of Periodization," C. E. Black, ed., *Rewriting Russian History: Soviet Interpretations of Russia's Past* (New York, 1956), 52–58.

Zagorovskii, V. P., "Belgorodskaia cherta" (avtoreferat of a dissertation submitted to Voronezh State University, 1969).

Zaozerskaia, E. I., *Razvitie legkoi promyshlennosti v Moskve v pervoi chetverti XVIII v.* (Moscow, 1953).

———. *U istokov krupnogo proizvodstva v russkoi promyshlennosti XVI–XVII vekov* (Moscow, 1970).

Zheludkov, V. F., "Vvedenie gubernskoi reformy 1775 goda," *Uchenye zapiski* (of Leningrad State Pedagogical Institute) 229 (1962), 197–226.

Zimin, A. A., "Sostav russkikh gorodov XVI v.," *Istoricheskie zapiski* 52 (1955), 336–47.

INDEX

absentee landowners, 19-20, 36, 48, 52, 83, 108-109, 110, 111, 251
Adams, J., 222, 225
administrative divisions: changes in Russia, 50, 54, 69, 73, 87, 88, 92-98, 101, 133, 155, 157, 175, 255, 256, 272; comparisons of populations in, 100-101, 156, 252, 254-57
agriculture: conditions for, 6, 42, 63, 64, 83, 89, 91, 92, 100-101, 110, 132, 151, 153-54, 156, 159, 162, 169, 181, 184, 191, 192, 208, 214, 258; in cities, 53, 62, 135-36, 148, 213; techniques for, 19, 49, 50, 92, 251; value of production, 28, 89, 118
Akhtyrsk, 211
alcoholic beverages, 110, 113, 118, 145, 196, 203, 213, 214
Alexander I, 95
American Indians, 239
annexation, 5, 24, 57, 58, 64, 86, 87, 90, 91, 97, 98, 99-100, 106, 107, 108, 158, 159, 160, 198, 199, 209, 210
architecture, 53, 130, 133, 137, 139, 140, 143, 148, 190, 208-209, 277, 278
archives, 25, 98, 105, 134, 139, 149, 160, 208
Arctic Ocean, 191
area of Russian Empire, 42, 50, 57, 90, 92, 156, 157, 159
areas of integration, 221, 254, 258-62, 263, 264, 265, 270, 279
Arkhangel'sk: city, 97, 128, 157, 168,

181, 183, 191, 200, 203, 205; guberniia, 101, 104, 121, 127, 169, 183, 184, 191
Armenians, 200
Astrakhan': city, 57, 58, 59, 73, 97, 129, 139-40, 155, 157, 193, 196, 198, 199, 200, 202, 207, 216; guberniia, 100, 104, 105, 193, 198-200, 218
Athens, 78, 80
Atlantic Ocean, 234
Austria-Hungary, 241
autocracy, 5, 56, 67, 68, 90
Azov Sea, 213

backwardness in history, 3, 4, 5-8, 18, 31, 41-42, 44, 55, 66-67, 83-85, 220, 276-79
Baltic region, 91, 95, 97, 99, 159, 210, 213, 217
Baltic Sea, 5, 51-52, 58, 87, 90, 185, 187, 189, 213, 219
barshchina, 106, 110, 115, 116, 118, 162, 173, 189, 214
Belgorod, 173, 175
Beloi gorod in Moscow, 141-42, 143, 144, 145, 148
Belorussia, 26, 91, 97, 99, 107, 159, 185, 210, 211, 212, 213
Black Plague, 28, 65, 78
Black Sea, 5, 42, 87, 90, 97, 108, 210, 213
boiars, 52, 53, 60
Bolkhov, 171, 174

borrowing from abroad, 6, 8, 38, 42, 44-45, 54, 55, 78, 80, 83-84, 130, 139, 146, 263
Boulet-Sautel, M., 81
Bukhara, 199, 207
Bulygin, I. A., 89, 124, 195, 196
bureaucracy, 47, 67, 69, 76, 103, 108, 110-11, 272
Byzantium, 5, 42

canals, 70, 91, 165, 181, 186, 215, 219, 234, 267, 268
capitalism: roots of, 20, 23, 24, 29, 31, 62, 70, 88; uklad of, 23, 28, 29, 30-31, 38, 86, 89, 120, 121, 130-31; as a Marxist stage, 9, 18, 19, 21
Caspian Sea, 199
Catherine II, 7, 69, 87, 95, 113, 130, 137, 146, 176
Caucasus, 90, 159, 198
Central Asia, 90, 128, 159, 197, 198, 207
centralization: administrative, 5, 6, 22, 35-36, 39, 46, 47, 53, 54, 56, 76, 82, 84, 93, 106, 156-57, 221, 240, 243, 244, 251-54, 260, 263-64, 266, 271-73, 278, 279, 280; commercial, 36-37, 64, 65, 74, 77, 82, 252, 253, 254, 263, 264, 266
central place theory, 13-14, 81-82
central places: definitions of, 3, 33-34, 41, 43, 46, 74-75, 81, 131, 132-33, 136, 138, 144, 153, 163, 231, 242-44, 252; distribution of, 13-14, 38, 39, 124, 149-56, 160, 218, 230, 242-54, 264, 265, 271, 272; order of appearance, 53, 65, 73-82
Ch'ang-an, 36, 64, 76
charters, 82
Cherepnin, L. V., 20, 22
Chernigov, 210, 211
China: as neighbor of Russia, 49, 90, 127; distribution of central places in, 13, 43, 46, 52-53, 218, 242-53; periodization of, 9, 19, 29, 30-31, 35-36, 42, 44, 49, 53, 54, 55, 56,

61, 63, 66, 67, 75-78, 83, 85, 87, 220
Chulkov, M., 119
churches: location of, 52, 53, 73, 104, 133, 136, 148, 176, 199; number of, 46, 53, 134, 137, 138, 141, 146, 179, 187, 188, 190, 209; land ownership of, 48, 51, 52, 54, 103, 187
city plans, 39, 47, 52-53, 62-63, 64, 68, 73, 80, 130, 131, 134, 136-49, 165, 176, 178, 199-200, 265, 266
city walls: inner and outer, 47, 48, 51-52, 60, 68, 80, 81, 133, 137, 141, 148, 199-200; gates in, 62, 134, 136, 139, 145, 146, 148, 200; length of, 52, 132, 134, 136, 140, 148; state of, 43, 63, 64, 136, 137, 143, 144, 148, 175, 198, 228
Clark, P., 83, 224, 225
class struggle, 26, 89, 116, 131
clergy, 67, 103, 111, 134; number of, 104-105, 106, 132, 135, 144, 195
colonies, 220, 237, 263, 268, 270
commercialization, 20, 23, 28, 37, 39, 49, 52, 53, 54, 62, 64, 86, 87, 89, 93, 221, 260, 266, 269, 270, 271, 272, 280
Commission on Commerce, 119
communism, 10
Constantinople (Istanbul), 55, 243
consumption, 6, 19-20, 43, 48, 81, 83, 106, 107, 111, 114, 122, 144, 157, 204, 253
corvée, 43, 52
Cossacks, 105, 209
Coulborn, R., 11
court peasants, 103, 104, 107, 162, 184, 195, 214
courtyards, 140, 142, 143, 144, 145-46, 199, 200
Crimea, 209
customs barriers, 71, 114, 257

Davis, D., 83
decentralization, 35, 46, 48, 49, 53, 54, 55, 56, 76, 77, 78, 80, 82, 84, 237, 263

demographic structure, 13, 98-102, 222, 224; enumerations of Russian population, 68, 88, 98-101, 102-103, 195, 208

Dictionnaire de la France, 230, 231

Dijon, 82

Dolgoruky, Yuri, 50

Don River, 129, 196

dvoriane, 60, 67-68, 95, 101, 103, 104-105, 106, 107-11, 112, 113, 114, 132, 134, 135, 137, 139, 140, 143, 144, 148, 151, 177, 181, 195

"economic" peasants, 103, 104, 162, 184, 214

Edo, 224, 237, 238, 243, 273

education, 67, 111

Eisenstadt, S., 11

Ekaterinburg, 201, 202, 205, 206

Elets, 171, 173, 174

Emmausskii, A. V., 203

Engels, F., 28

England: distribution of central places in, 222-30, 242-53; periodization of, 28, 30-31, 49, 54-55, 56, 57, 65-66, 78-85, 87, 220, 237

Eniseisk, 127, 202, 206, 208, 209

epidemics, 28, 31, 50, 100

ethnic minorities, 58-59, 105, 159, 191, 193, 197, 198, 199, 200, 202, 204

Everitt, A., 222, 224, 228, 229

evolutionary approaches, 4-5, 7, 9, 10, 12-13, 17, 28, 31, 38, 86, 90, 262, 263-64, 279-80

fairs: national, 71, 119, 120-21, 122, 127-29, 155, 174, 176, 191, 194, 195, 204, 207, 219, 229, 236-37; number of, 86, 88, 119-20, 121, 123, 133, 134, 153, 175-76, 163, 167, 168, 169, 175, 185, 188, 196, 203-204, 209, 213, 269; origin of, 61, 72, 82, 114, 270; specialized, 170, 177, 213, 229, 236; turnover at, 117, 118, 120-22, 126, 138, 156, 170, 174, 176, 179-80, 212-13

famines, 100

festivals, 61, 119, 151

feudalism: general treatment of, 11, 12, 76, 86, 131, 271; loyalties in Japan, 9, 256, 274; subdivisions of, 19-24, 26, 27, 32, 49

fires, 50, 136, 139, 146, 165, 176, 178, 189, 190

fish, 52, 129, 132, 176, 186, 187, 197, 198, 199

foreign trade, 24, 42, 44, 86, 89, 112, 113, 118, 155, 189, 191, 195, 198, 203, 207, 213, 220, 233, 237, 267, 268; of Novgorod, 51, 187; of St. Petersburg, 70, 191, 203; with China, 71, 90, 127, 203, 206, 209; with Europe, 71, 90, 181

fortifications, 43, 48, 60, 63, 133, 137, 175, 177, 185, 188, 195, 198, 206, 207, 209

France: distribution of central places in, 230-38, 242-53; periodization of, 28, 30-31, 49, 54-55, 56, 57, 65-66, 78-85, 87, 220

Frêche, Georges, 236

furs, 43, 57, 71, 90, 127, 208, 209

gardens, 135, 140, 146, 147, 148, 199, 200

Geographical Dictionary, 118, 124, 131, 134, 136, 139, 140, 152, 180, 230

geographical setting, 6, 8, 90-92, 156, 157, 267

Germany, 159, 236, 241

Golikova, N. B., 73, 140, 191, 199-200

gostinyi dvor, 63, 129, 133, 135, 137-38, 141, 145, 165, 176, 178, 186, 197, 200, 206, 207, 209, 236

Goubert, P., 231, 232

governor-generals, 95

governors, 94, 178, 199

granaries, 52, 170, 196, 200

Greece, 10, 28, 78, 80

Gromyko, M. M., 208

Hammond, M., 78, 80
Hanseatic league, 187
Helin, E., 231
hired labor, 23, 69, 70, 89, 106, 110,
   111, 112, 114, 115, 117, 144, 151,
   157, 162, 165, 214
historical sociology, 4, 10-12, 17, 18,
   265, 280
horses, 177, 180, 199
Hoskins, W. G., 224
household size, 101-102, 135, 139
housing, 108-109, 111, 117, 135, 137,
   139-49, 165-66, 174, 175, 184, 196,
   225, 278

Iakutsk, 127, 209
Iaroslavl': city, 58, 97, 122, 160, 162,
   165, 166, 167-68, 178-79, 190;
   guberniia, 104, 135, 161, 167-68
Iatsunskii, V. K., 25, 26
imperial family, 87, 103, 107
India, 13, 129, 199, 200, 207, 241,
   262, 269-70
Indonesia, 241
Industrial Revolution, 8, 28
inheritance, 48, 51, 52, 105, 108
intermediate marketing places, 34,
   35, 37, 61, 126, 133-35, 152, 155,
   224, 259-60
Iofa, L. E., 206, 207
Irbit fair, 121, 127, 128, 204, 205-206,
   207, 208
Irkutsk, 97, 127, 132, 138, 201, 207,
   208, 209
Italy, 236, 241
Ivan III, 59
Ivan IV, 65
Ivanovo, 136, 161, 166

Japan: distribution of central places
   in, 43, 52-53, 218, 237, 242-53;
   periodization of, 4, 9, 18, 29, 30-31,
   42, 44, 49, 53, 54, 55, 56, 57, 61,
   63, 66, 67, 75-78, 83-85, 87, 220, 228
Johnson, E.A.J., 13

Kabuzan, V. M., 96, 98, 99, 100,

107, 149
Kafengauz, B. B., 127, 129, 187
Kaluga, 97, 104, 108-109, 160, 162,
   166, 169-70
Kamakura, 64
Kamer'-Kollezhskii wall, 140, 144,
   148
Kapustina, G. D., 72
Karpachev, A. M., 26, 213, 214
Kazan': city, 57, 58, 97, 138, 139,
   193, 196-97; guberniia, 193, 196-97
Khar'kov, 129, 209, 211, 217
Khoroshkevich, A. L., 62
Kiev, 42-46, 53, 54, 55, 84, 155, 171,
   210, 211, 212
Kievan era, 41, 45-48, 50, 53, 55, 57,
   77, 85
King, G., 222, 224-25
King, P., 81
Kitai gorod in Moscow, 60, 129,
   141-45, 148, 200
Kizevetter, A. A., 113
Klokman, Iu. R., 26, 88, 170, 194
Kopanev, A. I., 58
Korea, 241, 242, 244, 269-70
Korocha, 171
Korrenaia fair, 122, 129, 176
Kostroma, 97, 104, 137, 162, 169,
   190, 217
Koval'chenko, I. D., 118
Krasnoiarsk, 202, 209
kreml', 43, 46, 47, 51, 52-53, 73, 134,
   136, 137, 139, 148, 199, 200, 209
Kremlin, 51, 60, 141, 142, 143, 148,
   200
Kronstadt, 183, 185
Kursk: city, 97, 129, 138, 139, 157,
   171, 172, 175, 176, 177; guberniia,
   122, 133, 137, 138, 173, 174, 175-76
Kusheva, E. N., 198
Kyoto, 53, 64, 84, 237, 238, 243, 273

Latysheva, G. P., 47
leadership, 7, 11, 39, 66, 68, 69, 87,
   92, 274
Lenin, V. I., 11, 26, 70
Lithuaniia, 65, 107

livestock, 59, 129, 150, 164, 168, 187, 199, 213, 229, 236
lodgers, 144, 145
London, 82, 83, 223-24, 225, 226, 243, 250, 257, 268, 272-73
Low Countries, 232, 236
Luppov, P. N., 205
L'vov, 212
Lyon, 233, 236, 243, 273

Makar'evskaia fair, 71, 121, 122, 128-29, 174, 194, 195, 199, 206, 219
Manchuria, 90
manufacturing, 14, 19, 23, 69, 71, 89, 113, 114, 118, 131, 136, 143, 144, 145, 154, 161, 166, 167, 168, 179; number of factories and plants, 179, 203, 205, 215
Marx, K., 10, 17, 18, 19, 26, 28
Marxist periodization, 5, 9-12, 17, 19-24, 27-31, 37-38, 83, 86, 264, 274, 280
Mediterranean Sea, 234
Meiji Restoration, 9
merchants: capital of, 20, 70, 104, 112, 117, 118, 163, 195; itinerant, 61, 112, 125, 132, 153; kuptsy, 104, 105, 106, 112, 114, 115, 117, 123, 125, 130, 134, 137, 143, 144, 148, 150, 180, 181, 195, 215; part-time, 69, 106, 113, 114, 132, 150, 265
meshchane, 104, 105, 106, 113, 114, 115, 123, 134, 144, 150, 180, 195, 215; location of, 125, 180
Mesopotamia, 78
mestechki, 212, 214
metals and mining, 43, 44, 71, 91, 113, 165, 168, 176, 179, 187, 188, 189, 190, 194, 199, 200, 203, 204, 205, 207
migration, 24, 38, 49, 57, 60, 70, 91, 100, 106, 113, 114, 115, 116, 144-45, 157, 160-61, 191, 192, 265, 273, 278
military: forces, 19, 42, 59, 70, 72, 99, 103, 110, 134, 139, 147, 177, 183,

191, 197, 198, 199, 219; foreign intervention, 24, 31, 48-49, 56, 58, 63, 90, 198, 274; quartering, 105, 106, 115, 146; service population, 63, 68, 72, 115, 206, 208; objectives, 5, 6, 87
mills, 116, 203, 214
Minsk, 211
moats, 43, 136, 198
modernization: contacts with, 3, 6, 8, 15, 220, 238, 275; preconditions for, 18, 38, 86, 87, 221, 274-75, 279, 283; process of, 6-7, 10, 238, 273, 278-79
Mogilev, 210, 211
Moldavians, 210
Mols, R., 231
monasteries, 46-47, 48, 51, 52, 60, 61, 63, 68, 103, 104, 133, 134, 137, 138, 148, 162, 179, 199, 200
monetary relations, 23, 52, 62, 72, 111, 148, 162; currency values, 89, 117; state budget, 87, 107, 111, 118
Mongols, 5, 22, 24, 41, 46, 48-53, 55, 56, 57, 187
monopolies, 52, 62, 69, 107, 112, 113, 114, 151, 252
Montpellier, 82, 232
Moscow: pre-1700, 50, 51, 76; land use of, 60, 73, 140-46, 148; population of, 41, 51, 59, 60, 106, 112, 144, 145-46, 160-61, 162, 182, 216, 243; luxurious living in, 60, 107, 111, 143, 158; guberniia, 69, 97, 101, 104, 124-25, 131, 134, 135, 136, 151, 161, 163-64, 165, 166, 170, 217
Moscow River, 134, 160
Mote, F. W., 136
motivation, 5-6, 116
Murav'eva, L. L., 71-72
Muscovy, 41, 57

Nadel, G. H., 9, 10
Nanking, 243, 272
national income, 116-17, 118

national market, 26-27, 37, 69, 70, 82, 88, 127, 129, 154, 155, 186, 209, 216, 262, 264, 267, 268, 269
natural resources, 6, 266
Near East, 129, 139, 159, 198
Nedosekin, V. I., 175-76
Nezhin, 211
Nisbet, R. A., 12
Nizhnii Novgorod: city, 50, 51, 58, 71, 97, 121, 169, 193, 194-95; guberniia, 108, 122, 128, 136, 152, 193, 194-95
Novgorod: autonomous region, 51-52, 57, 187; city, 42, 43, 46, 53, 58, 59, 60, 63, 97, 139, 181, 183, 186, 187, 188, 189; guberniia, 104, 121, 184, 186-88, 189
Novgorod Severskii, 209-10, 211
nunneries, 104, 138, 148, 179

obrok, 106, 110, 115, 116, 117, 118, 132, 144, 167, 173, 214
Odessa, 213
odnodvortsy, 173
officials, 19, 76, 103, 105, 106, 111, 115, 132, 135, 139
Oka River, 50, 160, 172, 174, 179, 181, 196
Olonets, 97, 121, 183, 184, 186, 189-90, 215
orchards, 135, 140, 147, 181, 200
Orel, 97, 101, 129, 137, 171, 172, 173-74, 177
Orenburg, 97, 105, 128, 138, 201, 202, 205, 206-207
Oriental despotism, 9, 19
Osaka, 237, 238, 243, 273
Ostashkov, 162, 165
Ostrogozhsk, 171, 178
Ottoman Empire, 90, 209, 241

palaces, 107, 111, 141, 199
Paris, 82, 232, 234, 237, 243, 257, 273
partitioning of landholdings, 24, 115
Patten, J.H.C., 225-28
Paul I, 95

Pavlenko, N. I., 25
Pavlovo, 136, 194
Peking, 90, 243, 272
Penza: city, 97, 137, 193, 194, 195-96; guberniia, 109, 124, 151, 193, 195-96
Pereiaslavl'-Zalesskii, 125, 136, 137, 162, 166, 167
periodic marketing: early development of, 36, 37, 47, 49, 55, 60, 62, 65, 72, 82, 85, 264, 269, 270; frequencies of, 61, 123, 124-25, 126, 133, 134, 138, 150, 185, 204, 225, 230, 235-36, 270; intensification cycle of, 13, 86, 88, 89, 94, 123, 127; locations of, 33, 61, 62, 112, 114, 123, 124, 125, 150, 151, 152, 167, 219, 229; switch to daily marketing, 8, 121, 126, 228, 236, 270, 277
Perm', 97, 127, 201-202, 204, 205-206
Persia, 199, 241
Peter I, 7, 66, 67, 113, 179, 186, 205, 210; reforms of, 67-68, 72, 88, 93, 130
Petrovsk, 193, 194, 197
Petrozavodsk, 183, 189-90
Pirenne, H., 31
Poitrineau, A., 236
Poland, 87, 90, 97, 209, 210, 211
pomest'ia, 68
population: decline, 28, 58, 214; density, 21, 50, 53, 57, 91, 92, 95, 97, 100, 101, 105, 132, 140, 144, 146, 151, 155, 157, 178, 181, 182, 183, 191, 200, 204, 210, 217, 218, 239, 244, 250, 258, 278; growth, 57, 64, 77, 96, 100, 108, 157, 172-73, 184, 192, 201, 214, 239, 265; in cities, 13, 14, 20, 31, 65, 77, 81, 82, 239-40, 242, 266-69; in Russian cities, 4, 7, 8, 45, 46, 48, 51, 52, 59-60, 64, 69, 72-73, 74, 77, 86, 88, 98, 105, 149, 152-53, 154, 212, 215-16, 217-18, 229-30, 268; of world, 14, 238, 240, 241, 280; of world's largest cities, 36, 242-43, 253, 280

Porshnev, B. F., 32
Portugal, 269, 270
posad: land use, 43, 52-53, 62, 134;
  rights of residents, 59, 68, 69-70,
  73, 105, 107, 112, 113, 114
post stations, 188
Pounds, N.J.G., 80
Pozdniakov, I. G., 29
primitive communalism, 9, 19-23,
  30, 37
princes, 22, 43, 44, 47-48, 49, 50,
  52, 93
production for orders, 23, 53, 62, 70
property, 19, 22, 158, 212, 266;
  ownership in cities, 53, 63, 68, 112,
  134, 144, 158; ownership of cities,
  48, 51, 56, 59, 95-96, 136, 154, 158,
  179
Pskov, 57, 58, 59, 60, 63, 97, 181,
  183, 184, 186, 187, 188-89
public buildings, 80, 133, 134, 136,
  139, 141, 147, 178, 187, 200
public squares, 47, 64, 130, 133, 134,
  135, 145
Pugachev, E., 89
Putivl', 171, 175

Rabinovich, M. G., 47
railroads, 90
Razgon, A. M., 89, 124, 125, 151, 167
raznochintsy, 103, 105, 106, 114,
  115, 134, 144
rebellions, 10, 20, 31, 89, 90
Red Square, 141, 142-43
regions of the Russian Empire, 91,
  96-97, 156-57, 214-19
Reinhard, M., 231
religion, 19, 35, 39, 52, 54, 55, 60,
  137, 139, 141, 142, 187, 199, 234
rents, 19, 62, 110, 111, 112, 116, 117,
  144, 251
retired soldiers, 103, 105, 106, 111,
  114, 208
Revel', 211, 213
Riabkov, G. T., 184-85
riady, 63, 64, 141, 145, 200
Riazan', 97, 122, 138, 172, 173, 180-81

Riga, 139, 155, 209, 211, 213
Roman Empire, 28, 54, 55, 56, 78,
  80, 81, 84, 85
Romanov dynasty, 87
rooms: number of, 143, 144
Rostov fair, 120, 122, 129, 168, 195
Rouen, 82, 232, 235
Rozhkov, M. K., 118
Rozhkova, M. K., 120, 121, 174
Rubinshtein, N. A., 89
Rubinshtein, N. L., 88, 119, 126
rural handicrafts, 42, 49, 71-72, 159,
  162-63, 167, 168, 213, 219, 228
rural-urban competition, 62, 88, 113,
  114
rural-urban dichotomy, 26, 32, 48,
  54, 131, 148-49, 156, 158, 252, 272-
  73
Russell, J. C., 13, 14, 81-82, 237
Ryndziunskii, P. G., 88, 92, 143
Rzhev, 138, 162, 164, 165

St. Petersburg: establishment of, 66,
  70, 72, 87, 130, 145, 165, 186, 216,
  224; guberniia, 69, 97, 135, 183,
  184, 185-86, 189, 215, 217; land
  use of, 111, 112, 140-41, 146-48;
  luxurious living in, 107, 111, 117,
  148, 158; population of, 41, 106,
  111, 182, 183, 185, 216-17, 219, 243,
  273
Sakharov, A. M., 25
salt, 52, 113, 118, 187, 198, 199
Saransk, 193, 195, 196
Saratov: city, 97, 156, 177, 193, 196,
  197, 198, 216; guberniia, 108, 126,
  192, 193, 197-98, 217
sela, 119, 133, 136, 151, 180, 181, 185
self-government in cities, 5, 7, 32-33,
  80, 130, 214, 225, 277-78
serfdom: consequences of, 5, 24, 100,
  251, 278; evolution of, 62, 67, 89,
  107, 274; household serfs, 106,
  111, 115, 117, 144, 195; serf industrial labor, 69, 70, 106, 115,
  116, 144, 151; number of serfs,
  103, 104, 108-109, 162, 173, 184,

serfdom (*cont.*)
189, 193, 197, 213, 214; obligations
of serfs, 18, 106, 110, 111, 115, 116,
162-63
serfowners, 24, 102, 115, 116, 118,
124, 151, 162, 173, 176, 189, 198;
holdings of, 95, 108, 109-10, 196,
213-14
Serpukhov, 125, 162, 163, 164
Shapiro, A. L., 25, 26, 62
Shepukova, N. M., 109
Sheremetev, Count, 136
Shul'ga, I. G., 209
Siberia, 95, 104, 159, 197, 200-209;
settlement of, 57, 58, 71, 90
Simbirsk, 97, 101, 193, 197
Skinner, G. W., 13, 14
Slack, P., 83, 224, 225
slaveholding, 9, 19, 30, 32, 89
sleighs, 92, 122, 181, 190, 206
slobody, 59, 68, 73, 133, 134, 151,
176, 200
Smith, C. T., 13
Smolensk: city, 57, 58, 60, 97, 155,
181, 183, 184; guberniia, 101, 109,
184-85
socialism, 10
social mobility, 6, 24, 265, 273
social stratification, 19, 22, 31, 38,
39, 51-52, 62, 67, 68, 87, 102-18,
133, 135, 143, 157-58, 221, 222,
225-28, 265, 280
soldier-cultivators, 63, 180
Sorina, Kh. D., 165
Soviet historiography, 6, 11-12, 17-18,
19-27, 28, 32-33, 49, 69, 70, 86,
88-90, 100, 127, 130-31, 160
Spain, 236, 241
stages of the urban network approach,
33-38, 41-42, 45, 55, 63-64, 74, 77,
83-85, 220-21, 238, 240, 262-63,
279-80, 281-82
Stalinism, 5, 11, 19
state peasants, 67, 114, 144, 162,
195, 198, 214; nonagricultural activities of, 106, 115, 116, 214;
number of, 103, 184, 193, 197,

202; obligations of, 18, 100, 106-107,
115, 162-63, 173
steamships, 90
stores: locations of, 63, 73, 83, 112,
133, 139, 270, 278; number of, 122,
125, 133, 134-35, 137-38, 141, 145,
151, 165, 168, 170, 190, 197, 215,
269; types of, 138, 148, 151, 176,
188, 208, 228-29
streets, 52, 63, 64, 130, 133, 136,
139-40, 146-47, 148, 176, 190;
names of, 53; number of, 135,
138, 143, 145-46, 179
strel'tsy, 68, 115
Stuzhina, E. P., 32
Sumy, 211
Svinskaia fair, 129, 174, 176
Sweden, 90, 186
Switzerland, 82
Syzran', 193, 197

table of ranks, 68
Tambov, 97, 126, 171, 176-77, 180
Tara, 202
Tatar raids, 58, 63, 90, 173
taxes, 19, 67, 68, 72, 102, 103, 107,
113, 115, 118, 165, 202, 205, 251,
253, 271, 272
textile production, 70, 71, 129, 131,
136, 144, 163, 167, 168, 169, 170,
232
Tikhomirov, M. N., 43, 46
Tikhonov, Iu. A., 62, 101
Tilly, C., 231
Time of Troubles, 65, 82
Tiumen', 117, 202, 206, 208
Tobol'sk, 97, 105, 127, 201, 202, 207,
209, 217
Tokugawa Ieyasu, 66
Tomsk, 201, 202, 207
Toropets, 183, 188, 189
Torzhok, 161, 162, 164, 165, 166
Toulouse, 82, 232, 234
transition to stage G, 42, 56, 66-74,
77, 78, 82, 252
transportation: networks, 50, 57, 64,
91-92, 95, 122, 155, 159, 181, 203,

205, 219, 250, 266, 267-79; technology, 8, 14, 19, 46, 90, 156, 266, 270; workers, 52, 70, 114, 115, 145, 162, 165, 192, 194

tribute, 22, 35, 43, 49, 263

tripartite periodization, 5, 9-10, 17, 27-31, 37-38, 83, 264, 280

Troitsk fair, 128, 206, 207

Troitskii, S. M., 107

tsar, 41, 59, 87, 103, 107, 214

tsekhovye liudi, 104

Tula: city, 97, 138, 139, 148, 171, 178-79, 209, 216; guberniia, 101, 102, 135, 137, 173, 174, 178-79, 181

Tver': city, 49, 51, 97, 125, 138, 139, 160, 162, 164, 165, 166; guberniia, 104, 112, 138, 161, 164-66, 170, 180, 215

Twitchett, D., 31

uezd: number of, 58, 72, 95, 96, 123, 124, 162, 171, 183, 193, 202, 211, 254-55, 261; maturation of, 50, 54, 62, 93, 94

Ufa, 202, 207

Ukraine, 91, 95, 97, 107, 159, 172, 174, 176, 209-10, 211, 212, 213; fairs in, 119, 120, 121, 129, 185, 212-13, 219

ulozhenie, 56, 59, 67, 113

United States, 11, 241

Urals, 71, 91, 97, 127, 128, 200-207, 217

urban sites, 43, 44, 50, 80, 136

USSR, 6, 42, 90

Ustiug Velikii, 63, 183, 190

usury, 52

Varangians, 5

Vartanov, G. L., 88, 114, 120, 121, 168, 179

Vazhskaia Blagoveshchenskaia fair, 127-28, 191

Viatka, 97, 104, 201, 202, 203-205, 217

Viaz'ma, 183, 184

villages, 116, 184-85; size of, 131, 258; types of, 35, 36, 48, 71, 119, 214, 226-28

Vitebsk, 211

Vladimir: city, 49, 97, 161, 166, 167; guberniia, 71, 89, 104, 123, 124, 126, 132, 136, 151, 161, 166-67, 181, 217

Vodarskii, Ia. E., 57, 69, 72

Volga River: cities on, 50, 58, 62, 160, 168, 191, 193-94, 197, 199; shipments along, 51, 57, 70, 128-29, 165, 181, 191, 194, 196, 197, 198, 204, 206, 215, 216, 219, 268

Vologda, 97, 126, 133, 183, 184, 188, 190, 217

Vol'sk, 193, 197

Voronezh, 97, 121, 171, 173, 177-78, 185

votchiny, 48, 51, 52, 68

wars, 10, 48, 50, 54, 58, 65, 72, 100, 157, 205, 214

weapons production, 43, 179, 189

Weber, M., 11, 32

White Sea, 57, 129

wholesale trade, 73, 113, 116, 122, 141

Wrigley, E. A., 224

Zemlianoi gorod in Moscow, 143, 144, 145, 148

Zimin, A. A., 63

Library of Congress Cataloging in Publication Data

Rozman, Gilbert.
  Urban networks in Russia, 1750-1800, and premodern periodization.

  Bibliography: p.
  Includes index.
  1. Cities and towns—Russia. I. Title.
HT145.R9R65   301.36'3'0947   75-3472
ISBN 0-691-09364-4